Dadisho' Qaṭraya's *Compendious Commentary* on *The Paradise of the Egyptian Fathers* in Garshuni

Texts from Christian Late Antiquity

43

Series Editor

George Anton Kiraz

TeCLA (Texts from Christian Late Antiquity) is a series presenting ancient Christian texts both in their original languages and with accompanying contemporary English translations.

Dadishoʿ Qaṭraya's *Compendious Commentary* on *The Paradise of the Egyptian Fathers* in Garshuni

Edited and Translated by

Mario Kozah

Abdulrahim Abu-Husayn

Suleiman Mourad

gorgias press
2016

Gorgias Press LLC, 954 River Road, Piscataway, NJ, 08854, USA

www.gorgiaspress.com

Copyright © 2016 by Gorgias Press LLC

All rights reserved under International and Pan-American Copyright Conventions. No part of this publication may be reproduced, stored in a retrieval system or transmitted in any form or by any means, electronic, mechanical, photocopying, recording, scanning or otherwise without the prior written permission of Gorgias Press LLC.

2016

ISBN 978-1-4632-0566-9   **ISSN 1935-6846**

Library of Congress Cataloging-in-Publication Data

A Cataloging-in-Publication Record is Available from the Library of Congress

Printed in the United States of America

◆ ܠܥܡܐ ܕܩܛܪܝܐ ◆

"To the People of Qatar"

(Isho'yahb III, Patriarch of the Church of the East d. 659. Letter 18)

Table of Contents

Table of Contents v
Acknowledgments vii
Introduction 1
    A Note on the Manuscripts 10
    List Of Witnesses 10
    Stemma Codicum 12
    Manuscripts 13
        Mario Kozah

Text and Translation 15
    English translation 16
      Mario Kozah, Abdulrahim Abu-Husayn,
        Suleiman Mourad
    Garshuni text 17
        Mario Kozah

Index of Biblical References 279
Index of Names, Terms and Subjects 283
Glossary of Proper Names and Key Concepts 287
Bibliography 293
Notes on the Garshuni Text 295
        Mario Kozah
Notes on the English Translation 349
      Mario Kozah and Suleiman Mourad

Acknowledgments

This book was made possible by NPRP grant NPRP 4–981–6–025 from the Qatar National Research Fund (a member of Qatar Foundation). The statements made herein are solely the responsibility of the authors.

INTRODUCTION

Mario Kozah
American University of Beirut

Dadishoʿ Qaṭraya is a seventh century Syriac author of monastic and ascetic literature, a Church of the East monk, he was a native of the Qatar region, as his demonym "Qaṭraya" indicates. Dadishoʿ seems to have become a monk at the otherwise unknown monastery of Rab-kennārē before dwelling for a time at the monastery of Rabban Shābūr and at that of the "Blessed Apostles."[1]

Dadishoʿ's name and works are to be found recorded at the beginning of the fourteenth century in the catalogue of ʿAbdishoʿ bar Brikā who states:[2]

> The renowned Dadishoʿ (ܕܕܝܫܘܥ ܚܣܝܐ) wrote a commentary (lit. commented) on the Paradise of the Occidentals [monks] (ܦܪܕܝܣܐ ܕܡܥܪ̈ܒܝܐ); he elucidated [the book of] Abbā Isaiah; he wrote a book on the [monastic] way of life (ܥܠ ܕܘܒܪ̈ܐ); treatises on the sanctification of the cell; consolatory dirges (ܣܘܬ̈ܪܐ ܕܚܘܠܡܢܐ); he also wrote letters and inquiries (ܐܓܪ̈ܬܐ ܘܫܘ̈ܐܠܐ) on stillness in the body and the soul (ܫܠܝܐ ܕܦܓܪܐ ܘܕܢܦܫܐ).[3]

---

[1] A. Scher, "Notice sur la vie et les oeuvres de Dadishoʿ Qaṭraya," *Journal Asiatique*, 10:7, 1906, pp. 103–111.

[2] As was first established by A. Scher in the above-cited article on Dadishoʿ Qaṭraya.

[3] J.S. Assemanus, *Bibliotheca Orientalis Clementino-Vaticana*, III/1. Rome, 1725, pp. 98–99.

The commentary on the twenty-six discourses of Abbā Isaiah has been edited and translated by René Draguet.[4] However, all the extant manuscripts of this work only reach the end of the commentary on the fifteenth discourse. Interestingly, a later anonymous commentary[5] in Syriac which is in fragmentary form incorporates sections from the subsequent discourses by Dadishoʿ proving that he did in fact complete this work. A more complete Garshuni translation exists of this anonymous commentary.[6] The anonymous commentary consists of a thematically arranged selection of excerpts and, according to R. Draguet's hypothesis,[7] was compiled in the first half of the eighth century by a disciple of Isaac of Nineveh. Could this disciple have undertaken this work at the Monastery of Rabban Shābūr with which both Isaac and Dadishoʿ were associated? It is certainly the case that disciples of Isaac were to be found in this very monastery as is attested by a fifteenth century Syrian Orthodox notice in which a pupil of Mar Dāzedeq (ܕܐܙܪܩ) named Būshīr (ܒܘܫܝܪ) appears to be a monk in Rabban Shābūr who is not only familiar with the teachings of Isaac but is able to send these teachings to Mar Dāzedeq.[8] This suggests that these teachings were to be found in written form at the monastery and that Būshīr considered them worthy enough of being disseminated, with the result that many others also became disciples of Isaac. Mar Dāzedeq writes in his letter to Būshīr:

> I know that the keys of the Kingdom have been gained by you in life, because you have filled our monastery with teaching that is filled with life. For we confess that we are pupils of Mar Isaac (ܘܐܠܡܚܣܝܐ ܣܝܢ ܘܡܪܝ ܐܝܣܚܩ) the bishop of Niniveh.[9]

---

[4] R. Draguet, *Commentaire du Livre d'abba Isaïe (logoi I–XV) par Dadišo Qaṭraya*, in *CSCO*, 326–327, Scr. Syr. 144–5. Louvain, 1972.

[5] R. Draguet, *Commentaire anonyme du Livre d'abba Isaïe (fragments)*, in *CSCO*, 336–337, Scr. Syr. 150–151. Louvain, 1973.

[6] Ibid., tr., p.xviii. Draguet refers to two manuscripts which contain this Garshuni translation: Paris syr. 239, ff. 226ʳ–280ᵛ and Cambridge D.d. 15.2 ff. 227ᵛ–269ʳ.

[7] Ibid., tr., pp. xxv–xxvi.

[8] I.E. Rahmani, *Studia Syriaca*, I. Charfet, 1904, p. ܟܓ.

[9] I.E. Rahmani, *Studia Syriaca*, I. Charfet, 1904, p. ܟܓ.

In addition to this commentary, the other writings by Dadishoʿ to survive are a letter to Abqosh[10] and a number of discourses or treatises on stillness.[11]

One very important work of his survives that is catalogued by ʿAbdishoʿ bar Brikā but which remains unedited and with no translation. This is, of course, Dadishoʿ's commentary on ʿNānishoʿ's *Paradise of the Fathers*,[12] which is the Syriac version of the *Paradise of the Egyptian Fathers* translated and compiled in the seventh century. Until recently this commentary was also only to be found surviving in an incomplete form in manuscripts at the British Library, Cambridge University Library and the Paris Bibliothèque Nationale.[13] However, the discovery of the complete text in the Metropolitan Library of the Church of the East in Baghdad has attracted the interest of a number of distinguished scholars and a critical edition and translation of this important text are now underway.[14]

What is, perhaps, less well known is that a Garshuni summary translation or Compendium of Dadishoʿ's commentary features in a number of manuscripts, one of which was first identified in Berlin by Eduard Sachau in 1899 and later clarified by Anton Baumstark as having been written by Dadishoʿ and not by Philoxenos of Mabbug.[15] On the very first folio the text itself

---

[10] An edition and French translation exists. See A. Guillaumont and M. Albert, "Lettre de Dadishoʿ Qaṭraya à Abkosh sur L'Hesychia," in E. Lucchesi and H.D. Saffrey, *Mémorial A-J. Festugière*. Geneva, 1984, pp. 235–245.

[11] Edited and translated by A. Mingana, *Woodbrooke Studies*, vol. 7, 1934, pp. 70–143/201–47.

[12] Some excerpts were published and translated by N. Sims-Williams, "Dādišoʿ Qaṭrāyā's Commentary on the *Paradise of the Fathers*," in *Analecta Bollandiana*, 112, 1994, pp. 33–64.

[13] Ibid., p. 33.

[14] A critical edition of Dadishoʿ's "Commentary on the *Paradise of the Fathers*" is being prepared by David Phillips. See R. Kitchen, "Dadisho Qatraya's *Commentary on 'Abba Isaiah'*. The *Apophthegmata Patrum* Connection," in *StPatr* 41, 2006, pp. 35–50.

[15] The manuscript is Berlin Syr. 244, ff. 1ʳ–112ʳ. See E. Sachau, *Verzeichniss der syrischen Handschriften der Königlichen Bibliothek zu Berlin*, vol. II. Berlin, 1899, p. 742; A. Baumstark, *Geschichte der syrischen Literatur mit*

attributes the work to Philoxenos of Mabbug, referred to as
Fīloksīnūs al-Siryānī:

> I begin with the Compendium (ܚܐܠܡܐ,ܐܙ) of the book of
> the stories (ܐܚܕܐܙ) of the Egyptian monks and its
> explanation (ܘܣܝܩܗ) by Fīloksīnūs (ܠܟܣܝܢܘܣܡܘܣ) the
> Syrian.[16]

Sachau was apparently the first to establish the relationship between this Garshuni abridged version or Compendium of Dadishoʿ's commentary and a Syriac abridged version to be found in the British Library[17] in 1899. He did not, however, identify the author of both texts as Dadishoʿ, leaving this important conclusion to be drawn by Anton Baumstark twenty-three years later in a brief (and mostly unnoticed) sentence to be found in his *History of Syriac Literature* published in German in 1922[18] where he identifies both as being authored by Dadishoʿ and not Philoxenos of Mabbug.[19] The same Garshuni Compendium was subsequently identified in a number of other manuscripts to be found in the Vatican, St. Petersburg, Jerusalem and Birmingham.[20] Although Alphonse Mingana published his *Catalogue of the Mingana Collection of Manuscripts* in 1933, it seems that Baumstark's conclusions had eluded him, as can be seen from his catalogue entries for the four manuscripts that include the Garshuni Compendium. In fact, it is only in the 1990s that this erroneous ascription is finally cleared up

---

Ausschluß der christlich-palästinensischen Texte. Bonn, 1922, p. 226, footnote 7, 8.

[16] Berlin Syr. 244, f. 1ʳ: ܐܚܕܘܣ ܚܐܠܡܐ,ܐܙ ܚܐܠܐܕ ܐܚܕܐܙ ܠܟܙܗܕܠ ܠܠܡܨܪܢܝܣ ܘܣܝܩܗ ܠܟܣܝܢܘܣܡܘܣ.

[17] BL Add. 17175. The same Syriac abridged version is also to be found in Vatican sir. 126.

[18] A. Baumstark, *Geschichte der syrischen Literatur mit Ausschluß der christlich-palästinensischen Texte*. Bonn, 1922, p. 226, footnote 7.

[19] The manuscript is Berlin Syr. 244, ff. 1ʳ–112ʳ. See E. Sachau, *Verzeichniss der syrischen Handschriften der Königlichen Bibliothek zu Berlin*. Vol. II. Berlin, 1899, p. 742; A. Baumstark, *Geschichte der syrischen Literatur mit Ausschluß der christlich-palästinensischen Texte*. Bonn, 1922, p. 226, footnotes 7, 8.

[20] For details see N. Sims-Williams, "Dādišoʿ Qaṭrāyā's Commentary on the *Paradise of the Fathers*," in *Analecta Bollandiana*, 112, 1994, pp. 38.

completely with an article by Nicholas Sims-Williams entitled: "Dādišoʿ Qaṭrāyā's Commentary on the *Paradise of the Fathers*" in *Analecta Bollandiana*, 112, 1994, p. 38. Interestingly, Sims-Williams points out[21] that the first scholar to argue that Dadishoʿ was the author of the Garshuni Compendium was in fact Baron Victor Rosen in his catalogue of Arabic manuscripts entitled *Notices sommaires des manuscrits arabes du Musée Asiatique* published in 1881,[22] forty-one years before Baumstark and unnoticed by Sachau and Mingana. Rosen's argument is based on internal evidence from the Garshuni Compendium manuscript he was describing, which is now to be found in the Asiatic Museum in St Petersburg. His argument is partly based on the identification of two books referred to and cited from in the Garshuni Compendium as having been composed by Dadishoʿ and uses the catalogue of ʿAbdishoʿ bar Brikā in order to corroborate this identification. The two works are the *Commentary on the Book of Abbā Isaiah* (كتاب تفسير انبا اشعيا), and *The Book of Perfection of Disciplines*, (كتاب التدبير الكامل). The identification of the *Commentary on the Book of Abbā Isaiah* as having been composed by Dadishoʿ is, of course, correct. On the other hand, *The Book of the Perfection of Disciplines* was in fact a monastic work, extant today in only three other known fragments,[23] written by Theodore of Mopsuestia. Theodore's works were translated from Greek into Syriac in Edessa in the first half of the fifth century and he enjoyed a great deal of authority in the Church of the East, being quoted extensively by authors such as Dadishoʿ. The confusion lies in the fact that all the names and titles of the doctrinal and monastic authorities specifically venerated by the Church of the East, such as Theodore of Mopsuestia, have been omitted or changed in the West Syriac manuscript witnesses and their Garshuni translations. Thus "Theodore the Blessed Interpreter" is often reduced to "the blessed interpreter" or "the

---

[21] Ibid., p. 34, footnote 5 and p. 38, footnote 25.

[22] V. Rosen, *Notices sommaires des manuscrits arabes du Musée Asiatique*, I. St. Petersburg, 1881, pp. 6–12.

[23] F. Graffin, "Une page retrouvée de Théodore de Mopsueste," pp. 29–34 in *A Tribute to Arthur Vööbus: Studies in Early Christian Literature and Its Environment, Primarily in the Syrian East*. Edited by Fischer, Robert H.. Chicago, Illinois: The Lutheran School of Theology at Chicago, 1977.

interpreter saint" or even changed to "Abba Evagrius," that is, Evagrius of Pontus, the universally revered monastic intellectual and author. The same is the case with Dadishoʿ himself who is transformed, as we have seen, into "Philoxenos the Syrian" at the outset of the Garshuni Compendium.

Clearly, the conscious attribution of this text to Philoxenos of Mabbug, one of the most important Syriac Orthodox theologians from the sixth century, in the rubric of many of these manuscripts, is an indication of the West Syriac Orthodox tradition to which they belong. Interestingly, a Syriac manuscript at the British Library (Add. 17264) reveals that a Syriac Orthodox copyist has omitted the name of Dadishoʿ who, as mentioned earlier, was a member of the Church of the East, and also omitted the name of his monastery but left his demonym "Qaṭraya," a very useful clue! In fact, an older Church of the East manuscript tradition also survives with Dadishoʿ Qaṭraya's name fully intact.

Unlike ʿNānishoʿ's *Paradise*, the Garshuni compendium is divided into four parts (ܐܓܙܐ / ܓܙܘ). In the copy to be found in the Vatican library[24] the first part is attributed to Philoxenos, the second to Barsanuphius, the third to Hieronimus and the fourth to Palladius.[25] The Berlin copy, however, as well as the oldest copy to be found in the Mingana collection[26] (c. 1480 CE) both clearly attribute the whole commentary to Philoxenos the Syrian (ܦܝܠܟܣܝܢܘܣ ܐܠܣܪܝܐܢܝ) at the very outset whereas the division of the parts and their attribution to Hieronimus (ܥܝܪܘܢܐܡܝܣ) for the third part[27] and Palladius (ܒܠܐܕܝܣ) for the fourth part[28] relate to Dadishoʿs reading of ʿNānishoʿ's *Paradise*. The first two parts do not seem to be attributed to anyone to judge from the rubric with

---

[24] Vat. ar. 85.

[25] See E. Tisserant, "Philoxène de Mabboug," in *DThC* 12, 1935, pp. 1521–1522.

[26] Mingana Syr. 403.

[27] Berlin Syr. 244, f. 29ᵛ: "The Compendium of the third part is complete, the part which belongs to ʿĪrūnāmīs who wrote the inquiries." ܟܡܠ ܡܟܬܨܪ ܐܠܓܙܘ ܐܠܬܐܠܬ. ܓܙܘ ܥܝܪܘܢܐܡܝܣ ܐܠܕܝ ܘܨܥ ܐܠܡܣܐܝܠ.

[28] Berlin Syr. 244, ff. 29ᵛ–30ʳ: "The fourth part which is the last of the stories of the solitaries written in the book *The Paradise*. From the last part which Balādīs wrote." ܐܠܓܙܘ ܐܠܪܐܒܥ ܘܗܘ ܐܠܐܟܝܪ ܡܢ ܐܟܒܐܪ ܐܠܡܬܘܚܕܝܢ ܐܠܡܟܬܘܒܗ ܦܝ ܟܬܐܒ ܐܠܦܪܕܘܣ. ܡܢ ܐܠܓܙܘ ܐܠܐܟܝܪ ܐܠܕܝ (sic) ܟܬܒܗ ܒܠܐܕܝܣ.

which the second part begins[29] although it may be argued, given the opening attribution, that they may be understood as both being attributed to Philoxenos. What must also be taken into consideration is that the Berlin, Mingana and Vatican Library copies are, all three, acephalous and refer to themselves as such. It remains to be verified whether the copy in St Petersburg is different in this regard as well as in the attribution of the parts, and consequently representing perhaps a different manuscript tradition. A preliminary investigation based on Rosen's catalogue entry, however, suggests that this is not the case.

It is not at all the case that the selected content which is commented upon in each of these parts can be located in the equivalent part of ʿNānishoʿ's *Paradise*. Take for example, the story of the vision of two great boats in one of which Abba Arsenius was travelling in silence with the spirit of God while in the second was Abba Moses and the angels of God who were feeding him honey from the comb. This is found in the third part of the *Paradise*,[30] but in the Garshuni Compendium in Berlin it appears on folios 3ᵛ–4ʳ[31] and thus in the first part of the commentary. More significantly, this four part division is not to be found in the full version of Dadishoʿ's commentary in Syriac as is apparent in the second most complete extant manuscript at the British Library (Add. 17264), the first part of which is damaged, but which is organized into two books, the first of which covers Books I–III of the *Paradise* while the second book corresponds to Book IV. It remains to be seen through comparative textual analysis whether the abridged version of the commentary in Syriac (or 'Epitome'), also to be found in the British library (Add. 17175), is, like the Garshuni Compendium,

[29] Berlin Syr. 244, f. 25ʳ: "That [which] was abridged from the second part is complete and God is my strength." ܬܡ [ܡܐ] ܐܟܬܨܪ ܒܚܣܒ ܡܢ ܐܠܩܣܡ ܐܠܬܐܢܝ ܘܐܠܠܗ ܐܠܡܥܝܢ ܒܗ ܀

[30] Ernest A.W. Budge, *The Book of Paradise*…, 2 vols. London, 1904, vol. 1, pp. 597–8.

[31] Berlin Syr. 244, ff. 3ᵛ–4ʳ: "He saw two boats in a river and Arsānīyūs was in one of them in silence and the spirit of God was with him and Anbā Mūsā was in the other and the angels and saints were with him and were feeding him honey from a comb." ܦܪܐܝ ܡܪܟܒܝܢ ܦܝ ܢܗܪ ܃ ܘܐܪܣܐܢܝܘܣ ܦܝ ܐܚܕܗܡܐ (sic) ܦܝ ܐܠܣܟܘܬ ܘܪܘܚ ܐܠܠܗ ܡܥܗ ܃ ܘܐܢܒܐ ܡܘܣܐ ܦܝ ܐܠܐܟܪ ܘܐܠܡܠܐܝܟܗ ܘܐܠܩܕܝܣܝܢ ܡܥܗ ܘܗܡ ܝܛܥܡܘܢܗ ܥܣܠ ܡܢ ܫܗܕ.

divided into four parts or follows the same ordering.³² What might be concluded at this stage is that both the full version and the Epitome in Syriac as well as the Garshuni Compendium all seem to be acephalous for different reasons. The full Syriac version (Add. 17264) is acephalous due to the fact that the first two quires are lost, while the first 19 folios of the Epitome in Syriac (Add. 17175), although partially mutilated at the beginning, appear to contain lost material from the beginning of Dadishoʿ's full commentary.³³ This hypothesis, first proposed by N. Sims-Williams was recently confirmed in an article by David Phillips.³⁴ Basing his conclusion on the recent discovery of the most complete text to date (found in the Metropolitan Library of the Church of the East in Baghdad) comprising the full Syriac version of the commentary that includes most of the missing section at the beginning³⁵ Phillips states:

> Until the discovery of G [=the Baghdad MS] the initial logia (ff° 1r°–19v°) were not immediately identifiable in DQC [=Dadishoʿ's full commentary] and Sims-Williams suggested, that they were "based on lost material" from DQC I. His hypothesis has been vindicated by the material now made available by G: the initial logia in g [=Add. 17175] do indeed find parallels in DQC as attested by the Baghdad manuscript.³⁶

In contrast, the Garshuni Compendium actually begins towards the end of the answer to question I/14 and includes the six concluding

---

³² D. Phillips, "The Syriac Commentary of Dadishoʿ Qatraya on the *Paradise of the Fathers*. Towards a Critical Edition," in *BABELAO* 1, 2012, pp. 1–23, states on p.16: "The beginning and end are missing and there are no subdivisions into books. No numbering system has been applied to questions and answers, but each question-and-answer group has been supplied with a title written vertically in the margin."

³³ See N. Sims-Williams, "Dādishoʿ Qatrāyā's Commentary on the *Paradise of the Fathers*," in *Analecta Bollandiana*, 112, 1994, p. 38.

³⁴ D. Phillips, "The Syriac Commentary of Dadishoʿ Qatraya on the *Paradise of the Fathers*. Towards a Critical Edition," in *BABELAO* 1, 2012, pp. 1–23.

³⁵ Ibid., p. 12: "…there are some missing folios at the beginning and the end."

³⁶ Ibid., p. 16.

topics,[37] which makes it most likely the case that the Garshuni Compendium is either an elaboration of the Epitome or the product of a direct contact with an acephalous full Syriac version. This is further verified by the fact that the end of the first part of the Compendium refers to what it calls "the first copy" (ܢܣܟܗ ܐܠܐܘܠܗ) which states that "forty inquiries" (ܐܪܒܥܝܢ ܡܣܐܠܗ) are missing:

> The first part is complete with God's aid and it is mentioned in the first copy that forty inquiries are missing at its beginning.[38]

Given that the material at the beginning of the full Syriac version and of the Epitome has been established[39] as coming at the end of the answer to question I/14 (ܐܪܒܥܬܥܫܪ) and not forty (ܐܪܒܥܝܢ) could this error, which originates in II/14 of the full Syriac version, have been inherited by the Garshuni Compendium indirectly through the Epitome? There is also, however, the possibility that the error may have come directly from the full Syriac version if the Garshuni Compendium in fact reveals itself to be different from the Epitome. Given that the Epitome is not completely preserved in the British Library manuscript (Add. 17175) which is damaged at the beginning and end, the publication and translation of the Garshuni Compendium will help reconstruct this Epitome as well as reveal any material that has been preserved in the Garshuni but has been lost in both the Epitome and the full Syriac version of Dadisho's commentary.

Further, the Garshuni Compendium does not mark the end of the literary journey of Dadisho''s commentary for, in fact, an Ethiopic (Geʿez) translation of this Compendium survives in

37 These six topics are listed simply as numbers in the Garshuni. Berlin Syr. 244, f. 4r : ܐܠܬܐܢܝ ; f. 4v : ܐܠܬܐܠܬ ; f. 8r : ܐܠܪܐܒܥ ; f. 11r : ܐܠܚܐܡܣ ; f. 12r: ܘ̱.

38 Berlin Syr. 244, f. 18v: ܟܡܠ ܐܠܓܙܘ ܐܠܐܘܠ ܒܡܥܘܢܬ ܐܠܠܗ ܘܘܓܕ ܦܝ ܢܣܟܗ ܐܠܐܘܠܗ ܐܢܗ ܢܩܨ ܡܢ ܐܘܠܗ ܐܪܒܥܝܢ ܡܣܐܠܗ.

39 See N. Sims-Williams, "Dādišoʿ Qaṭrāyā's Commentary on the *Paradise of the Fathers*," in *Analecta Bollandiana*, 112, 1994, p. 37.

numerous copies and is yet to be fully edited or translated.⁴⁰ The importance of investigating the history of the translation process of Dadishoʿ's commentary from Syriac into Arabic and subsequently into Geʿez is that it will provide a very rare opportunity to acquire valuable insights into the transmission of knowledge and cultural material from an originally Syriac work into other languages and cultures over the course of many centuries, from the seventh century to the most recent Garshuni and Ethiopic manuscripts of the eighteenth and nineteenth centuries. Furthermore, it will trace the changing use of the text and its intent which in both the Garshuni and Geʿez versions seems to be to immerse the novice monk in the spiritual lore of the monastic vocation, and to saturate his mind and spirit with advice and warnings about the pitfalls of aiming to be perfect while remaining nevertheless an imperfect human being. Only complete editions of the Syriac, Garshuni, and Geʿez versions of Dadishoʿ's commentary on the *Paradise* will bring to light the significance and impact of the work of this great literary survivor from Beth Qaṭraye.

A Note on the Manuscripts

A significant step towards this overall goal is the full critical edition and translation presented here of Dadishoʿ Qaṭraya's *Compendious Commentary* on *The Paradise of the Egyptian Fathers* in Garshuni. The edition is based on the oldest extant copy, Mingana Syr. 403, dated c. 1480 and uses all of the other copies to be found in the Mingana collection (Mingana Syr. 174, Mingana Syr. 370, Mingana Syr. 457). In addition to these, two other manuscripts are used: Berlin Syr. 244 and Vat. ar. 85. What follows is the list of witnesses:

List Of Witnesses

A   **Mingana Syr. 403**

The Commentary is to be found in folios 1r–93v of this manuscript. It is written by one hand in a clear West Syriac *serṭo* script. The headings are written in red. It was copied from a manuscript that was written from another manuscript

---

⁴⁰ See W. Witakowski, "Filekseyus, the Ethiopic version of the Syriac Dadisho Qatraya's Commentary on the Paradise of the Fathers," in *Rocznik Orientalistyczny*, 59, 2006, pp. 281–296.

preserved in the "Monastery of St Antony" dated 1545 of the Greeks, 1234 AD (this date is given in the colophon of C, f. 115r below). We are further informed that the work was translated from Syriac into Arabic by one who was not much accustomed to such translations. No date is given. Alphonse Mingana estimates it to be from about 1480 AD it would thus represent the oldest extant complete copy.

B   **Berlin Syr. 244**

The Commentary is to be found in folios 1v–113v of this manuscript. It is written in a thick West Syriac *serṭo* script with punctuation and Garshuni *rukokho* and *qushoyo* dots in red. Dated 2016 of the Greeks or 1705 AD (f.156v).

C   **Mingana Syr. 174**

The Commentary is to be found in folios 44v–114v of this manuscript. At the end of the previous treatise (f. 44v) the names of the copyists of the whole manuscript appear as Joseph, son of Alous al-Munayyir from the Khazraj quarter of the town of Mosul, and Joseph son of Hanna Zati the brother of the deacon Stephen. No date is given. It was copied from a manuscript that was written from another manuscript preserved in the "Monastery of St Antony" dated 1545 of the Greeks, 1234 AD (f. 115r). Written in a clear West Syriac *serṭo* script of about 1840 AD according to Mingana's estimate. Headings, important words, punctuation, and Garshuni *rukokho* and *qushoyo* dots in red.

D   **Mingana Syr. 370**

The Commentary is to be found in folios 72r–142v of this manuscript. It is acephalus and begins in the Fourth Section. The date of the manuscript is given as 1999 of the Greeks or 1688 AD (f. 71v). It is written in a clear West Syriac *serṭo* script. Headings only are written in red. Broad margins. The copyist's name has disappeared in a lacuna.

E   **Mingana Syr. 457**

The Commentary is to be found in folios 72r–146r of this

manuscript. Like D it is acephalus beginning at the exact same point as D in the Fourth Section. It is dated (ff. 71v and 146r) 4th of May and 6th July respectively of the year 1843 AD and copied by Ephrem son of Zakkār from the family of Kass Ibrahim. It is written in a clear West Syriac *serṭo* script. Headings, punctuation, and Garshuni *rukokho* and *qushoyo* dots in red.

F   **Vat. ar. 85**

The Commentary is to be found in folios 3r–250v of this manuscript. The text is written in the Arabic script. No date but probably nineteenth century. The text is referred to on at least two occasions as *Bustān al-Ruhbān* (f. 54r, f. 42v) although, of course, it bears no direct resemblance to the more well-known Coptic spiritual handbook for monks which bears the same title. The text is in a question and answer format and is divided into four parts attributed to Philoxenos (f. 3r), Barsanuphius (f. 54r), Hieronimus (f. 92r) and Palladius (f. 119r) respectively. Only the first part attributed to Philoxenos is directly related to MSS A–E and even here the text often represents a reading of the Garshuni. In fact the first part as found in this text is almost double in length. The direct correspondence ends on f. 30r, marking the end of the first part in the other manuscripts, after which only a very loose correlation is discernible most notably in the fourth part (f. 119r) which is similarly attributed to Palladius. Most probably Coptic in origin and incomplete at the end.

Stemma Codicum

This edition is based on a collation of five of the most important available witnesses (ABCDE) and partial reference to F which represents a later paraphrase of the original text written in the Arabic script. While a complete stemma must await a full collation of all the available witnesses the below diagram may be proposed as the most probable. The two main points of uncertainty are whether B shares an ancestor with AD or whether it is independently derived from α, and whether E is in fact a direct descendant of D rather than a descendant of a sibling of D. E is acephalus beginning at the exact same point as D in the Fourth Section. Regarding the latter question, the places where D is in error but E is not could be argued to be correctible errors. At present, therefore, the relationship of D to E is uncertain. In the stemma below, the Greek letters represent hypothetical texts which are not extant. Their place chronologically is not significant, but represents only the textual relationship between their descendants. The sole exception to the rule that hypothetical manuscripts are not anchored in time is the ancestor of both A and C, whose date is given in the colophon of C and may very well be the archetype α.[41]

MANUSCRIPTS

1. Mingana Syr. 403 = A
2. Berlin Syr. 244 = B
3. Mingana Syr. 174 = C
4. Mingana Syr. 370 = D
5. Mingana Syr. 457 – E
6. Vat. ar. 85 = F

---

[41] C, f. 115^r.

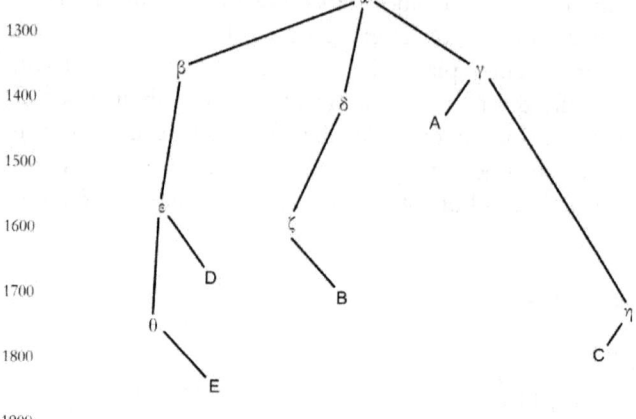

TEXT AND TRANSLATION

Dadisho' Qaṭraya's *Compendious Commentary on The Paradise of the Egyptian Fathers*

Translators: Mario Kozah, Abdulrahim Abu-Husayn, Suleiman Mourad

1   In the name of the Father, the Son and the Holy Spirit, the One God. I commence by summarizing the Book of the Egyptian Fathers[1] and its commentary written by Philoxenos the Syrian,[2] the bishop of Mabbug, assisted by their holy prayers. The first fifteen questions and their responses:

2   **The brothers asked**: we shall begin at the start of the story: there were two brothers who were the sons of a merchant.[3] When he passed away, they divided up the inheritance and each of them got five thousand dinars. It occurred to them to please God through perfect righteousness. The first one distributed his share [of the inheritance] between the churches, monasteries, the wretched and the needy. He learned a handicraft to earn his living; while always persisting in stillness, prayer and fasting. The second one built a monastery where fellow monks gathered, welcoming there with joy the strangers, the poor, the elderly, the sick, and all who happened to be present, and he would give them respite. Thus he spent all his money.

Some brothers favored what one of the two brothers did while others favored the way of life of the other. They asked Abba Pambo which one of the two is better. He replied: "They are both perfect because the first worked like Elijah while the other acted according to Abraham's way of life." Some questioned this asking, "How could they be equal since the first accomplished our Lord's command for the Perfect which states: 'If you aspire to perfection, sell all that is yours, give it to the poor and follow me'."[4] Others answered saying, "The second is the blessed by virtue of our Lord saying: 'Who then is the servant who is wise and faithful, whom his master appoints over his household, to give them his food at the proper time? Blessed is that servant, whom, when his master comes, he will find doing this. Amen, I say to you, he will set him over everything he has'."[5]

DADISHOʿ QAṬRAYA'S *COMPENDIOUS COMMENTARY* ON *THE PARADISE OF THE EGYPTIAN FATHERS*

EDITOR: MARIO KOZAH

1 (a1r/b1v/c44v/f3r) بسم الاب والابن والروح¹ القدس الاه² واحد. ابتدي باختصار كتاب اخبار الرهبان المصريين وشرحه لفيلكسينوس السرياني اسقف منبج بمعونة صلواتهم المقدسه الاول خمس عشر ورده.³

2 **قالوا الاخوه** نبتدي من بداية السيرة. كان اخوان ولدا⁴ رجّل⁵ تاجر. ولما تنيّح⁶ اقتسما ميراثه فصار لكل منهما خمسة الاف⁷ دينار فخطر على⁸ قلبهما (f3v) ان يرضوا⁹ الله بكمال البر. ففرق احدهما نصيبه¹⁰ على الكنايس والاديره والمساكين والمحتاجين وتعلّم¹¹ صنعة اليد لقوت يومه وداوم الهدوا¹² والصلاة والصوم. والاخر بنّى ديراً وجمع عندهُ اخوه. وكان يقبل الغربا¹³ والفقرا والشيوخ والمرضى¹⁴ بفرح. وكل من يتفق وينيّحهم.¹⁵ وهكذا¹⁶ فرق جميع مالهُ فصار بعض الاخوه يفضل عمل الواحد وبعضهم يفضل تدبير الاخر. فسالوا الطوباني انبا بموي¹⁷ ايهما افضل فقال هما¹⁸ كاملان لان الاول عمل مثل ايليا¹⁹ والاخر عمل²⁰ كتدبير²¹ ابرهم.²² فقال بعضهم كيف يتساويان (c45r) والاول كمل (f4r) وصية ربنا التي (b2r) للكاملين القايله²³ ان كنت تريد ان تكون كاملاً²⁴ بع كل ما لك وادفعهُ للمساكين واتبعني. والاخرُ اجابوا قايلين ان الثاني هو المغبوط لقول ربنا من هو الوكيل الحكيم الامين الذي يقيمه سيدهُ على بيته ليعطيهم طعامهُ²⁵ في حينه. طوبا لذلك²⁶ العبد الذي ياتي سيده فيجده يعمل هكذى.²⁷ الحق اقول لكم انه يقيمهُ على جميع ما لهُ.

He [Abba Pambo] said, "Give me a little time so that I may inquire from God." A few days later, they came to him. He said to them: "I saw them [the two brothers] standing before God in the Paradise of Eden."

3 **The master stated**: "As for intent, they were equal since both intended to please God the way each of them considered fit to accomplish God's will. Thus they were equal in their intent to love and obey God. As for the way of life, the one who gave up everything and followed the Lord had the better way, since he removed the causes of falling into what distances one from God and was not preoccupied with any thoughts that may prevent communion with God. The way of life in Christianity is of two types: the way of the Upright and the way of the Perfect. The way of the Upright is how Abraham, Sarah, Zacchaeus and Martha lived. The way of the Perfect is how Elijah, Matthew, Hannah, and Mary, Martha's sister, lived. The way of life of Matthew and Elijah is better than the way of life of Abraham and Zacchaeus. The work that Hannah and Mary did, is better than that of Sarah and Martha; not where intent is concerned, but in the way of life. For Abraham was perfect in his intent of love for God and people while wandering in the world. God willed this since He intended that Christ be his descendant. Thus also King David, who was modest and pious. However, the way of life of Elijah was better than theirs."

When a brother asked Abba Nastir about the way of life he should follow,[6] he answered him: "It is written that Abraham used to love strangers and God was with him. David was humble and God was with him. Every act which is of God, do it and God be with you." He did not say to him go back to the world, get married, and serve strangers as Abraham did, and be humble towards your subordinates like David. Rather he meant that one should, in monastic life, do deeds of God because monastic life according to the Fathers consists of three parts: stillness with exertion, sickness with gratitude, and service with joy and vitality. He who is in stillness is always content and his heart boils over with the love of God like Elijah. He fasts and prays without interruption and endures in fighting the invisible and the visible Satan. He does this for God and not for men. He who is in perpetual sickness acts like David in forgiveness and like the patience of Job in forbearance

فقال اصبروا عليّ²⁸ قليلاً²⁹ حتى استعلم من الله. وبعد ايام اتوا اليه ³⁰ (a1v) فقال لهم ³¹ رايتها قايمين قدام الله في فردوس النعيم ³² عدن.

قال المعلم ³³ (f4v) اما في الضمير فكانا متساويان لانهما اضمرا ان يرضيا الله بحسب ما راه كل واحد³⁴ منها انهُ يوصل الى تكميل³⁵ ارادة الله. فتساوَيا³⁶ في النيةِ³⁷ في محبة الله وطاعته.³⁸ واما في التدبير فالذي ترك كلشي³⁹ وتبع الرب تدبيره افضل لانه قطع اسباب السقوط في ما يبعد عن ⁴⁰ الله ولم يشغل فكرهُ بشيّ ⁴¹ يمنع⁴² اتصالهُ بالله. وتدبير النصرانيه على قسمين. تدبير الصالحين (b2v) وتدبير الكاملين. فتدبير الصالحين هو عمل ابراهيم وساره وزكى⁴³ ومرتا. وتدبير الكاملين هو تدبير اليا⁴⁴ ومتى وحنّه ومريم اخت مرتا. وتدبير متى⁴⁵ وايليا⁴⁶ افضل من تدبير (f5r) ⁴⁷ ابرهيم⁴⁸ وزكى.⁴⁹ وعمل حنه⁵⁰ ومريم افضل من⁵¹ عمل ساره ومرتا ليس في الضمير بل في التدبير لان ابرهيم⁵² كان كاملاً في⁵³ ضميره في حب الله والناس في تقلبه⁵⁴ في العالم والله اراد هذا لانه (ان يكون⁵⁵) مزمع ان يكون⁵⁶ المسيح من نسله. وكذلك داوود⁵⁷ الملك كان متضعًا وبارًا. لكن تدبير اليا⁵⁸ كان افضل من تدبيرهما. ولما سال اخ انبا نستير⁵⁹ عن تدبير يتدبر فيه⁶⁰ قال له⁶¹ مكتوب ان ابرهيم⁶² كان يحب الغربا وكان الله معهُ. وداوود⁶³ كان متضعًا⁶⁴ والله كان معه. وكل فعلٍ يكون لله اصنعه والله يكون معك. وما قال لهُ ارجع الى العالم وتزوّج واخدم (f5v) الغربا مثل ابرهيم.⁶⁵ واتضع لمن تروس⁶⁶ عليه مثل داوود.⁶⁷ بل قصد منه ان (c45v) يتدبر في الرهبنه بعمل من الاعمال التي لله لان تدبير الرهبنه عند الابا (a2r) على ثلائة اقسام. الهدوا⁶⁸ مع المجاهده والمرض (b3r) ⁶⁹ مع الشكر والخدمه مع فرح⁷⁰ ونشاط. فالذي في الهدوا يلزم القناعه ويغلي قلبه في حب الله مثل ايليا ويصوم ويصلّي⁷¹ بلا فتور ويصبر⁷² لقتال الشيطان الخفي والظاهر. ويعمل ذلك من اجل الله لا من اجل الناس. والذي في المرض الدايم يتشبّه في الغفران بداوود وفي طول الروح بصبر⁷³ ايوب

and his thanksgiving to God. He never tires of the one he serves or of what may be disagreeable to him. He who is unable to remain in stillness and is not perpetually sick, as a consequence he serves the sick brother, the frail old man, or the brother who is in permanent stillness, for the sake of God only and not for a worldly purpose. Rather, he abandons his whims and carries out the will of the one he serves lovingly and joyfully not grudgingly and with grumblings, and serves him for the sake of Christ as if serving Christ. A man such as these [aforementioned] three if they were such, are equal in reward as is the case of the above-mentioned two brothers. Since the two brothers were perfect in their way of life, each in his own way. The first in stillness and the second in service.

For this reason Abba Pambo said: "If it were not for one brother's fasting and prayers he would not have reached the compassion and service of the other. And if it were not for the service rendered with upright intention by the other, he would not be equal to the one in stillness."[7]

The Blessed Antony said: "There are those who spend many years in stillness in their cells without learning how to sit still there for one single day; which means that he did not regard himself as sinful, helpless, and ignorant but justified himself and blamed others."[8]

Perfect stillness is the best way of life just as the spirit of God is better than the spiritual saintly angels. For a certain brother went to join Arsenius but he did not accept him or grant him repose because he cherished solitary stillness. He then went to Abba Moses who accepted him in joyful welcome. Upon hearing this, a certain brother exclaimed: "How can it be O Lord that the one runs away from people for your sake while the other accepts people for your sake!" He then saw two boats in a river. In one boat was Arsenius in stillness and the spirit of God was with him and in the second was Abba Moses accompanied by the angels and saints feeding him honey from the comb.[9] The way of life of stillness is better because it is superior to human nature and this is the way of life of the virtuous, the solitaries, and the wandering itinerant [monks].

وشكرهُ⁷⁴ لله. ولا يضجر على خديمهِ ولا من عدم ما⁷⁵ يوافقهُ. وان كان (f6r)⁷⁶ ما يقدر⁷⁷ يمكث في الهدوا⁷⁸ ولا مرضهُ دايم ولذلك يخدم الاخ المريض والشيخ الضعيف او⁷⁹ الاخ الدايم⁸⁰ من اجل الله فقط وليس من اجل غرض دنياني. بل يقطع هواه ويصنع ارادة الذي يخدمهُ بالحب والفرح لا بالتكره والتذمر بل يخدمه⁸² من⁸³ اجل المسيح كانه يخدم المسيح. لان⁸⁴ انساناً فهولاي⁸⁵ الثلثه⁸⁶ اذا كانوا هكذى⁸⁷ (b3v) كانوا متساويين في المجازاه كما تقدم من⁸⁸ حال الاخوين لانهما كانا كاملين في تدبيرهما في حال⁸⁹ الوحده. ⁹⁰ الواحد في الهدوا⁹¹ والاخر في الخدمه. ولهذا قال انبا بموي⁹² لولا صوم الواحد وصلاته ماكان يصل الى (f6v) رحمة وخدمة الاخر. ولولا خدمة الاخر بنية مستقيمه ماكان يساوي الذي في الهدوا.⁹³ وقد⁹⁴ قال الطوباني انطونيوس ان ثم⁹⁵ من يسكن قلايته في الهدوا⁹⁶ سنين كثيره ولا يعرف كيف الجلوس فيها يومٌ واحدًا.⁹⁷ يعني انه ما يحسب نفسه خاطيًا وعاجزًا وجاهلًا بل يبرّر نفسه⁹⁸ ويلوم اخرين. فاما⁹⁹ الهدوا¹⁰⁰ الكامل فهو التدبير الافضل. كما ان روح الله افضل من الملايكه الروحانيين القديسين. لان بعض (a2v) الاخوه مضى الى ارسانيوس¹⁰¹ فما قبلهُ ولا نيّحهُ من اجل محبته لهدوا الوحده. فمضى¹⁰² الى انبا موسى (f7r)¹⁰³ فقبلهُ بفرح وبشاشه. فلما سمع بعض الاخوه قال يا رب كيف واحد يهرب من الناس من اجلك. واخر يقبل الناس (c46r) من اجلك. فراى مركبين في نهر وارسانيوس¹⁰⁴ في احدهما في الهدو وروح الله معه. وانبا موسى في الاخر والملايكه والقديسين¹⁰⁴ معهُ وهم يطعمونهُ عسل.¹⁰⁵ من شهد. فتدبير الهدوا¹⁰⁶ افضل لانهُ اعلاٰ من الطبع البشري. وهو تدبير الافاضل¹⁰⁷ الحبسا والسواح والمنتقلين.

4   **The Second Section:**

The Brothers asked: why did Abba Pambo state, "If it were not for the fasting of one he would not have been equal to the compassion of the other."[10]

5   **The Exegete replied**: "It has been explained above how both of them were correct in their way of life, according to each one's ability. But this should not be stated absolutely. Anyone who gives up all that he owns and sits in stillness but does not fast continuously and does not pray without interruption is not equal to the one who has possessions but has perfect compassion and servitude. The one in stillness could be sick and thankful but cannot because of his sickness be in continuous fasting and prayers. If that brother who has compassion and servitude were living in the world with a wife and children and carried out his service and compassion to the best of the ability of someone living in the world, the Fathers would not regard him in terms of his work and reward as equal with his brother in this solitude just as they did not regard the way of life and reward of Matthew the tax collector as equal with the way of life of Zacchaeus the chief tax collector. Both intended to please God. The extent of the purity of intent and way of life in performing virtuous deeds is matched by the purity of the reward. A man may give up all he owns and live the solitary life with fasting and prayer but his intent is not correct because he seeks glory among the people. And he may also be of correct intent but his way of life is lacking because of laxity in his zeal rather than poor health. Similarly, another man may bring with him his possessions into solitary life and through them relieve the needy but in order to gain glory among people. He may perform this deed for the sake of God but not for the sake of goodness or his love of people but because he does not wish to force himself given the difficulty of stillness."

6   **The Third Section:**

The Brothers asked: "We would like you to demonstrate to us with evidence how it is that one who lives in the world does not deserve to be equal with the solitaries in terms of reward: one who has a wife, children, and possessions and whose way of life is excellent since he gives charity to the poor, releases the imprisoned, frees the enslaved, relieves the afflicted, establishes the right of the

4 الثاني[108] قالوا[109] الاخوه[110] فلماذا قال انبا بموي[111] لولا صوم الواحد ما سَاوَى رحمة الاخر. ولولا خدمة الاخر بنيّة مستقيمه ما سَاوَى[112] اخاه.

5 قال المفسر[113] لما تقدم شرحه (f7v) من استقامة كل واحدٍ منها في تدبيره[114] حسب قدرته. وليس ينبغي ان يقال هذا مطلقاً. ان كلمن[115] يبعد من جميع ما لهُ[116] ويجلس في الهدو ان لم يصُم[117] دايمًا[118] ويصّلي بلا فتور ما يساوي الذي لهُ القنيه[119] والرحمه والخدمة التامه. لان الذي في الهدو قد يكون مريضاً شاكرًا. ولا يقدر لاجل مرضه ان يكون صايمًا مصليًا[120] دايمًا. ولو كان ذلك الاخ الخديم الرحيم في العالم وله زوجه واولاد وهو يصنع الخدمه والرحمه حسب ما يقدر[121] من هو في العالم.[122] (b4v) لما كانت الابا[123] يساوونهُ[124] في عمله وجزايه باخيه الذي في هذه[125] الوحده. كما لم يساووا[126] تدبير[127] وثواب متى العشار بتدبير زكى[128] مقدم العشارين. وكلها[129] قصدًا[130] ان (a3r) يرضيا الله.[131] وبقدر[132] نقاوة[133] النيه والتدبير في عمل الفضايل يكون نقاوة[134] المجازاه. فقد يتعرى[135] انسان من كل قنيته ويتدبر بهذه[136] الوحده بالصوم والصلاه. لكن نيته[137] غير مستقيمه لانه يكون[138] طالبًا لمجد الناس. وقد يكون مستقيم النيه ايضًا وتدبيره ناقص[139] لرخاوه همته الا[140] لضعف جسده. وكذلك[141] قد ياتي اخر بقنيته معه الى الوحده[142] وينيح[143] بها (f8v) المحتاجين لكن من اجل تمجد[144] الناس. وقد يفعل ذلك من اجل الله لكن ليس من اجل[145] جوده ومحبتهِ للبشر بل من اجل انه ما يشا ان يغصب[146] نفسه على صعوبة الهدو ❖❖❖

6 الثالث[147] قالوا[148] الاخوه (c46v) نريد ان تبين لنا بشهاداتٍ كيف لا يستحق المساواه بالمتوحدين في المجازاه. من هو في العالم وله (b5r) زوجه واولاد وقنيه وتدبيرهُ[149] جيّد.[150] فيصدق على المساكين ويخلّص الماسورين ويعتق المستعبدين وينيح المضرورين وينصف

oppressed in the face of oppressors, is generous with the righteous, rules justly between the meek and powerful, does not take a bribe for a judgment nor interest on a loan. He brings up orphans, supports widows, and visits the imprisoned and the sick. He serves God to the best of his ability."

7   **The Exegete replied**: "This is known from the words of the Lord and the way of life of the Fathers. For the Lord called the saints 'the children of light', and he called lay persons 'the children of the world'. Since he stated that, 'The children of this age are wiser than the children of light'[11] in their ignorance. This is because their virtue is easy to practice since it concerns matters that are external to their selves, whereas the virtue of the children of light is difficult to practice because it relates to the thoughts of their souls and the organs of their body. For they offer themselves as a living and holy sacrifice according to the exhortation of Paul the Apostle.[12] They act according to the commandment of our Lord who said: 'If you want to be perfect, sell all your possessions and give to the poor, take up the cross and follow me',[13] that is, serve me within yourself and not with what is external to you, and die to the desires and concerns of the world. Seek, therefore, to serve the Lord alone such that you are not distracted from this by worldly affairs, in view of his words, 'Where I am there my servant will be; he who serves me, the Father will honor',[14] and, Love the Lord alone to the exclusion of all others,[15] and his words, 'He who loves father or mother or woman or children more than me is not worthy of me'.[16] They departed from their race and nation, and resisted their desires in order to accomplish his will when he said, 'He who does not hate his father and his mother and his brothers and his sisters and his wife and his children and indeed even himself, he cannot be my disciple'.[17] They denied themselves and endured satanic trials and natural tribulations for the sake of his words, 'Whoever wants to follow me, let him deny himself and take up his cross every day and let him come after me'.[18] These are the words that the Lord spoke to those who departed from the world and sought him alone bearing all afflictions unto death, joyful in their proximity to the Lord. As for the lay, the Lord said to them: 'Make friends for yourselves by means of unrighteous wealth, so that when it fails they may receive you into their eternal dwellings',[19] that is, just as you receive in your homes the ascetic servants of God who own

المظلومين من الظالمين ويكرم الصديقين ويعدل في الحكم بين[151] الضعفا والاقويا.[152] ولا ياخذ على الحكم رشوه (f9r)[153] ولا على القرضه[154] ربا. ويربي الايتام ويقوم[155] بالارامل ويزور المحبوسين والمرضى. ويخدم الله على[156] قدر قدرته.[157]

قال المفسّر[158] هذا معروف من اقوال الرب وتدبير الابا. فان الرب دعا[159] القديسين بني النور وسمى العلمانيين[160] بني العالم. اذ قال ان بني هذا الدهر احكم من بني النور[161] في جلهم.[162] وهذا لان فضيلتهم سهلة[163] العمل لانها بالامور الخارجه عن ذواتهم. وفضيلة[164] بني النور صعبة العمل لانها بافكار (a3v) نفوسهم واعضا اجسادهم فهم يقربون ذواتهم ضحايا[165] ناطقه مقدسه بوصية[166] الرسول بولس.[167] (b5v) وعاملون بامر ربنا القايل ان[168] تريد[169] (f9v) ان تكون كاملاً بع[170] كل ما لك وادفعهُ للمساكين واحمل الصليب واتبعني. اي اخدمني بذاتك لا بما هو[171] خارج عنك. ومت من شهوات العالم وهمومه. فطلبوا[172] خدمة الرب وحده حيث لا يعوقهم عنها الامور العالميه ناظرين الى قوله حيث اكون انا هناك يكون[173] خادمي. ومن يخدمني يكرمه الاب. واحبوا الرب وحده وتركوا[174] محبة غيره لقوله من احب ابا[175] او امًّا[176] او امراةً[177] او بنتًا[177] اكثر مني فما يستحقّني. وفارقوا جنسهم ووطنهم وقاوموا اهويتهم ليكملوا ارادته لقوله من لم يبغض[178] اباه وامه واخوته وخواته (f10r) وزوجته واولاده نعم حتى ونفسه لا يقدر ان يكون لي تلميّذا. ورفضوا نفوسهم واحتملوا التجارب الشيطانيه والمصاعب الطبيعيه لاجل قوله من اراد ان يتبعني فليكفر بنفسه ويحمل صليبهُ كليوم[179] ويّتبعني. فهذه الاقوال قالها الرب للذين تركوا العالم وطلبوه وحده صابرين على كل[180] (b6r) المضايق[180] الى الموت مسرورين بالتقرب الى الرب. (c47r) فاما العلمانيون[181] فلهم قال الرب اتخذنوا لكم اصدقا من مال الظلم حتى فنى يقبلونكم في مظالهم الابديه.[182] اي (a4r) كما تدخلون بالزهاد العباد الذين (f10v) ليس لهم

nothing of this world and you relieve them with what you possess, so too will they bring you into the Kingdom of Heaven because of what you did to them. Concerning the repentant lay persons and devout ascetics the Lord said, 'My son, you are always with me and everything that I have is yours. But it is right for us to celebrate with your brother because he was dead, and he is alive again'.[20] The older son signifies the devout ascetics who are with God from their youth to old age. His Kingdom belongs to them. The younger son signifies those who return to God from among the lay. They have a fitting share of the Kingdom as was revealed. This is a small sample of the many sayings of the Lord revealing the precedence of the devout ascetics. As for demonstrating this through the way of life of individuals, Zacchaeus the chief tax collector excelled in virtue giving half of his wealth to the poor and the one whom he extorted anything from he would pay back four times the required amount joyfully and with enthusiasm such that the Lord entered his home and rewarded him with salvation. Yet his goodness and reward are not equal to the goodness and reward of Matthew the tax collector since he did not act in a similar fashion, rather he performed just one act as witnessed by the Book. This was that when the Lord called him he left everything and followed him, living with him a life of poverty and sacrificing himself to obey him. Similarly, Martha was hard-working in the service of the Lord and his disciples whereas Mary sat listening to the words of the Lord without being distracted by anything from him. Rather, she neglected the affairs of this world and wholeheartedly embraced the affairs of the next world. When Martha requested from the Lord that he tell her sister Mary to help her he replied that Mary has chosen a good lot for herself which cannot be appropriated from her. Just as Martha did not recognize the way of life of her sister Mary so too lay persons who perform pure virtues physically and with their wealth do not sense the invisible way of life of the solitaries in stillness. Just as the soul is inherently superior to the body so too the invisible spiritual way of life is superior to the visible bodily one. And just as the actions of the spiritual angels is superior to the actions of human beings and their love of God is superior to the love of creatures so too the actions of the solitaries is superior and better than the actions of lay persons. The love of the lay is also divided up between their women, children, possessions, and occupations, and the seed of their virtues is, in the

شي من هذا العالم الى بيوتكم وتنيحوهم مما لكم هكذا يدخلون بكم الى ملكوت السماء.[183] لما فعلتموه معهم وعن العلميين التايبين والمتزهدين المتعبدين قال الرب انت يا ولدي معي في كلحين.[184] وكما لي هو لك. فينبغي ان نفرح مع اخيك لانه كان ميتًا فعاش. فالابن الاكبر اشار به الى[185] الزهاد العباد الذين هم مع الله من[186] صبايهم الى اخرتهم. فملكوته لهم. والابن الاصغر اشار به الى الراجعين الى الله من العلمانيين.[187] فلهم قسم صالح من الملكوت كما بيّن. فهذا قليل من كثير من اقوال الرب. وقد تبين[188] فيها فضل الزهاد العباد.[189] (f11r) فاما بيان ذلك من (b6v) تدبير الاشخاص فان زكى[190] مقدم العشارين بالغ في الفضيله فدفع نصف ماله للمساكين. ومن غصبه[191] شيٍ[192] دفع له عوض الواحد اربعه[193] بفرحٍ ونشاط حتى ان الرب دخل الى بيته واوجب له الخلاص. وليس بره واجره مساويين لبر واجر متى العشار لانه[194] لم يصنع كذلك وانما عمل عملا واحدا كما شهد الكتاب. وهو ان الرب دعاه فترك كلشيٍّ[195] وتبعهُ وعاش معهُ في عيشةٍ ضيقه. وبذل نفسه في طاعته.[196] وكذلك مرتا[197] كانت مجتهده في خدمة الرب وتلاميذه. ومريم[198] جالسه تسمع كلام الرب[199] ولم تشتغل عنهُ بشي. (a4v) بل اهلت امور (f11v) هذا العالم واقبلت بكليتها الى امور العالم الاخر. ولما طلبت مرتا من الرب ان يقول لمريم اختها تعينها قال لها ان مريم اختارت لها نصيبًا[200] صالحًا لا ينزع منها. وكما ان مرتا ما كانت تعرف تدبير اختها (b7r) مريم. هكذى[201] العلمانيون الذين يعملون الفضايل الطاهره باجسادهم واموالهم. ما يحسون[202] بالتدبير الخفي الذي المتوحدين[203] في الهدو. (47v) وكما ان[204] النفس افضل في الطبع من الجسد هكذى[205] التدبير الخفي النفساني افضل من التدبير الظاهر الجسماني.[206] وكما ان عمل الملايكه الروحانيين اعلا من عمل[207] البشريين ولمحبت الملايكه الروحانيين اعلا من عمل البشريين[208] ولمحبة[209] الله[210] افضل من (f12r) المحبة المخلوقين.[211] هكذى[212] عمل المتوحدين اعلا وافضل[213] من عمل العلمانيين. ومحبة العلمانيين[214] مقسومة ايضًا[215] على نسايهم واولادهم وقنايهم[216] وصناعاتهم[217] وزرع فضايلهم

words of our Lord, choked with the thorns of this world[21] which are its cares and concerns. As for the solitary who has left behind the love of all creatures, he has one love for one beloved who is Christ the Creator. Whereas they fear many things and take pride in many things, he only fears this One alone and does not exult except in Him. As for demonstrating the superiority of the solitaries through the teachings of the Fathers it is written in *The Paradise*[22] that a divine vision occurred to Saint Paphnutius which said to him, 'Go to a certain village and enter the home of the head and learn from[23] him the perfect way of life'.[24] He departed immediately and when he entered his home he compelled him to reveal his way of life to him. The man revealed it to him for the sake of God's command saying, 'For the last thirty years I have kept myself away from my wife. I had intercourse with her three times and have three sons by her who, behold, serve me in the love of strangers and the poor. I never allowed the inhabitants of my village to surpass me in welcoming a stranger and no poor man or stranger ever left my home empty-handed. I never passed a wicked judgment upon anyone and never committed an abominable deed against anyone. I never sowed my field before helping the weak with their sowing. There was never enmity in my country which I did not resolve'. Paphnutius praised his way of life, kissed him upon the head, and said to him, 'May the Lord bless you out of Zion and may you see the prosperity of Jerusalem.[25] You have acted well but you lack one thing which is the prime virtue, namely, divine wisdom which no person can acquire if he does not deny himself and the whole world, carry the cross of our savior and follow him'. Immediately and without the members of his household knowing he accompanied the blessed man to the mountain and entered the life of solitude. After a short period of time his life came to an end in this state and Paphnutius saw his soul going up to Heaven accompanied by angels who were praising God and saying, 'Blessed is the one whom you select, O Lord, and whom you bring to dwell in your habitation'.[26] He had never heard of anyone who had a virtuous way of life in this world like him and who only became perfect through the solitary way of life. And God called the blessed Arsenius, the father of kings, from Heaven saying: 'O Arseni, flee from people and you will live'.[27] He did not say to him: 'Give to charity and live an upright way of life in the world and you will be saved', even though he was able to

مخنوق كقول ربنا بشوك ²¹⁸ هذا العالم الذي هو همومه واهتمامه. واما المتوحد فترك محبات المخلوقات جميعها. وله محبة ²¹⁹ واحده ²²⁰ في محبوب واحد هو المسيح الخالق ²²¹ واوليك يخافون من اشيا ²²² كثيره ²²³ ويتعزون باشياء ²²⁴ كثيره. وهذا يخاف من هذا الواحد وحده ولم يتعزا ²²⁵ بغيره. واما بيان فضل المتوحدين من تعاليم الابا فقد كتب في الفردوس ان منظرا (b7v) الهيًا ²²⁶ (f12v) صار على القديس ببنوده. وقال له امض ²²⁷ (a5r) الى الضيعة ²²⁸ الفلانيه وادخل الى بيت الريس وعلمه تدبير الكمال. فمضى لساعته ولما دخل عندهُ الزمهُ ان يكشف له تدبيرهُ. فكشف لهُ لاجل امر الله وقال ان لي ثلاثين ²²⁹ سنه من حيث انقطعت من ²³⁰ زوجتي. وثلاث ²³¹ دفعات عرفتها فصار لي منها ثلثة ²³² بنين. وها هم يخدموني ²³³ في محبة الغربا ²³⁴ والمساكين. وما تركت اهل ضيعتي يسبقوني ²³⁵ لقبول غريب. ²³⁶ وما خرج مسكين ولا غريب من بيتي ويدهُ فارغه. وما اخذت بوجه ²³⁷ احد ²³⁸ في الحكم ولا فعلت قبيحًا مع احد. وما زرعت حقلي حتى ساعدت (f13r) الضعفا في زراعاتهم. وماكان في بلدي خصومه الا واصلحتها. فمجد ببنودهِ ²³⁹ تدبيرهُ وقبل راسهُ وقال لهُ يباركك الرب من صهيون وترى خيرات اورشليم. ²⁴⁰ جيد ²⁴¹ صنعت. وانت عاجز واحده وهي راس الخيرات وهي الحكمة الالهيه التي لا يقتدر ²⁴² الانسان يقتنيها اذ لم يرفض نفسه والعالم كله ويحمل صليب مخلصنا ويتبعهُ. فمن ساعته بغير علم اهل (b8r) بيته صحب الطوباني الى الجبل وصار في ²⁴³ الوحده. وبعد زمان قليل كمل حياته فيها فنظر ببنودهِ ²⁴⁴ نفسه تصعد مع الملايكه ²⁴⁵ الى الفردوس وهم يمجدون الله قايلين (c48r) طوبى ²⁴⁶ لمن تختاره يا رب وتقربه ليسكن (f13v) ديارك. فما سمع بان احد تدبر في هذا العالم بالفضيله مثل هذا. ولم يكمل الا في تدبير الوحده. والطوباني ارسانيوس ²⁴⁷ ابو الملوك (a5v) دعاه الله من السما قايلا يا ارساني ²⁴⁸ اهرب من الناس وانت تحيا. فما قال له اعمل صدقه وتدبر مستقيمًا في العالم وانت تخلص مع

accomplish this more than others as he also possessed wealth and wisdom. Rather, God said to him: 'O Arseni, flee, keep silence, and live a life of [contemplation in] silence, for these are the principal things which keep a man from sins'."

8 **The Fourth Section:**

The Brothers asked: "If the virtuous lay man does not equal the perfect servant of God, would he equal the novice or mid-rank servant of God?"

9 **The Exegete replied:** "No, because our Lord has classified the way lay people pursue virtue according to three categories, and the solitaries according to three categories in his parable about the sower.[28] He said: 'Some fell on the path, and the birds came and ate them'. These are the ones who might see something or hear something that draws them to virtue, or grace might alert their heart and they decide to do good, but then the Devil would secretly fight them in their thoughts and the intensity of their energy wanes because of their laziness. He said: 'Some fell on a rock and sprang up quickly, but when the heat of the sun intensified they withered'. These are like the one who reads in the books or hears from teachers that the Kingdom of Heaven is prepared for the righteous and Hell is prepared for the sinners. He seeks the Kingdom and fears Hell. He starts to work, but a short time later he hits some hurdles and ceases his work. He said: 'Some fall among thorns, and thorns grew and choked them'. They are the majority of lay people who love the good but the cares of the world and its preoccupations choke their thoughts and they do not bear fruit. This means that they cannot complete a hidden virtue such as constant peaceful prayer nor escape from the concealed tricks of the devil and his secret fights. For this reason, the Fathers said that without escape from the world, ceasing conversation with people, and pursuing stillness, prayer without interruption or distraction cannot exist, not even any of the other virtues by which purity of the heart is acquired and by which contemplation of God is achieved. These are the three categories of lay people. He then classified the solitaries' virtue in three steps. He said: 'Others fell into good soil, they sprouted, and some yielded thirtyfold, others sixtyfold, and others a hundredfold'. He meant by soil the soul, and described in general terms the solitaries' way of life as sound. He

تمكنه²⁴⁹ من ذلك اكثر من غيره. كما²⁵⁰ كان له من الغنى والحكمه وانما قال الله له يا ارساني اهرب واسكن واسكت لان هذه اصول²⁵¹ الابتعاد من²⁵² الخطايا.

8 **الرابع قالوا الاخوه**²⁵³ فاذا كان العلماني الفاضل ما يساوي العابد²⁵⁴ الكامل فهل يكون مثل العابد المتوسط المبتدي.

9 (f14r) **قال المفسر**²⁵⁵ لا لان²⁵⁶ ربنا قد جمع تدبير فضيلة العلمانيين على ثلثة²⁵⁷ اقسام²⁵⁸ (b8v) والمتوحدين على ثلثة²⁵⁹ اقسام²⁶⁰ في مثل الزارع.²⁶¹ قال فبعض وقع على الطريق نجا الطير واكله. فهولا²⁶² هم الذين يبصرون او يسمعون شيًا يجتذبهم الى الفضيله. او تنبيه النعمه سريرتهم فيريدون ان يصنعوا خيرًا. فيحاربهم الشيطان خفيًا في افكارهم. فتبرد²⁶³ حرارة نشاطهم لاسترخاهم. قال وبعض سقط على الصخره فنبت من ساعته. ولما احترت الشمس يبس. وهولاي²⁶⁴ ممن يقرا في (f14v) الكتب او يسمع من المعلمين²⁶⁵ ان ملكوت السماوات²⁶⁶ معده للصالحين والجحيم معده للخاطيين فيوثر²⁶⁷ الملكوت ويخاف من الجحيم فيبتدي في العمل.²⁶⁸ فيعرض بعد زمان قليل ضيق فيبطل عمله. قال وبعض وقع (a6r) بين الشوك فصعد الشوك²⁶⁹ وخنقه. فهولاي²⁷⁰ هم اكثر العلمانيين²⁷¹ المحبين للخير. فان هموم العالم واهتماماته²⁷² تخنق افكارهم فلا يثمرون.(d72r/e72r) اي لا يقدرون ان يكملوا فضيله خفيه كالصلاة²⁷³ الدايمه الهاديه. ولا²⁷⁴ ان ينجوا من²⁷⁵ مخادعات الشيطان الباطنه²⁷⁶ وقتالاته الخفيه²⁷⁷. ولهذا قالت الابا ان بغير الابتعاد من العالم وانقطاع (f15r) الكلام مع الناس ومداومة الهدو لا تكون²⁷⁸ صلاه²⁷⁹ بلا (c48v) فتور ولا طياشه ولا باقي الفضايل التي منها تقتني²⁸⁰ نقاوة القلب التي يكون بها النظر الى الله. وهذه²⁸¹ اقسام العلمانيين الثلثه.²⁸² ثم رتب ايضا فضيلة المتوحدين في ثلثة²⁸³ درجات. قال واخر سقط في ارض جيدة. فاثر فيها واحد ثلثين.²⁸⁴ واخر ستين. واخر ماية. فعنى بالارض النفس. ووصف جملة تدبير المتوحدين بالجودة.

meant by thirtyfold the labor of the novices, sixtyfold the labor of those in mid-rank, and hundredfold the labor of the Perfect. It is like a field in which one crop is grown, nonetheless an ear might yield thirty seeds, whereas another sixty, and another hundred. Irrespective, all of these are treated as one raised before the altar and blessed, thus becoming the body of Christ. Likewise with people, if their intentions and way of life are the same, they become equal in the Kingdom, even if the Perfect dies in his old age, the mid-ranked in his middle age, and the novice in his youth. That is because God rewards according to the uprightness of intention, striving to do good, and for that to be only for the sake of his love of God almighty. This after all relates to a person's choice and perseverance. As regards someone's death in youth or surviving till late in life, it is not in his hands, but rather it is according to God's economy through wisdom that we cannot grasp. Mark, the disciple of Abba Silvanus, became strong in his virtue even though he died young.[29] But his father Sava became strong in perfection and died in his old age, as will be explained later. We are not saying that lay people's preoccupations do not convey virtues. For our Lord did say that the seeds sprouted and grew between thorns. But we say that worldly preoccupations and their pursuit suffocate their thoughts and they do not bear fruit for the virtuous, perfect and concealed soul which are continuous reflection, love towards our Lord, contemplation of him, remembering his reward and punishment, striving to fulfill his will and all his commandments, constant meditation, and prayer without interruption or distraction. If the solitary wavers in doing good acts or falls into evil either because of the weakness of his nature or excessive effort, he is nevertheless close to repentance and attaining grace through divine aid as long as he remains in solitude. For there was a brother who pursued virtue intensely but then wavered in his salvation while at the monastery of Pachomius.[30] His name was Silvanus. He started playing and singing without fear or shame. Pachomius ordered him to remove the robe of monastic life, dress like lay people and leave the monastery. Silvanus asked him to forgive him this failure and let him stay. He promised him that from this point forward he would not pursue a futile life. Brother Silvanus kept striving, and Pachomius had a vision in which he saw a throng of angelic saints coming to him at the time of his death. They took his soul with great joy as if it was an accepted offering or luxurious incense.

واشار بالثلثين على ^{285} عمل المبتدين. وبالستين الى عمل المتوسطين. وبالمايه الى تدبير الكاملين.
وكما ان حقلاً واحداً ينبت ^{286} فيه نوع واحد. (f15v) ومع هذا فسنبله يكون فيها ^{287} ثلثون ^{288}
حبه.(d72v) واخرى ^{289} ستون. واخرى مايه. ويصير عن ^{290} الجميع بالسوا جز ^{291}, واحد ^{292}.
ويرفع على المذبح ^{293} ويقدس فيصير ^{294} (e72v) جسد المسيح. هكذى ^{295} العباد اذا تساوت نياتهم
وتدبيرهم ^{296} (b9v) يتساووا ^{297} في الملكوت. ولو مات الكامل في شيخوخيته والمتوسط في
كهوليته والمبتدي (a6v) في شبوبيته. ^{298} لان الله يجازي بحسب استقامة ^{299} النية ^{300} والاجتهاد
في البر وان يكون ذلك من اجل حبه لله ^{301} تعالى فقط. لان هذا راجع ^{302} الى اختيار الانسان
وعزمه. واما موته في بداياته ^{303} او حياته الى نهايته فليس هذا راجعا اليه (f16r) بل لتدبير الله
بالحكمة التي لا ندركها. فمرقس تلميذ انبا سلوانا تقوى في فضيلته ومات في شبابه. وساوى اباه
الذي تقوى بكماله وتنيح في شيخوخيته كما سياتي شرحه في موضعه. ولسنا نقول ان هؤم ^{304}
العلمانيين لست ^{305} لهم فضايل فان ربنا ^{306} قال ان زرعه نبت وطلع بين (d73r) الشوك وانما نقول
ان هموم العالم واهتمامهم يخنق افكارهم فلا يثمرون ثمارا لروح الفاضله الكامله الخفيه التي هي التفكر
الدايم والمحبه ^{307} الى ربنا ^{308} والنظر اليه ^{309} والتذكر ^{310} (e73r) لوعده ووعيده والاجتهاد في تكميل
ارادته وجميع وصاياه. والهذيذ الدايم (b10r/f16v) والصلاه بلا فتور ولا طياشه. والمتوحد اذا
توانا ^{311} (c49r) في عمل البر او سقط ^{312} من ^{313} الشر اما لضعف الطبع او لشدة الجهاد فهو
قريب من التوبه وادراك النعمه بالمعاصده ^{314} الالهيه ^{315} ما دام في الوحده. فقد كان اخ نشيط في
الفضيله ثم توانا في خلاصه ^{316} في دير بكوميوس ^{317} اسمه سلوانوس ^{318} حتى انه صار يلعب ويغني
بلا خوف ولا حيا. فامره ^{319} بكوميوس (a7r) ان يقلع اسكيم الرهبنه ويلبس لباس العلمانيين
ويخرج من الدير. فساله سلوانس ^{320} ان يغفر له هذه الدفعه ويتركه. وعاهده انه من الان لا
يحيى ^{321} حياة ^{322} سقمه. ^{323} فجاهد الاخ (d73v) سلوانس. ^{324} وشاهد ^{325} بكوميوس ^{326}
انه (f17r) راى جمعا من الملايكه القديسين اتوا اليه عند نياحته وقبلوا نفسه بفرح عظيم مثل
ذبيحة مقبوله وبخور فاخر.

Another father was virtuous in his beginning.[31] But then he wavered in his salvation so much so that he would enter the house of a great man named Job and steal what food he found. The saint learned about this but remained joyfully patient, but at the time of his death he called for him. He held his hands, kissed them, and placed them on his eyes saying: 'O my brother, I kiss these two hands as thanks to their grace because of which I enter the Kingdom of Heaven'. That brother became remorseful and left to live in the wilderness. He pursued the good energetically so much so that he was nicknamed the energetic one. Another brother battled fornication.[32] He became enamored with the daughter of the priest of idols, and asked her father to marry her. He consulted his idol. The devil replied saying: 'If he were to renege the robe of monastic life and the sacrament of baptism give her to him'. When the brother did so, the grace of the soul departed from his mouth as a dove and ascended to Heaven. But because the compassionate God knew that he reneged on account of the weakness of his nature and the intensity of the Devil's fight against him and not on account of his desire and his passion for it, he made the Devil who was behind his reneging to be the cause of his repentance. He [the Devil] told the priest: 'Do not give your daughter to him because his god is still with him, and if he repents he will accept him'. When the brother heard this, he became remorseful and left to the wilderness to a saintly old man. In three weeks his repentance was accepted and the grace returned to his soul and resided in it. So as soldiers fighting for the sake of God are not reproached for what befalls them of wounds as long as they persevere in the war, but they are reproached if they were to flee and return to their homes before the conclusion of war. Likewise are the solitaries. This is their rule in God's war."

10 **The Fifth Section:**

The Brothers asked: "If the solitaries who waver were to straighten their ways they become superior to the virtuous lay people. Would they be superior to them if they do not straighten their ways too?"

11 **The Exegete replied:** "The virtuous among the lay people are better than those who do not straighten their ways from among the solitaries, as in the case of Zacchaeus over Judas Iscariot. The

وابا³²⁷ اخر كان في بدايته فاضلا. وبعد ذلك توانا³²⁸ في خلاصه حتى³²⁹ كان يدخل عند رجل عظيم اسمه ايوب ويسرق (e73v) ما يجده من قوته.³³⁰ وعلم به القديس وصبر بفرح وعند نياحته استدعاه. وصار يمسك (b10v) يديه³³¹ ويقبلها³³² ويضعها³³³ على عينيه. ويقول يا اخي انا اقتبل هاتين اليدان³³⁴ شكرا لنعمتها التي من اجلها ادخل الى³³⁵ ملكوت السما. فندم ذلك الاخ ومضى وسكن في وسط الغاب.³³⁶ ونشط في البر حتى انه (f17v) دعي النشيط. واخ اخر صار معه حرب الزنا. فهوى بنت كاهن الاصنام وطلب زيجتها من ابيها. فشاور³³⁷ الهه³³⁸ فاجابه³³⁹ الشيطان قايلا ان كان³⁴⁰ يكفر باسكيم الرهبنه وسر المعموديه ادفعها له. ولما فعل الاخ³⁴¹ خرجت نعمة الروح من فيه شبه حمامه (d74r) وصعدت الى السما. والله الرحيم من اجل معرفته بانه من ضعف طبيعته وشدة³⁴² جهاد (a7v) الشيطان له كفر³⁴³ لا بشهوته وايثاره فاضطر الشيطان الذي كفره صار سببا لتوبته. فقال لذلك³⁴⁴ الكاهن لا تدفع له بنتك لان الهه³⁴⁵ بعد معه وان تاب فهو يقبله. فلما سمع الاخ (f18r) هذا ندم ومضى الى البريه عند شيخ قديس وفي ثلث³⁴⁶ جمع (e74r) قبلت توبته وعادت نعمة (c49v) الروح وسكنته. فكما ان الجند (b11r) المجاهدين ما داموا ثابتين في الحرب لا³⁴⁷ يلامون على ما يصيبهم من الجراحات. وانما يلامون اذا هربوا³⁴⁸ ورجعوا الى بيوتهم قبل كمال الحرب هكذى³⁴⁹ المتوحدون هذا حكمهم في حرب الرب.³⁵⁰

10 **الخامس قالوا الاخوه**³⁵¹ فاذا كانت المتوانيون³⁵² سن المتوحدين³⁵³ انا استقام ندبيرهم كانوا ارفع من العلمانيين الفاضلين فهل يكونوا³⁵⁴ ارفع منهم وان لم يستقيم تدبيرهم.

11 **قال المفسر**³⁵⁵ بل افضل (d74v) العلمانيين افضل ممن (f18v) لم يستقيم تدبيره من المتوحدين. ففضل³⁵⁶ زكى³⁵⁷ على يهودا الاسكريوطي.³⁵⁸

wicked solitary is the one who constantly upsets the brothers, frequents the towns and becomes a cause for the outsiders to doubt and the loss of believing lay people. There was a brother who had a good reputation among people, but would anger God a lot. At the moment of his death, he sent to him a terrifying angel holding forceps with three prongs. One of the saints saw this in a vision and heard a voice from God saying: 'The soul of this one did not leave me peaceful not even for a single hour, so do not be merciful to him'. He stabbed the iron forceps into the heart of the wicked solitary and punished him. He took his soul and cast it in Hell, the abode of demons. So what you seek to know measure it according to this. Abba Sylvanus saw in a vision lay people taken up to the Kingdom of Heaven. These are the ones to whom the Lord said that he will say to them: 'Come you who are blessed by my father, inherit the Kingdom prepared for you, because I was hungry and you fed me, thirsty and you gave me drink, naked and you gave me clothing, a stranger and you sheltered me, and sick and in prison and you visited me. For everything that you have done to one of my weak brothers who believe in me, you have done it to me'.[33] He also saw solitaries taken down to Hell, like that brother who had a good reputation but constantly angered God. Also the brother who had a pot full of gold but when he was sick the brothers took care of him and spent their own money on him. The pot was buried with him, and fire appeared on his grave as the sign of Hell that is prepared for him.[34] Likewise are the solitaries who are full of weakness and haughtiness who return to the world [after] they were captured by grace. They did not leave the world at once as did Lot, for he was ordered to leave quickly and not look back. But his wife when she looked back perished.[35] Similarly with Elisha, for when Elijah threw his mantel at him, he at once left the world and accompanied him.[36] And Matthew, for when the Lord said to him: 'Come', he left everything and followed him.[37] As for the other ones, they wrong God's grace which draws them either by their will and desire, even though they might vow and promise God, or because they waver and neglect their divine calling. The prompting of grace abandons them and their energy cools down. We ask God for his success and aid. Amen."

12 **The Brothers asked:** "Very good. You have shown us from the divine books, teachings of the Fathers, evidence of existence, and

والمتوحد الشرير هو الذي يسجس ³⁵⁹ الاخوه دايمًا ³⁶⁰ والذي يتقلب ايضا في المدن ويكون سببا لتشكيك البرانيين وخسارة العلمانيين المومنين. كان اخ له ذكر صالح ³⁶¹ بين الناس. وكان يغضب الله كثير ³⁶² وعند موته ارسل اليه ملاك مخيف وبيده كلبتان بثلثة ³⁶³ روس. ³⁶⁴ وواحد (a8r) من القديسين راى هذا في الرويا. وسمع صوت ³⁶⁵ من الله قايلا (e74v) ³⁶⁶ ما نيحتني نفس هذا ولا ساعة ³⁶⁷ واحده ³⁶⁸ فلا تشفق عليه. فغطس الكلبتين (b11v) الحديد في قلب المتوحد الشرير وعاقبه (f19r) واخذ نفسه والقاها في الجحيم مسكن الشياطين. وما يطلب وحل على ³⁶⁹ هذا المطلوب. ان ابا سلوانا راى في الرويا علمانيين يذهب بهم الى ملكوت السما ³⁷⁰ وهم الذي ³⁷¹ قال الرب انه سيقول لهم تعالوا يا مباركي ابي ارثوا (d75r) الملك المعد لكم. لاني جعت فاطعمتموني وعطشت فسقيتموني وعريان وكسيتموني ³⁷² وتغربت ³⁷³ فاويتموني ومرضت وحبست فزرتموني. ³⁷⁴ لان جميع ما صنعتموه باحد اخوتي هولاي ³⁷⁵ الصغار المومنين بي ³⁷⁶ في صنعتموه. وراى ايضا متوحدين ينزلون الى الجحيم مثل ذلك ³⁷⁷ الاخ الذي كان له ذكر ³⁷⁸ صالح (f19v) وكان يغضب الله دايما والاخ الذي كان له قدر مملوه ذهبا. وفي مرضه كانت الاخوه يخدمنوه ³⁷⁹ وينفقون عليه من مالهم. فدفنت القدر معه في القبر وصارت النار تظهر على قبره علامة الجحيم (e75r) المعده ³⁸⁰ له. وكذالك ³⁸¹ ذو ³⁸² الانحلال والكبريا من المتوحدين الراجعين الى العالم والذين اصطادتهم ³⁸³ النعمه (c50r) وما خرجوا من العالم من ساعتهم مثل ما ³⁸⁴ خرج لوط لانه (h12r) ³⁸⁵ امر ان يخرج بسرعه ولا يلتفت. وزوجنه لما التفتت تلفت. ومثل ما ³⁸⁶ فعل اليشع (a8v) فانه لما رمى عليه اليا ³⁸⁷ رداه. فمن ساعته ترك العالم وصحبه. (f20r) ومتى فانه لما قال الرب له تعال ترك كل شي وتبعه. فاما غير هولاي ³⁸⁸ فيظلمون ³⁸⁹ نعمة الله التي تجتذبهم ³⁹⁰ حتى انهم قد يندرون ويعاهدون الله اما بارادتهم وشهوتهم واما من اجل ³⁹¹ انهم يتوانون ويهملون دعوتهم الالهيه. ³⁹² وتتوانى ³⁹³ عنهم ³⁹⁴ تحريك النعمه وتبرد حرارتهم. فنسال ³⁹⁵ الله توفيقه وعونه امين. ³⁹⁶

12 قالوا ³⁹⁷ الاخوه ³⁹⁸ جيدا جدا بينت ³⁹⁹ لنا من الكتب ⁴⁰⁰ الالهيه ومن ⁴⁰¹ تعاليم الابا ومن شهادة الوجود ومن

logic that the worshiping solitaries—the Perfect, mid-ranked or novices—are better than the virtuous lay people, and that those solitaries who do not recant their sins go down to Hell and those lay people who do virtuous acts go to the Kingdom of Heaven. But now we will ask about the issues that we could not understand."

13   **The Exegete replied:** "You, by the Lord's aid, inquire and I, by the Lord's strength, explain. We all thank our Lord's grace that teaches you to seek and grants me to explain."

14   **The Brothers asked:** "What about that which was said about Ammonius that during the time when he fought the desire of fornication he would heat iron and place it on his organs?"[38]

15   **The Exegete replied:** "He, when the Devil fought him, would punish his body by inflicting pain on the organs where the sin is stirring in order to stop the stirring of natural disposition and the instigation of the Devil. When they tried to force him to become bishop, he cut off his left ear.[39] He did so to show his physical disability and to fight the demon of vainglory. So if the pleasure was instigated by the demon of fornication, he burnt his penis. In the struggle against [bad] thoughts, he adhered to prayers and fasting, the mortification of the soul by humility and the tiring of the body through works in the service of God and people so much so that Abba Evagrius said about him: 'I have never seen someone who experienced pain more than he'.[40] He is not Amnonius the Virgin or the bishop who was the disciple of Antony. He is rather the one who went with Abba Evagrius to Abba John of Lycus, the prophet from Upper Egypt, and asked him about the invisible light of the mind. He answered him: 'The mind by its natural disposition emanates a light, and has something from outside that lightens it'."[41]

16   **The Brothers asked:** "When the souls of the righteous depart from their bodies, do they proceed to Paradise or to Heaven?"[42]

17   **The Exegete replied:** "To Paradise."

18   **They asked:** "How did Antony then see the souls of Paul and Ammon ascending to Heaven?"

19   **He replied:** "Paradise is called Heaven because of its elevation from Earth. The Apostle [Paul] called Paradise the third heaven.[43]

قياس العقل ان المتوحدين المتعبدين الكاملين والمتوسطين (f20v)[402] والمبتديين افضل من العلمانيين الفاضلين. (e75v)[403] وان من لم يرجع من[403] شروره من المتوحدين ينزل الى الجحيم. ومن يعمل الفضايل من العلمانيين يمضي الى ملكوت السموات[404] ومن الان نسال[405] لما[406] تعسر[407] علينا فهمه من (d76r) المسايل.[408]

13 (b12v) **قال المفسر**[409] انتم بمعونة[410] الرب تستخبرون وانا بقوة الرب افسر. ونحن جميعا[411] نشكر نعمة ربنا[412] الذي يعلمكم ان تطلبوا ويدفع لي ان افسر.

14 **قالوا**[413] **الاخوه** ما هو الذي قيل عن امونيس[414] انه كان في وقت قتال الزنا[415] يحمي الحديد (f21r) ويضعه على اعضاه.[416]

15 **قال المفسر**[417] انه كان في محاربة[418] الشيطان له يعاقب جسده بايلام الاعضا التي تكون (a9r) بها الخطيه. لكي يبطل[419] حركة الطبع وتحريك الشيطان. ولما ارادوا ان يغصبوه[420] الاسقفه[421] قص اذنه الشمال. وهذا فعله لنقص[422] شخصه[423] وفي مجاهدة شيطان المجد الباطل. وهكذى[424] اذا كان لزه شيطان الزنا يكوي عضو التناسل. وفي مجاهدة الافكار يلازم الصلوات[425] والاصوام. وسحق (f21v) النفس بالاتضاع واتعاب الجسم بالاعمال التي في خدمة (c50v) الله والناس (e76r) حتى قال عنه انبا وغريس ما رايت احدا[426] عبر[427] الاوجاع اكثر منه. وليس هو امونيوس (d76v) البتول. ولا هو الاسقف تلميذ انطونيوس. بل هو الذي مضى مع (b13r) وغريس الى انبا[428] يوحنا الاسيوطي النبي الصعيدي وساله عن النور الخفي الذي للذهن. فقال له[429] ان الذهن[430] من طبعه ينبع نورا. ومن خارج[431] له شي[432] ينوره.

16 **قالوا**[433] **الاخوه** اذا خرجت نفوس الابرار من اجسادهم هل يمضون الى الفردوس ام الى السما.

17 **قال المفسر**[434] الى الفردوس.

18 **قالوا**[435] فكيف[436] انطونيوس (f22r) راى[437] نفس بولص[438] ونفس امون صاعدتان[439] الى السما.

19 **قال** والفردوس من اجل[440] ارتفاعه على الارض يدعى بالسما[441] والرسول قد دعا[442] الفردوس السما الثالثه.

The first [heaven] comprises the celestial spheres, about which God said in the Torah of Moses: 'In the Beginning, God created the heaven and the earth'.[44] The second [heaven] comprises the firmament that God used to split the waters.[45] The third [heaven] comprises Paradise, as called by Paul the Apostle. The souls of the righteous rest in Paradise until God brings about the [Last] Judgment, and then they will achieve union with Christ in the Kingdom of Heaven. What proves this is what our Lord said to the thief on his right: 'Today, you will be with me in Paradise'.[46] And his words that when he comes in his glory, he shall place the righteous on his right, praise them and make them inherit his Kingdom."[47]

20 **The Brothers asked:** "Why did Antony say to his disciple Paul: 'Depart and seclude yourself so that you learn fighting the demons'?"[48]

21 **The Exegete replied:** "Because fighting the demons happens in thoughts. The combatant benefits from the stillness of seclusion. Through this, one also acquires fervent and durable prayer, as well as the purity of the heart. There, the combat is for the glory of God."

22 **The Brothers asked:** "Why did Abba Macarios the Alexandrian never spit on the ground for sixty years, from the day he was baptized until he died?"[49]

23 **The Exegete replied:** "Because he received the holy sacraments. This is why one should drink the water and eat the bread of benediction after one receives the sacraments. The Fathers used to say to us: 'If one of you has to spit after he receives the sacraments, but before he drinks or eats, let him swallow it. If he disdains that, let him then wipe it in his garment'."

24 **The Brothers asked:** "Why did Elijah build a nunnery, bring to it three hundred nuns and place himself as their head, but after a few years, he could no longer resist the thoughts of fornication, so he withdrew to the desert? Why did God send to him three angels who relieved him of the yearnings and instructed him to return to the nunnery to lead the sisters and look after them?"[50]

25 **The Exegete replied:** "There are three reasons [for this]. The first was because of his [Elijah's] kindness, worthiness, and chastity. For when he realized their number, and that they prefer to live in chastity but could not withdraw to the desert because they would

فالاوله⁴⁴³ هي الافلاك التي قال الله عنها في التوره⁴⁴⁴ على لسان موسى. في البدي⁴⁴⁵ خلق الله السما والارض. والثانيه هي الجلد الذي⁴⁴⁶ فصل الله به⁴⁴⁷ بين المياه.⁴⁴⁸ والثالثه⁴⁴⁹ هي (a9v) الفردوس. كما دعاها الرسول بولص.⁴⁵⁰ ونفوس⁴⁵¹ الابرار تكون⁴⁵² في الفردوس الى ان ياتي (d77r/e76v) ربنا المجازاه.⁴⁵³ وحينيذ⁴⁵⁴ تكون⁴⁵⁵ لهم الشركه مع المسيح في ملكوت السموات. ويدل على ذلك قول ربنا للص⁴⁵⁶ اليمين. (b13v/f22v) اليوم تكون معي في الفردوس. وقوله⁴⁵⁷ اذا جا في مجده يقيم الابرار عن يمينه ويمدحهم ويورثهم ملكوته.

20 **قالوا**⁴⁵⁸ **الاخوه** لماذا قال انطونيوس لبولا تلميذه امضي واجلس في الوحده حتى تتعلم⁴⁵⁹ قتال الشياطين.⁴⁶⁰

21 **قال المفسر** لان حرب الشياطين⁴⁶¹ في الافكار والمناظر⁴⁶² انما يكون في هدو الوحده. ومنها⁴⁶³ تقتني⁴⁶⁴ الصلاه الدايمه الحاره.⁴⁶⁵ ومنها يقتني نقاوة القلب. وبها⁴⁶⁶ يكون النظر لمجد الله.

22 **قالوا**⁴⁶⁷ **الاخوه** لماذا ما بصق⁴⁶⁸ انبا مقار الاسكندراني على الارض ستين سنه منذ تعمد والى ان⁴⁶⁹ تنيح.

23 **قال المفسر**⁴⁷⁰ من اجل تناوله السراير المقدسه. (f23r) ولهذا ينبغي ان يشرب الماي⁴⁷¹ ويوكل⁴⁷² خبز البركه بعد تناول السراير.⁴⁷³ وقد كانوا⁴⁷⁴ الابا يقولون⁴⁷⁵ لنا (d77v) اذا جا لاحد بصاق بعد ان يتقرب قبل ان يشرب او ياكل (c51r) فيبلعه. وان ابت نفسه (e77r) فليمسحه في ثيابه.

24 **قالوا**⁴⁷⁶ **الاخوه** لماذا بنى⁴⁷⁷ اليا⁴⁷⁸ ديرا وجمع فيه ثلثماية راهبه. وصار لهن مدبرا.⁴⁷⁹ وبعد سنين اشتد عليه قتال (b14r) الزنا فخرج الى البريه فارسل الله اليه⁴⁸⁰ ثلثة⁴⁸¹ ملايكه رفعوا عنه الوجع (a10r) وكلفوه⁴⁸² يمضي الى الدير ويدبر الخوات ويهتم بهن.⁴⁸³

25 (f23v) **قال المفسر**⁴⁸⁴ لثلاث⁴⁸⁵ اسباب. الاول لرحمته وحريته وطهارته. فانه لما راهن مع كثرتهن⁴⁸⁶ يوثرن⁴⁸⁷ ان يعيشن⁴⁸⁸

41

not find someone to look after their needs there, he increased in spiritual love and built for them a nunnery, looked after them and led them. The second was because God did not ward off from him the stirrings of physical yearnings and demonic struggles [in order] to show people, angels and demons his ability to disregard yearnings, resistance to the devil, love of virtue, and obedience to God. The third was because there is a group who have a corrupt belief and who say unconsideringly: 'This is good and this is bad'. They also allege that their good comes from the good and their evils come from the devil. Others claim that sin became innate in us from our father Adam; they allege that their sins are natural in them. When God willed to undermine these views, he made a group chaste from their birth. He also removed in others the intense conflict with [their] instinctive nature and struggling with demons in order to demonstrate his might and the unity of his divinity."

26 **The Brothers asked:** "What did Paphnutius advise when he said: 'The gravity of transgressions by tongue, sense, act and all the body corresponds to the person's arrogance'?"[51]

27 **The Exegete replied:** "The transgression through sense is to fail in your thoughts as stated by the blessed Mark: 'Let not your heart arrogantly think it knows scriptures lest your mind fall into blasphemy'.[52] The transgression with the tongue is to do what one of the brothers did on account of his arrogance in the Scetis Desert:[53] he cursed Mar Evagrius and the holy Fathers. The transgression through act is to do what the same brother did by committing fornication on account of his arrogance. The transgression with all the body is to do what the same brother did on account of his arrogance, and was caught by thieves who tied him up, placed him on a haystack and set him on fire."

28 **The Brothers asked:** "Why was it said that the mind that ceases from the remembrance of God is taken over by the demon of fornication and the demon of wrath? Why did Palladius[54] ask: 'How can the human mind be constantly with God?' and was answered by Diocles: 'Any action or learning that preoccupies the soul for fear of God then its mind is with God'. What did he mean by action and learning?"

بطهاره ويعسر عليهن ⁴⁸⁹ الخروج الى البريه لعدم من يهتم بهن ⁴⁹⁰ في حاجة الجسد غلى ⁴⁹¹ في ⁴⁹² الحب الروحاني وبنى ⁴⁹³ لهن ⁴⁹⁴ ديرا ⁴⁹⁵ واهتم بهن ⁴⁹⁶ ودبرهن. ⁴⁹⁷ والثاني لان الله لم يضبط عنه حركة ⁴⁹⁸ الاوجاع الطبيعيه والقتلات ⁴⁹⁹ الشيطانيه ليظهر الناس ⁵⁰⁰ والملايكه والشياطين ⁵⁰¹ مقدار جهاده في بغضة ⁵⁰² الاوجاع وعصيانه الشيطان ⁵⁰³ ومحبته للفضيله وطاعته (d78r) لله. والثالث لان قوما رايهم فاسد يقولون بالهين خير وشرير وينسبون خيرهم ⁵⁰⁴ للخير وشرورهم (f24r) الشرير. ⁵⁰⁵ واخرين يقولون ان الخطيه سرت فينا من ادم ابينا وينسبون خطاياهم ⁵⁰⁶ (e77v) انها طبيعيه فيهم. ولما اراد الله ان يبطل هذه ⁵⁰⁷ الارا ⁵⁰⁸ جعل قوما ⁵⁰⁹ من بدايتهم (b14v) اعفا وابطل شدة حرب الطبع وقتال الشياطين عن قوم ⁵¹⁰ ليظهر ⁵¹¹ قوته ⁵¹² وحدانية لاهوتيته. ⁵¹³

26 **قالوا** ⁵¹⁴ **الاخوه** ما هو الذي اشار اليه ببنوده ان زلات اللسان والحس والفعل وجميع الجسد تكون على قدر تعظم ذلك ⁵¹⁵ الانسان.

27 **قال المفسر** ⁵¹⁶ الزله التي بالحس (f24v) هي السقوط بالفكره كما قال الطوباني مرقس لا يتكبر قلبك في معرفة الكتب ليلا يسقط عقلك في روح التجديف. والزله التي (a10v) باللسان كما زل احد الاخوه من اجل ⁵¹⁷ كبرياء وشتم مار ⁵¹⁸ وغريس والابا القديسين ⁵¹⁹ ببرية الاسقيطي. ⁵²⁰ والزله التي (d78v) بالفعل كما هو زل ⁵²¹ ايضا بسبب الكبريا ووقع ⁵²² في الزنا. والزله التي ⁵²³ بجميع الجسد كما زل هو ايضا من اجل كبرياه فوقع في يدي ⁵²⁴ اللصوص فكتفوه (c51v) وجعلوه في وسط التبن واحرقوه بالنار.

28 **قالوا** ⁵²⁵ **الاخوه** لماذا قيل ان العقل الذي يسقط من تذكار (e78r) الله يتسلمه شيطان (f25r) الزنا وشيطان ⁵²⁶ (b15r) الغيظ. ولما قال فلاديس ⁵²⁷ فكيف يقدر عقل بشري ⁵²⁸ ان يكون مع الله دايما. فاجاب دموقلاس ⁵²⁹ اي فعل او فهم اشتغلت به النفس من اجل مخافة الله فهو عقلها مع الله. ⁵³⁰ فما هو الفهم والعقل ⁵³¹ الذي قاله.

29   **The Exegete replied:** "Apart from prayer without feebleness and distraction, the learning that is conducted for fear of God is to remember God's promises and read his scriptures. The act undertaken for fear of God is to carry out his commandments and what leads to the fulfillment of his demands. It is as if [Diocles] had said to him: 'If you cannot attach your thought constantly to the remembrance of God, reflection on his divinity, might, wisdom, excellence of his mercy, his love and glory, and if you cannot pray without feebleness and distraction because of disruptions, weakness of the mind, or struggling with demons which is hard to carry out—and a virtuous act—then slow down your thought and start slowly by remembering God's promises. Bring yourself to rest, for when your [thought] is rested and a bad idea stirs in it, raise it [your thought] to the remembrance of God. The prayer without feebleness and distraction is achieved as those who pray with their body. When they tire of standing and reciting, they rest their bodies by sitting down and they enlighten their minds with reading. When they are rested, they go back to perform the prayer while standing. The mind is with God when it is thinking of God, his commandments and what fulfills his will. But if it thinks of sinful ailments or worldly things that it does not [really] need, then it is with the devil'."

30   **The Brothers asked:** "Why do [some] people not have the divine light in their hearts until their hearts have been purified through prolonged [good] works and struggles [with the devil], whereas others receive the light of grace even before they withdraw from the world to the desert, like the light that shone in the heart of Abraham on the seventh day of his marriage and he left his bride and withdrew from the world?"[55]

31   **The Exegete replied:** "The Fathers have said that the light has categories; each category [is given] to a person in accordance with his progress in his intention and resolution. Grace is kindled in the person's heart out of love of God, so he hates the glory of this world and comes without any expectation to this work. At the beginning, grace gives him the love of works, facilitates for him adversities, and does not allow the struggles of the demons to exceed his capacity. Only after extensive labor and immense humility is his heart cleansed and he deserves to see Christ in the likeness of light. As he progresses towards encountering our Lord

29 **قال المفسر**⁵³² اما ما سوى الصلاة التي بلا فتور ولا طياشه فان الفهم الذي بمخافة الله هو بذكر⁵³³ مواعيد الله وقراة كتبه. والفعل الذي بمخافة الله هو عمل وصاياه وما يودي الى تكميل ارادته. فكانه قال له ان كنت ما تقدر تربط (d79r) فكرك دايما في تذكار الله والتفكر في ربوبيته وقدرته وحكمته وجودة⁵³⁴ (f25v) رحمته⁵³⁵ ومحبته ومجده. وان تصلي بغير فتور ولا طياشه من اجل القواطيع.⁵³⁶ او لضعف⁵³⁷ العقل. او حرب الشياطين العظيم (a11r) قتاله. هذا العمل الفاضل. فانزل بعقلك وقتا وقتا⁵³⁸ الى تذكار مواعيد الله. وريح ذاتك (b15v) فاذا استراح او تحرك فيه فكر ردي (e78v) ارفعه الى ذكر الله. والصلاه التي بغير فتور ولا طياشه كما الذين يصلون جسدانيا اذا تعبوا في⁵³⁹ الوقوف والترتيل اراحوا اجسادهم بالجلوس واناروا عقولهم بالقراة.⁵⁴⁰ واذا استراحوا وقفوا في خدمة الصلاه. فاذا افتكر العقل في الله او في وصاياه وتكميل ارادته كان⁵⁴¹ (f26r) مع الله. واذا افتكر في اوجاع الخطيه او في العمليات التي لا حاجة له بها كان مع الشيطان.

30 **قالوا**⁵⁴² الاخوه⁵⁴³ لم كانت العباد⁵⁴⁴ ما يضي لهم⁵⁴⁵ نور⁵⁴⁴ (d79v) الهي⁵⁴⁵ في قلوبهم حتى تتنقى⁵⁴⁶ قلوبهم بالاعمال والحروب زمانا طويلا. واخرون من قبل خروجهم من العالم الى البريه يضي لهم نور النعمه. كما اضا⁵⁴⁷ في قلب ابراهيم⁵⁴⁸ في اليوم السابع من عرسه. وحينيذ⁵⁴⁹ ترك العروس⁵⁵⁰ وخرج من العالم.

31 **قال المفسر**⁵⁵¹ ان الآبا قالوا ان النور اقسام وان كل قسم لكل واحد على قدر ربحه (b16r) في نيته وعزيمته.⁵⁵² فان (c52r)⁵⁵³ النعمه تغلي في قلب الانسان في حب الله. فيبغض مجد (f26v) هذا العالم وياتي بلا قنيه لهذا⁵⁵⁴ العمل. وفي البدايه تعطيه (e79r) النعمه محبة الاعمال وتسهل عليه المصاعب. ولا تدع عليه⁵⁵⁵ (a11v) من حرب الشياطين⁵⁵⁶ اكثر من قوته ومن⁵⁵⁷ بعد تعب كثير واتضاع عظيم يطهر قلبه ويستحق ان يرى المسيح في منظر النور.⁵⁵⁸ وكما يتقدم للقا ربنا

through works and struggles, likewise our Lord comes to encounter him in the form of light until they are united. If he is firmly fixed in the Lord through his love, the Lord is firmly fixed in him through His light, as the Lord has said,[56] and the Prophet [David] too: 'My soul thirsts for you, O living God. When shall you come that I may behold your face?'[57] He also said: 'I walk in your way without transgression, so when shall you come to me?'[58] Some walk fast in straight paths and others walk slowly in corrupt paths. Contemplate the words of the Prophet: 'All your waves and your gales have gone over me',[59] 'You made me cross in water and fire and brought me out to rest'.[60] But the solitaries who deserve [to receive] the light before they depart from this world, if they returned to live among the brothers they would grow dim through myriad trials. Through the effort of many works they earn the purity of the heart and glow with the divine light during prayer, as the Fathers said."

32 **The Brothers asked:** "Why did Paul the Apostle say: 'Whoever aspires to the office of bishop aspires to a noble task?'[61] [Why did] the blessed commentator[62] counsel his friend in the book of priesthood and ask him to attain the rank of priesthood? Why did Saint Paulinus, Bishop of Antioch,[63] when he saw the many disruptions after fifteen days of assuming his see in the city, pray to God who told him in a vision [to] leave?"

33 **The Exegete replied:** "There is nothing more loved and esteemed by our Lord than the purity of the righteous. Because of it, he granted his gifts of priesthood and others. The Apostle [Paul]–when he saw that the least in competence in his knowledge and leadership would seek priestly leadership for the love of leadership and vainglory, but he might be turned down because of this, whereas whoever has virtuous knowledge and righteous work avoids leadership the result of his humility and preference for stillness–feared that the teaching of Christianity would be impaired or harmed through the lack of correct instruction and worthy leadership. He said this thing but did not compel anybody; rather he left it to their desire after he set down the conditions of the episcopacy. It is therefore desirable that whoever seeks a position of leadership–be it spiritual, episcopal, priestly, or an abbotship– does not seek it for leadership's sake and its power. It is also desirable that only he who has moral competence and expertise in the Holy Scriptures seek it. For then, he will be deserving of his

في الاعمال والحروب هكذى ^{559} ربنا ياتي القايه ^{560} بالنور حتى يجتمعا. واذا اثبت ^{561} في الرب (d80r) بمحبته ثبت ^{562} الرب فيه بنوره كما قال الرب وكقول النبي ان نفسي عطشانه اليك يا الله ^{563} الحي. ^{564} حتى متى تاتي وانظر وجهك. ^{565} وقال انني امشي في طريقك بغير ^{567} عيب. فالى متى تاتي (f27r) الي. ^{568} الا ^{569} ان بعض هولاى ^{570} يمشون سريعا ^{571} في ^{572} طرق مستقيمه وبعضهم ^{573} يمشون بطيا في طرق معوقه. ^{574} وتاملوا قول النبي جميع (b16v) امواجك ورياحك جازت علي. واجزتني ^{575} في الما والنار واخرجتني الى الراحه. والمتوحدون الذين يستحقون النور قبل خروجهم من هذا ^{576} العالم اذا رجعوا بين الاخوه اظلموا في تجارب ملونه. وبالجهاد ^{577} في اعمال كثيره يستحقون طهارة (e79v) القلب. ويضون بالنور الالهي في وقت الصلاه كما قالوا الابا.

32 **قالوا** ^{578} **الاخوه** (f27v) ^{579} الرسول لماذا بولص ^{579} الرسول يقول من اشتهى الاسقفيه فاشتهى ^{580} عملا صالحا والمفسر الطوباني وعظ صديقه في كتاب الكهنوت وساله ان يكمل درجة الكهنوت. والقديس بولا اسقف انطاكيه. بعد خمسة عشر يوما لجلوسه على كرسيه بالمدينه لما (a12r) راى كثرة الصداع صلا ^{581} لله فقال له في الرويا ابتعد.

33 **قال المفسر** ^{582} ليس شيا محبوبا (d80v) وكريما عند ربنا ^{583} مثل نقاوة الابرار. ومن اجلها اعطا ^{584} مواهبه الكهنوتيه وغيرها. والرسول لما راى من له حكمة له في علمه وتدبيره يطلب رياسة الكهنوت من اجل محبة الرياسه والمجد الباطل (f28r) ولهذا قد ^{585} (b17r) يمنع ^{586} منها. ومن له علم فاضل ^{586} وعمل صالح ^{587} يهرب من رياسة ^{588} من اجل اتضاعه وايثاره الهدو. حاف ^{589} ان يتعوق او تنضر ^{590} (c52v) التلمذه ^{591} النصرانيه لعدم التعليم المستقيم والتدبير الصالح. فقال هذا القول ولم يجبر ^{592} احدا ^{593} بل فوض ذلك لشهوتهم بعد ان قرز ^{594} شروط الاسقفيه. فينبغي ^{595} لمن اثر (e80r) رياسة روحانيه اما اسقفيه ^{596} او قسيسيه او رياسة دير ان لا يوثرها من اجل رياستها ^{597} وسلطانها. وينبغي ^{598} ان لا يطلب لها الا من اقتنى حكمة خلقيه. ودربة بالكتب ^{599} المقدسه. وهو محق في

trusteeship and successful in his leadership. He will also have virtues that benefit those who take him as a guide and follow his leadership, such as love, forgiveness, humility, solace, discernment and knowledge. As for the blessed commentator, he asked his friend to attain the rank of priesthood for five reasons. The first reason was because he had accepted the rank of priesthood. The second reason was because many of those who feared God had chosen him. The third reason was because of his virtuous work. The fourth reason was for his good leadership. The fifth reason was because of his great humility and conviction, which made him evade taking up leadership. But when he was compelled to assume it, he constantly sought to distance himself from it. As for [Bishop] Paulinus, he was righteous, modest and sought stillness. When he realized that leadership would not win him anything because of constant worries and running affairs, he asked our Lord with tears and in agony to permit him to leave the leadership of priesthood and turn to what he was able to do and in which he could benefit. Our good Lord answered his supplication for two reasons. The first was for his benefit. The second was to deter the insolence of the inept and ignorant from seeking the leadership of priesthood, for they would realize that God's will for human beings is that they should be where it is beneficial for them."

34 **The Brothers asked:** "The author[64] of the book *The Paradise* said about the blessed Eustathius that his body became dry as a result of fasting, prayer and vigil, so much so that the sun could be seen through his ribs."[65]

35 **The Exegete replied:** "I have seen a saint who was strong and could walk, but his body was dry as a result of great asceticism, so much so that one thought he had no liver or spleen in his belly. His ribs could be seen under transparent skin. Because of this, Macarius said: 'As fire dries out moisture in wood and burns it, so too the fear of God. If it settles in a person, it dries his flesh and desiccates his bones'.[66] In *The Book of the Perfection of Disciplines* [*Kitāb al-Tadbīr al-Kāmil*],[67] having said that any account fails to relate their perfection, the blessed commentator said about the two solitary biological brothers who lived in Antioch that because of their prolonged asceticism and labor, their bodies weakened and waned, so much so that if a person looked at them, he would think he was seeing shadows, not real human beings. Also, Palladius said about

امانته وموفق في تدبيره. وله فضايل ينتفع بها (b17v) من يقتدي (f28v) به ويروسه مثل الرحمه والمغفره والاتضاع والسهوله والافراز والمعرفه. واما المفسر الطوباني فسال صديقه ان يكمل درجه الكهنوت لخمس اسباب.[600] الاول لانه كان قد قبل درجة الكهنوت. والثاني لان كثيرين خايفين من الله اختاروه. والثالث (b18r/d81r) من اجل[601] عمله[602] الفاضل. والرابع لتدبيره الصالح. والخامس (a12v) بسبب اتضاعه العظيم وقناعته. ولذلك كان يهرب من الرياسه. ولما اغتصب وجعل فيها صار يوثر الابتعاد منها. فاما بولا فانه كان بارا متضعا[603] موثر الهدو.[604] فلما راى انه لا يربح في الرياسه لكثرة (f29r) القلق والاهتمام سال[605] ربنا بدموع وتوجع ان يفسح له في ترك رياسة الكهنوت. ويصير الى ما يقدر عليه ويربح فيه. (e80v) وربنا الصالح اجاب سواله لامرين. احدهما لربحه والاخر ليكف[606] جسارة الجاهل العاجز عن طلب رياسة الكهنوت. اذ[607] يرى ارادة الله للانسان ان يكون فيما له فيه ربح.

34 **قالوا الاخوه** ان كاتب[608] الفردوس قال من اجل الطوباني اسطاتيس[609] انه يبس جسده من الصوم والصلاه[610] والسهر حتى ان الشمس كانت تبين[611] من بين اضلاعه.

35 **قال المفسر**[612] (f29v) انا رايت قديسا وهو قوي ويمشي. يبس جسده من كثرة النسك حتى يظن انه ليس في بطنه كبد ولا طحال. وربما تبان اضلاعه من تحت الجلد الصافي. ولهذا قال مقاريوس[613] كما ان النار[614] تنشف رطوبة[615] الخشب وتحرقه هكذى[616] مخافة الله اذا سكنت، (d81v) في انسان تنشف لحمه وتجفف (b18v/c53r) عظامه. والمفسر الطوباني قال في كتاب التدبير الكامل عن اخوين بالطبع متوحدين ساكنين في انطاكيه. بعد قوله ان كل قول يعجز عن سيرة كماهم.[617] انهم[618] من طول نسكهما وتعبها (a13r) ضعف جسدهما واضمحل حتى انها اذا نظر اليها (f30r) انسان (e81r) فيظن[619] انه يرى خيالا[620] لا بشرٍ[621] حقيقا.[622] وبلاديوس قال عن

the brother who lived in Jerusalem that he appeared as a shadow because of the economy of his labors.[68] We must believe what is recounted about the saints from those honest informants, even though they do not live in our own time."

36 **With the assistance of God, the First Part is complete.**

It is stated in the original copy that the first forty questions are lost.

37 **From the Second Part.**

38 **The Brothers asked:** "Explain to us the saying of Abba Macarius, the priest: 'I never gave the Eucharist to Mark the mourner. It was an angel who gave him the Eucharist from the altar. I only used to see the angel's hand giving him the Eucharist'."[69]

39 **The Holy Man replied:** "At the beginning, in the deserts of Egypt, it was the head of the monastery alone who conducted the mass until his death, as Palladius said: 'There were eight priests running the affairs of the Parnouj Monastery.[70] But as long as the first was alive, none of the others would assume the function of the priesthood or any of the hermits in the caves. One priest only conducted for them the service of the sacraments'.[71] In another place, there were a priest and a deacon serving an entire year. As for the priest Macarius, he conducted the mass alone, and he saw the angel's hand as a link between him and Mark, as one of the seraphs did when it took the burning coal from the altar and placed it in the mouth of the Prophet Isaiah.[72] The angel did this because angels do not have authority to conduct the service of the Eucharist and communicate it to people. But because of Mark's great purity and humility, he was made an example for others. His life attested that he had reached in four virtues what no other had attained. Two of them were because of his will and effort: his purity in body and soul and his great humility. Two others were gifts from God: memorizing the Old and New Testaments by heart and knowing their true explanation, and taking the Eucharist from the angel's hand. This is the great Graeco-Egyptian Mark whose knowledge and way of life was not surpassed by any of the solitaries in Egypt. It was he who wrote the book against those who claimed that Melchizedek was the son of God. He is to be differentiated from Mark the Syrian whose original name was

الاخ الذي يسكن في اورشليم ⁶²³ انه كان يرى ⁶²⁴ مثل الظل ومن ⁶²⁵ تدبير اعماله. فينبغي لنا ان نصدق ما يقال عن القديسين من المخبرين الصادقين وان لم يكونوا في زماننا. ⁶²⁶

36 تم ⁶²⁷ الجز الاول بمعونة الله وذكر في نسخة ⁶²⁸ الام ⁶²⁹ انه عدم من اوله اربعون ⁶³⁰ مساله.

37 من الجز الثاني.

38 **قالوا** ⁶³¹ **الاخوه** فسر لنا قول انبا مقار القسيس. انني ما قربت قط مرقس الكييب بل ملاك كان يناوله من المذبح. ويد الملاك لا غير كنت اراها تناوله.

39 **قال الشيخ** ان الزمان الاول في براري مصر كان الذي يروس الدير هو الذي يقدس القداس الى يوم وفاته. كما قال بلاديس. ⁶³² ان ثمانية قسوس كانوا يدبروا دير برنوج. وما دام الاول حيا ما يكهن احد منهم. وان المنفردين في (b19r/d82r) مغاير ايضا. كان قسيس واحد يكمل لهم خدمة الكهنوت. وفي موضع اخر كان قسيس ⁶³³ واحد وشماس ⁶³⁴ واحد يخدمان سنه كامله. فالقسيس مقاريوس كان وحده يقدس. وكان يرى يد الملاك واسطه بينه (e81v) وبين مرقس. كما فعل واحد من السارافيم ⁶³⁵ لما اخذ من على المذبح الجمرة النار ووضعها في فم اشعيا النبي. (a13v) وكان الملاك يصنع هكذى لانه لا سلطان للملايكه ⁶³⁶ ان يقدسوا القرابين ويدفعوها للبشر. ومن اجل عظم طهارة مرقس واتضاعه ليتشبه به غيره وشهدت سيرته انه كان له اربعة فضايل بلغ فيها ما لم يصل اليه غيره. اثنتان لارادته واجتهاده. وهما طهارته في جسمه ونفسه واتضاعه العظيم. واثنتان موهبه من الله وهما حفظ العتيقه والحديثه في (c53v) قلبه ومعرفته تفسيرهما الحقيقي. واخذه القربان من يد الملاك. وهذا هو مرقس الكبير اليوناني المصري الذي لم يكن في جميع المتوحدين بمصر اعلم منه في المعرفة والتدبير. وهو الذي عمل الكتاب في الرد على الذين قالوا ان ملكيزادق ⁶³⁷ هو ابن الله. وليس هو مرقس السرياني الذي كان يدعى اولا

Malchus⁷³ and lived the remainder of his life in Syria, nor is he Mark the Less, the disciple of Sylvanus."⁷⁴

40   **The Brothers asked:** "The book *The Garden*⁷⁵ states that when the priest of the Scetis Mountain went down to the monasteries that were around Alexandria he found the brothers gathered for the fortieth-day anniversary of the death of one and the third-day anniversary of the death of another?"

41   **The Exegete replied:** "Saint Antony had said to Eulogius and his leprous companion: 'Do not part company for both your deaths are near'. When the priest arrived to where they were, he found them [the monks] gathered for the fortieth-day anniversary of the death of Eulogius and the third-day anniversary of the leper."⁷⁶

42   **The Brothers asked:** "It is written in the life of Abba Moses the Black that for some time he joined his band of companion robbers and did sinful things with them. A good thought came to him. How was the good thought capable of delivering him from bad habits, and from his companions and demons? If this was from the grace of God or from himself, how is it that it did not occur before, but only at that time?"⁷⁷

43   **The Exegete replied:** "Every virtue that a person does, as our Lord said, is accomplished with God's help, such as in His saying: 'You can do nothing',⁷⁸ meaning nothing good. Grace follows what is similar and apt. As when Paul's inclination was to the splendor of truth and he was apt in his effort to spread the truth, thus he was elected. Grace attracts people to virtue through three mediums: thought, education, and reading. Doing good deeds is accomplished through grace and a person's will. Before a person's thought leans towards good or evil, it [grace] neither assists him nor abandons him. Father Abraham, when his thought cast off the unbelief of his fathers and it longed for knowing the truth, grace immediately illuminated his thought. Likewise with Abba Moses when his thought leaned [towards the good], grace then assisted him."

44   **The Brothers asked:** "Why did the saintly Fathers become accustomed all the time to pursuing virtue, and struggling with yearnings and the devil, yet Abba Isidore the priest said to Abba

40 **قال الاخوه** ان كتاب[639] البستان يقول ان قسيس جبل النطرون لما نزل الى الاديره التي حول الاسكندريه[640] وجد الاخوه مجتمعين في اربعين الواحد وثالث الاخره. ملخس وكل حياته في الشام. ولا هو (b19v) مرقس الصغير تلميذ (d82v) سلوانا.[638]

41 **قال المفسر** ان القديس انطونيوس (e82r) قال لاولاجه ورفيقه المجدم لا تفترقا فقد قرب اجلكما. فلما وصل القس الى موضعها وجدهم مجتمعين في اربعين اولاجه.(a14r) وثالث المجدم.[641]

42 **قال**[642] **الاخوه** ان سيرة انبا موسى[643] الاسود مكتوب. انه كان بعض الايام يتقلب مع اصحابه اللصوص فيما كانوا يصنعوه من الشرور. فاتته فكرة صالحه. فكيف قدرت[644] فكرته تخلصه من العوايد الرديه ومن اصحابه ومن الشياطين. فان كان هذا من نعمة الله او منه فلمذا لم يكن ذلك من قبل وانما كان[645] في ذلك الوقت.

43 **قال المفسر** كل فضيلة يعملها الانسان كقول ربنا انما تتم بمعونة الله. كقوله لستم تقدرون تعملون شيا.[646] اي جيدا. النعمه تتبع المثل والتاهل. كما لما كان ميل بولص الى نضرة[647] الحق وكان متاهلا لما صدر عنه من[648] الاجتهاد في اشاعه الحق انتخب. والنعمه تجتذب الناس الى الفضيله بثلثة[649] اسباب. في الفكره وفي التعليم وفي القراة. (b20r/d83r) وفعل الخير يتم من النعمة واختيار ارادة الانسان. من قبل ان تميل فكرة الانسان للخير وللشر ما تساعده ولا تتخلا عنه. فالاب ابراهيم لما رذلت فكرته كفر[650] ابايه واشتهت معرفة الحق. فالوقت (e82v) انارت النعمه فكرته. وكذلك[651] انبا موسى لما مالت فكرته حينيذ ساعدته النعمه.

44 **قال الاخوه** لماذا الابا القديسون يدرجوا في كل حين في عمل الفضيله ومحاربة الاوجاع والشيطان. (a14v/c54r) والقس انبا ايسيدرس مع انبا

Moses: 'Do not obstinately dispute with demons for there is a limit even in our works of ascetic life'?"[79]

45 **The Exegete replied:** "This was because at the beginning he [Abba Moses] believed that only through his excessive works and hardships will he gain the upper hand over the demons. When they discovered this, they increased in their struggles with him covertly and overtly. Abba Isidore wished to teach him humility and make him realize that hardships alone are insufficient without the grace of the Holy Spirit that comes through baptism and the Eucharist. It is similar to the sick in body. The doctor orders him to take medicine, and also instructs him not to sleep, move around, eat heavy food, and other conditions for taking the medicine. The cure is not achieved though by any of these conditions. Rather, it is achieved through the medicine. Similarly, the sick in spirit is not cured by his works, be it stillness, silence, fasting, vigils, honesty and humility. Rather he is cured and defeats the demons by the grace of the Holy Spirit. Whoever struggles with yearnings and demons must fulfill our Lord's commandments. He should not focus on the success of his work. The wanderer travels between monasteries to benefit [others] or derive benefit in terms of spiritual matters, and the hungry to receive bodily benefit."

46 **The Brothers asked:** "Why did the solitary Fathers stretch their hands in prayer and raise them to Heaven?"

47 **The Exegete replied:** "This is because Paul the Apostle said: 'I desire that in every place men pray, lifting up their hands in purity without rage or bad thoughts'."[80]

48 **The Brothers asked:** "Is it because of this that the commentator stated that lifting up hands implies lifting up thoughts to Heaven, to the Lord, with love and purity?"

49 **The Exegete replied:** "This is not said to the many, but rather only to the solitaries and perfect ones. They do not only lift up their thoughts, but also their eyes and hands. The many are incapable of lifting up their thoughts to God. It is easier for them to lift up their hands and eyes to Heaven. Everyone emulates the prophets and Christ, glory to him, and his Apostles and saints. David said: 'I stretch out my hands to you',[81] 'let the lifting up of my hands be as an evening sacrifice',[82] and 'I lifted up my eyes to

موسى قايلا لا تلاجج الشياطين.^652 لان لنا عمال والتدبير حدا.

45 **قال المفسر** لانه كان في مباديه يظن انه من كثرة اعماله واتعابه فقط يقوى على الشياطين. ولما عرفوا هذا زادوا في محاربته خفيا وظاهرا. فاراد انبا ايسيدرس ان يعلمه الاتضاع ويعرفه ان الاتعاب بمفرده غير كافيه. من دون نعمة الروح^653 القدس الحاصله بالمعموديه والقربان. وهذا كالذي هو مريض في جسده. فيامره الطبيب بشرب دوا. ويامره مع ذلك ان يمتنع من النوم والحركة^654 والغذا الغليظ وباقي شروط شرب الدوا. وليس يحصل الشفا بشي من هذه الشروط. انما يحصل بالدوا. وكذالك^655 المريض في نفسه لا يشفى^656 بمجرد^657 اعماله (b20v) من (d83v) سكوت وصوم وسهر وصدقه واتضاع. وانما يشفي ويغلب الشياطين بنعمة روح القدس. فمن يحارب مع الاوجاع والشياطين يجب ان يعمل وصايا ربنا. ولا ينظر الى النجح بعمله.(e83r) لكن ان المنتقل يدور على الاديرة يفيد او ليستفيد امورا^658 روحانيه. وجايع ليستفيد امورا^659 جسمانيه. (a15v/c54v)

46 **قال الاخوه** لماذا الابا المتوحدين يبسطون ايديهم في الصلاه ويرفعوها نحوا السما.

47 **قال المفسر** لقول بولص الرسول اشا^660 ان تصلي الرجال في كل موضع رافعين ايديهم بطهارة بلا غضب ولا افكار رديه.

48 **قال الاخوه** ولهاذا قال المفسر ان رفع الايادي هو رفع الافكار الى السما. الى الرب بمحبه وطهاره.

49 **قال المفسر** ليس هذا يقال للكثيرين وانما يقال للمتوحدين والكاملين. وليس يرفعون افكارهم فقط. بل واعينهم وايادهم. ^661 واما الاكثرون فيعسر عليهم رفع الافكار الى الله. ويتيسر لهم رفع الايدي والاعين الى السما. والكل يتشبهون بالانبيا وبالمسيح له المجد. وبرسله وقديسيه. فان داوود يقول بسطت^662 اليك يدَّي. وليكن رفع يدَّي قربانا^664 للمساء.^665 ورفعت عيَّني^663

you, O Lord'.⁸³ You find Christ too lifting up his hands, eyes and thoughts.⁸⁴ Paul said: 'Seek the place above where Christ is seated'.⁸⁵ The Fathers lift up their hands and eyes to Heaven to help with lifting up their thoughts to God. Thus did Moses do when he fought the Amalekites.⁸⁶ It is also written that Abba Sisoes of Thebais used to stand in prayer and stretch out his hands. His mind would be caught up to our Lord for a long while.⁸⁷ And if someone came, he would lower his hands [but] his mind would be caught up. He struggled greatly with this."⁸⁸

50   **The Brothers asked:** "Why did the wanderers say to a brother: 'If you wish to become a wanderer like us, sit first in your cell and weep for your sins, then you will become like us'."⁸⁹

51   **The Exegete replied:** "This is because whoever distances himself from the world cuts off the activity of yearnings while in solitude and ties his thought to God. He thus attains the rank of wanderers."

52   **He added:** "The phantom-like angel cut open the belly of the wanderer and showed him the pain of his liver, then returned him to his previous condition.⁹⁰ Similarly, the angels cut the testicles of Elijah, head of the nunnery, when he fought the desire [of fornication]."⁹¹

53   **He also added:** "The strength of the demons' struggle with every person is in accordance with their work, labor, effort, way of life, and endurance. When someone asked if he could stay with him in the desert, Abba Apellen replied: 'You cannot endure the trials of the demons'. But when he prevailed upon him he received him and he lived in a cave beside him. The demons came to him at night. At first, they corrupted his thoughts, and finally they wanted to scare him. Apellen came to him and drew around the cave the sign of the cross. Only then could he live in it. Just as not all the Apostles were given [the power] to exorcise all the demons, likewise, not all solitaries have the capacity to withstand the struggle with powerful and wicked demons. Only the humble and perfect are capable of this."⁹²

54   **The Brothers asked:** "Why did the two brothers who lived three years in the Scetis Desert where Abba Macarius was never visit him or anyone else?"

اليك يا رب. (a16r) والمسيح تراه رفع يديه. وتراه رفع (c55r) عينيه وافكاره. (b21r/d84r)
وبولص قال اطلبوا ما فوق موضع جلس المسيح. والاباء يرفعون ايديهم واعينهم الى السماء 666
معاونة لرفع افكارهم الى الله. هكذا عمل موسى في حرب العمالقه. فقد كتب ان انبا (e83v)
شيشاتي التبايسي كان يقف في الصلاه ويبسط يديه فيخطف عقله الى عند ربنا وقتا طويلا. 667
واذا حضر احد حط يديه فيخطف عقله وهذه 668 الحال تعبه جدا.

50 **قال الاخوه** لماذا قالوا السواح لاخ ان كنت تقدر ان تكون سايحا مثلنا اجلس في قلايتك
وابك 669 على خطاياك. فتكون مثلنا.

51 **قال المفسر** لان الذي بعد من العالم قطع منه حركة 670 الاوجاع في الوحده وربط فكرته بالله هو
في منزلة السواح.

52 **وقال ايضا** ان الملاك بالخيال شق بطن السايح واراه وجع كبده ورده كما كان. وكذالك الملايكه
شقت انثي ايليا ريس دير راهبانات لما صار معه قتال الشهوه.

53 **وقال ايضا** كل انسان فعلى قدر عمله وتعبه وجهاده وتدبيره وصبره يكون مقدار قوة جهاد
الشياطين له. فان انبا ابلوا[ن] لما ساله واحد ان يسكن معه في البريه قال له ما تقدر تصبر
لتجارب الشياطين. فلما الزمه وداه معه وسكن في مغاره الى جانبه. فاتاه 671 الشياطين في
الليل. وفي (d84v) (b21v/a16v) الاول نجسوا افكاره. وفي الاخر ارادوا ان يخيفوه. لجا
اليه ابلوا[ن] وجعل حول المغاره رسم الصليب دايره. وحينيذ قدر ذاك ان يسكن فيها. وكما ان
ما (e84r) كل الرسل اعطيوا 672 ان يخرجوا كل الشياطين. كذالك ولا كل المتوحدين يقدرون
يثبتون لحرب الشياطين الاقويا 673 الاشرار. وانما يقدر على ذالك 674 من كان كاملا متضعا.

54 **قال 675 الاخوه** لماذا الاخوان الذان سكنا في الاسقيطي عند انبا مقار ثلث سنين ما مضيا اليه
ولا الى غيره.

55   **The Exegete replied:** "Because the older one was a perfect and humble worker. Had he visited him, he would have revealed his perfection and been glorified. As for the younger one, he was learning from the older one."[93]

56   **The Brothers asked:** "The stories concerning the life of Abba Bessarion attest that he lived in desolate places and mountains. One day he came to a monastery, sat at its door and said: 'Thieves robbed me at sea. The storms thundered and waves rose up against me. I have been deprived of the possessions of my house and shorn of my ancestors' wealth and glory'."[94]

57   **The Exegete replied:** "He meant by the sea the life of solitude, by storms the trials, by waves the yearnings, by thieves the demons, and by his ancestors the Father, the Son and the Holy Spirit, the One God, in whose form and likeness we were created, as he said in the Torah,[95] and as our Lord said in the Gospel: 'Be perfect as your heavenly Father, for he is perfect'.[96] By possessions of his house [he meant] the possessions of his soul which it had the result of its nature and divine grace; its nature is what the Creator had planted in it: desire, will, and ability to know the truth and perform pious acts if it chose to. These are the things that the Prophet had said that a person in honor squanders out of ignorance[97] of them and is driven out with mindless beasts and becomes like them. As for what comes from grace, they are baptism and spiritual gifts. It is written: 'Faith without work is dead',[98] and 'He who does not have, even what he has is taken away from him'.[99] That is, he who has no work that befits faith, then faith is taken away from him in the sense that he would not benefit from it, like one who does not have faith at all. As for his ancestors' wealth, [he meant] the virtues that make us resemble our heavenly Father, and make us inherit his Kingdom through faith, hope, and love of God and people. Welfare, mercy, patience, purity, magnanimity, humility, knowledge, and spiritual prayer; these possessions are drowned by the seas of worldly desires, and suffocated by the concerns and preoccupations of the world. Vainglory steals them. When the blessed one became mindful that many of the solitaries lacked these spiritual possessions, the law of brotherly love stirred in him. He began to weep and wail for them as though he was crying for his own self. As though he was miserable and his possessions had perished and what he had was stolen from his house. He would ask

55 **قال المفسر** لان الواحد الكبير كان عاملا كاملا متضعا. ولو مضا اليه اظهر كماله ومجد. واما الصغير فكان يتعلم من الكبير.

56 **قال الاخوه** ان اخبار سيرة انبا بسيرين تشهد بانه كان في القفر والجبال ساكنا. وانه في بعض الايام (c55v) وصل الى دير وجلس عند بابه قايلا. ان اللصوص وقعوا علي⁶⁷⁶ في البحر والزوابع ثارت. والامواج علت علي. وافتقرت⁶⁷⁷ من⁶⁷⁸ قنية بيتي. وعدمت غنا اباي ومجدهم.

57 **قال المفسر** اشار بالبحر الى زمان تدبير الوحدة. وبالزوابع الى التجارب. وبالامواج الى الاوجاع. وباللصوص الى الشياطين. وبابايه الاب والابن والروح⁶⁷⁹ القدس الاله الواحد الذي بصورته وشبهه خلقنا. (b22r/d85r)⁶⁸⁰ كما قال في التوراه. ولقول ربنا في الانجيل كونوا كاملين مثل ابيكم⁶⁸¹ السماوي⁶⁸² فهو كامل. وقنية بيته هي قنية نفسه التي كانت (a17r/e84v) لها من طبعها ومن النعمه الالهيه. فالتي من طبعها هي التي غرسها فيها الخالق. وهي الشهوه والارادة والقدرة لمعرفة الحق وعمل البر اذا اختارت.⁶⁸³ وهذه هي التي قال النبي عن الانسان الذي يضيعها في كرامة وجهلها طرد مع البهايم التي لا عقل لها وشبه بها. والتي من النعمه هي المعموديه والمواهب الروحانيه. وقد كتب ان الايمان بلا عمل ميت⁶⁸⁴ وان من ليس له فالذي معه يوخذ منه. اي من ليس له العمل الملايم للايمان فالايمان يوخذ منه.⁶⁸⁵ بمعنى انه⁶⁸⁶ لا يكون منتفع⁶⁸⁷ به كمن لا ايمان له. وقنية ابيه هي الفضايل التي تشبهنا بابينا السماوي⁶⁸⁸ ويجعلنا نكون وارثين لملكوته بالايمان والرجا والمحبه لله والناس. والسلامة والرحمه وطول الروح والطهر والجود والاتضاع والمعرفه والصلاة الروحانيه. وهذه القنيات تغرقها⁶⁸⁹ بحار الشهوات العالميه وتخنقها هموم واهتمام الدنيا. (b22v) ويسرقها المجد الباطل. والطوباني (d85v) لما راى بعين عقله ان كثيرا من المتوحدين قد عدموا هذه القنايا⁶⁹⁰ الروحانيه. نخسه ناموس محبة الاخوه. فجعل يبكي وينوح عليهم كمن (e85r) يبكي على نفسه. وكانه مسكين قد غرقت قنيته. وسرق ما له من بيته. وكان يسال من⁶⁹¹

God to make them worthy of the fortune of his love and the possessions of his blessings."

58 **The Brothers asked:** "What are the nine virtues of that person?"

59 **The Exegete replied:** "I believe they are: possessing very little, abstinence, fasting always till the evening, holding vigils, saying the seven hourly prayers day and night, reading the holy books between the prayers, gentleness, humility, and loving people. These virtues are acquired through great labor and enormous struggle. By them one defeats all yearnings. By possessing very little one defeats the love of silver. By abstinence one defeats gluttony. By fasting one defeats desire. By nightly vigils one defeats sleep. By prayers one defeats thoughts. By reading books one defeats foul speech and idle talk. By gentleness one defeats rage and anger. By humility one defeats vainglory and pride. By love of people one defeats hatred, jealousy, enmity and most evils. The tenth virtue, which even he who has the nine virtues is incapable of attaining, is exceeding continuously all bounds in loving our Lord. It is only acquired through inner prayer in the mind without feebleness or distraction, and through constantly exorcising the thoughts of yearnings and the tricks of demons from the first moment they occur in the heart. For this virtue is more perfect than all virtues and the strong and wicked demons often fight the solitaries so that they do not attain it or endure in it. For this reason too, the works that lead to it are the most laborious and difficult of all the virtues. This is why blessed Mark said that because of the opposition of demons to this work he could not quickly become perfect in the love of Christ, which is attained by the unity of thought and exceeding all bounds [in loving] God.[100] Saint Evagrius said: 'If you defeat the frivolousness of thoughts and endure in the remembrance of God, then you deserve perfection which is in the love of Christ and people, and by which you defeat all yearnings that attach primarily to the love of the self. Whoever possesses this perfection longs to leave this world, depart from this body, and proceed to the Lord who loved him. He will be in Paradise, the home of the pure and abode of the Perfect, which is superior to yearnings, demons, struggles and defeats, and the place of repose from the toils of virtue, until the appearance of Christ, eternally enjoying his glory'."[101]

الله ان يجعلهم مستحقين لغنا حبه (a17v) وقنية خيراته.

58 (c56r) **قال الاخوه** ما هي التسع فضايل[692] التي لذلك[693] الانسان.

59 **قال المفسر** اظن[694] انهم قلة القنيه الامساك الصوم الى المسا دايما. السهر صلاوات الساعات السبع نهار وليلا. قراة الكتب المقدسه بين صلوات[695] الساعات الوداعة الاتضاع حب الناس. وهذه الفضايل اقتناها بتعب[696] كثير وحرب عظيم. وبها غلب جميع الاوجاع فبقلة القنيه غلب محبة الفضه. وبالامساك غلب البطنه. وبالصوم غلب الرغبه. وبالسهر غلب النوم. وبالصلوات[697] غلب الافكار. وبالقراة في الكتب غلب الكلام الردي والحديث الباطل. وبالوداعه غلب الغضب والحرد. وبالاتضاع غلب المجد الباطل والكبريا. وبمحبة البشر غلب البغضه والحسد والعداوه واكثر الشرور. والفضيلة العاشره التي (b23r/d86r) يعجزها صاحب هذه التسعه هي الغلوة الدايمه في محبة ربنا. وهذه انما تقتني من الصلاة الخفيه في الذهن[698] التي تكون (e85v) بغير فتور ولا طياشه. ومن داوم[699] طرد افكار الاوجاع وخدع الشياطين من اول حركاتهم في القلب ومن اجل ان هذه الفضيله اكمل[700] من كل الفضايل. فالشياطين الاقويا الارديا يجاهدون المتوحدين بالاكثر على ان لا يصلوا اليها ولا يثبتوا فيها. ولهذا كانت الاعمال الموصله اليها اتعب اعمال الفضايل واصعبها. (a18r) ولهذا قال الطوباني مرقس انه من اجل مضاددة الشياطين لهذا العمل ما قدر سريعا يكمل في حب المسيح. الذي يقتني من اجتماع الفكرة والغلوة التي لله. وقال القديس وغريس ان غابت[701] طياشة الافكار وثبت في ذكر الله فانت تستحق الكمال الذي في حب المسيح والناس. الذي بها تغلب جميع الاوجاع التي تتعلق اولا بمحبة النفس والذي يملك هذا الكمال فهو يشتهي ان ينصرف من هذا العالم ويفارق هذا الجسد. ويصير الى الرب الذي احبه. ويكون في الفردوس مسكن الابرار وبلد الكاملين.(c56v) الذي هو اعلا من الاوجاع والشياطين. والحروب والسقوط. موضع (e86r/d86v) النياح من اتعاب الفضيله الى ظهور المسيح الذي ينتعم في مجده نعيم لا ينتهي.

60 **The Brothers asked:** "Explain to us the way of life of that holy man who had baskets and small stones?"[102]

61 **The Exegete replied:** "It is the economy of the mind that leads the solitary to purity of the heart. His labor was that he placed a basket to his right and a basket to his left. For every good thought that occurred to him, he would place a stone in the one to his right, and for every foul thought that occurred to him, he would place a stone in the one to his left. This was in addition to his assiduousness in carrying out his duties, prayer and labor. Because of this virtuous work, the demons were envious of him and would stir in his heart many evils. The holy man would refuse to eat if his good thoughts did not surpass the bad ones, and he would suffer in spirit and body. Not only does the soul suffer from the toils of the body because of its unity with it, but also the demons that fight it suffer even more. When Evagrius fought the demon of fornication, he took off his clothes and stood under the sky all night long. He exhausted the demon of fornication to such an extent that he fled from him.[103] The suffering of saints exhausts demons because the angels, by God's command, make them suffer. A demon once intended to separate two biological brothers. When the younger lit a lamp, the demon threw it down with the stand, and extinguished it. The [older] brother smote him [the younger] on his cheek. He [the younger] prostrated before him and said: 'My brother, be patient with me and I will light it'. When God saw the patience of the youth and his humility, he commanded the angel of that youth who tied that demon up in the cell and punished him until the next day. As restitution for one slap that this brother bore calmly from his brother because of the work of the demon, the angel fettered that demon and flogged him all night long."[104]

62 **The Brothers asked:** "Why do demons fear the works of solitaries, as the Fathers said: 'If you want demons to fear you, then reject desires'?"

63 **The Exegete replied:** "For three reasons. The first reason is that when our Lord rejected the three yearnings that the devil employed to fight him—namely, desire, love of money and vainglory, which comprise all types of yearnings—and through his endurance during [the trial] in the desert, and [through] stillness, fasting and prayer he defeated the devil. Those who follow his lead destroy the thoughts

60 **قال الاخوه** فسر لنا تدبير عمل ذلك (b23v) الشيخ صاحب القفف والحصا الصغار.

61 **قال المفسر** هو تدبير الذهن [702] الذي يوصل المتوحد [703] الى نقا القلب. وعمله هو انه وضع قفه عن يمينه وقفه عن شماله. وكل فكرة صالحه تاتي عليه يضع حصاه في التي عن يمينه. وكل فكرة رديه تاتيه يضع حصاة في التي عن شماله. وهذا مع مداومته في خدمته وصلاته وعلمه. ولاجل غاية هذا العمل الفاضل. كانت الشياطين يحسدونه ويحركون في قلبه شرورًا (a18v) [704] كثيره. والشيخ ما كان ياكل اذ لم تزد [705] افكاره الصالحه على الرديه ويتالم بالنفس والجسد. وليست النفس فقط تتالم في اتعاب الجسد من اجل اتحادها به. بل والشياطين الذين يقاتلونها يتعبون بالاكثر. فان وغريس لما حارب معه شيطان الزنا تعرى ثيابه ووقف تحت السما طول الليل. فاتعب شيطان الزنا حتى انه هرب عنه. فاتعاب القديسين تتعب الشياطين. لان الملايكه بامر (e86v) الله تعذبهم. فان شيطانا اراد ان يفرق بين الاخوين جسدانيين. فلما وقد الصغير السراج رماه الشيطان هو والمناره فطفاه. فضربه اخوه على خده. فصنع له مطانيه وقال له يا اخي طوّل عليّ روحك وانا اقده. فلما راى الله صبر الصبي واتضاعه امر ملاك ذلك [706] الصبي. فربط ذلك [707] الشيطان في القلايه وعاقبه (b24r/d87r) الى الغداه. فعوض ضربة واحده صبر عليها ذلك الاخ من اخيه بفعل الشيطان. ربط الملاك ذلك الشيطان وجلده طول الليل.

62 **قال الاخوه** لماذا تخاف الشياطين من اعمال المتوحدين. (c57r) كقول الابا ان اردت ان تخاف مناك الشياطين فارذل الشهوات.

63 **قال المفسر** لثلاثة اسباب. الاول لان ربنا لما رذل الاوجاع الثلثه [708] التي تجمع اصناف الاوجاع. وهي الشهوه. محبة المال. والمجد (a19r) الباطل. التي بها حاربه الشيطان. وفي ثباته في البريه. والهدو. والصوم والصلاه غلب الشيطان. فالذين يسلكوا في اثره يهدمون افكار

of sin and the Lord chases demons away from them. For demons do not only fear the cross of Christ, but also making its sign. They are not defeated and do not run away from the works of Christ alone, but also from those who follow his works. The second reason is that if the solitaries succumb to the tricks of demons through sinful thoughts and enjoy them their souls darken because of distance from God. They are saddened, humiliated, weakened and censured. But if they do not succumb to their tricks, cast off thoughts when they occur, and appeal to their Lord to aid them, the demons are disbanded and humiliated, and they depart. Likewise, the blessed Mark said: 'As whoever seeks to fornicate with someone else's wife is struck with fear and runs away when he hears the husband's voice, so too the demon is struck with fear and runs away when he hears us calling upon God'.[105] The third reason is because they attain proximity to God by obedience to God and love of Him. Demons thus keep at a distance from them. For the Lord had said to those who love him: 'I have given you power over all the forces of the Enemy; and nothing will harm you'."[106]

64 **The Brothers asked:** "Why do demons flee sometimes at the mention of Christ's name and the sign of the cross, but at other times they do not?"

65 **The Exegete replied:** "They flee because of what was said earlier. As for why they do not flee at other times, and do not fear a name, sign, or prayer but stand firm, and might not only cause fear, but also strike at the solitaries—that is because they have taken from the Lord power for their success. Saint Pachomius was once walking with Theodore at night. The devil appeared to them as an astounding phantom. They prayed for him to be driven away from them, but he boldly persisted and said to them: 'Do not exhaust yourselves with prayer in vain, for I was given power to tempt you'.[107] It is necessary that we do not stop making the sign of the cross, calling the name of Christ and praying if demons appear to us. If they leave, it is because of the Lord aiding us. But if they do not, it is because the Lord has released them for our ultimate success."

66 **The Brothers asked:** "Three demons came to Evagrius in the likeness of priests and disputed with him,[108] and angels came in the likeness of lay people[109] to the head of the Cells[110] for that [holy

الخطيه. ويطرد الرب شياطين عنهم. وكما تخاف الشياطين ليس من صليب المسيح فقط. (e87r) بل ومن رسم مثاله. هكذى 709 وليس يغلبون ويهربون من اعمال المسيح فقط. بل ومن اعمال التابعين له في اعماله. الثاني كما ان المتوحدين اذا قبلوا خداع الشياطين بافكار الخطيه واستلذوها تظلم نفوسهم بالبعد من الله. ويحزنون ويفتضحون ويضعفون ويلامون. هكذى اذا لم يقبلوا خداعهم وابعدوا الافكار من اول حركاتها. 710 ويدعون رهم لعونهم. فالشياطين تنحل وتفتضح وتنصرف. كما قال الطوباني مرقس. مثل ما يفزع ويهرب الذي يريد (b24v) ان يزني بزوجة (d87v) غيره اذا سمع صوت الزوج. هكذى يفزع الشيطان ويهرب اذا سمعنا ندعوا الله. الثالث. لان بطاعة الله ومحبته يحصل لهم القرب من الله. فتبتعد الشياطين منهم. وقد قال الرب لمحبيه 711 قد اعطيتكم سلطانا على جميع قوات العدو ولا يضركم شي. 712

64 قال الاخوه لماذا تاره 713 تنصرف الشياطين باسم المسيح ورسم الصليب وتاره لا ينصرفون.

65 قال المفسر اما انصرافهم فلما تقدم واما كونهم لا ينصرفون مرات ولا يخافون من اسم ولا رسم ولا صلاه بل يثبتون وقد لا يخيفون 714 فقط. لكن ويضربون (a19v) المتوحدين. فذلك 715 انما يكون اذا اخذوا من الرب سلطانا لريهم. فقد كان القديس بكوميوس (e87v) يمشي مع ثادرس 716 ليلا فترايا لهم الشيطان في خيال 717 عجيب. فصليا (c57v) ليبطل عنها وهو يظهر لها جسارة. وقال لا تتعبا بطالا 718 وتصليا. فاني قد اخذت سلطانا 719 على تجربتكما. فينبغي لنا ان لا نبطل رسم الصليب. وتسمية المسيح والصلاه. اذا ترات 720 لنا الشياطين. ان انصرفوا من اجل عون الرب لنا وان تباطوا باطلاق من الرب لربحنا.

66 قال الاخوه ان ثلثة 721 شياطين دخلوا عند وغريس في زي قسوس وتجادلوا معه. وملايكه مضوا في زي علمانيين الى ريس القلالي من اجل

man] who had the baskets and stones. They all prostrated before the cross, kissed it and prayed. Was this true or not?"

67 **The Exegete replied:** "As for the angels, they prostrated, kissed and prayed in themselves and as forms, just as the souls and bodies of the Perfect prostrate, pray and kiss. The demons, however, did so through their deceitful phantasms, because, unlike angels, demons do not have power to take on real forms."

68 **He added:** "At first, youths work for the glory of people. But then grace shows them the eminence of God's glory, so that they reach the point of obedience and love of him alone. Evagrius said: 'If your disciple is defeated, cure him without anger. But if he is victorious, praise him, because praise increases the force of the brave'."

69 **The abridgment of the Second Part is complete, thanks to God's favor towards me.**

70 **From the Third Part.**

71 **The Brothers asked:** "Paul the Apostle said: 'Love never falls'.[111] But a group reached the heights of the love of God and then fell?"

72 **The Exegete replied:** "Their arrogance was the reason for their fall."

73 **They asked:** "What is arrogance?"

74 **He replied:** "That a person considers himself righteous and better than sinners."

75 **They asked:** "How can the righteous and virtuous person consider himself a sinner and less than the deficient?"

76 **He replied:** "In many ways, such as to think that he cannot love God as God has loved him, nor be humble for God's sake as God has been humble for his sake, nor be humble and love God like the prophets and saints, nor be perfect with his obedience and will.[112] For it is written: 'God loved the world', meaning that the Father loved the sinners, 'so much so that he sent his only Son to die for their sake'.[113] The only Son became man and handed himself over to crucifixion and death on their behalf. The Holy Spirit hovers over them as a bird over its chicks and a mother over her children. It is also written that the Lord said: 'Learn from me for I am gentle

صاحب القفف (b25r/d88r) والحصا. وكانوا يسجدون للصليب⁷²² ويقبلونه ويصلون. فهل كان ذالك حقا ام لا.

67 **قال المفسر** اما الملايكه فكانوا يسجدون ويقبلون ويصلون بذواتهم وبخيالاتهم. كما تسجد وتصلي وتقبل نفوس الكاملين مع اجسادهم. واما الشياطين فكانوا⁷²³ يفعلون ذلك بخيالاتهم الكاذبة. فليس للشياطين⁷²⁴ سلطان ان يركبوا خيالات حقيقيه من الاستقصات كما تصنع الملايكه.

68 **قال** ان الصبيان يعملوا في المبادي من اجل مجد الناس. وبعد ذلك تريهم النعمه شرف مجد الاله ليضحوا في طاعته ومحبته وحده.. وقال وغريس (e88r) تلميذك فداوه بلا حرد. وان غلب فمجده. فان التمجيد يزيد الشجاع قوه.⁷²⁵

69 تم⁷²⁶ اختصر عليه من (a20r) الجز الثاني ولله المنه علي.⁷²⁷

70 من الجز الثالث.

71 **قال**⁷²⁸ **الاخوه** ان بولس⁷²⁹ الرسول يقول الحب ما يسقط البته. وقوم قد ارتفعوا الى علو محبة الله ثم سقطوا.

72 **قال المفسر** ان عظمتهم كانت سبب سقوطهم.

73 **قالوا** وما (b25v) هي العظمه.

74 **قال** ان يحسب الانسان نفسه ان بار وافضل من الخطاه.

75 **قالوا** وكيف يمكن البار (c58r) الفاضل ان يحسب ذاته خاطيا وانقص (d88v) من الناقصين.

76 **قال** باشيا⁷³⁰ كثيره. منها من يتامل انه لا يقدر يحب الله كما احبه. ولا ان يتضع من اجله كما اتضع هو من اجله. ولا ان يتضع له ويحبه كالانبيا والقديسين. ولا ان يكمل طاعته وارادته. لانه قد كتب ان الله احب العالم. يعني ان الاب احب الخطاه حتى دفع ابنه الوحيد للموت من اجلهم. والابن الوحيد تاانس واسلم نفسه للصلب⁷³¹ والموت عنهم. والروح القدس يرف عليهم كالطير على فراخه وكالوالده مع بنيها. وكتب ايضا ان الرب قال تعلموا مني فاني وديع

and humble in heart'.[114] Another way is to think that possibly those he believes to be sinners are more righteous and humble than him, and that in those virtues where he considers himself more perfect than them he is actually less perfect but does not know it. Just like the Pharisee who invited our Master to a banquet and said: 'If this man were a true prophet, he would know what kind of woman she is and that she is a sinner'.[115] The Pharisee and others at that time thought that she was a sinner, but our Lord who knows everything and at all times saw that she was righteous. He said: 'Her many sins are forgiven because she has shown great love'.[116] Similarly, [the parable of] the other Pharisee who thought himself more righteous than the tax collector when they prayed, but the Lord said that the tax collector was more righteous than him.[117] Another way is to think concerning the person who believes himself to be more righteous and better than him, that it is possible that their states have been reversed, as in the states of Judas[118] and the thief on the right.[119] If you are righteous and wise, and you love God and are loved by him, remember that brother Solomon who was [righteous] in his youth, but then in old age became ignorant and a lover of pleasures. If you are a prophet, remember how that prophet lapsed and erred when that false prophet prevailed over him and fed him bread, and was then killed by lions.[120] If you are an apostle who exorcises demons and performs miracles, remember how Judas subsequently fell because of his love of silver and was called a demon and a son of perdition.[121] If you see a murdering bandit, say: 'How would I know. He might be admitted to Paradise before me, like the thief on the right'. If you witness a sinful fornicator, say: 'How would I know, he might in the future love Christ and weep for his sins more than I do'. He who always thinks in this way never falls from the love of our Lord but when he tends towards pride he falls from on high."

77 **The Holy Man said:** "When the solitary possesses perfect humility, by denigrating himself at all times and in every act, he is released from struggling, whether at the beginning of the struggle, in the middle of it, or at the end of it, as Mark the mourner said. Abba Sisoes said: 'If the solitary attains humility, he attains perfection'."[122]

78 **He added:** "In ranking the solitaries' way of life, they first become weary through bodily labors, then through the struggle with

ومتضع بقلبي. ومنها ان يفكر في انه يجوز ان يكون اوليك الذين يظن (e88v) انهم خطاه هم ابر منه باتضاعهم. والذي يرا انه اكمل[732] منهم هو انقص منهم في بعض الفضايل وهو لا يدري. كذلك[733] الفريسي الذي دعا سيدنا الى الوليمه وقال لو (b26r) كان هذا نبيا لعلم[734] حال هذه الامره[735] انها خاطيه. فكان الفريسي وغيره الى ذلك الوقت (a20v) يرون انها خاطيه. فاما ربنا العارف بكل الاشيا[736] في كل الاوقات فراى[737] انها باره. فقال ان خطاياها الكثيره مغفوره لها[738] لانها احبت كثيرا وكذلك[739] الفريسي الاخر المصلي[740] الذي حسب انه ابر من (d89r) المصلي الاخر العشار. وقال الرب ان العشار ابر منه. ومنها ان يفكر ان الذي يظن انه ابر وافضل منه يجوز ان ينتقل حالها الى خلاف ماكانا عليه. كحال يهودا[741] ولص اليمين. فان كنت بارا حكيما محبا لله محبوبا منه فتذكر ذلك الاخ سليمان الذي كان هكذا[742] في صباه وصار في كبره جاهلا ومحبا للشهوه. وان كنت نبيا فتذكر كيف زل ذلك[743] النبي وخالف لما اطغاه واطعمه الخبز ذلك[744] النبي الكذاب فكسره السبع. ولو كنت رسولا تخرج الشياطين وتصنع البراهين فتذكر كيف سقط يهوذا في محبة الفضه. (c58v) بعد ذلك[745] حتى انه دعى (e89r) شيطانا وابن الهلاك. وان رايت لصا[746] قاتولا فقل من اين اعلم (b26v) ان كان هذا يسبقني الى الفردوس مثل لص اليمين. وان ابصرت زانيا خاطيا. فقل من اين اعرف ان كان هذا عتيدا ان يحب المسيح ويبكي على خطاياه اكثر مني. فمن يفكر هكذى دايما ما يسقط من محبة ربنا. ومتى مال الى الكبريا سقط من العلا.

77 **قال الشيخ** ومتى اقتنى المتوحد الاتضاع الكامل. وهو ان يحتقر نفسه في كل وقت وفي كل (a21r/d89v) فعل بطل عنه القتال. ان كان اول الحرب. او في وسطه. او في اخره كما قال مرقس الكبيب. وقد قال انبا شيشاي اذا وصل المتوحد الى الاتضاع وصل الى الكمال.

78 **قال** ترتيب تدبير المتوحدين انهم في الاول يتعبون في الاعمال الجسمانيه وبعد ذلك[747] في حرب

thoughts. After that, they acquire purity of heart. After that they experience the light of their mind, and then through its light they experience the light of Christ through spiritual sight. Some can see this light before they withdraw from this world which would be a guide for them to withdraw from the world to the monastery of the solitary. As for ranking the solitary's struggle with the devil, first [it occurs] in thoughts. After defeating bad thoughts, [it occurs] in physical sight through terror and then blows. But in some cases, demons might at first fight a solitary through terror and blows. This occurs to those who are beset by many sins in the world, such as Abba Moses the Black. The demons boldly fight him visibly through terror and blows for two reasons. One reason is because he did not know at first about the struggle with thoughts, and the other reason is because God's aid had abandoned him. This was in order for the intensity of his repentance, endurance, and effort to transpire."

79 **The Brothers asked:** "What does the saying of Abba Apollo mean: 'If the snake's head is crushed, all its body is dead'?"[123]

80 **The Exegete replied:** "He meant by 'the snake's head' the first thought of any sin that is stirred in the solitary's heart by the devil. He meant by 'its body' the many thoughts of the solitary that tolerate that deceiving [first] thought and provoke committing a sin."

81 **The Brothers asked:** "Why did that brother ask Abba Apollo to pray to God to grant him grace, and when he prayed for him, he was given the gift of humility, denigration [of one's self] and love?"[124]

82 **The Exegete replied:** "That brother had devoted much effort for these virtues, but the Lord did not wish to grant them to him without him asking God for them through grace, because if he took them from God through grace, he would be humbled through them. For this reason our Lord wished that the brothers attain their perfection through the counsel of the Fathers and their prayers for them."

83 **The Brothers asked:** "Why was the demon of pride found on the shoulders of Abba Apollo despite his labors, perfection, and God choosing him and sending him to save many?"[125]

الافكار وبعد ذلك⁷⁴⁸ يقتننون نقا القلب. وبعد ذلك⁷⁴⁹ يعاينون نور اذهانهم. وحينيذ يعاينون بنورها نور المسيح في رويا الروح. وقد يرى هذا النور احاد من قبل ان يخرجوا من هذا العالم. ويكون لهم مرشدا للخروج من العالم الى الدير المتوحد. ومراتب قتال الشيطان للمتوحد اما اولا⁷⁵⁰ ففي الافكار. واما من بعد غلبة الافكار الرديه. ففي النظر الحسي بالتخويف ثم (b27r) بالضرب. وقد (e89v) تقاتل الشياطين بعض المتوحدين في الاول بالتخويف والضرب. وهذا يكون لمن يتقلب في العالم في شرور كثيره مثل انبا موسى⁷⁵¹ الاسود. وتجسر الشياطين عليه وتقاتله ظاهرا بالتخويف والضرب لامرين.⁷⁵² احدهما لانه ما كان يعرف حرب الافكار في مباديه. والاخر لتخليه معونة الله عنه. وهذه لتظهر مقدار قوة (d90r) توبته وصبره ومجاهدته.

79 **قال الاخوه** ما معنى قول انبا بلوا[ن]⁷⁵³ اذا رض راس الثعبان فكل جسده يكون مايتا.

80 **قال المفسر** يعني براس الثعبان الفكرة الاولى التي يحركها الشيطان في قلب (a21v) المتوحد لاي خطية كانت. ويعني بجسده الافكار (c59r) الكثيره للمتوحد التي تقبل تلك الفكره الخداعه وتحرك على فعل الخطيه.

81 **قال⁷⁵⁴ الاخوه** لماذا طلب ذالك⁷⁵⁵ الاخ من انبا بلوان يصلي عليه لله ليعطيه النعمه. ولما صلى عنه اوعطيت له الموهبة الاتضاع والمحقره والحب.

82 **قال المفسر** ان ذالك⁷⁵⁶ الاخ كان قد قدم مجاهدات كثيره من اجل هذه الفضايل ولم يشا الرب ان يعطيها له من غير ان يطلبها من الله انعاما. لانه (b27v) اذا اخذها من الله انعاما اتضع فيها ولذلك اراد ربنا ان تصعد الاخوه الى (e90r) كهالم بوساطة مشورة الابا وصلاواتهم⁷⁵⁷ عنهم.

83 **قال⁷⁵⁸ الاخوه** لماذا وجد شيطان الكبريا على كتفي انبا بلوا[ن] بعد⁷⁵⁹ اتعابه وكماله واختيار الله له وارساله لخلاص الكثيرين.

84 **The Exegete replied:** "The Fathers said that after defeating all the demons and yearnings, the struggle with pride and vainglory remains with the Perfect until death, from God, so that they may persevere in their efforts and perfection. When God said to him: 'Go to the desert near the delta and teach a people so that they may glorify me and do good works'. Abba Apollo said: 'O Lord, free me from pride so that I do not become arrogant with the brothers and lose all the good.' God ordered him to stretch his hand to his neck, throw down what he found on his shoulder, and bury it in the sand. He found a small Ethiopian screaming 'I am the demon of pride' and buried him in the sand. The Fathers say that [for each] yearning which a person becomes a slave of, a demon sits on the organ through which he commits the act. So you will find the demon of fornication sitting on the testicles of him who is a slave of the yearning of fornication. He who is a slave to rage, the demon of rage sits on his heart. He who complains and says foul words, it sits on his tongue. He who becomes somnolent while praying, it sits on his eyes; and the thief, it sits on his right."

85 **The Brothers asked:** "Why did the holy man censure the solitaries who wore silk and grew their hair, even though many have been saved by doing this?"[126]

86 **The Exegete replied:** "He did not censure the Perfect, but only those who lacked the concealed virtues who behaved in this manner vaingloriously."

87 **The Brothers asked:** "Why were there many solitaries at the outset of the preaching of Christianity, especially in Egypt, but now there are a few?"

88 **The Exegete replied:** "Because the Lord sent his Apostles and commanded them to make disciples of people through faith, and teach them the way of perfection. He granted them many great signs to fulfill this. Hence, the full effects of his power were revealed to those who believed and labored. Just as the number of those who believed was in the thousands and more, in all towns and regions, so too those who labored, as is written in the lives of the monks: Abba Hor led a thousand solitaries,[127] and Isidore a thousand. Abba Ammon led three thousand solitaries, and Pachomius three thousand. Abba Serapion had ten thousand. The bishop of the great city of Bahnasa[128] said that in his see, under his

84 **قال المفسر** ان الابا قالوا ان من بعد غلبة جميع الشياطين والاوجاع يثبت مع الكاملين الى الموت قتال الكبريا والمجد الفارغ تخلية من الله حتى يثبتوا في (d90v) جهادهم وكمالهم ولما قال الله له امض الى البريه القريبه من الريف وتلمذ لي شعبا يمجدني ويصلح للاعمال الصالحه. قال انبا بلوا[ن] يا رب ارفع عني الكبريا ليلا اتكبر على الاخوه واخسر جميع الخير. فامره الله ان يمد يده على عنقه ويحط ما يجده على كتفه ويدفنه (a22r) في الرمل. فوجد حبشيا صغيرا فدفنه في الرمل وهو يصيح انا شيطان الكبريا. والابا يقولون ان الوجع الذي يتعبد له الانسان يجلس شيطان على العضو ^{760} الذي به يعمل الفعل. فالمتعبد لوجع الزنا. نظروا شيطان الزنا ^{761} (b28r) جالسا على انثيته. والمتعبد للغضب يجلس شيطان الحرد على قلبه. والذي يتذمر ^{762} ويتكلم بالكلام الردي. يجلس على لسانه. والذي ينعس في الصلاه يجلس (e90v) ^{763} على عينيه. والسارق يجلس على يمينه.

85 **قال الاخوه** لماذا كان الشيخ يلوم المتوحدين الذين يلبسون الحرير ويربون الشعر. وكثيرين قد نجيوا (c59v) بهذا ^{764} العمل.

86 **قال المفسر** انه ماكان يلوم الكاملين. بل العادمين الفضايل المخفية الذين كانوا يفعلون ذلك من اجل المجد الفارغ.

87 **قال الاخوه** لماذا صار في مبادي ^{765} البشاره (d91r) المسيحيه كثيرون متوحدون. لاسيما في ارض مصر. والان هم قليلون.

88 **قال المفسر** لان الرب ارسل رسله وامرهم ان يتلمذوا الناس بالايمان. ويعلموهم تدبير الكمال. ومنحهم الايات الكثيره العظيمه لتكميل ذالك. ^{766} فظهرت اثار قدرته باسرها ^{767} للذين ^{768} امنوا والذين عملوا. فكما كان الذين يامنون الوفا ^{769} وربوات. وكل ^{770} مدنا واقاليم. كذالك الذين عملوا كما كتب (b28v) في سير الرهبان ان ابا هور راس ^{771} على الف من المتوحدين. وايسيدرس على الف. وانبا امون كذا ^{772} يدبر ثلثة ^{773} الاف متوحدين (a22v) وباكوم ثلثة ^{774} الاف. ^{775} وانبا سرافيون كان تحت يده عشرة الاف. وقال اسقف مدينة البهنساء ^{776} الكبرى ان في كرسيه تحت

leadership, there were ten thousand solitaries and twenty thousand nuns. Also, at the beginning of the preaching of Christianity, people took the Apostles as models because Christ was a solitary and said: 'learn from me',[129] 'whoever does not take up his cross and follow me is not worthy of me',[130] and 'if you wish to be perfect, give all your possessions to the poor and follow me'.[131] Paul the Apostle used to say: 'Imitate me, just as I also imitate Christ',[132] 'I wish that all people were like me in purity',[133] and 'It is well for a man not to touch a woman',[134] because 'He who has a wife concerns himself with how to please her', but he who does not have one 'concerns himself with how to please God, his Lord'.[135] Those who take as models the very most virtuous whom they see who have made a great impact through grace are better than those who imitate by listening to old stories."

89 **The Brothers asked:** "Why did some of the saintly Fathers ask God [to reveal to them] the saint they resembled, and he used to send them to lay people inferior to them, such as dispatching Antony to the shoemaker, Macarius to the two women,[136] Paphnutius to the singer thief,[137] and Laban to the shepherd?"

90 **The Exegete replied:** "As for their asking God, that was because they had liberty with him, like the liberty John son of Zebedee had with our Lord when he placed his head on his chest and asked him about the one who would betray him.[138] They also meant by asking, namely to know which saint they resembled, that their fear be removed, their trust and hope be strengthened and fervor in the love of our Lord increased. As for God sending them to lay people below them in perfection, that was in order to consolidate their humility, and recompense those lay people for the labor of their righteousness and to strengthen their hope, and to make others emulate them when they realized that they would be like the upright solitaries if they exerted themselves in good works."

91 **The Brothers asked:** "Evagrius used to counsel the brothers not to quench their thirst with water?"[139]

92 **The Exegete replied:** "Because our Lord said: 'When the unclean spirit has gone out of a person, it wanders through waterless places seeking rest, but finds none. Then it returns to that person'.[140] The Fathers also used to say: 'Whoever does not minimize his food, especially drinking water, cannot defeat the spirit of fornication or

سلطانه عشرة الاف متوحد. وعشرين الف راهبه. وايضا ففي مبدا (e91r) البشاره تشبهت الناس بالمبشرين. لان المسيح كان متوحدا. وقال تعلموا مني. ومن لا يحمل صليبه ويتبعني ما يستحقني. فان اردت ان تكون كاملا فادفع كلما⁷⁷⁷ لك للمساكين واتبعني. وبولص الرسول كان يقول تشبهوا بي كما اتشبه بالمسيح. واريد ان يكون جميع الناس مثلي في الطهاره.⁷⁷⁸ وحسن بالرجل ان لا يقرب امراه. (d91v) لان الذي له زوجه يهتم كيف يرضيها. والذي ليس له يهتم كيف يرضي الله ربه. والذين يتشبهون بمن يرونهم افاضل في الغايه القصوى ولهم من النعمه الاثار الكبرى اكثر من الذين يتشبهون بسماع الاخبار بعد زمان (c60r) اطول.

89 **قال الاخوه** لماذا كان بعض الابا القديسين (b29r) يطلبون من الله لمن يشبهون. كان يرسلهم الى قوم عالميين⁷⁷⁹ ناقصين عنهم. كما انفد انطونيوس للاسكاف. ومقاريوس للمراتين⁷⁸⁰ وببنوده⁷⁸¹ للص الزامر ولبوين الى عند الراعي.

90 **قال المفسر** اما طلبهم من الله فلا دلا لهم عليه. كما اوجب ادلال يوحنا ابن زبدي⁷⁸² على سيدنا. انه اتكى على صدره وساله عن مسلمه. وقصدوا بهذا السوال وهو لمن من⁷⁸³ القديسين يشبهون. زوال خوفهم وقوة (e91v) اتكالهم (a23r) ورجايهم وزيادة حرارتهم في حب ربنا. واما ارسال الله اياهم الى العالميين⁷⁸⁴ الذين هم انقص منهم في الكمال. فليثبتهم⁷⁸⁵ في الاتضاع. وليفيد اوليك العالميين⁷⁸⁶ العزا عن اتعاب برهم. ويقوي رجاهم. وليفيد غيرهم التشبه بهم. اذا علموا انهم يساوون المتوحدين الابرار اذا اجتهدوا في عمل البر.

91 **قال الاخوه** ان (d92r) وغريس يوصي الاخوه ان لا يشبعوا من الما.⁷⁸⁷

92 **قال المفسر** لان ربنا قال ان الروح النجس اذا خرج من الانسان يطوف مواضع⁷⁸⁸ ليس فيها ماء⁷⁸⁹ يطلب راحه فلا يجد. (b29v) فيرجع⁷⁹⁰ الى ذالك⁷⁹¹ الانسان. والابا قالوا ان من لم ينقص من طعامه وبالاكثر من شرب الما.⁷⁹² ما يغلب روح الزنا. ولا

reach perfect chastity'. There is nothing like thirst to dry out the bodily organs, inhibit sexual discharge at night, ejaculation and flow, and calm dirty thoughts during the day. Even he who fasts and minimizes his food will not settle if he drinks too much water, because drinking too much water fills the stomach and the bodily organs with moisture. Thus, the devil finds a way to deceive him through thoughts during the day and dreams at night. Evagrius said: 'If you seek purity, reduce your food and minimize drinking water, then the purity of the heart will shine. Your mind will also shine like a star that you see during your prayer'."[141]

The abridgment of the third part is complete: a section from Hieronymus who wrote down the questions and a section from Palladius because he wrote during the time of Theodosius the Great.[142] Palladius also wrote during the time of his son Arcadius.[143] Thanks and gratitude to God.

93 **The Fourth and last Part of the stories of the solitaries written in the book *The Paradise*, from the last part written by Palladius.**

94 **The Brothers asked:** We begin, with the help of our Lord, to ask in sequence. Why did the saintly Fathers teach us above all else to leave the world and live in a monastery, and then leave communal life and dwell in solitude in a cave?"

95 **The Exegete replied:** "Because these are the foundations upon which one builds and from which one proceeds to the high palace of the good. In communal life, they begin by loving people. But in solitude, they become perfect in the love of our Lord. As the Lord and the Apostle [Paul] said: 'Love is the fulfilling of the law'.[144] At first, the person leaves the world and ceases to love it because, as it is written, the love of the world is contrary to the love of God.[145] Whoever does not hate his father, mother, wife, children and himself—meaning his sexuality, habits and desires—cannot fulfill the love of God and become a disciple of Christ. True love cannot be accomplished in the world because it is resisted by natural love which is love of sex, habitual love which is love of what is familiar, or egoistic love which is love of the sensual. But after his departure from the world with his heart and entire body, he enters the monastery, the communion of brotherhood, to carry out with them Christ's commandments: fasting, prayer, nightly vigils, reading, and

يكمل العفه. فليس شيا ينشّف الاعضا⁷⁹³ ويمنع من جنابة الليل والفيض والسيلان ويهدي الافكار الدنسه في النهار مثل العطش. حتى ان من صام وقلل طعامه. لم يستقر مع كثرة شرب الماء.⁷⁹⁵ لان⁷⁹⁶ كثرة الماء⁷⁹⁷ تملا البطن. وتزيد الاعضاء⁷⁹⁸ رطوبه. فيجد الشيطان سببا لخداعه في افكار النهار (c60v) واحلام الليل. قال وغريس اذا اردت الطهاره فانقص من (e92r) الطعام. وضيق عليك في شرب الماى. وحينيذ تضي طهارة القلب. ويضي عقلك مثل كوكب⁷⁹⁹ تراه في صلاتك..

كمل مختصر الجز الثالث جزو عيروناميس الذي وضع المسايل. وجزوا لبلاديس. لانه كتب في زمان تاودسيوس الكبير. وبلاديس (a23v) كتب في ايام ارغاديوس ولده. ولله الشكر والمنه..

93 **الجز الرابع وهو الاخير من اخبار المتوحدين المكتوبه في كتاب (b30r) الفردوس من الجز الاخير⁸⁰⁰ الذي⁸⁰¹ كتبه بلاديوس.**

94 **قال الاخوه**⁸⁰² (d92v) قالوا الاخوه⁸⁰³ نبتدي بعون ربنا نسال بترتيب. لماذا قبل كل شي الابا القديسون علمونا الخروج من العالم والمقام في الدير. ثم الخروج من الشركه والانفراد⁸⁰⁴ في المغاره.

95 **قال المفسر**⁸⁰⁵ لان هاذين هما الاساس الذي يبنى عليه. ويصعد منه الى الجوسق العالي الذي للبر.⁸⁰⁶ لانهم في المجمع يتدون بحب الناس. وفي الانفراد يتكملون في حب ربنا. لان الحب هو كمال⁸⁰⁷ الناموس كما قال الرب والرسول ففي الاول يخرج الانسان من العالم. ويكف من محبته. لان محبة العالم هي ضد لمحبة الله كما كتب. ومن لا يبغض اباه (e92v) وامه وزوجته واولاده ونفسه. اي جنسه وعاداته⁸⁰⁸ وشهواته ما يقدر يكمل محبة الله ويصير تلميذا للمسيح. ولان الحب الحقيقي لا يتم في العالم لما يقاومه من الحب الطبيعي الذي هو (b30v) محبة الجنس. والاعتيادي الذي هو محبة المالوف. والايمي الذي هو محبة اللذات. وبعد خروجه من العالم بقلبه وكليته. يدخل الى دير مجمع شركة الاخوه (a24r) ليصنع معهم وصايا المسيح. الصوم. والصلاه. والسهر. والقراة.

other works by which the brother fulfills the love of brotherhood, such as tending to the sick and serving the saints, welcoming strangers, and being obedient to the holy men and superiors. Also, at the beginning of his departure from the world, he does not have the capacity to struggle, given how numerous the thoughts of the demons are. Thus, in the community of brotherhood the person is trained in the way, starting with visible struggles and partial weariness. After this training, the grace of solitude in the cell occupies him so that he attains the prospect of fulfilling all the higher commandments by which the perfect love which belongs to God is shaped. This is the utmost goodness and the highest palace of virtue. This labor just mentioned involves the remembrance of God, his graces, promises, commandments and punishments, continuous contemplation of him and conversation with him through prayer without feebleness and distraction, abhorrence of yearnings and cutting off foul thoughts from the moment they occur in the heart. Through this labor the solitary acquires the purity of the heart, for Christ to dwell in him, who said: 'I and my Father will come and make our home in him'.[146] At that stage, he sees in himself the light of his mind and becomes worthy to witness the light of the Lord of Glory, who is worshipped."

96 **The Brothers asked:** "How long does the brother have to stay in the monastery [before] entering the solitary cell?"

97 **The Exegete replied:** "It depends on his form, level, fitness of his body, and vigor of his labor under the authority and knowledge of the learned and experienced holy Fathers. The Holy Synod[147] established that the brothers who possess perfect stature, are trained in knowledge and vigorous labors, love fervently, are disciplined through humility, and together with all this [also] love the stillness of the cell, it is enough for them to have three years of training in the works of purity through which love of neighbor is engendered. After that, they must enter stillness which is the smelting furnace, where they mold the invisible works through which love in God is perfected. As for those who come to the monastery in their youth and lacking in training, knowledge, vigor and energy of love, it is good for them to stay eight, nine or ten years in the community. Then they will be worthy of stillness in the cell. Blessed Mark said about his subordinates: 'This is what the law means by saying: "Six days shall work be done, but the seventh is

وباقية العمل الذي يكمل به محبه الاخوه. مثل خدمة المرضى ⁸⁰⁹ والقديسين. (d93r) وقبول الغربا. وطاعة الشيوخ والروسا. ⁸¹⁰ وايضا فلانه ما يقدر في اول خروجه من العالم يقاتل مع كثرة افكار الشياطين. فيتدرب الانسان بمعرفة التدبير بين جماعة الاخوه. والابتدا بالحروب الظاهره والملل ⁸¹¹ الجزوي. ⁸¹² وبعد هذا التدرب ⁸¹³ تسكنه النعمه في الوحده في (c61r) القلايه. حتى يكون له فرجة لعمل جميع الوصايا العاليه التي يتقوم بها الحب الكامل الذي لله. وهذا هو غاية البر. واعلا جوسق الفضيله. وهذا العمل المذكور هو تذكار الله ونعمه. ومواعيده ووصاياه ووعيده. (b31r) والنظر (e93r) الدايم اليه. والمحادثه معه. وذلك ⁸¹⁴ بالصلاة التي بغير فتور ولا طياشة فكر. وبغضة الاوجاع وقطع الافكار الرديه من ابتدا حركبها في القلب. وبهذا العمل يقتني المتوحد طهارة القلب. حتى يسكن فيه المسيح. القايل انا وابي ناتي ونصنع فيه مسكنا. وحينيذ يرى في ذاته النور الذي لذهنه. ويستحق ان يرى النور المسجود له رب المجد.

قال الاخوه كم ينبغي للاخ ان يقيم في المجمع ⁸¹⁵ ويدخل الى قلاية الوحده. ⁸¹⁶

قال المفسر كما يليق بشكله ودرجته وتدرب قامته ونشاط عمله وهذا تحت سلطنة ⁸¹⁷ معرفة الابا الشيوخ العارفين (a24v/d93v) المجربين. وقد راى المجمع المقدس. ان الاخوه الذين يكونون في قامة ⁸¹⁸ كامله ومتدربين في المعرفه ونشاط الاعمال ويغلون في الحب. ومرتبيين ⁸¹⁹ في الاتضاع. ويكونون مع هذه كلها يحبون الهدو في القلايه. يكفيهم ثلاث ⁸²⁰ سنين التدرب ⁸²¹ بالاعمال الطاهره التي منها يتقوام حب القريب. ومن بعدها ينبغي لهم ان يدخلوا الى الهدو ⁸²² الذي هو الكور. الذي فيه يصوغون الاعمال الخفيه التي بها ⁸²³ يكمل ⁸²⁴ الحب الكامل في الاله. فاما الذين ياتو الى الدير وهم في ⁸²⁵ سن الصبا. وناقصون في التدرب ⁸²⁶ (e93v) في المعرفه (b31v) والنشاط وحرارة الحب. فجيد لهم ان يصيروا ثمانية وتسعة وعشر سنين في المجمع. وحينيذ يستحقون الهدو (c61v) في القلايه. وقد قال الطوباني مرقس في الروس التي له. هكذى الناموس يرمز بقوله في ستة ايام يجب العمل. وفي السابع ⁸²⁷

rest.'"[148] Namely, that it is necessary to work in the community for six years, and in the seventh, stillness and rest from the labor of purity is achieved."

98   **The Brothers asked:** "What are the means by which grace calls the brothers to monastic life?"

99   **The Exegete replied:** "By several means. Among them is the warning of the conscience, just as Moses the Black's conscience warned him and he repented. Also included among them is recitation, as Antony and Simeon the Stylite who upon hearing the reading of the Gospel in church departed from the world. Included among them too is hearing the words of the sermon, just as Abba Serapion and others who by their teachings brought back many bandits and fornicators. Included among them as well are the fears and struggles brought by the hands of angels, as with Abba Evagrius. And included among them is God's call, just as he called Arsenius."[149]

100   **The Brothers asked:** "Why did the book *The Paradise* relate the story of Arsenius at the beginning of the book before the holy men's teachings about departing from the world to the monastery and then the monk's leaving the community to the stillness of the cell?"

101   **The Exegete replied:** "Because he was called by God to the monastery and from the monastery to the cell.[150] That is why they began with the story of his life and organized their teachings around it. His story is as follows. In the world he was tormented by many afflictions, so he cried out to God from the pain of the heart, saying: 'O Lord, direct me how to live'. He heard God's voice say to him: 'Arseni, escape from the world' (meaning people) 'and you will live'. When he came to the community, he was borne down by his senses and the distraction of his thoughts. God said to him: 'Escape, live in silence and live in stillness'. Thus, when he abhorred evil and loved good, God became his teacher, first in monastic life and finally in solitary life."

102   **The Brothers asked:** "Explain to us the meaning of the two calls."[151]

103   **The Exegete replied:** "The first call is 'escape and you will live'. It means that if you wish to be saved from the death of breaking the

يستريح. على انه ينبغي العمل في المجمع ست سنين. وفي السابعه يكون الهدو والراحه من العمل الطاهر.

98 **قال الاخوه** ما هي الاسباب التي بها تدعو النعمه الاخوه الى الرهبنه.

99 **قال المفسر** باسباب كثيره. منها تنبيه السريره. كما نبهت انبا موسى الاسود سريرته (d94r) فتاب. ومنها القراة مثل انطونيوس وسمعان العامودي الذين من سماع قراة الانجيل في البيعه خرجا[829] من (a25r) العالم. ومنها سماع كلام الوعظ كما رد انبا سرافيون وغيره بتعاليهم كثيرين[831] من اللصوص والزواني. ومنها المخاوف والشدايد على ايدي الملايكه مثل ابا وغريس. ومنها استدعى الله كما دعى ارسانيوس.

100 **قال الاخوه** لماذا كتب كتاب الفردوس خبر ارسانيوس في بداية الكتاب قبل تعليم المشايخ على الخروج من العالم الى الدير (b32r) وخروج الراهب من المجمع الى الهدو في القلايه.

101 **قال** (e94r) **المفسر** من اجل انه دعي من الله الى الدير. ومن الدير الى القلايه.[832] فلهذا ابتدوا بسيرته ورتبوا عليها[833] تعليمهم. وخبره مكتوب هكذى. انه كان في العالم مضطهدا من هموم كثيره. فصرخ الى الله من وجع قلب قايلا. يا رب دبرني كيف احيا. فسمع صوت الله يقول له ارساني اهرب من العالم اي الناس وتحيا. ولما صار في المجمع كان مضغوطا من حواسه وطياشة[834] افكاره. قال الله له اهرب واسكت واهدى. فلما ابغض الشر واحب الخير. صار الله له معلما. اولا[835] في الرهبنه واخيرا في الوحده.

102 **قال الاخوه** فسر لنا ما[836] معنى هاتين الدعو.[837]

103 **قال المفسر** الدعوة الاولى وهي اهرب وتحيا. معناها[838] ان اردت (d94v) ان تخلص من موت مخالفة

commandment, leave your possessions, family and country and live as a stranger in the desert among those who cultivate my commandments, and you will live, as it is written: 'I loved your commandments so make me live by your grace'.[152] As for his saying in the second call 'escape', that is, from the community, and his saying 'live in silence and live in stillness', that is, do not allow many to come in to you, to converse with you and preoccupy you, because seeing and hearing a great deal of talk causes mental distraction. What is meant is silencing the tongue from conversing with people in their presence, and the stillness of the mind from conversing with them in their absence. For one might think about beautiful women and men with the desire of fornication. Accordingly, he would converse with them in his mind with yearning. He might also think about other things and become angry in his heart with some people and accuse them, he might seek through delusional thoughts honor and glorification from others, or think about managing wealth and leadership. For this reason when they asked Saint Macarius: 'How must the novice live in the stillness of his cell?' He replied: 'He should not think about any person at all. He will not gain anything if he does not restrain his inner senses from conversing with people and recollect his thoughts in stillness'."[153]

104 **The Brothers inquired:** "It is written that a brother said to Arsenius: 'My father, my thoughts disturb me and tell me: "You cannot fast and work, so leave your cell and serve the weak, which is the greatest commandment"'. He said to him: 'Eat, drink, sleep, do no work, and from your cell do not go out'. After sitting for three days, he became weary of idleness, so he took some palm leaves and split them. The following day, he soaked them and started weaving them. When he became hungry, he said: 'I will eat when I am done'. When he finished, he said: 'I will read a little and then eat without a worry'. In this way, he progressed little by little with God's help until he reached his first rank and acquired power over thoughts.[154] Thus is written in the last part of the teachings of the holy men: 'Stillness in the Cell'."

105 "It is also written in the teachings of the holy men: 'Love and Mercy'. A brother asked a holy man saying: '[There were] two brothers, one was living in the stillness of his cell, fasting six days at a time and laboring a great deal, whereas the other served the place

الوصيه. اترك قناياك واهلك وطنك وتغرب في البريه عند (c62r) الذين يعملون وصاياي وتحيا. كما كتب احببت وصاياك فاحيني بنعمتك. وقوله (a25v) في الدعوه (b32v) الثانيه اهرب. اي من المجمع. وقوله اسكت واهدي. اي ولا تدع كثيرين يدخلون اليك ويتحدثون معك ويقلقونك. لان من النظر وسماع الكلام الكثير يكون طياشة الافكار. والمقصود سكوت اللسان من الحديث مع الناس في حضورهم (e94v) وهدو العقل من الحديث معهم في غيبتهم. فانه قد يتفكر في ذوي الحسن والجمال من النسا والرجال بشهوت الزنا. فيتحدث معهم في عقله بالم. وقد يتفكر في امور اخرى. فيغضب في قلبه على قوم ويلومهم. ويطلب من قوم توقيرا وتمجيدا في هذيذ افكاره. وتاره يفتكر في تدبير مال وتدبير رياسه. ولهذا لما سالوا القديس مقاريوس كيف ينبغي المبتدي ان يكون في هدو قلايته. قال لا يكون له تذكر بانسان بالجمله. فليس يريح شيا ان لم يضبط حواسه الباطنه من الحديث مع الناس. ويجمع افكاره في هدو.

104 **قال الاخوه** مكتوبا ان اخ قال لارسانيوس يا ابي افكاري تقلقتي. وتقول لي ما تقدر تصوم وتعمل فاخرج من قلايتك واخدم الضعفا. (b33r/d95r) وهذه هي الوصية العظيمه. فقال له كل واشرب وارقد ولا تعمل. ومن قلايتك لا تخرج. فلما جلس ثلثة ايام مل من البطاله. فاخذ قليل سعف وشققه. وفي يوم الاخر بله وابتدا ان يضفره. ولما جاع قال افرغ واكل. ولما فرغ قال اتلوا قليلا واكل بلا هم. وهكذى تقدم قليلا قليلا بعون الله. (a26r) حتى وصل الى طكسه الاول. واخذ سلطانا على الافكار. (e95r) فهكذى مكتوب في الجز الاخر في تعليم الشيوخ. (c62v) الهدو في القلايه.

105 ومكتوب ايضا في تعليم الشيوخ الحب والرحمه. ان اخا سال شيخ قايلا. ان اخين احدهما في هدو قلايته يصوم ستة ايام ويتعب نفسه كثيرا. والاخر يخدم الموضع

[the sick]¹⁵⁵ a lot. Whose labor is more acceptable before God?' He answered: 'If that one who fasted were to hang by his eyelids he would not equal before God the one who served'."¹⁵⁶

106 **The Brothers asked:** "Do the sayings of the Fathers contradict each other, if not what is the explanation?"

107 **The Exegete replied:** "The sayings of the Fathers are not contradictory. Rather, they counsel each person by what they know, through guidance and experience, to be more proper and suitable for him. They agreed to treat as equal he who is in a state of good stillness, the thankful sick, and he who serves with energy and joy. As for the sick, or those in stillness, or in the monastery, if a demon knows this, he becomes envious of them and comes up with tricks to deprive each one of the three from his virtue through the desire of the virtue of the other. He would make stillness desirable and service hard for those who serve the solitaries living in stillness, but they themselves have no ability to live in stillness, thus he makes them lose both virtues. He would make living in stillness hard and service desirable for those living in stillness but have no ability to serve, thus he deprives them of gaining both. In the same way, the sick realise the loss, after fasting, prayer and service to the point of losing patience and thankfulness. They are deprived of the reward of sickness and cannot do good works. He makes each one of the three prefer to move to do the other's work, not because of its virtue, but rather to seek respite from the labor of his [original] work and in order to be defeated in his effort. Because the Fathers know the causes of sicknesses—the result of the grace of their own guidance by grace and training from experience—they prescribe for each one the remedy that is proper for him. Abba Arsenius knew that that brother was vigorous in the solitary life of stillness and that the devil fought him with boredom and by cooling his fervor in order to make him leave his cell. [He knew] that if he endured in his cell a short time, boredom would leave him and the fervor of his activity would return, but if he left his cell, he would be deprived of his life of stillness and have no ability to endure in the service of the sick, thus he would lose both virtues. He [Arsenius] advised him to do what was mentioned above. As for the brother who asked the holy man about the two brothers, he was granted by God the gift of serving the sick and the weak holy men. The devil intended to deprive him of his crown,

كثيرا. فمن منها تعبه مقبول قدام الله أكثر من صاحبه. فأجابه لو ان ذلك الصايم[846] يتعلق بجفون عينيه لم يتساوى قدام الله مع الذي يخدم.

106 **قال الاخوه** وهل اقوال الابا متضادده. والا فما التفسير.

107 **قال المفسر** ليست اقوال الابا متضادده. (b33v) وانما هم يشيرون على كلواحد كما يعلمون[847] بالهداية والتجربه. انه اصلح واوفق له. فقد اتفقوا على مساواة الذي يكون في هدو حسن. والمريض الشاكر. والذي يخدم (d95v) بنشاط وفرح اما المرضى او الذين في الهدو او الدير. ولا علم شيطان هذا حسدهم. واحتال في[848] ان يعدم كل واحد من الثلثه[849] فضيلته بشهوة فضيلة الاخر. فيحسن الهدو ويصعب الخدمه للذين يخدمون المتوحدين في الهدو. ولا قدره لهم في الهدو ليخسّرهم الفضيلتين. ويصعب الهدو ويفضل الخدمه عند الذين في الهدو ولا قدره (e95v) لهم في الخدمه. ليعدمهم[850] ربح الامرين. وهكذى يرى المرضى[851] الخساره بعد[852] الصوم والصلاه والخدمه لينحلوا من الصبر والشكر. فيعدموا[853] فايدة المرض ولا (a26v) يقدروا على عمل البر. فيجعل كل واحد من الثلثه[854] يوثر الانتقال الى عمل الاخر. ليس من اجل الفضيله لكن من اجل الراحه من اتعاب عمله. وانهزاما في جهاده فلمعرفة الابا باسباب الامراض لما لهم من نعمة هداية النعمه ودرية التجربه. يصفون لكل (c63r) واحد ما يصلحه من (b34r) الادويه. فانبا ارسانيوس عرف ان ذلك[855] الاخ نشيط في وحدة الهدو. وان الشيطان جاهده بالملل[856] وبرد حرارته ليخرج من قلايته وانه اذا ثبت في قلايته زمانا قليلا عبر عنه الملل.[857] وعادة اليه حرارة نشاطه. (d96r) واذا خرج من قلايته يهلك تدبير هدوه. ولا يقدر ان يثبت في خدمة المرضى.[858] فيخسر الفضيلتين. فاشار عليه كما تقدم. واما الاخ الذي سال الشيخ عن الاخوين. فكان قد اعطى من الله موهبة خدمة المرضى والشيوخ الضعفا. فقصد الشيطان ان يعدمه اكليله

thus he made the life of stillness [appear] beautiful to him in order to deprive him of what he had and seek what he cannot attain, [knowing] that he could not return to his previous situation. The holy man advised him to do what is more advantageous for him."

108 **He also said:** "Whoever lives in the world cannot see all his sins because his heart is preoccupied with the world and its concerns, even if he showed compassion toward the needy and was a peacemaker between enemies. For the Lord has given blessedness to those too when He said: 'Blessed are the compassionate',[157] and 'the peacemakers'.[158] As for whoever leaves the world, enters the cell after his training in the monastery and devotes himself to [spiritual] battle, he thinks about his sins, sees his deficiencies, and recognizes his yearnings. If he abhorred them, drove away his foul thoughts, asked for forgiveness and aid, persisted in secret prayer, then his heart would be purified and he would become like an adorned mirror. He would see the light of our Lord Jesus Christ who said: 'Blessed are the pure in heart for they will see God'."[159]

109 **The Brothers asked:** "What is the meaning of Abba Sisoes' saying to Abba Ammon: 'The freedom of my thoughts is sufficient for me'?"[160]

110 **The Exegete replied:** "Abba Sisoes spent his entire life living in a remote desert. After he became old and weak, the Fathers brought him to the monastery of the brothers. They would come to him seeking some profitable counsel and helpful prayer. However, he was not used to making conversation, and his thoughts became unfocused because of his recollection of conversations with the brothers and worrying about matters. Abba Ammon saw that he was sad at having come from the desert and said to him: 'You should not be sad about living among the brothers. Your body has become weak and you cannot labor any more as you did in the desert'. He answered him with dread, saying: 'The freedom of my thoughts in the desert was enough for me. This is not impeded by old age or by sickness, for you to think that [greater] ease of attaining purity of mind is [to be found] with you, which is [in fact] acquired in the life of stillness and conversation with God, through constant and concentrated prayer, the remembrance of Christ and gazing upon him, and through exultation of the soul in loving him and his commandments, desiring his benefits and glory, meditation

فحسّن له الهدو لكي يعدم ما بيده. ويطلب ما لا يصل اليه. ولا (e96r) يقدر على العوده الى ما كان له. فاشار عليه الشيخ بالاوفق لـه.^859

108 **وقال ايضا** ان الذي في العالم ليس يبصر خطاياه كلها. لان قلبه يشتغل باهتمام العالم وهمومه. ولو فيه رحمة المحتاجين وفعل السلامه بين المتباغضين مع ان الرب قد دفع لهولاى^860 ايضا الطوبا بقوله طوبا للرحما ولفاعلي السلامه. فاما الذي يخرج من العالم (b34v/a27r) ويدخل الى هذه القلايه من بعد تدربه في الدير ويتفرغ للجهاد. فانه يتفكر في خطاياه. ويبصر نقصه. ويعرف اوجاعه. فاذا ابغضها وطرد افكاره الرديه وطلب الغفران والعون. وداوم^861 الصلاة الخفيه. نقى قلبه وصار مثل المراة المجلوه فيرى نور ربنا يسوع المسيح القايل طوبا النقيه^862 قلوبهم. فانهم يعاينون الله.

109 **قال الاخوه** ما معنى (d96v) قول انبا شيشاي لانبا امون تكفيني حرية افكاري.

110 **قال المفسر** ان انبا شيشاي كان عمره كله مقيما في بريه^863 بعيده. ومن بعد كبره وضعفه احضره الابا الى دير الاخوه. فصاروا يدخلون اليه من اجل (c63v) كلمة المنفعه ومعونة الصلاه. وما كان معتادا بالحديث. فابتدا^864 (e96v) ان تطيش افكاره في تذكار حديث الاخوه وهم الاشيا. فراه انبا امون حزينا على مجيه من البريه. فقال ماكان ينبغي ان تحزن على جلوسك بين الاخوه. لان جسدك قد ضعف. فلا تقدر تتعب كما كنت في البريه. فاجابه برهبة قايلا. حرية افكاري في البريه كانت تكفيني. وهذه ما (h35r) تـ:ـاق من الكبر. ولا من المرض فترى عندك هينه^865 نقاوة العقل التي تقتني في الهدو والمخاطبه مع الله. في الصلاه التي بغير فتور ولا طياشه. وتذكار المسيح والنظر اليه. وفرح النفس بمحبته ومحبة وصاياه. وشهوة خيراته ومجده. والهذيذ^866 في عظمته. والتعجب من اتضاعه. فهذه الامور (a27v) وامثالها لا يمنعها الكبر والضعف. لكنها تهلك من الخلطة^867 الدايمه مع الناس. ومن الاهتمام بغيرها.

111 **قال الاخوه** ذلك^868 الرجل صياد الوحوش (d97r) الذي ابصره انبا شيشاي الذي كان يسكن

upon his greatness, and admiration of his humility. These and matters like them are not impeded by old age or weakness. They are, however, destroyed by constant mingling with people and being preoccupied with matters other than them'."[161]

111 **The Brothers asked:** "That hunter of wild beasts whom Abba Sisoes saw when he was living in the cave of Antony and who said to him: 'I have been alone for eleven months, I have not seen a human being until you today'. Was he a human being or an angel?"[162]

112 **The Exegete replied:** "I believe he was an angel because a man does not hunt wild beasts alone, and no lay person would live in the inner desert for eleven months. Rather, the servant of Abba Sisoes was absent from him for ten months, thus he did not see a human being [for some time]. The devil attacked him by means of pride. God, who takes care of his saints, commanded one of the angels to appear to him in the shape of a human being, who admonished his thought and stopped his pride. He went into his cell and slapped his face, saying: 'I could not even do what this lay person has done'."

113 **The Brothers asked:** "A brother came to Abba Sarmata and asked him: 'What work should I undertake my father, for I am inept. I eat, drink and go to bed with troubled thoughts, and I am worried and weak-spirited?' He replied: 'Endure in your cell and do what you can without getting upset. The little labor that you do is comparable to the numerous works that Antony performed in the mountain. And I believe that if you sit in the cell for the sake of the name of God, you will also be found in Antony's place'.[163] How can a brother, an inept beginner, who eats, drinks and finds joy in dirty thoughts, be the equal of the great Antony in terms of extensive good works, and [also] in [terms of] reward?"

114 **The Exegete replied:** "God prescribed through Moses bodily commandments for the Jewish people. They are acknowledged [as fulfilled] through words and works, not through intention and will as in the spiritual commandments which he prescribed for Christians through his only Son. For our Lord Jesus Christ has said to those who believe in Him: 'You have heard that it was said to the people long ago', meaning the Jews, '"You shall not murder,"' meaning by act, and '"You shall not commit adultery,"' meaning

في مغارة انطونيوس. وقال له لي احدعشر شهر⁸⁶⁹ وحدي ما رايت انسانا الا انت اليوم. ترى كان انسانا او ملاكا.

112 **قال المفسر** اظن انه ملاك. لان انسانا واحدا لا يصيد الوحوش. وعلمانيا لا (e97r) يقيم في البرية الداخله احدعشر شهرا. وانما انبا شيشاي كان قد ابطا عنه خديمه عشرة شهور. فلم يرى انسانا فقاتله الشيطان بالافتخار. فامر الله (b35v) المهتم بقديسيه واحدا من الملايكه تراا⁸⁷⁰ له بشبه انسانا⁸⁷¹ وبكت فكرته ومنعه من الافتخار. فدخل الى قلايته ولطم وجهه قايلا ولا مثل هذا العلماني عملت.

113 **قال الاخوه** ان اخا مضى⁸⁷² الى انبا سرمطا وقال له ما اصنع (c64r) يا ابي لاني متوان. اكل واشرب وانام في افكار⁸⁷³ مسجسه. وانا قلق وانا صغير النفس. قال له اصبر في قلايتك وهما قدرت اعمل بلا سجس. وهذا العمل القليل الذي تعمله هو مثل العمل الكثير الذي كان يعمله انطونيوس في الجبل. وامن انك اذا قعدت في القلايه من اجل اسم الله. توجد انت ايضا في موضع انطونيوس. فكيف يمكن ان يكون اخ مبتد متوان⁸⁷⁴ ياكل ويشرب ويتلذذ في (d97v) افكار رديه. يساوي العظيم انطونيوس في (a28r) العمل الطويل الجيد وفي المجازاه.

114 **قال المفسر** ان الله وضع وصايا جسديه على يد موسى لشعب اليهود. تعرف من الكلام والاعمال لا من النيه (e97v) والارادة كالوصايا⁸⁷⁵ الروحانيه التى وضعها للمسيحيين (b36r) بيد ابنه الوحيد. لان ربنا يسوع المسيح قال للمومنين به. قيل للاولين اي اليهود. لا تقتل اي بالفعل. ولا تزن⁸⁷⁶ اي

bodily. 'But I say to you do not become enraged', meaning do not kill or commit adultery with your eye and heart. For He also said: 'If anyone is angry with his brother without cause, he will be subject to judgment',[164] meaning the judgment of execution, and 'if someone looks at the wife of his brother with lust he has already committed adultery with her in his heart'.[165] In the former, He [God] prescribed bodily punishment for the bodily act. In the latter, He promised spiritual requital for the spiritual act and what comes from intention and will. The bodily act is temporal, but the spiritual is not temporal. It can be that the bodily act is sometimes hindered temporally, but not the spiritual, because temporal matters cannot impede intention and will. Because of this, the Fathers said: 'Whoever wants to do something but cannot is equal to the one who is able and does'. As to the fact that the goodness [of deeds] is not [judged] according to the work of the body, this is shown in the work of Martha and her sister Mary. Our Lord praised the work of Mary more so than that of Martha, because Martha with her body served material matters, I mean food, but Mary with her spirit served spiritual matters, I mean listening to the words of the Lord. As to the fact that the goodness [of deeds] is not [about] age and service, it is shown in Christ who loved John more than Peter, and the youth of blessed Mary did not hinder her from becoming blessed among women and full of grace more so than old Elizabeth[166] and the Prophetess Anna who spent eighty-four years fasting and praying in the Temple.[167] As to why the goodness [of deeds] is not about how much is offered, this is because the Lord said about the woman with the two copper coins that she gave more than the rich,[168] the tax collector did good as a result of his humility more so than the Pharisee despite his fasting, giving of alms, and praying,[169] the sinful woman showed her great love by her tears at just that moment and the Lord praised her, favored her and pardoned her many sins,[170] and the thief on the right who spoke judgement on himself at the time of death and appealed to the Lord to remember him when he comes into his Kingdom, as a result of which he became worthy of Paradise.[171] These are the children of the eleventh hour who begin work in the vineyard at the last hour but the Lord gives them a full day's wage along with those who have borne the burden of the day and its scorching heat,[172] meaning from their youth until their old age. These were the instances the Fathers relied on to direct the

بالجسد. وانا اقول لكم لا تغضب. اي لا تزني لا تزني اي بنظرك وقلبك. لانه قال. لان من غضب على اخيه باطلا وجبت عليه الدينونه اي دينونة القتل. ومن نظر الى امراة اخيه واشتهاها فقد زنى^877 بها في قلبه. ^878 ففي الاول وضع القصاص جسمانيا على الفعل الجسماني. وفي الاخير يوعد بالمجازاه الروحانيه على العمل الروحاني. والذي يكون بالنيه والارادة. والعمل الجسداني هو زماني. والروحاني غير زماني. وقد يحصل في الزمان معاوقة عن الفعل الجسماني واما الروحاني فلا. ^879 لان الزمانيات لا تقدر تمنع النيه والاراده. ولهذا قال بعض الابا. ان الذي يريد ان يفعل شيا ولا يقدر يساوي الذي يقدر ويفعل. اما ان البر ليس هو على قدر عمل (d98r) الجسد. فذلك^880 يبين من عمل مرتا ومريم اختها. فان ربنا مدح عمل مريم اكثر من عمل مرتا. لان مرتا خدمت بجسدها الجسدانيات (e98r) اعني الاغذيه. ومريم خدمت بروحها (b36v) الروحانيات اعني سماع (c64v) كلام الرب. (a28v) واما ان البر ليس هو يتقدم^881 السنين والخدمه. فيدل عليه كون المسيح احب يوحنا اكثر من بطرس ومريم المغبوطه ما اعاقها صباها ان تكون مباركه في النسا. وممتليه نعمه اكثر من اليصابات العجوز. ومن حنه النبيه التي لازمت الصوم والطلبه في الهيكل اربع وثمانين سنه. واما ان البر ليس هو بكثرة ما يقدم. فلان الرب قال عن صاحبة الفلسين انها قدمت اكثر من الاغنيا. والعشار تبرر من اجل اتضاعه اكثر من الفريسي مع كثرة^882 صومه وصدقته وصلاته. والخاطيه اظهرت^883 كثرة^884 حبها بدموعها في الوقت الحاضر. فمدحها الرب وفضلها وغفر لها خطاياها الكثيره. ولص اليمين دان ذاته عند موته وابتهل الى الرب في ان يذكره اذا جا في ملكوته. فاستحق الفردوس. فهولا^885 هم اصحاب الحادية عشر ساعة.^886 الذين يدخلون في الاواخر الى عمل الكرم. (d98v) فيعطيهم الرب اجرة النهار بكماله مع الذين قاسوا ثقل النهار وحره اي من صباهم الى كبرهم. (b37r) فعلى هذه الامور اعتمد الابا في تدبير

brothers. They used to console them with good hope during their trials, thus instead of sadness, weariness and hopelessness which arise as a result of struggling with the devil, they would acquire patience through hope and the joy of comfort. When Abba Sarmata saw the brother about to lose hope as a result of his trial, he knew that the vigor of the solitaries might be impeded with periods of weariness and weakness with regard to the labors of the body, and with periods of struggle with thoughts and hopelessness concerning the works of the mind. For this reason he consoled him during his trial and said to him: 'Even though your works have presently decreased as a result of struggling with demons, yet your intention is correct in living in stillness in your cell for God and has not diminished. By it, you resemble Antony. Just as your intention resembles his intention, so too does your reward resemble his reward. Your little work, given the circumstance of your trial, endurance in your cell, your lack of knowledge, your weakness, and little training compared to the perfection of Antony's knowledge, his strength and training, is equal in God's eyes to the great work of Antony. For this reason, your rewards are also equal'. As for his saying: 'Do not get upset', this means 'Do not obey your thoughts which distress your mind through sadness and hopelessness'. He then consoled him, saying: 'And I believe that if you sit in your cell for Christ until your trial passes, you will attain the fervor of love and strength to do works'."

115 **The Brothers asked:** "It is written that one of the Fathers came to Arsenius to see him. He knocked on the door, but when he [Arsenius] opened and saw him, he threw himself on the floor face down. He said to him: 'O father, get up so that I may kiss you'. He replied: 'I will not get up until you leave'. Despite insisting a great deal, he did not get up. Thus he left him and went away?"[173]

116 **The Exegete replied:** "Those who love stillness and prefer the life of constant solitude in the cell in the remote desert do not see anyone other than their disciples, despite old age and weakness. This is what the wanderers advised Abba Macarius the Egyptian, saying to him: 'If you cannot be like us, stay in your cell and weep for your sins'. Abba Arsenius chose the life of complete stillness. He wept so much that the hair on his eyelids fell off. His cell was ten parasangs[174] away in the Scetis Desert. When Macarius of Alexandria asked him: 'What is the purpose of your living away

الاخوه. (e98v) فكانوا يعزونهم في زمان تجربتهم بالرجا الصالح. ليقتنوا عوض الحزن والملل وقطع الرجا. هذه التي تكون من قتال الشيطان.⁸⁸⁷ صبر الرجا وفرح العزا. فانبا سرمطا لما راى الاخ⁸⁸⁸ في تجربته قد قرب من قطع الرجا وعرف ان المتوحدين قد ينعاق نشاطهم في اعمال الجسد اوقاتا من الملل⁸⁸⁹ وانحلال (a29r) الاعضا.⁸⁹⁰ وفي اعمال الذهن اوقاتا⁸⁹¹ من حرب الافكار وقطع الرجا.⁸⁹² فلهذا عزاه في وقت تجربته. وقال له ان كانت اعمالك انتقصت الان من شدة حرب الشياطين. الا ان نيتك مستقيمه في الهدو في قلايتك من اجل الله ما نقصت. وبها تشبه انطونيوس. وكما تشبه نيتك نيته كذالك⁸⁹³ يشبه جزاك جزا. وعملك القليل (c65r) في حال تجربتك مع ثبوتك في قلايتك ونقص معرفتك وضعف قوتك وقلة دربتك. بالنسبة الكمال معرفة انطونيوس. وقوته ودربته. يساوي عند الله عمل انطونيوس الكبير. ولهذا ايضا يساوي جزاكما. (d99r) وقوله (b37v) لا تتسجس اي لا تطاوع افكارك التي تسجس عقلك بالحزن وقطع الرجا. ثم عزاه بقوله. وانا امن⁸⁹⁴ انك ان صبرت في قلايتك من اجل المسيح حتى تعبر تجربتك فانت تنال حرارة الحب (e99r) وقوة الاعمال.

115 **قال الاخوه** مكتوب ان احد الابا جاء⁸⁹⁵ الى ارسانيوس لينظره. فلما دق الباب وفتح له وراه⁸⁹⁶ رمى بنفسه على الارض على وجهه. فساله قايلا قم اقبلك ايها الاب. فقال ما اقوم حتى تمضي. فلج عليه كثيرا فلم⁸⁹⁷ يقوم. فتركه ومضى.

116 **قال المفسر** ان الذين يـ:ـرون الهدو ويوثرون الوحده الدايمه في القلايه في البريه البعيده. ولا يرون احدا غير تلاميذهم. ومن بعد الكبر والضعف. وبهذا اشار السواح على (a29v) انبا مقار المصري⁸⁹⁸ وقالوا له ان كنت ما تقدر ان تكون مثلنا امكث في قلايتك وابك⁸⁹⁹ على خطاياك. فانبا ارسانيوس اثر الهدو الكامل. وكان يبكي حتى انتتف شعر عينيه. وكانت قلايته بعيده في برية الاسقيطي عشرة فراسخ. ولما قال (b38r) له مقاريوس الاسكندري لاي شي جلست بعيدا

from us?' He replied: 'I cannot be with God and people at the same time. For God's will is one but people's will is diverse',[175] because of their mortality, disposition, lack of knowledge, weakness of instincts, and numerous yearnings. We cannot free ourselves from them and conquer them, and also please God's will with our own unless we live in the stillness of solitude, away from the sight of people and conversation with them. However, the angels are capable of this because they are great and the inhabitants of the next world. They are in unison because their will is unified in loving God and glorifying him, and because there are no hindrances or obstructions to this. Because Arsenius chose the life of stillness, he was preoccupied with cutting off the causes that impede him. And because he was of noble stock, read the Holy Scriptures and teachings of the philosophers a great deal, and walked in the way of virtue more than many, his fame became widespread. The old, the virtuous, and those near and far used to come to him, even that noble lady came to him from Rome to see him.[176] It is written that Timothy, Patriarch of Alexandria, came to him with bishops to talk to him. They returned sad because he did not sit down patiently and speak with them.[177] On another occasion Patriarch Theophilus came to him with a number of bishops and when they asked him to speak a profitable saying to them he said: 'If I tell you, will you comply by it?' They replied: 'Yes'. He said: 'Do not come to the place where Arsenius is'.[178] For this reason, he did not show his face to that father who asked him to get up to kiss him: in order that others might be discouraged from coming to him."

117 **The Brothers asked:** "Why did he [Arsenius] distress that faithful woman who came by God's guidance from Rome to Egypt to see him and ask for his prayers as one of the prophets and apostles, as she mentioned to Patriarch Theophilus. And yet he [Arsenius] replied: 'I pray to God to uproot your memory from my heart', and as a result she became sad and sick?"[179]

118 **The Exegete replied:** "Because vainglory harms the virtuous more than all other yearnings. It also gives birth to pride. Abba Evagrius calls it the burdock,[180] because it pricks from every direction. It makes the weak strong, the strong weak, the old young, the young old, and employs its deception through the robe of Christ or robe of silk. Regarding it Abba John the Seer said: 'It is

منا. قال له ما اقدر آكون مع الله والناس معا. لان ارادة (d99v) الله واحدة واراده⁹⁰⁰ الناس مختلفه. لما فيهم من الميتوته والميلان وقلة المعرفه وضعف الطبايع. وكثرة الاوجاع. فلا نقدر ننعتق منها ونظفر بها.⁹⁰¹ ونرضي ارادة الله بارادتنا. الا في هدو (e99v) الوحدة والبعد من النظر الى الناس والحديث معهم. وانما⁹⁰² اقتدر الملايكه فهم ربوات. واهل العالم العتيد وهم مجتمعون لاتحاد ارادتهم في محبة (c65v) الله وتمجده. وعدم الموانع والقواطع عن ذلك.⁹⁰³ فلايثار ارسانيوس الهدو كان يهتم بقطع الاسباب التي تعوقه. ولانه من جنس الملوك وكثير القراة في الكتب المقدسه وتعليم الفلاسفه. وساير في تدبير الفضيله اكثر من كثيرين شاع خبره. وكان الكبره والفضلا والقربا والبعدا. ياتون اليه حتى ان تلك المراة العظيمه اتت اليه من روميه لتنظره. وكتب⁹⁰⁴ طياطوس بطريرك الاسكندريه (b38v) مضى اليه ومعه اساقفه للحديث فرجعوا⁹⁰⁵ من عنده وهم حزانا. لكونه ما قعد (a30r) معهم للحديث بطول روح. ومرة اخره⁹⁰⁶ مضا⁹⁰⁷ اليه تااوفيلوس البطريرك ومعه اساقفه. ولما سالوه ان يقول لهم كلام منفعه. قال فاذا قلت لكم تحفظونه. قالوا نعم. قال موضع ارسانيوس لا تمضوا اليه. ولهذا⁹⁰⁸ الراي ما ارى وجهه لذلك⁹⁰⁹ الاب الذي (d100r) ساله ان يقوم ليقبله حتى يمتنع غيره من المضي اليه.

117 **قال الاخوه** فلمذا احزن تلك المراة⁹¹⁰ المومنة التي اتت (e100r) بتدبير الله من روميه الى مصر حتى راته. وطلبت صلاته. مثل واحد من الانبيا والرسل كما قالت لثاوفيلوس⁹¹¹ البطرك. فقال اصلي لله ان يقلع ذكرك من قلبي فحزنت ومرضت.

118 **قال المفسر** لان المجد الفارغ يوذي⁹¹² الفضلا اكثر من باقي الاوجاع وهو يولد الكبريا. وانبا وغريس يدعوه القرطب. لانه يلدع من كل ناحيه. فيصنع الضعيف قويا. والقوي ضعيفا⁹¹³ والشيخ صبيا والصبي شيخا (b39r) ويستعمل مكره مع لباس المسيح. ومع لباس الحرير. ومن اجله قال انبا يوحنا النبي انه

not defeated easily or in a short period of time. Whoever is entangled in it, his thought roams ceaselessly after his desire and is divided [in his mind] to a boundless degree'.[181] It does not vanish in a short period of time for it is a bond that is hard to untie. The blessed Mark says that [even] one who possesses much wisdom and learning can hardly diagnose this yearning and recognize its offshoots are born from it and accompany it, such as faithlessness, for it is born from it as our Lord said in the Gospel: 'How can you believe when you attain your glory from each other and do not seek the only glory of God'.[182] Also, such as envy, jealousy, deception, love of superiority, hate, hypocrisy, contemptuousness, complaint, falsehood, and other hidden yearnings. The demon of vainglory is indeed full of deception and evil. Those who come to struggle with this yearning after having defeated all other yearnings, if they defeat it too, attain purity of the heart and perfection, such as Paul the Apostle, who ridiculed glory,[183] being humiliated, praise and commendation, such that he said: 'I for the sake of Christ have been crucified to the world and the world has been crucified to me'.[184] Those who are like this disparage the honors of the world and consider them losses so much so that they may distress someone who honors them, as Arsenius did with the lady from Rome. So too Theodore: when a governor came to see him, he spoke to him carelessly, his hood lobbed over his shoulders and his chest exposed because his clothes were torn. When the governor left, a holy man asked him: 'Why did you do that with a man like this who came to you to be blessed and gain profit from you, and you threw him into doubt?' He replied: 'We do not seek to please people. Whoever wishes can profit, and whoever wishes can doubt'."[185]

119 **The Brothers asked:** "Why did Abba Moses the Black consent that strangers come to him even though he loved the life of stillness?"[186]

120 **The Exegete replied:** "Because before he became a monk, he used to do harm to people. Thus he desired to relieve people through his toil during the period of his repentance."

121 **The Brothers asked:** "That holy man who saw angels with Abba Moses in the boat in the form of human beings, how did he see the

لا ينغلب بسهوله ولا في زمان قليل. وان المرتبط به يطيش فكره (c66r) خلف لذته بغير فتور. وينقسم بغير حد. وما ^{914} يزول في وقت يسير وهو رباط صعب انحلاله. والطوباني مرقس يقول ان الكثير الحكمه والادب بالحراء ^{915} يقدر يدل هذا الوجع. ويعرف فروعه التي تتولد منه وتصحبه. مثل قلة الايمان فانه يتولد منه كما قال ربنا (a30v) في الانجيل. فكيف ^{916} تقدرون ان تومنوا. وانما تمجدون بعضكم من بعض. ومجد الله الواحد ما (d100v) تطلبون. ومثل الحسد. والغيره. والمكر. ومحبة الغلبه. والبغضه. والمراياه. ^{917} وعبودية نظر العين. (e100v) والتذمر والكذب والاوجاع المخفيه فشيطان المجد الباطل كثير المكر والشر. والذين ^{918} وصلوا الى قتال هذا الوجع من بعد غلبة بقية الاوجاع. اذا غلبوه وصلوا الى نقا القلب والكمال. كبولص الرسول. الذي كان (b39v) قد استهان بالمجد والاهانه. والسبح والمديح. حتى قال. انا من اجل المسيح مصلوب للعالم ^{919} والعالم مصلوب لي. فالذين هم هكذى يحقرون كرامات العالم ويعتدونها خسرانا حتى انهم قد يحزنون من يكرمهم. كما فعل ارسانيوس مع الروميه. وتاادري ^{920} الذي اتاه رييس ^{921} ليراه. فتكلم معه بتهاون وقلنسوته ^{922} مرميه على اكتافه وصدره مكشوف. لان ثيابه كانت مقطعه. ولما مضا ^{923} الرييس ^{924} قال له شيخ لم صنعت هكذا ^{925} مع رجل مثل هذا اتى اليك ليتبارك وينتفع منك. فشككته. فاجابه لسنا نطلب مرضاة ^{926} الناس. فمن اراد ينتفع ومن اراد يتشكك.

119 قال الاخوه ^{927} فلماذا انبا موسى ^{928} الحبشي كان يقبل الغربا مع محبته الهدو.

120 قال المفسر لانه كان يودي الناس (c66v) قبل رهبنته. فاحب ان ينجح ^{929} الناس بتعبه في وقت توبته.

121 قال الاخوه ان ذلك (a31r) الشيخ نظر الملايكه مع انبا موسى في المركب (d101r/e101r) بشبه البشر. فكيف نظر

Spirit of God with Arsenius in the boat,[187] and how did the other holy man see it in baptism and in the monastic garb?"[188]

122 **The Exegete replied:** "The Gospel testifies that [John] the Baptist saw the Holy Spirit in the form of a dove.[189] The stories of the Apostles testify that the Holy Spirit descended upon the disciples in the form of tongues of fire.[190] Accounts also testify that the grace of the Spirit appeared upon the head of one of the saints in the form of a star of light, and to another in the form of a virgin who fortified and strengthened him during his temptation. It appears in many forms to those who see it."

123 **The Brothers asked:** "It is written that when the assembly used to leave the church Abba Sisoes would quickly escape to his cell. Some brothers said that there was a demon in him. However, he was doing the work of the Lord. What is the meaning of their saying and his work?"[191]

124 **The Exegete replied:** "These [monks] were lazy. Demons fight those who labor by means of such [monks]: who speak such abuse or in other ways. As for the work of God that he used to do, it was his escaping from conversation in order to pray in his cell, as in the advice of Abba Isaiah who said: 'If the gathering is dismissed and they leave the table, do not sit and talk to anyone–neither worldly nor profitable speech–rather, enter your cell and weep for your sins'. Abba Macarius also said: 'If the community is dismissed, escape like this', and he would place his hand over his mouth. Thus each one used to flee in silence."[192]

125 **The Brothers asked:** "Why did the early Fathers kiss each other, then pray, then kiss each other again?"

126 **The Exegete replied:** "In the beginning, the solitaries when they opened the door and saw a father or brother, they would prostrate on their face to him then kiss him, then enter and pray, then kiss each other again and sit together. This is what Arsenius did to that man when he saw him and prostrated to him, but because he chose the life of stillness, he did not get up to kiss him or asked him to come in, even though the holy man said to him: 'Get up so that I may kiss you', but he did not.[193] When the demons started to come to the solitaries in the form of brothers in order to kiss them and impede their spiritual work, the brothers began to pray first,

روح الله مع ارسانيوس في المركب. (b40r) وكيف راها الشيخ الاخر على المعموديه واسكيم الرهبنه.

122 **قال المفسر** الانجيل يشهد ان المعمد راى روح القدس شبه حمامه. وقصص الرسل تشهد بان روح القدس حل على التلاميذ شبه السنة نار. والاخبار تشهد ان نعمة الروح ظهرت على راس واحد من القديسين شبه كوكب نور. ولاخر شبه عذرى وعزته وقوته في تجربته. فهي تظهر للناظرين في اشباه مختلفه.

123 **قال الاخوه** مكتوب ان انبا شيشاي كان عندما تنصرف الجماعه من الكنيسه. يهرب الى قلايته سريعا. وكانت اخوه[930] يقولون ان به شيطانا. فاما هو فكان يصنع عمل الرب. فما معنى قولهم وعمله.

124 **قال المفسر** هولاي[931] كانوا محلولين. وبوساطة مثلهم تقاتل الشياطين العمالين تاره بالشتيمه هكذى وتراه بغيرها. واما عمل الله الذي كان يصنعه فهو هربه من الحديث الى الصلاه في قلايته. كوصية انبا اشعيا القايل اذا سرح الجمع قاموا عن المايده فلا تجلس او تتكلم مع انسان. لا كلام العالم ولا كلام (b40v) منفعه. بل ادخل الى قلايتك وابك على خطاياك. وانبا مقاريوس قال. اذا (e101v) انحل المجمع[932] اهربوا هكذى. ويضع يده على (d101r) فمه. فكان كل واحد[933] يهرب وهو ساكت.

125 (a31v) **قال الاخوه** لماذا كانوا الابا الاولون يقبلون بعضهم بعضا. وبعد ذلك يصلون ثم يقبل بعضهم بعضا.

126 **قال المفسر** ان المتوحدين في الاول (c67r) كانوا عندما يفتحون الباب ويرون الاب او الاخ يخرون له على وجوههم ثم يقبلونه. وبعد ذلك يدخلون ويصلون. ثم يرجعون يقبل بعضهم بعض[934]. ويجلسون. وهكذى صنع ارسانيوس مع ذلك لما راه سجد له ولا يثاره[935] الهدو لم يقم ليقبله ويدخل معه. وقال له الشيخ ايها الاب قم لاقبلك فلم يقم. فلما صارت[936] الشياطين تمضي الى المتوحدين المتشبهين بالاخوه ليقبلونهم ويبطلوهم من عملهم الروحاني صار الاخوه يقبلون الصلاه.

because if the phantasm was demonic it would vanish by the power of the prayer. One of the blessed was praying the midnight prayer when a demon came to him and called out through the window of his cell: 'I am your friend so and so'. He opened the door, and when he entered they kissed each other. The demon turned into a long dog, stretched its body from the floor to the head of that brother, placed its hands around him, blew in his face, and bit his neck. But he was not scared. Instead he said: 'It appears to be you, O devil! Your salutation resembles that of your disciple Judas'."[194]

127 **The Brothers asked:** "Antony said: 'As the fish die if they are taken out of water, likewise the monk dies if he lingers outside his cell'."[195]

128 **The Exegete replied:** "That is, he dies in spirit because the life of the soul is proximity to the living God, and this is accomplished through the constant remembrance of God. If he lingers in the city, his remembrance of God is interrupted through observing and conversing with people a great deal. He forgets the toil of virtues and desires repose. His heart becomes distressed by cravings and falls into the yearnings which cause his death, namely, being distant from the Living God."

129 **The Brothers inquired:** "The Fathers gathered near the monasteries on the day of our Lord's resurrection in the Scetis Desert: wanderers, roamers, hermits and solitaries. They agreed that the hardest of struggles is when the monk leaves his cell, because all other struggles rapidly cease."

130 **The Exegete replied:** "That is because perseverance in the life of stillness in the cell is accompanied by hope, and leaving it ruptures hope. So as long as he is in the cell, he overcomes yearnings one by one through the grace of Christ's succor. But if he becomes weary and leaves, the labor ceases."

131 **The Brothers inquired:** "Abba Theodore and Abba Luca spent fifty years resisting their thoughts which urged them to move away from their place. They would say: 'We shall move in the winter'. But when winter came, they would say: 'Until the summer'. They continued in this way to the end of their lives."[196]

132 **The Exegete replied:** "The demons fight the Fathers a great deal to [make them] leave [the life of] stillness because they know how

حتى ان كان الخيال شيطانيا بطل بقوة الصلاه. فبعض الطوبانيين⁹³⁷ كان في الصلاه نصف الليل. نجا اليه شيطان وصاح به من طاق قلايه⁹³⁸ انا فلان صديقك. ففتح الباب ولما دخل الواحد قبل الواحد الاخر. فصار⁹³⁹ الشيطان شبه كلب طويل وبسط قامته من الارض الى راس ذلك⁹⁴⁰ الاخ وعانقه بيديه ونفخ في وجهه ونهش في (b41r) عنقه فلم يفزع. بل قال (e102r) له كانك انت هو يا شيطان سلامك يشبه سلام يهوذا تلميذك.

127 **قال الاخوه** ان انطونيوس قال كما يموت السمك اذا خرج من الماي.⁹⁴¹ كذالك يموت الراهب اذا ابطا خارج قلايته.

128 (d102r) **قال المفسر** اي يموت بروحه. لان حياة⁹⁴² النفس هي القرب من الله الحي. وهذا (a32r) يكون بتذكار الله دايما. فاذا ابطا في المدينه انقطع تذكاره⁹⁴³ لله بكثرة نظره وكلامه الناس. وينسى اتعاب الفضايل. ويحب الراحه. ويتنجس قلبه بالشهوات. ويسقط في الاوجاع التي بها يكون موته. الذي هو البعد من الله الحي.

129 **قال الاخوه** ان الابا اجتمعوا في عيد قيامة⁹⁴⁴ ربنا في الاسقيطي. السواح والمنتقلين والحبسا والمنفردين. قريبا من الاديره⁹⁴⁵ واتفقوا على ان ترك الراهب قلايته اصعب القتالات. (c67v) لان باقي القتالات تبطل سريعا.

130 **قال المفسر** لان المداومه لهدو القلايه يصحبها الرجا. والخروج منها يكون مع قطع الرجا. فما دام في القلايه فهو يغلب واحدا واحدا من الاوجاع بنعمة معونة المسيح. واذا مل وخرج بطل من العمل.

131 (b41v) **قال الاخوه** انبا تاادري وانبا لوقا اداما خمسين سنه يدفعان (e102v)⁹⁴⁶ افكارهما.⁹⁴⁷ لانهما كانا يريدان الانتقال من موضعهما. فكانا يقولان الى الشتا نمضي. واذا جا الشتا يقولان الى الصيف. وبقيا هكذا⁹⁴⁸ الى انقضا حياتهما.

132 **قال المفسر** ان الشياطين تقاتل الابا كثيرا بالخروج من الهدو لمعرفتهم

richly rewarding it is. Some Fathers used to play with the thoughts of the demons, like these two. But many were disturbed by the demons such that they left their cells and lost their way as happened in our days to one who was perfect in the divine way of life. He was given the gift of exorcising demons, but struggling with the desire to move overcame him so much so that he could not stay in his cell for more than a week. As a result his disciples built for him places in the desert, and he would move from one cell to another. Grace protected him from drifting in the cities. This happened to him so that he would not grow proud and as a punishment for contradicting the will of his teacher. For his teacher said to him: 'If you do not remain in my place after my death, then moving around will overcome you until your death'. And so it was, for at the age of ninety years he would mount a donkey and his disciples would take him around the cells. The Fathers wondered at his situation, and the brothers learned a lesson from him. It is because of this that Abba Macarius the Great, when he thought of asking Christ to show him the wanderers feared that he would have to struggle with the urge of constantly moving. He endured five years praying to know whether it [the thought] was from God or from the devil. After that, he went and saw them."[197]

133 **The Brothers inquired:** "Antony said: 'He who dwells in the desert is liberated from three battles: speaking, seeing and hearing. He is left with the battle of the heart'."[198]

134 **The Exegete replied:** "As those who leave the life of stillness fall if they add to struggling with the senses struggling with the heart, likewise those who live in stillness fall if they add to struggling with the heart struggling with the senses. For example, the brothers who were visited by women were defeated when [actually] seeing the form of the face with the eye was added to seeing through the heart. The struggle of those living in stillness is harder, as Evagrius said: 'Demons fight those who dwell in the stillness of solitary life directly and not through a medium. But they fight those in the monastery who seek to perfect the economy of the mind by means of dissolute brothers. There is a big difference between inner struggle through the inner senses and external struggle through the eye in the external senses'."

بكثرة ربحه.⁹⁴⁹ وبعض الابا (d102v) كانوا يتلاهون في افكار⁹⁵⁰ الشياطين. كهاذين⁹⁵¹ وكثير منهم هزت بهم الشياطين حتى خرجوا من قلاليهم فطاشوا. كما جرى في ايامنا لواحدا كاملا في التدبير الالهي. منح (a32v) موهبة اخراج الشياطين. فانه قوي عليه حرب الانتقال. حتى انه ما كان يبات في قلايته⁹⁵² اكثر من الجمعه. حتى ان تلاميذه بنوا له مواضع في البريه وكان ينتقل من قلايه الى قلايه. وحرسته النعمه من الدوران في المدن. وهذا جرى له حتى لا يتكبر. وجزا مخالفته وصية شيخه. لان معلمه قال له ان لم تثبت في موضعي بعد وفاتي فالنقله تنبسط عليك الى حين موتك. وكذلك كان صار له تسعون سنه. (b42r) كان يركب حمار ويدور به تلاميذه القلالي. حتى كانوا⁹⁵³ الابا يتعجبون منه والاخوه يتادبون به. ولهذا كان انبا مقار الكبير لما تفكر في ان يريه المسيح السواح خاف من قتال النقله. (e103r) فصبر خمسة سنين يصلي ليعرف هل ذلك من الله ام من الشيطان. وبعد هذا مضى⁹⁵⁴ وراهم.

133 **قال الاخوه** ان انطونيوس قال ان الذي يجلس في البريه خلص من ثلثة⁹⁵⁵ حروب. الكلام. والنظر. والسماع. وبقي له حرب (c68r) القلب.

134 **قال المفسر** كما ان الخارجين من الهدو اذا ازدادوا على قتال الحواس قتال القلب سقطوا كذلك⁹⁵⁶ الذين (d103r) في الهدو. ولو زاد على قتال القلب قتال الحواس لسقطوا. كالاخوه الذين دخلت عندهم النساء.⁹⁵⁷ فلما ازدادوا على نظر القلب نظر العين لصورة⁹⁵⁸ الوجه غلبوا. وقتال الذين في الهدو اصعب. كما قال وغريس (a33r) ان الذين يسكنون في هدو الوحده. تقاتلهم الشياطين بذواتهم بلا واسطه. والذين في المجمع ويريدون تكميل تدبير الفكر يقاتلونهم بوساطة الاخوه المنحلين. (b42v) وكثير بين القتال بالذات بالحواس الباطنه وبين القتال بوساطه العين في الحواس الضاهره.

135 **The Brothers inquired:** "What is the meaning of Antony's saying: 'The cell is for the solitary like the place of the three boys in the furnace of Babylon'?"[199]

136 **The Exegete replied:** "As fire has two characteristics—one is burning heat and the other is delightful light—likewise endurance in the cell has two characteristics.[200] The first is the heat of fighting demons to begin with through increased weariness, anxiety and fear. The other is serenity of perfection and enlightening of the heart through purity from yearnings by which one arrives at the revelations of light. Just as He sent to the boys an angel who called out and untied their binding in the furnace, because they endured being bound and thrown in the furnace and resisted the king for the sake of God, likewise God sends the novice brother help if he endures in the struggle of solitude and in resisting the devil for the sake of God, and makes him deserving of His perfect love and witnessing His glorious light."

137 **He also said:** "Looking at Jesus with whom endurance begins for us. If we suffer with Him, we are then glorified with Him. If we endure with Him, we will be in His Kingdom with Him, as the Apostle said.[201] Pray for those who persecute you as our Lord did,[202] and as with the love of Stephen.[203] When the solitary thinks about these matters, he defeats yearnings. He should not reciprocate a person's evil with evil and harbor hate towards him. Rather he should rejoice if someone curses him and pray for him."

138 **The Brothers inquired:** "Some brothers cursed Abba Moses. He was asked: 'Did your heart become troubled?' He replied: 'Yes I was troubled, but did not say a word'."[204]

139 **The Exegete replied:** "Solitary life requires two things, that neither the senses of the body are troubled nor the senses of the soul. The first is as one who is angry in his mind but does not respond with his tongue, as Abba Moses did. The second is more perfect, namely, that he is neither angry in his heart nor does he respond with his tongue, as Abba John the Less and those like him did. Once, a person ridiculed him and cursed him while sitting among the brothers, but he did not frown. They asked him: 'Did your heart not become angry when you were cursed?' He replied: 'As you have seen, I am at peace outwardly and likewise inwardly'. This is the point where yearning is transcended. Abba Moses

135 **قال الاخوه** ما معنى قول انطونيوس ان القلاية للمتوحد⁹⁵⁹ موضع الثلثة⁹⁶⁰ فتيه من اتون بابل.

136 **قال المفسر** كما ان النار لها خاصتان الواحده الحراره المحرقة والاخرى النور المفرح. (e103v) هكذى مداومة القلايه لها خاصتان. الاولى حرارة حرب قتال الشياطين في البدايه بكثرة الملل والقلق والتخويف. والاخرى نياح الكمال ونور القلب بنقاوة من الاوجاع الذي به يصل الى مناظر النور. فكما ارسل للفتيه⁹⁶¹ ملاك ندا وحل رباطهم في الاتون. لما ان صبروا على ان يربطوا و يطرحوا في الاتون. وقاوموا الملك من اجل الله. هكذى⁹⁶² الاخ المبتدي يرسل الله اليه معونه (d103v) اذا صبر على قتال الوحده ومقاومه الشيطان من اجل الله. ويجعله يستحق محبته الكامله وينظر نوره الممجد.

137 **وقال ايضا** النظر الى يسوع الذي صار لنا (b43r) بداية الصبر. فان نحن تالمنا معه. فنحن نتمجد معه. وان صبرنا معه فنحن نملك معه. كما قال الرسول. واطلبوا بالصلاه الغفران للذين يضايقونكم كما فعل ربنا. وكمحبة استفانوس (a33v) واذا (c68v) افكر المتوحد في هذه الامور فهو يغلب الاوجاع. وليس انه ما يجازي انسانا شرا بدل الشر ويحقد عليه. بل ويفرح اذا شتمه انسان ويصلي عليه.

138 **قال الاخوه** ان اخوه شتموا انبا موسى. فقيل له ما تسجس قلبك. قال تسجست (e104r) ولكن ما تكلمت.

139 **قال المفسر** كما ان الوحده بامرين. ان لا يتسجس حواس الجسد ولا حواس النفس. والاول مثل ان حرد بضميره ولا يكافي بلسانه كما عمل انبا موسى. والثاني اكمل. وهو ان لا يحرد بقلبه. ولا يكافي بلسانه كما كان انبا يوحنا القصير ونظراه. فان واحدا عيره وشتمه وهو جالس بين الاخوه. فلم يعبس. فقالوا له ما غضب قلبك لما شتمت. فقال كما رايتم محتدي⁹⁶³ من خارج وهكذى انا من داخل. فهذا حد عبور الوجع. وانبا موسى (b43v)

admitted that he had not yet reached that perfection at that time, but restrained his thoughts and was silent. He revealed this as a sign of humility. As for the Prophet Moses, when he was cursed by his sister, he asked God to forgive her and to be healed from her punishment."[205]

140 **The Brothers inquired:** "The Fathers advise us to learn from the holy men, except that one [of the holy men] said to a brother: 'Go and sit in your cell and it will teach you'."[206]

141 **The Exegete replied:** "They do not contradict each other. Abba Macarius the Great said: 'At the beginning when you enter your cell, keep doing for some time what you used to do when you were in the community: fasting, praying, reading, and other things. After that, you will be prescribed the level that suits someone like you, either in terms of increase or diminution. That is, in as much as what appears to them from him in the stillness of the cell, they guide him accordingly either in terms of adding to or diminishing from what he used to do in the community. This is the meaning of his saying: "Sit in your cell and it will teach you everything"'."

142 **The Brothers inquired:** "Abba Agathon placed a stone in his mouth for three years until he held his peace."[207]

143 **The Exegete replied:** "Every time he went out to the monastery or sat to listen to the reading he would place a small pebble in his mouth so that he would not fail through his tongue by talking about it. But if he met someone who had a profitable counsel for him, he would put it in his hand. Likewise if he stood with the brothers during prayer, or sat at the table, he would place it in his sleeve. But when he left the meal, he would put it back in his mouth. When God saw his perseverance, He granted him control over his tongue. When the Fathers heard about this, they began to emulate him. One would place a ring in his mouth, and another would place a small cross. Another would reprimand himself upon entering his cell for the failings of his tongue, beg God for forgiveness, and go back to holding his peace. When he found respite from struggling and holding his peace, he would glorify God."

144 **On Fasting.**

اعترف انه لم يصل (d104r) الى ذلك الوقت الى هذا الكمال. لكنه ضبط افكاره وسكت. واظهر ذلك ⁹⁶⁴ على سبيل الاتضاع. فاما موسى النبي فانه لما شتم من اخته طلب لها الغفران من الله. والشفا من قصاصها.

140 **قال الاخوه** ان الابا يوصون على التعليم من الشيوخ. الا الذي قال لبعض الاخوه امض واجلس في قلايتك وهي تعلمك.

141 **قال المفسر** لم يتضاددوا. فان انبا مقار الكبير قال في اوايل دخولك الى قلايتك اعمل كما كنت تعمل في تدبير الجمع ⁹⁶⁵ زمانا (a34r) معروفا. وفي الصوم والصلاه والقراه. وغير ذلك. ⁹⁶⁶ وبعد ذلك يدفع لك الترتيب الذي (c69r) يوافق مثلك (e104v) من زياده او نقص. يعني بقدر ما يظهر لهم منه في هدو القلايه. يدبرونه بحسبه من زياده على ما كان يعمله ⁹⁶⁷ في الجمع. او نقص عنه. وهذا هو مقصود قوله اجلس في قلايتك وهي تعلمك كل شي. ⁹⁶⁸

142 **قال الاخوه** ان انبا اجاثن ⁹⁶⁹ جعل في فمه حجرا ⁹⁷⁰ مدة ثلثة ⁹⁷¹ سنين. حتى بقى بغير كلام.

143 **قال المفسر** في كل وقت كان يخرج (b44r) الى المجمع او يجلس لسماع القراة كان يضع حصاة صغيرة في فمه. لكيلا يسقط بلسانه بتذكارها. واذا لقيه من يكلمه كلمة منفعه ياخذها بيده. وكذلك ⁹⁷² اذا وقف مع الاخوه في الصلاه. واذا جلس على الميده يضعها في عبه. واذا خرج من الاكل اعادها (d104v) الى فيه. ولما نظر الله حرصه ⁹⁷³ اعطاه الغلبة على لسانه. ولما سمع الابا تشبهوا ⁹⁷⁴ به فمنهم ⁹⁷⁵ من وضع خاتم في فمه. ومنهم من وضع صلبا صغيرا. ومنهم من كان يحاسب نفسه عند دخوله الى قلايته على سقطات لسانه. ويتضرع الى الله عنها. ويعود الى تحفظه. وبعد ما ⁹⁷⁶ استراح من القتال والتحفظ ومجد الله.

144 في الامساك.

145 **The Brothers asked:** "Why is it harder for Christians–solitaries and others–to struggle with demons during the Great Fast more so than during other days?"

146 **The Exegete replied:** "For three reasons. The first is that the devil's fight with our Savior was during this fast, and our Lord gave us the ability to defeat him. This is why he is more furious during this time and harasses us. The second is that during this time Christians begin resisting desires and struggling with yearnings. This is why demons fight them more. The third is that during Lent, our Lord grants those fasting an increase in the grace of succor to do what accompanies fasting in terms of good works. Their fighting increases by the same extent as the increase in succor. This is their habit."

147 **The Brothers asked:** "What is the difference between struggling, its tenacity, its hardship, its agony, its success [over us], and its defeat?"

148 **The Exegete replied:** "Struggle is when the devil stirs in the heart of the solitary the recollection of one of the yearnings, such as fornication, rage, or vainglory. The solitary should not let it linger in his heart. Rather, he should become angry with himself because of it and chase it away at once through prayer. For if he lets it linger in his heart and is not angry with himself because of it and does not chase it away through prayer then this is laziness not struggling. If the thought of something lingers in the heart then this indicates a love of it. If the struggle at a given time increases more than what is usual at other times then this is the agony of the struggle. If the urge to recall yearnings continues without interruption, then this is the continuance of the struggle. If a fall occurs during the struggle then this is the hardship of the struggle. If a person is fought with a yearning, and the struggle persists and becomes more painful and difficult so much so that the person gives up, is defeated and does not resume struggling with the yearning, then this is the victory of the struggle. But if a person endures in struggling, through its agonies and tenacity, from beginning to end, until it leaves off and in the meantime he does not fall, then this is the defeat of the struggle. At that time the spiritual warrior will be overshadowed by the power of the most

145 **قال الاخوه** لماذا يصعب (e105r) للنصارى^{977} المتوحدين وغيرهم قتال الشياطين في الصوم الكبير اكثر من بقية الايام..

146 (a34v) **قال المفسر** الثلثة^{978} اسباب. الاول لان في مثل هذا الصوم كان قتال الشيطان مع مخلصنا. ودفع لنا سيدنا ربح غلبتنا له. فلهذا يحنق فيه بالاكثر. ويضيق علينا. والثاني لان فيه يستعد (b44v) النصارى الصبر عن الشهوات. والقتال للاوجاع. فلهذا تزيد الشياطين في (c69v) مقاتلتهم^{979} والثالث لان في الصوم العام يدفع ربنا للصايمين زياده في نعمة المعونه على عمل ما يلازم الصوم من البر. فبقدر زيادة^{980} المعونه يزيد قتالهم. فهذه عادتهم.

147 **قال الاخوه** اي شي هو الفرق بين القتال ومداومته وصعوبته وضيقته وغلبته. والغلبه عليه.

148 **قال المفسر** القتال هو ان يحرك الشيطان في قلب المتوحد تذكار شي من الاوجاع. مثل الزنا (d105r) والغضب والمجد الباطل. فلا يدعه المتوحد يبطي في قلبه. بل يجرد على ذاته من اجله ويطرده من وقته بصلاه. فان تركه يبطي في قلبه ولا يجرد على ذاته من اجله ولا يطرده بصلاه فهذا انحلال لا قتال. فان الفكره بشي اذا ابطات^{981} في القلب دلت على^{982} المحبه له. فاذا زاد القتال في وقت عن (e105v) العاده في باقي الاوقات فهو ضيق القتال. واذا دامت حركة^{983} تذكار الاوجاع بغير انقطاع فهو مداومة القتال. واذا حصل في اثنا القتال (b45r) سقوط^{984} فهو صعوبة (a35r) القتال. واذا قوتل الانسان ببعض الاوجاع ودام عليه القتال وضاق وصعب حتى ان الانسان ينحل ويغلب^{985} ولا يعود يقاتل الوجع. فهذا الانغلاب القتال واذا ثبت الانسان في القتال في ضيقته وداومه من اوله الى اخره الى ان ينحل القتال ولم يسقط في اثنايه. فهذا هو غلبة القتال. وحينيذ يظلل المجاهد قوة

High, his heart will be purified and the light of his mind will dawn, after which the signs of victory [appear]."

149 **The Brothers inquired:** "It was said that Paphnutius refused to drink wine and that he once chanced upon thieves while they were drinking. Their leader forced him to drink a cup with prostrations. Paphnutius said to him: 'I believe in God, and because of this one cup He will forgive you your sins'."208

150 **The Exegete replied:** "The Holy Spirit alerts sinners in different ways: once through thought, once through reading, once through learning, and once simply through seeing the saints like this. When the leader of the thieves saw Saint Paphnutius, grace alerted his thought, and the secret space of his soul appeared on his face. Paphnutius saw, through the Spirit, that the leader of the bandits was called in his thought by grace to repent. He said: 'Because of this cup', meaning what I am doing for love of people, 'God will forgive you your sins', meaning the acts that he committed because of his hate of people. Hope changed his thought from evil to good, and he repented with his companions, and they swore an oath to God that they would not hurt anyone again."

151 **The Holy Man also said:** "The Perfect become detached from their senses during their prayers and reading such that they forget about their bodily nourishment. Sometimes, their thought is snatched up by the wonders of God–a day, or two or three–such that they do not feel physical exhaustion."

152 **He also said:** "The Egyptian monks used to only eat their bread dry. When a stranger came, they would cook food knowing how dry the bread was. They would observe the cooking fire and find comfort in their thought knowing that it is lit to cook the food for their repose. That is why one of them said to his disciple: 'Is it not sufficient for you to observe the fire?'"

153 **He also said:** "In their illnesses, they would seek a repose that would cure them, knowing from experience what validates the words of the Apostle: 'When you are sick, you are strong',209 and 'Your power is made perfect in weakness'."210

154 **The Brothers inquired:** "A brother asked a holy man about comfort. He answered him: 'Eat grass, wear grass and sleep on grass'."211

العلي وينقا قلبه ويشرق نور ذهنه. وبعده هي (c70r) علامات الغلبه.

149 **قال الاخوه** قيل ان ببنوده كان يمتنع من شرب الخمر. وانه عبر على لصوص وهم يشربون. وان راسهم اغصبه على شرب كاس خمر بمطانيات. فقال له ببنوده فانا امن بالله من اجل هذا الكاس الواحد يغفر لك خطاياك.

150 **قال المفسر** بانواع[986] كثيره تنبه روح (d105v) القدس[987] الخطاه. مره بالفكره. ومره بالقراه ومره بالتعليم. ومره بنظر القديسين فقط هكذى. فان القديس ببنوده لما راه (b45v)[988] مقدم اللصوص نهبت النعمه فكرته. فاباصر محل نفسه الخفي ظاهرا على وجهه. فرا (e106r)[989] ببنوده بالروح ان مقدم القطاع قد دعته النعمه في فكرته الى التوبه. فقال انا من اجل هذا الكاس[990] يعني الفعل الذي صنعته بمحبة الناس ان الله يغفر لك خطاياك. يعني الافعال التي صنعها ببغضة الناس. فغير الرجا[991] فكرته من الشر الى الخير وتاب هو واصحابه. وعاهدوا الله انهم لا يعودون يوذون احدا.

151 (a35v) **وقال الشيخ** ان الكاملين يكونون في صلوتهم[992] وتلاوتهم خارجين عن المحسوسات. حتى انهم ينسون طعامهم الجسداني. وفي بعض الاوقات قد تخطف فكرتهم الى عجايب الله. يوم واثنين وثلثه[993] حتى انهم ما يحسون باتعاب الجسد.

152 **وقال ايضا** ان الرهبان المصريين كانوا لا ياكلوا خبزهم الا يابسا. فاذا اتفق حضور غريب طبخوا من[994] اجل يبس الخبز. وكانوا ينظروا نار الطبيخ يجدون في فكرهم نياحا. لمعرفتهم بانها من اجل الطبيخ (b46r/c70v) الذي يتنيحون[995] به. فلهذا قال احدهم لتلميذه اما يكفيك نظر النار.

153 **وقال** انهم في امراضهم كانوا يختارون نياحا يشفيهم منها. لما وجدوا بالتجربه (d106r) من تحقيق قول الرسول. اذا مرضت حينيذ تقوى. وقوتك[996] انما تكمل بالضعف.

154 **قال الاخوه** ان اخا سال شيخا عن الراحه. (e106v) فقال له كل عشبا[997] والبس عشبا. وارقد على عشبا.

111

155 **The Exegete replied:** "He asked him about life, meaning 'How do I manage my life in my cell'. He answered him: 'Humble your bodily life and focus on your spiritual life'."

156 **The Brothers inquired:** "Some Fathers direct keeping the commandments both when in isolation and in an assembly. Others see that they should [only] be kept when in isolation, and participating with the community when in assembly."

157 **The Exegete replied:** "The Perfect who have traversed from need to self-discipline do not keep any commandment that interrupts their way of life according to what is revealed to be in their interest in each individual case. As for the majority, they should always maintain self-discipline."

158 **The Brothers inquired:** "Two holy men passed by a river and sat to eat.[212] One dipped his bread-cake in the river water whereas the other took water in his hand and sprinkled [it over] his bread-cake. The first asked the other: 'Why did you not dip it?' He replied to him: 'Let not your heart take pleasure in many possessions'."[213]

159 **The Exegete replied:** "The meaning of this is that you should not abandon your habits if you find more than what you need. Rather, you should restrain your thought, despite the presence of the river, as though you were in your cell so that your mind is not corrupted and your restraint not the result of a lack but out of choice."

160 **On Drunkenness.**

161 **The Holy Man said:** "Drunkenness causes rage and lust. Rage with a deficiency in the mind produces profanity, enmity, and belligerence. Lust with the weakening of inhibition gives rise to fornication and other things. Because the demons fight solitaries more than lay people, they should be more vigilant. The solitaries should not only cease drinking wine because of the obvious yearnings that are produced by it, but also because it delights the human heart, as David said.[214] Drunkenness also causes one to forget sorrow, as his son Solomon said,[215] and one is then denied the blessedness that was promised to those in sorrow and who mourn.[216] The [demon] fighting us finds the weakness in his opponent, presses him and defeats him. Through many sorrows we are barely capable of guarding our souls, and this with great difficulty. The Fathers permitted the brothers to drink three cups,

155 **قال المفسر** انما ساله عن الحياة.⁹⁹⁸ اي كيف ادبر حياتي في قلايتي. فقال له تهاون بحياتك⁹⁹⁹ الجسمانيه واهتم بحياتك الروحانيه.

156 **قال الاخوه** ان بعض الابا يامر بحفظ القوانين في حال الانفراد والاجتماع معا. وبعضهم يرى بحفظهم في الانفراد. ومشاركة الجماعه في حال الاجتماع.

157 **قال المفسر** اما الكاملون الذين قد عبروا الاحتياج الى التحفظ فلا قانون عليهم يقطعهم من تدبيرهم (a36r) بحسب ما يظهر لهم من المصالح في حال حال. واما الكثيرون فينبغي ان يتحفظوا دايما.

158 (b46v) **قال الاخوه** ان شيخين مرا بنهر. فجلسا لياكلا. فغطس احدها كعكته في ماي النهر. والاخر اخذ ماي بيده ورش كعكته. فقال له لماذا لم تبلها. فاجابه لا يفرح قلبك بالقنية الكثيره.

159 **قال المفسر** معنى هذا لا تخرج من عادتك اذا وجدت اكثر من حاجتك. بل ضيق على فكرتك مع وجود النهر كحالك في قلايتك لكيلا ينحل ذهنك ويكون ضيقك للعدم بغير اختيارك.

160 في السكر.

161 (d106v) **قال الشيخ** ان السكر يكون سبب¹⁰⁰⁰ للغضب¹⁰⁰¹ والشهوه. فالغضب مع نقص العقل (c71r) يولد الشتيمه والخصومه (e107r) والقتال. والشهوه مع ضعف الضابط لها تولد الزنا وغيره. ولان الشياطين تقاتل المتوحدين اكثر من العلمانيين فيجب¹⁰⁰² عليهم ان يتحرزوا بالاكثر. فليس ينبغي للمتوحدين ان يتركوا شرب الخمر لاجل ما يتولد عنه من الاوجاع الظاهره فقط. بل لكونه يفرح قلب الانسان. كما قال داوود. والسكر ينسي الحزن كما قال (b47r) سليمان ولده. فيعدم الطوبا التي قيلت للحزنا والباكيين. ويجد المجاهد لنا انحلالا من خصمه فيشتد عليه ويغلبه. لان بالاحزان الكثيره والكاد ان نحفظ نفوسنا. ولهذا بصعوبه كثيره. فسح الابا¹⁰⁰³ للاخوه يشربوا ثلثة¹⁰⁰⁴ اقداح

either during the holy feasts or once in a while. Whoever drinks more than three cups has violated God's law that prohibits drunkenness and gluttony,[217] human nature by inhibiting the mind from functioning according to its nature, and the saintly Fathers by disobeying their guidance and advice."

162   **The Brothers asked:** "A holy man was given a cup of wine but turned it down saying: 'Take this death away from me'. But why did they also not drink?"[218]

163   **The Exegete replied:** "He possibly gave up drinking wine because he had the yearning of fornication, which Abba Pachomius had.[219] When he took the cup in his hand, saw the color of [the wine] and smelt it, he felt the desire. He then passed it back and called it the cup of death, meaning the death caused by sin. The brothers also gave it up in agreement with the holy man."

164   **The Brothers inquired:** "One day, wine was brought to the Scetis Desert, and each was given a cup. One [monk] ran away to hide, but the roof collapsed under him. He fell down, and they heard his voice. They went to him and found him lying [on the ground]. They chastised him saying: 'You deserve this, you who seek vainglory'. The head of the monastery said to them: 'Leave my son for he did well. As the Lord lives, this breach will not be built in my days so that the people might know that because of [refusing to] drink a cup [of wine] a breach occurred in the Scetis Desert'."[220]

165   **The Exegete replied:** "The devil was envious of his great asceticism and wished to trap him, so that he either regreted [his action] or was glorified [because of it]. But the Lord protected him. When the devil's intention was not fulfilled, he stirred up the lazy brothers to curse him so that they all might fail. But when the head of the monastery recognized the envy of the Enemy and the virtue of the brother, he wanted the brothers to remember this [incident] so that they might be wary of the devil's struggle against virtue through him or through others, and to emulate those who are steadfast."

166   **The Brothers inquired:** "A holy man said: 'Decrease your human knowledge and your belly then you will find rest'."[221]

167   **The Exegete replied:** "A human being is composed of a soul and a body. The greatest yearning of the body is the love of gluttony,

162 **قال الاخوه** شيخا دفع له كاس خمر فرده وهو يقول خدوا مني هذا الموت. فلم شربوا هم ايضا.

163 **قال المفسر** لانه كان قد ترك شرب الخمر وربما كان معه وجع الزنا الذي كان مع انبا بأكوم. فلما اخذ الكاس بيده ونظر لونه (d107r/e107v) وشم رايحته حس باللذه. فرده وسماه كاس الموت اي موت الخطيه. والاخوه تركوه موافقة الشيخ.[1007]

164 **قال الاخوه** (b47v) في بعض الايام احضر (c71v) الى الاسقيطي خمر. فدفع[1008] لكل واحد كاس فهرب واحد[1009] ليختفي. فانخسف[1010] به سطح ووقع. فسمعوا صوته ومضوا اليه فوجدوه مرميا فلاموه قايلين جيدا حل بك هذا يا من يطلب المجد الباطل. فقال لهم راس[1011] الدير اتركوا ولدي فانه صنع جيدا. وحي هو الرب ما تبنى هذه الثغره[1012] في ايامي. حتى تعرف الناس ان من اجل شرب كاس صارت ثغره في الاسقيطي.

165 **قال المفسر** ان الشيطان حسد نسكه[1013] العظيم. فاراد يوقعه اما ان يندم واما ان يتمجد. والرب حفظه. فلما لم تتم ارادة[1014] الشيطان حرك الاخوه المحلولين على شتمه ليخسر (a37r) هو وهم. وريس الدير لما عرف بحسد العدو وفضيلة الاخ اراد بقا تذكار ذلك عند الاخوه. ليحذروا[1015] مقاومة الشيطان الفضيله بنفسه وبغيره. ويتشبهوا[1016] بالمتمسكين.[1017]

166 **قال الاخوه** ان شيخا قال نقص معرفتك الانسانيه ومعدتك فتجد راحه.

167 **قال المفسر** ان الانسان مركبا من نفس وجسد. وراس (b48r) الاوجاع الجسد محبة البطنه.

and the greatest yearning of the soul is love of vainglory. They are defeated by the humbling of the self. If a person defeats all the greatest yearnings, he finds rest. As for his saying: 'Decrease your human knowledge', this means human wisdom that is acquired through reading and education, and which the Apostle called the 'Wisdom of words'.[222] He [also] said: 'Whoever wants to be wise must be a fool to himself',[223] as though he was to say to him: 'Scorn the wisdom of this world and acquire the wisdom of God whose pinnacle is the fear of God and proper understanding for whoever adheres to it', in the words of the Prophet."[224]

168 **On Prayer, Night Vigil and Remembrance.**

169 **The Brothers asked:** "On the eve of Sundays Arsenius used to turn his back to the [setting] sun, raise his hands to Heaven, and pray until the sun dawned in his face.[225] Why did he say to his disciples: 'Demons are fighting us and I fear they will carry me off while asleep, so labor in vigil alongside me this night and alert me if I become drowsy'?"[226]

170 **The Exegete replied:** "The solitaries toil in the labors of virtue according to the strength of their natural disposition, and at the end they receive through grace a strength that exceeds their natural disposition. In the labors of the body, there is nothing more difficult than the nightly vigil. It subdues the body and purifies the soul. This is why the Fathers turn to it during their old age. It is written that Abba Macarius the Alexandrian kept vigil for twenty nights, and Antony asked God to grant him this gift for a suitable period of time so that he might understand the strength of the Enemy. And in order that they do not grow proud through this gift, God leaves them to their natural disposition. They then become weak and recognize the limit of their strength and the extent of the strength they had from grace. This is why weakness befell Arsenius during that night such that he sought the assistance of his disciples. This also occurred to King David, for he killed the mighty Philistine alone, with the Lord's help,[227] but when he fought the Gittite, Abishai son of Zeruiah helped him to kill him,[228] so that he [David] would not grow proud."

171 **The Brothers inquired:** "A perfect holy man used to see hidden things. He saw a brother meditating on the remembrance of God

وراس اوجاع النفس (e108r) محبة المجد الفارغ. تغلب بحقرية‏[1018] الذات.‏[1019] واذا (d107v) غلبت روس اوجاع الانسان وجد الراحات. وقوله نقص معرفتك الانسانيه يعني الحكمة البشريه التي تقتني من القراة والتعليم. التي سماه الرسول‏[1020] حكمة الكلام. وقال من اراد ان يكون حكيما فليكن عند نفسه جاهلا. وكانه قال له ارذل حكمة هذا العالم واقتني حكمة الله التي راسها مخافة الله. والفهم صالح لمن عمل به كما قال النبي.

168 على الصلاه والسهر والتذكار.

169 قال الاخوه (c72r) ان ارسانيوس كان في ليالي الاحد يخلي الشمس خلف ظهره ويرفع يداه الى السما ويصلي حتى تشرق الشمس في وجهه. فلماذا قال لتلاميذه ان الشياطين يحاربونا‏[1021] واخاف يسرقوني في النوم. فاتعبوا معي في هذه الليله. بالسهر فاذا نعست انهوني.

170 قال المفسر ان المتوحدين يتعبون في اعمال الفضيله. (a37v) بقدر قوة (b48v) طبعهم. وفي الاخر ينالون من النعمه قوه فوق طباعهم. وليس في عمل الجسد اصعب من السهر. وهو يقمع الجسد وينقي النفس. ولهذا ترغب اليه الابا في زمان شيخوخيتهم.‏[1022] فقد كتب ان انبا مقار الاسكندري سهر عشرين ليله. (e108v) وانطونيوس طلب من الله حتى دفع له هذه الموهبه زمانا معروفا. حتى يفهم قوة عدو. وليلا يتكبروا (d108r) في هذه الموهبه يتركهم الله بمقتضى طباعهم.‏[1023] فينحلون ويعرفون مقدار قوتهم. والقوة التي كانت معهم من النعمه. فلهذا صار الانحلال لارسانيوس في تلك الليله حتى استعان بتلاميذه. وهكذا‏[1024] كما جرى لداوود الملك. فانه وحده قتل الجبار الفلسطيني بمعونة الرب. وفي الاخر لما تقاتل معه الجثى‏[1025] ساعده ابيشوش بن صوريا حتى قدر يقتله. وهذا حتى لا يتكبر.

171 قال الاخوه ان شيخا كاملا كان ينظر الاشيا الغايبه. وراى اخا في هذيذ ذكر الله

while a demon was trying to enter [his cell] but could not. When he ceased his meditation, the demon got in."[229]

172 **The Exegete replied:** "The soul because of its union with the body sees the *sensibilia* through the eye of the body. But if it is purified from yearnings and reaches perfection, which is the union with God, then it can see the hidden spiritual things through God's grace, as angels see things and are not hindered by bodies. The inability of the demon to enter is because he talks to the mind, struggles with it and tricks it. Thus when he [the demon] saw the mind of the praying brother caught up in meditation with God, protected in his love and fear, he did not enter for fear of getting burnt by the light of his mind and the fervor of his prayer, love and fear. For a certain demon said about a brother: 'I left him and I was burnt'.[230] Another said about a brother: 'When I entered his cell, he stood in prayer and broke me with a terrific breaking'."[231]

173 **The Holy Man also said:** "It is necessary for solitaries to be without a flaw on the path of virtue. This is so that even if wicked demons or people wanted to denounce them, they would not find anything to say other than [concerning] the perfection of their virtue, such as Daniel and his companions,[232] and the pious martyrs.[233] For they were persecuted unjustly but endured for the sake of goodness and the truth not for the sake of wicked acts which they had committed."

174 **The Brothers inquired:** "A disciple of Abba Sisoes knocked on his door but he shouted from inside saying: 'Flee and do not enter now for the place is not empty'."[234]

175 **The Exegete replied:** "There are three moments in which the Fathers do not want their disciples to enter: the moment when their thought is caught up in the wonders of God, the moment when their conscience is fixated on the remembrance of God, and the moment when the struggle with demons is intensified in the conscience or through phantasms. If their thought is caught up with marveling at God, they would not recognize their disciples entering and conversing with them, as with Abba Sylvanus when his thought was drawn to Heaven through prayer for half the night and he saw God's glory.[235] His disciple entered [his cell] a number of times but he did not sense him for nine hours until his soul was released from that wonderful vision. If their thought is elevated

وشيطانا يريد الدخول اليه فلا يقدر. فلما سكت من هذيذه دخل.

172 **قال المفسر** ان (b49r) النفس من اجل اتحادها بالجسد تشاهد المحسوسات بعين الجسد. واذا تطهرت من الاوجاع ووصلت الى الكمال الذي هو الاتحاد بالله. حينيذ تنظر الروحانيات الغايات بنعمة الله كما تشاهد الملايكه الاشيا (a38r) ولا يعوقهم الاجساد [1026] وامتناع الشيطان من الدخول. لانه انما يتكلم مع العقل ومعه يقاتل وله يخدع. فلما راى عقل الاخ المصلي مشغولا في الهذياذ مع الله [1027] محميا في محبته وخوفه. لم (c72v/e109r) يدخل اليه خوفا من الاحتراق بنور عقله. وحرارة صلاته ومحبته وخوفه. فان شيطانا قال عن اخ. اني خرجت من عنده وانا محترق. واخر قال عن اخ. [1028] لما دخلت الى (d108v) عنده وقف في [1029] الصلاة وكسرني كسرة [1030] عظيمه.

173 **وقال الشيخ** ينبغي للمتوحدين ان يكونوا [1031] في طريق الفضيله بغير عيب. حتى ان ارادت الشياطين او الناس الاشرار يلومونهم لا يجدون ما يذكرونه غير كمال فضيلتهم. مثل دانيال ورفقته والشهدا الابرار. فانهم ضيقوا عليهم ظلما. وصبروا من اجل الخير والحق. لا من اجل (b49v) شرور صنعوها.

174 **قال الاخوه** ان تلميذ انبا شيشاي دق عليه الباب فصرخ من داخل قايلا اهرب ولا تدخل الان. فليس المكان فارغا.

175 **قال المفسر** في ثلثة [1032] اوقات ما يريدوا الابا ان تدخل تلاميذهم اليهم. وقتَ ان تخطفَ فكرتهم في عجايب الله. وقت يشخص ذهنهم في تذكار الله. وقت اشتداد قتال الشياطين معهم في الذهن او في المناظر. فاذا اختطفت فكرتهم في العجوبه في الله. ما يعرفون يدخلون تلاميذهم اليهم وكلامهم معهم. (a38v) مثل انبا سلوانا لما اختطفت فكرته في صلاة نصف الليل الى السما. ونظر تسبحة الله ودخل اليه تلميذه دفعات وما عرف به الى (e109v) تسع ساعات. حتى انحلت نفسه من ذلك [1033] المنظر العجيب. واذا ارتفعت فكرتهم

above this sensed world and they attain meditation with God, they may sense their disciples but would not to be hindered by them while in the felicity of meditation, as with Abba John the Less. For when a brother came to him to take baskets, he said to him in the end: 'Take and leave for I am not free'.[236] On another occasion he soaked a plait to weave it into two baskets. He wove it into one basket without noticing until the plait was all used up.[237] If they were preoccupied with struggling, they did not allow their disciples to enter lest they were hindered from recognizing the struggle, then fighting and overcoming it. Abba Sisoes, when his disciple knocked on his door, was in divine meditation or struggling with a demon. He forbade him from entering lest he hindered him."

176 **The Holy Man also said:** "On many occasions we commit many evils. God in His mercy gives us respite and does not oppress us with temptations. Rather, He waits for us to repent. If we do good, He does not delay our reward, as a loving father."

177 **The Brothers inquired:** "A Holy Man said: 'Whoever [does not] love all the brothers equally and discriminates between them has not yet become perfect'."[238]

178 **The Exegete replied:** "He meant that he desires good to all. He loves the good and is delighted for them in their goodness. He asks [forgiveness] for the sinners and is saddened by their evil. He pities the poor, weak and ignorant and grieves for them. He forgives those who offend him and seeks to win them over. He sets everyone before himself and honors them because all people are [created] in the noble image of God, and he should not differentiate in this between a friend and an enemy. He should not befriend the good man and praise him, and hate the sinner and reject him. This completes what has been predestined for him. There is no difference in the heart of the Perfect between a gentile or Jew, slave or freeman. All people are Christ without any differentiation."

179 **The Brothers inquired:** "Three holy men went to Abba Sisoes. One of them asked him: 'How can I escape from the river of fire?' The second one asked: 'How can I escape from the gnashing of teeth and worms that never perish?' The third one asked: 'What should I do? For the recollection of the outer darkness has troubled me?' He answered them: 'I do not concern myself with

من هذا العالم (c73r) المحسوس وصاروا في الهذيذ مع الله. قد يحسون بتلاميذه. لكنهم ما ينعاقون معهم في نعيم (d109r) الهذيذ. مثل (b50r) انبا يوحنا القصير. فانه لما جا اليه اخ ياخذ قفف. قال له في الاخر خذ وامض ما انا فارغ. ومرة اخرى بل ضفيره ليخطها قفتين فخاطها[1034] قفه واحده وما علم حتى فرغت الضفيره. واذا كان معهم قتال ما يدعون تلاميذهم يدخلون اليهم ليلا ينعاقون من معرفة الحرب ومجاهدته وغلبته. فانبا شيشاي لما قرع تلميذه بابه. كان في هذيذ الهي او في قتال شيطاني. فمنعه من الدخول ليلا يعوقه.

176 **وقال الشيخ** اننا نعمل اوقات كثيره شرور كثيره. والله برحمته يمهلنا ولا يضيق علينا بالتجارب. بل ينتظر توبتنا. واذا عملنا خيرا فما يوخر مجازاتنا مثل الاب المحب.

177 **قال الاخوه** قال بعض الشيوخ. ان الذي يحب جميع الاخوه بمساواه بل يميز واحد على واحد ما كمل بعد.

178 **قال المفسر** يعني انه يحب الخير للجميع. فحب[1035] الابرار ويفرح لهم ببرهم. ويسل من اجل الخطاه (a39r) ويحزن لشرهم. (e110r) ويشفق على المساكين[1036] الضعفا والجهال ويتالم (b50v) معهم. ويغفر للمسيين اليه ويريد رجهم ويفضل الكل على نفسه ويكرم لانهم صورة الله المكرمه الناس كلهم. ولا يفرق[1037] في ذلك بين صديق وشرير. فلا يود البار ويمدحه. ويبغض الخاطي ويزله. (d109v) فهذا يكمل عليه المكتوب. ليس في قلب الكاملين فرق بين الشعوبي[1038] واليهودي والعبد والحر. بل كل الناس المسيح بغير فرق.

179 **قال الاخوه** ان ثلثة[1039] شيوخ مضوا الى انبا شيشاي. فقال له احدهم كيف اقدر اخلص من نهر النار. وقال الثاني كيف انجوا من صرير الاسنان والدود الذي لا يموت. وقال الثالث ماذا اصنع لان تذكار الظلمة البرانيه (c73v) قد اقلقني. فاجابهم انا لا اهتم

any of these. I believe that God is merciful and that he will be merciful towards me'. They were grieved [at his answer]. He then said to them: 'I was jealous of you, O my fathers, for your minds are dominated by this recollection because of your perfection. What should I do? for the hardness of my heart does not allow me to recollect the Punishment. That is why I sin all the time'. They said: 'As we had heard, even so have we seen'."[239]

180 **The Exegete replied:** "Abba Sisoes was so perfect that whenever the holy men mentioned him to Abba Poemen he would say: 'Do not refer to him because his perfection is beyond description'. When great holy men came to him, he would first converse with them as one who is deficient. Thus when those three holy men mentioned to him what they possessed concerning the recollection of Hell, but heard from him that which did not correspond with what they had heard about his rank, they complained. But when he righted matters, they realized that his former words were out of humility, and the latter out of perfection. Thus they said: 'As we had heard about your humility, knowledge and perfection, even so have we seen and understood'."

181 **The Brothers inquired:** "Abba Or and his companion used to wear lamb skins. One said to the other: 'If the Lord were to visit us what should we do?' They then returned to their cells weeping."[240]

182 **The Exegete replied:** "Their saying 'were to visit us' was either because of death or because of grace which come upon saints in the cell and reveal to them not only the Paradise of the good but also the Hell of the wicked. This they cannot have unless they are in a state of isolation. Thus when these two remembered this, they abandoned conversation and ran back weeping to the life of stillness."

183 **The Brothers asked:** "A brother asked a holy man saying: 'I desire to have the tears that I heard the holy men [have] but am unable and become sad as a result'. He said to him: 'The Israelites only entered the Promised Land after living in the desert for forty years, and tears resemble the Promised Land'. How can tears resemble the Promised Land when not only the Perfect holy men weep but we also find boys and novices weeping profusely?"[241]

بواحدة من هذه. وامن ان الله رحيم ويصنع معي رحمه. فصعب عليهم. فقال غزت ^{1040} منكم يا ابوتي لان عقلكم مسلط على هذا التذكار لكمالكم. فماذا ^{1041} اصنع انا لان قساوة قلبي ما تتركني اتذكر العقوبه. ولهذا انا اخطي كل وقت. فقالوا كما سمعنا كذالك راينا. ^{1042}

180 (b51r) **قال المفسر** انبا شيشاي كان كاملا حتى ان الشيوخ كانوا اذا ذكروه عند انبا بجمن يقول لهم ^{1043} اتركوا هذا. لان كماله (e110v) يعلو الوصف. وكان اذا اتى ^{1044} اليه الشيوخ العظما يتكلم معهم كناقص اولا. فلما ذكر له هولاي ^{1045} الشيوخ الثلثه ^{1046} ما اقتنوه من تذكار جهنم. وسمعوا ما لا يوافق درجته (a39v) التي سمعوها شكوا. فلما تلا فاهم علموا ان كلامه الاول بالاتضاع والاخير في الكمال. وقالوا كما سمعنا عن اتضاعك ومعرفتك وكمالك كذالك راينا وفهمنا.

181 (d110r) **قال الاخوه** ان انبا اور ورفيقه كان لباسهما جلود غنم. فقال احدهما للاخر. ان كان الرب يفتقدنا ماذا نصنع. ومضيا الى قلايتها باكيين.

182 **قال المفسر** قولهما يفتقدنا اما لاجل الموت واما لاجل النعمه التي تزور القديسين في هذه القلايه. وتكشف لهم ليس نعيم الابرار فقط بل وجحيم الاشرار. وهذه لا تكون (b51v) لهم الا في حال انفرادهم. ولهذا فلما تذكرها هاذان تركا الكلام. واسرعا الى الهدو باكيين.

183 **قال الاخوه** ان اخا سال شيخا قايلا. اني اشتهي الدموع كما اسمع عن الشيوخ فما اقدر عليها فاحزن. فقال له ان بني ايسرايل لم يدخلوا ارض الميعاد الا بعد ان اقاموا في البريه اربعين سنه. والدموع هي تشبه ارض الميعاد. فكيف تكون الدموع تشبه ارض الميعاد وليس (c111r) الشيوخ الكاملين فقط هم الذين يكون. (c74r) بل ونجد صبيانا ومبتدين يكون ايضا بكا ^{1047} كثيرا.

184 **The Exegete replied:** "There is a big difference between the weeping of holy men and the Perfect and the weeping of boys and novices. Some weep profusely because of the moisture and heat of their constitution, such as women and boys. Their weeping comes easily. Some weep because of the pain in their heart, either the result of their rage or intensity of their pain and sorrow. Some weep out of happiness, such as the one who meets his companion after a long time. As for the saints, their tears flow because their hearts are satiated with the ache of remorse for their sins and because of their inability to attain their virtuous intent. In addition, because of the long period they spend coercing their souls to sigh and yearn for weeping. In conclusion, the tears of the perfect holy men are a gift of grace and not derived from natural instinct. Since tears are accompanied by pride, the Fathers warned those who have them a great deal saying: 'If you are granted the streamlet of tears, do not become arrogant'. Whoever receives the gift of tears must use them to cleanse his sins, win when struggling, and improve his way of life. Tears are of two types, the type that belongs to novices and the type that belongs to the Perfect. For example, the fear and love of God: novices love God's graces and fear His commands, as slaves. But the Perfect love God and fear His grandeur, as children who fear their father."

185 **The Brothers asked:** "Some philosophers went to try the solitaries. They asked a certain holy man: 'What is it that you do which is superior to what we do? You fast and we [also] fast, you are pure and we are [also] pure?' They replied: 'We guard our minds'. They said: 'We cannot protect our minds'. What is the protection of the mind, and why are philosophers incapable of protecting their minds?"[242]

186 **The Exegete replied:** "That is, protecting their minds from being distracted by foul thoughts, and worldly thoughts in general. They always suspend them before God when remembering Him, remembering His graces, promises and commandments. They do not allow them [minds] to converse with demons nor to be drawn into their ruses or sinful thoughts. Rather, the mind should be entirely focused on God, preoccupied with Him and conversing with Him through fervent prayer. This protection is strange to the philosophers because they do not practice asceticism for the sake of God. Instead, they fast to refine their bodies, they abstain from

184 **قال المفسر** فرق كثير[1048] بين بكا الشيوخ والكاملين وبكا[1049] الصبيان والمبتديين. فثم من يبكي كثيرا من رطوبة وحرارة مزاجه. مثل النسا والصبيان. فبكاهم (a40r) هين. وثم من يبكي من وجع قلبه. اما لحرارة غيظه او لشدة المه وحزنه. وثم من يبكي لفرحه مثل الذي يجد صاحبه بعد (d110v) زمانا طويل. اما القديسين فلامتلا قلوبهم بوجع الندم على خطاياهم والعجز التكميل مرادهم من الفضيله تفيض دموعهم. وايضا (b52r) فلطول المده التي يغتصبون نفوسهم فيها بالتنهد والتوجع على البكا. وبالجمله فدموع الشيوخ الكاملين موهبه من النعمه وليست من الطبع. ولان الدموع يكون معها التكبر. حذرت الابا صاحبها منه كثيرا قايلين. اذا كان لك ينبوع الدموع فلا تتكبر. ومن نال موهبة الدموع فيها يغسل خطاياه. ويغلب القتال. ويحسن تدبيره. والدموع نوعان.[1050] نوع المبتديين. ونوع الكاملين. كالمخافة من الله والمحبه له. فان المبتديين يحبون خيرات الله ويخافون[1051] احكامه كالعبيد. والكاملين يحبون الله[1052] ويخافون عظمته. كالاولاد الذين (e111v) يخافون اباهم.[1053]

185 **قال الاخوه** ان فلاسفه مضوا ليجربوا المتوحدين. فقالوا لبعض الشيوخ. ما الذي تعملونه افضل منا. انتم تصومون ونحن نصوم. انتم اطهار ونحن اطهار. فقالوا نحن نحرص عقولنا. فاجابوا ما نقدر نحن نحفظ عقولنا. فما هو حفظ العقل. ولم لا تقدر الفلاسفه يحفظون عقولهم.

186 **قال المفسر** اي يحفظون عقولهم من (a40v) الطياشه. في الافكار الرديه.(b52v) وبالجمله في الافكار العالميه ويوقفونها دايما قدام الله في ذكره. وتذكار خبراته ومواعيده (c74v) ووصاباه. ولا يدعونها تتكلم مع الشياطين. ولا تميل الى (d111r) خداعهم. ولا الى افكار الخطيه. بل يكون العقل بكليته ناظر الى الله. وفيه همه ومعه مخاطبته في صلاته بلا فتور. وهذا الحفظ الفلاسفه منه بعدا. لانهم لا يتنسكون من اجل الله. وانما يصومون لتلطف اجسادهم ويتركون

greasy food to enlighten their minds and sharpen their understanding, and they abstain from marriage in order not to be distracted from the teaching of wisdom. Their understanding is worldly and their aim is worldly wisdom. Their thoughts roam aimlessly after what they cannot ascertain through them. What hinders them from protecting the mind is their association with people and conversation with them. Their meditation is on worldly wisdom. Protecting the inner senses cannot be achieved without guarding and controlling the external senses."

187 **The Brothers inquired:** "Some brothers came to Antony and said to him: 'Give us a commandment to keep'. He said: 'It is written that "Whoever strikes you on one cheek, turn to him the other."'[243] They replied: 'We are unable'. He said: 'Stick to one [cheek]'. They replied: 'We are unable'. He said: 'Do not requite [the strike] with blows'. They replied: 'We are unable'. He then said to his disciple: 'Prepare for them some cooked food for they are sick'."[244]

188 **The Exegete replied:** "That is, their souls are sick and need to be cured, as with those who are physically sick and need treatment with cooked food."

189 **A marginal note on Saint Antony:** Whenever his disciple told him that brothers had come, he would ask him: "Are they from Jerusalem or Egypt?" meaning "Are they heavenly or earthly?" If he replied "From Jerusalem," he would come down and speak to them. But if he replied "From Egypt," he would ask that they be fed and allowed to depart.[245] Thus when he spoke to them and found them to be earthly and decadent, he said to his disciple: "Feed them," meaning "They are seeking nourishment for their bodies not for their souls."

190 **The Exegete said:** "The heads of monasteries should not lose hope in weak brothers concerning their way of life and hastily distance themselves from mixing with them because of the slackness of their conduct. They should instead concern themselves with their salvation through prayer, tears, heartache, humility, and patient education, at times through counseling, and other times through admonishment as the Apostle advised,[246] so that they might find favor before God, as Pachomius did with Sylvanus, and Isidore with one of his sons."

الاطعمه الدسمه لتنور عقولهم وتدق افهامهم. ويتركون الزيجه حتى لا يشتغلون عن تعليم الحكمه. فهمهم دنياني ومطلوبهم حكمة عالميه وافكارهم طايشه خلف ما لا يدركونه بها. ويعوقهم من حفظ العقل اجتماعهم بالناس وحديثهم معهم. وهذيذهم (e112r) في حكمة العالميه وحفظ الحواس الباطنه لا يمكن من دون حراسة الحواس الظاهره وضبطها.

187 **قال الاخوه** ان اخوه مضوا الى انطونيوس وقالوا له اعطنا وصيه نحفظها. فقال مكتوب من لطمك على خدك حول له (b53r) الاخر. فقالوا ما نقدر. فقال فاثبتوا بالواحد. فقالوا ما نقدر. فقال لا تكافوا بالضرب.[1054] قالوا ما نقدر. قال لتلاميذه هيي لهم قليل طبيخ فانهم مرضًا.[1055]

188 **قال المفسر** اي[1056] هم مرضًا[1057] النفوس. اي محتاجون لشفايها. كما ان المرضى الاجساد محتاجون لمداواتها بالطبيخ.[1058]

189 **حاشيه** القديس انطونيوس. (a41r) كان اذا اخبره تلميذه بحضور الاخوه يقول له ام هم من اورشليم ام مصر. اي هم سماييون[1059] ام (d111v) عالميون. فان قال له من اورشليم نزل وتحدث معهم. وان قال من مصر اطعمهم ودعهم يمضون. فلما تحدث مع هولاء وجدهم[1060] عالميين منحطين. قال لتلميذه اطعمهم. اي انهم طالبون غذا اجسادهم لا غذا نفوسهم.

190 **قال المفسر** ينبغي لمقدمي الاديره ان لا يقطعوا رجاهم من الاخوه الضعفا في تدبيرهم ويبتعدوا (c75r) عاجلا من الاختلاط بهم من اجل رخاوة عادتهم (e112v) بل يهتموا بخلاصهم بالصلاه والدموع. وتالم القلب والاتضاع والتعليم بطول روح. تاره بالوعظ. وتاره بالتانيب (b53v) كما اوصا الرسول لكي يجدوا داله قدام الله. كما صنع باكوميوس مع سلونا[1061] وايسيدرس مع احد اولاده.

191 **The Brothers inquired:** "A holy man saw someone carrying a dead person. He said to him: 'Leave off carrying the dead and go carry the living'."[247]

192 **The Exegete replied:** "Meaning carry the Lord because He is the life from the death of sin. This resembles the saying of Abba Macarius: 'You should carry, O sister, the Lord in your heart as Mary carried Him in her womb'."

193 **A marginal note:** One might say that he meant carrying the cross of Christ and following Him, as He commanded,[248] or carrying His yoke and learning from it gentleness and humility, as He commanded,[249] or obeying the word of God because when He was told: 'Blessed is the womb that bore you',[250] he replied: 'Blessed rather is he who hears the word of God and obeys it'."

194 **The Brothers asked:** "Why are sinners and the good equally stricken with illnesses and trials?"

195 **The Exegete replied:** "God's commands in this world are in accordance with what God told Prophet Jeremiah[251] and Saint Antony: no one other than Him knows them, neither angels nor people. They, nevertheless, teach it throughout the whole world to people endowed with reason. Solomon the Wise once wondered at this and said: 'If what happens to the fool happens to me too, why then did I seek further wisdom? This is absurd and distressful'."[252]

196 **A marginal note:** One can say that sinners are punished for a sin that was committed or are hindered through pain from committing a sin that would have been committed were it not for the pain. As for the good, it is to show the weak their endurance and gratitude so that they might imitate them and thus increase their goodness and reward. It might also be said that some illnesses are natural and that both the wicked and the good share a natural predisposition for them. This could be a dispensation from God so that the good do not become proud, as the Apostle said about himself.[253] In conclusion, there is no doubt that God's dispensation and commands cannot be perceived by anyone. As for the intended purpose of anything, it can only be known by Him.

197 **The Brothers asked:** "Why do some people, who are the majority, find repentance after some time, whereas others are never granted repentance?"

191 **قال الاخوه** ان شيخا راى انسانا يحمل ميتا. فقال له دع حمل الميته وامض احمل الحياة.[1062]

192 **قال المفسر** اي احمل الرب. لانه هو الحياة[1063] من موت الخطيه. وهذا كقول انبا مقار. يجب عليك ايها الاخت ان تحمل الرب في قلبك كما حملته ماريام في بطنها.

193 **حاشيه** ويجوز انه كان اراد احمل صليب المسيح واتبعه كما امر. او احمل نيره وتعلم منه الوداعه والاتضاع كما امر. او اعمل بكلام الله. لانه لما قيل له. طوبى[1064] للبطن[1065] الذي حملك.[1066] قال محلا طوبى لمن يسمع كلام الله (d112r) ويحفظه.

194 (a41v) **قال الاخوه** لماذا يقع الخطاه والابرار في الامراض والمحن بمساواه.

195 **قال المفسر** احكام الله في هذا العالم كما قال الله لارميا النبي والقديس انطونيوس ما يدركها (b54r) احد[1067] غيره. لا الملايكه ولا الناس لكنهم فيعلمونها في العالم الكامل للناطقين. وقد تعجب من هذا (e113r) سليمان الحكيم حتى قال اذا كان يصادف الجاهل مثل الذي يصادفني فلماذا[1068] تحكمت زايدا. هذا هبا وشقوة قلب.

196 **حاشيه** يجوز ان يقال ان الخطاه يقاصصون عن اثم وقع. او يمنعون بالام عن اثم لولاه لوقع. واما الابرار فليظهر الضعفا صبرهم وشكرهم فيفتقدوا بهم. ويكون ذلك زياده في برهم وثوابهم. وقد يقال ان بعض الامراض طبيعيه. والاشرار والابرار مشتركون في الطبع القابل لها. وقد يكون ذلك للابرار تدبير من (c75v) الله لكيلا يتكبروا. كما قال الرسول عن نفسه. وبالجمله فلا شك ان تدبير الله وحكمه لا يدركه احد.[1069] فاما وجه الحكم[1070] في شي[1071] شي فلا يعرف الا من جهته.

197 **قال الاخوه** لماذا قوم وهم الاكثرون يجدون زمانا التوبه. وقوما لا يعطون زمانا التوبه.

198 **The Exegete replied:** "Knowing this is difficult because our Lord came to call sinners to repentance, as He said.²⁵⁴ He granted [the possibility of] repentance to each person up to the hour of death. What we can say is that those [sinners] were granted a long period of time but they did not repent, and He knew from them that they would perhaps increase in hypocrisy and sin. This may be what it means, so that the majority do not become slack and fall, in the hope of repentance at the end."

199 **The Holy Man also said:** "When the solitary begins the struggle with thoughts, his soul starts to become pure and enlightened with the light of grace. Evagrius said: 'As the devil asked God to hand over Job to him,²⁵⁵ likewise, when each soul starts to become enlightened and refined, the devil asks that grace be withdrawn a little and withheld from it in order to expose the extent of its steadfastness and love of God. He then overwhelms it with many evils'."

200 **The Brothers inquired:** "Arsenius while in prayer in his cell called his disciple Daniel and said to him: 'Relieve your father as much as you can, so that when he goes to our Lord he may make entreaties on your behalf and good will occur to you'."²⁵⁶

201 **The Exegete replied:** "When Arsenius prayed, his heart attained spiritual visions, his soul was filled with joy, and he boiled over in the love of Christ. On one occasion, he thought about what some people said: that people's souls after they leave their bodies do not perceive and do not glorify God. Rather, they are like a sleeper, without any sense or movement until the Resurrection. He then became very sad believing that his soul would be incapable of glorifying God and delighting in Him until the Resurrection. However, when this thought occurred to him while in prayer and he became worthy of the divine vision, he learned from the vision that after its departure from the body, his soul would not be incapable of praising God, rather it would orbit in Paradise in joy and calm with the souls of the righteous, glorifying God until the Day of Resurrection, and it would find repose from arduous works, struggling and falling, and find serenity in the hope of perfection at the Resurrection. He then called Daniel, who served him in his old age and knew his secrets, and said to him with great joy: 'Gratify my old age so that if I go to Paradise I would ask the Lord to

198 **قال المفسر** هذا معرفته عسره. لان ربنا انما جا (b54v) ليدعوا الخطاه الى التوبه. كما قال. وقد اعطى¹⁰⁷² التوبه لكل انسان الى ساعة الموت. والذي يمكن ان نقوله¹⁰⁷³. ان هولاي اعطيوا زمانا (d112v) طويلا فلم يتوبوا (a42r) وعلم منهم انهم¹⁰⁷⁴ ربما يزدادون نفاقا واثما. وان هذا يكون القايل لكيلا يتهاون الكثير ويسقطوا. موملين التوبه اخيرا.

199 **وقال الشيخ** ان المتوحد (e113v) عندما يبتدي في حرب الافكار تبدى نفسه تنقا وتنور بنور النعمه. وقال وغريس. كما طلب الشيطان من الله من اجل ايوب هكذى¹⁰⁷⁵ من اجل كل نفس تبتدي تنور وتنسلق¹⁰⁷⁶ يطلب الشيطان ان تخلي النعمه عنها قليلا فيتوانا عنها ليظهر ثباتها وحبها في الله. وحينيذ يغلب عليها شرورا كثيره.¹⁰⁷⁷

200 **قال الاخوه** ان ارسانيوس في صلاته في قلايته دعى دانيال تلميذه وقال له نيح اباك ما قدرت. حتى اذا مضى¹⁰⁷⁸ الى ربنا يسال فيك. ويصير لك خير.

201 **قال المفسر** ان ارسانيوس كان في صلاته يصير¹⁰⁷⁹ قلبه في مناظر الروح. وتمتلي نفسه فرحا. ويغلي في حب المسيح (c76r) وفي بعض الاوقات يفتكر (b55r) ما قيل من بعض الناس ان نفوس الناس من بعد انتقالها من اجسادها ما تدرك ولا تمجد الله. بل تكون كما النايم بلا حس ولا حركه الى القيامه تحزن كثيرا. لكون نفسه تعدم تمجد الله. والفرح به الى القيامه. ولما عرض له هذا الفكر في الصلاه واستحق الرويا الالهي. وتعلم من النظر ان بعد انتقالها من الجسد لا تعدم نفسه تسبحة الله بل تدور (e114r) في الفردوس في الفرح والنياح مع ارواح (d113r) الصالحين. وتمجد الله الى يوم الانبعاث. وتجد الراحه من الاعمال المتعبه. (a42v) ومن قتال وسقوط. وتتنيح برجا الكمال في القيامه. فدعا دانيال الذي كان يخدمه في شيخوخيته ويطلع على اسراره كمن غلب عليه الفرح. وقال له نيح شيخوخيتي حتى اذا مضيت الى الفردوس سالت الرب ان

protect you. Thus I learned from our Lord in the vision: that if I leave the body, I would go to Paradise and there I would glorify Him, and would find favor with Him'. This story resembles what the abbot of the monastery said to his blind disciple: 'Pray for me for if I find favor with our Lord in Paradise, I will make entreaties to Him on your behalf, and on Sunday, your eyes will open'. After his death, the eyes of the blind disciple were opened and he glorified God. I have heard from some brothers who served their saintly teachers well that after the death of their Fathers, they found support in their labor and liberation from temptations through their prayers more so than when they were with us. I have demonstrated this in an extensive explanation in the *Commentary on the Book of Abba Isaiah* in the twenty-fifth chapter,[257] with the aid of our Lord."

202 **The Brothers asked:** "Two brothers were living in a monastery; one of them possessed nothing and his way of life was harder, while the other was obedient and humble. The monks wished to know which of the two was greater. They then went down to a river which had crocodiles. The obedient and humble monk entered and stood in their midst, and they prostrated to him. He then invited his companion [to enter] who said: 'Forgive me for I have not yet attained your level of faithfulness'. How is it that the laborer who possessed little was fearful but the obedient and humble monk was not?"[258]

203 **The Exegete replied:** "Humility has two additional characteristics to other virtues. One of them is that to the same degree it brings its possessor down, grace exalts him high. For our Lord said: 'Who humbles himself will be exalted'.[259] The second is that he does not fear demons, wicked people, wild beasts or reptiles, as Evagrius said: 'He who is humble is without fear'. Similarly, he who is obedient for the sake of God is obeyed by everything because he has severed his desire and obeyed his father through submission to God. For everything submits to God. In fact, faith arises with obedience and humility. 'Everything is possible for the believer', as the Lord said.[260] As for the laboring brother, he rejoiced in his labor, did not depend on obedience, and his faith was not strong. As a result nothing submitted to him."

204 **On the Classification of the One who Struggles.**

يحفظك. هكذى تعلمت من ربنا في الرويا. انني اذا خرجت من الجسد امضي الى الفردوس وهناك امجده. ويكون لي عنده داله. وهذا الخبر يشبه قول رييس الدير الذي قال لتلميذه[1080] الاعمى صلي علي فان وجدت داله عند ربنا في الفردوس (b55v) سالته من اجلك. وفي يوم الاحد تنفتح عينيك. ومن بعد نياحته انفتحت عيني الاعمى ومجد الله. وانا سمعت من بعض الاخوه الذين خدموا معلميهم القديسين جيدا. ان من بعد نياح اباييهم وجدوا عونا في العمل. وخلاصا في التجارب بصلوتهم.[1081] اكثر من الوقت الذي كانوا فيه عندنا. وقد بينت هذا بشرح طويل في تفسير كتاب انبا اشعيا في الميمر الخامس العشرين[1082] بعون ربنا.

202 **قال الاخوه** كان اخوان في دير احدهما لا (e114v) يقتني[1083] شيا وفي تدبير اصعب. وكان الاخر طايعا متضعا. واراد[1084] الرهبان ان يعرفوا ايهما افضل. فنزلا الى النهر وكان فيه (c76v) تماسيح. فدخل الطايع المتضع ووقف بينهم فسجدوا له. ودعا صاحبه فقال له اغفر لي ما وقفت بعد في درجة امانتك. فكيف العامل القليل القنيه خاف والطايع المتضع ما خاف.

203 **قال المفسر** الاتضاع له خصلتان ازيد من باقي الفضايل (a43r) احدهما انه بقدر ما يحط صاحبه الى العمق (b56r) ترفعه النعمه الى العلوا. فان ربنا قال من يضع نفسه يرتفع. والثانيه انه ما يخاف من الشياطين. ولا من الناس الاشرار. ولا من الوحوش والهوام. كما قال وغريس. ان المتضع يكون بلا خوف. وايضا المطيع من اجل الله يطيعه كلشي لانه قطع هواه واطاع اباه خضوعا لله. فالله يخضع له كلشي.[1085] والاصل ان الايمان يكون مع الطاعه والاتضاع. وكلشي[1086] يكون للمومن[1087] مستطاع.[1088] كما قال الرب. فاما الاخ العامل فكان يفرح بعمله. فلم يعتمد على الطاعه. ولم يكن ايمانه قويا. فلم تخضع له الاشيا.

204 في ترتيب المجاهد.

205 **The Brothers inquired:** "Abba Poemen said: 'The devil has three powers which precede sin: error, neglect, and desire. Neglect follows error, desire follows neglect, and sin follows desire. If the solitary does not fall into error, neglect will not come to him, if he is not negligent, desire will not arise in him, and if he does not desire, he will, through the help of Christ, not fall [into sin]'."[261]

206 **The Exegete replied:** "Just as visible war has an order – first, the foot soldiers shoot arrows, second, the cavalry line advances to the line of enemy fighters and they fight each other with swords – so too the hidden war between demons and solitaries has an order. If the devil wishes to distance the solitary from God, he does not stir in him from the outset of the struggle the recollection of sin – fornication, for example, or anger, or any other of these spiritual yearnings – since the thought of the solitary would be alert through the remembrance of God and he would pray for the departure of the thought that was planted in him by the devil, and it would take flight. The devil would also flee beaten as if scorched by fire every time, as he said. But if he sees the solitary in his prayer or in meditation, he envies him and rushes to stop his thought from connecting with God and make him forget His remembrance. This is forgetfulness caused by error, which is the first power of the devil. After this, he stirs in him the recollection of things that he thinks are not sinful, and preoccupies his mind with them. This is neglect, which is the second power of the devil. After this he stirs in him the recollection of sin – either desire, anger or other. If he is defeated in the three levels of the struggle then he is easily deceived and manipulated to commit sin. But if he prays with fervor and tears, the struggle leaves off, either at the first, or the second, or the third level. This is the classification of their fight with the novice solitaries. However, with the Perfect, he seeks to draw them away from the remembrance of God to contemplating His creation, so as to drag them down from on high to below. For just as God is greater than His creation, so too His remembrance is greater than its recollection. Evagrius said: 'It is through the constant remembrance of God that the knowledge of God is born'.[262] And through the recollection of creation [the devil] lures them to the comprehension of spiritual books."

207 **The Brothers inquired:** "A holy man said: 'There are those who give all their thoughts to the Enemy, those who give ten [thoughts]

205 **قال الاخوه** قال انبا بجمن. الشيطان.[1089] ثلث قوات تتقدم الخطيه. الطغيان. والتواني. والشهوه. (e115r) فالتواني يتبع الطغيان. والشهوه تتبع التواني. والخطيه تتبع الشهوه. وان لم يسقط المتوحد في الطغيان ما ياتيه التواني. وان لم يتوانا ما تاتيه[1090] الشهوه. وان كان (b56v) ما يشتهي ما يسقط بعون المسيح.

206 **قال المفسر** كما ان الحرب الظاهر له ترتيب. ففي اوله ترمي الرجاله بالنشاب (d114r) وفي الثاني تتقدم صف الخياله الى الصف المقاتل له ويتقاتلان بالسيوف. كذالك الحرب الخفي بين الشياطين والمتوحدين له ترتيب. فاذا اراد الشيطان[1091] ان يبعد المتوحد من الله. ليس يحرك فيه من اول القتال (a43v) تذكار الخطيه. الزنا مثلا او الغضب او غيره من هذه الاوجاع النفسانيه. لان فكرة المتوحد (c77r) تكون مستيقظه في تذكار الله. فيصلي على انصراف الفكرة التي زرعها فيه فتنصرف وينصرف الشيطان منكسرا كالمكوي بالنار. كما قال مرة بعد مره. لكنه اذا راى المتوحد في صلاته او في هذيذه يحسده. فيسرع ان يقطع فكرته من الارتباط بالله. وينسيه تذكاره. وهذا هو نسيان الطغيان. وهو قوة الشيطان الاولى. وبعد هذا يحرك فيه تذكار (b57r) الاشيا التي ما يظن انها خطيه. ويشغل عقله بها. وهذا هو (e115v) التواني وهو قوة الشيطان الثانيه. وبعد هذا يحرك فيه تذكار الخطيه. اما الشهوة او الغضب او غيره. فاذا انغلب في درجات المعركة الثالثه[1092] سهل انخداعه وانطياعه لفعل الخطيه. فان صلى بحرارة ودموع انصرف عنه الحرب. اما في الاولى[1093] او الثانيه الى الثالثه. وهذا ترتيب قتالهم مع المتوحدين المبتدين واما مع الكاملين. فبان يميلهم من تذكار الله الى الفكرة في مخلوقاته ليحطهم من الاعلى الى الادنى. لان كما ان[1094] الله اعظم من مخلوقاته.[1095] تذكاره اعلا من تذكارها. وقال وغريس. (d114v) ان من تذكار الله الدايم تتولد معرفة[1096] الله. ومن تذكار المخلوقات. او[1097] كان يميلهم الى فهم الكتب الروحانيه.

207 **قال الاخوه** قال شيخ ثم من يدفع جميع افكاره (a44r) للعدو[1098] وثم من يدفع عشره

but take one, those who give one and take ten, and those who give nothing'."²⁶³

208 **The Exegete replied:** "When the devil stirs the Perfect one to recollect sin he would chase him away and distance him at once. This is the one who gives none of his thoughts to the Enemy. As for the intermediate [solitary], the thought lingers in him a little, but he then remembers God, His love and His fear, and hastens to chase it away and distance it after having been drawn to it. This is the one who gives one [thought] but takes ten. As for the novice, he becomes greatly preoccupied with the thought, but in the end his intention would reproach him for his neglect and accepting the foul thought, he would then chase it away and seek aid from God after having found it agreeable and enjoyable. This is the one who gives ten and takes one. As for the dissolute and negligent one, he enjoys [the thought] and does not reject it. He might even fulfill it through action without any shame or fear. This is the one who gives all [his thoughts] to the Enemy."

209 **The Brothers inquired:** "Abba Sisoes said: 'The minute a yearning stirs in you, cut it off'.²⁶⁴ Abba Poemen said: 'If thoughts stir in you, give and take with them so that you may be tested and molded in the struggle against them'.²⁶⁵ He said to someone else: 'Cut them out immediately and do not approve of them'."²⁶⁶

210 **The Exegete replied:** "The strong wise men are not harmed if the stirring of yearnings linger in them, because they are not fond of them or obedient to them. They would allow them to linger in them in order to recognize them and train how to struggle against them. As for those who are deficient and weak, they should never let them linger in them at all. They should instead cast them off the minute they begin to stir in their hearts. The Fathers instruct the weak to cut them off at their start, but order the strong to leave them to the extent that they can train in the struggle against them. But they do not order anyone to observe this with respect to the difficult yearnings, such as fornication, anger, and demonic possession. They order both the strong and weak to cast these off the moment they begin to stir and chase them away with natural indignation and intense prayer. However, they order the strong to be patient a little with yearnings that do not originate in the animal predisposition, such as love of silver and vainglory, and such as

208 **قال المفسر** (b57v) ان الكامل اذا حرك فيه الشيطان تذكار الخطيه طرده وابعده لوقته. فهذا (c77v) هو الذي لا يدفع للعدو¹¹⁰⁰ ولا واحدا¹¹⁰¹ من افكاره. فاما المتوسط فان الفكره تبطى معه قليلا. ثم يذكر الله وحبه ومخافته فيسارع الى طردها وابعادها بعد ميله (e116r) لها. وهذا هو الذي يدفع واحده¹¹⁰² وياخذ عشره. واما المبتدي فانه يتوسوس بالفكره كثيرا. وفي الاخر تبكته نيته من اجل توانيه وقبوله الفكرة الرديه فيطردها. ويطلب عونا من الله من بعد موافقته لها والتذاذه بها. وهذا هو الذي يعطي عشره وياخذ واحده. واما المنحل المتواني فيلتذ¹¹⁰³ بها ولا يطرحها. وقد يكملها بالفعل بلا حيا ولا خوف. وهذا هو الذي يدفع الكل الى العدو.

209 **قال الاخوه** ان انبا شيشاي قال. في¹¹⁰⁴ الوقت الذي يتحرك فيك الوجع اقطعه. وقال انبا بمن اذا تحرك فيك افكار لحذ معها واعط.¹¹⁰⁵ لتكون ممتحنا مسبوكا في جهادها. وقال¹¹⁰⁶ لاخر اقطعها للوقت ولا (b58r) توافقها.

210 **قال المفسر**¹¹⁰⁷ الحكما الاقويا ما يتاذون (d115r) اذا توانت فيهم حركة¹¹⁰⁸ الاوجاع. لانهم لا يكونوا بمحبه معها وطوعا لها. وانما يتركونها تبطي معهم من اجل معرفتها والتدرب بجهادها. واما الحله¹¹⁰⁹ الضعفا فما ينبغي لهم البته يدعونها تبطي فيهم. (a44v) بل يلقونها عنهم من ابتدا حركتها في قلوبهم. فالابا يامرونهم للضعفا¹¹¹⁰ بقطعها من بدايتها. ويامرون الاقويا بتركها مقدار ما يتدربوا (e116v) بجهادها. وليس يامرون احدا بهذا في الاوجاع الصعبه مثل الزنا والغضب والعارض. فانهم يامرون الاقويا والضعفا ان يلقوا هذه عنهم من اول حركتها (c78r) ويطردوها¹¹¹¹ بالغضب الطبيعي والصلاه الحاده. وانما يامرون الاقويا بالصبر قليلا¹¹¹² على الاوجاع التي لا اصل لها في الطبع الحيواني مثل محبه الفضه. والمجد الباطل.

forgetfulness and neglect mentioned above, not out of love and approval of them, but rather in order to benefit from struggling against them. It is on a similar subject that Evagrius said: 'There is a demon called Shadow who sticks to the solitary from the start causing his mind to wander from city to city, from house to house, from one thing to another, so that his mind becomes intoxicated with the fatigue of wandering. [This demon] is then able to overwhelm him, and cast him into the hands of the demon of sorrow, or desire, or anger. In this way, he corrupts the purity of his intention'."[267]

211 **The Brothers inquired:** "A brother asked a holy man to teach him how to weave. He showed him how, then prayed and offered him food. He ate and departed, then came back early in the morning. The holy man said to him: 'Why did you not take your weaving and left me in the tribulation of worry?'"[268]

212 **The Exegete replied:** "We learn from this that the solitary [living] in stillness requires great caution and immense purity. Just as those who purify skins from all dirt and hair with enormous effort so that they become suitable to write the laws of God on them, so too those [who live] in stillness should purify their minds with enormous effort, through watchfulness and prayer, from the filth of foul thoughts so that they may be sealed with the spirit of God. Since the palm leaves for weaving were with the holy man and the brother left without taking them, the devil found a cause by which to distract the thought of the holy man: why did he not give the plait to the brother since he had woven it and kept the brother's work with him? Thus his mind was hindered from pure prayer. Similarly the saint who was hindered from prayer all night long the result of distraction because of a small sentence he had heard during the day outside his cell such that he said: 'A small sentence has disabled my remembrance and thought, even though I have memorized fourteen books'. Abba Isaiah said: 'It is necessary that whoever [lives] in stillness must guard himself from hearing a word that would pain him internally just as a pregnant woman guards against that which would harm what is in her womb'."[269]

213 **The Brothers inquired:** "Two brothers fought until they bled and Abba Poemen was sitting by but he did not say anything to them. Abba Job came in and said to him: 'Why did you leave them to

وليس محبه وموافقه لها لكن للخيره بمجاهدتها. ومثل النسيان والتواني المقدم ذكره. وعن مثل هذا قال وغريس. ثم شيطان يدعى الظل (b58v) يثبت مع المتوحدين ما باكر ويطيش عقله من مدينه الى مدينه. ومن بيت الى بيت. من شي الى شي. ليسكر عقله من تعب الدوران[1113] وحينيذ يستطيع عليه ويلقيه في يدي شيطان الحزن. او الشهوه. او الحرد.[1114] وبهذا يفسد نقا نيته.

211 **قال[1115] الاخوه** اخا سال شيخا ان يعلمه الظفيره. (d115v) فاراه العمل وصلى وقدم له طعاما فاكل وراح وعاد باكرا. فقال له الشيخ لماذا ما اخدت ظفيرتك وتركتني في تجربة الاهتمام.

212 **قال المفسر** نتعلم من هذا ان المتوحد في الهدو محتاج الى تحفظ كثير ونقا عظيم. كالذي (e117r) ينقون (a45r) السلوخ من جميع الوسخ والشعر[1116] بتعب كثير. حتى يصلح لان يكتب فيها ناموس الله. وهكذى الذي في الهدو يجب ان ينقوا عقولهم بتعب عظيم في الحفظ والصلاه من اوساخ الافكار الرديه[1117]. حتى تقبل بروح الله. ومن اجل ان سعف الظفيره كان عند الشيخ ومضا[1118] الاخ ولم ياخذها. فوجد الشيطان عله (b59r) يشغل بها فكرة الشيخ. كيف لم يدفع الظفيره للاخ لانه ظفرها. بل ترك عمل الاخ عنده. فانعاق ذهنه عن الصلاة النقيه. كذلك[1119] القديس الذي انعاق عن الصلاة[1120] (c78v) طول الليل من الطياشه من اجل كلمه صغيره سمعها في النهار خارج قلايته. حتى قال كلمه صغيره بطلت على تذكاري وفكرتي. وانا احفظ اربعة عشر كتابا. وقال انبا اشعيا. ينبغي للذي في الهدو ان يتحفظ من ان يسمع كلمة توله في باطنه. كتحفظ المراة الحامل بما يوذي ما في بطنها.

213 **قال الاخوه** تقاتل اخوان حتى خرج دمهما. وانبا بجن جالس ما كلمهما. فدخل انبا ايوب. فقال له لماذا تركتهما (d116r)

fight?' He replied: 'They are brothers and will be reconciled. Consider me not to be here'."²⁷⁰

214 **The Exegete replied:** "A brother of Abba Poemen became attached to a group outside his monastery. Abba Poemen was not happy about this, he then went to Abba Ammon and told him. He [Ammon] said to him: 'Are you still alive, O Poemen? Go and sit in your cell and think in your mind that you are in the grave, and you have been dead for a year'. For Abba Poemen had six natural brothers who were solitaries like him and living with him. Abba Job was the eldest amongst them. One was committing foul deeds and was not obeying Abba Poemen. He went and mixed with corrupt brothers. He [Poemen] counseled him but he did not accept, and his mind became distracted with worry thinking about him. He fled to Abba Ammon as a result of his soul's distress and revealed to him the reason behind his distress. He said to him: 'He will not accept or change, and you are being harmed. Therefore, consider yourself as dead: do not discern, do not counsel, and do not chastise'. Thus [the next time] he had a fight with one of his brothers as was his custom, he pretended not to know according to the advice of his teacher. Abba Job had no idea about what had happened [with Abba Ammon]. Thus when he saw that Abba Poemen had ignored his brothers, he blamed him, but it was not an opportune time to disclose to him the full reason, he [Poemen], therefore, answered him in a wise manner that convinced him. It is the habit of the Fathers to withhold their advice from those who do not heed them. For instance, blessed Mark said: 'He who does not listen to one word, do not coerce him. Rather, the gain that he shunned you yourself will receive through your patience, more than his becoming upright'. Also, Abba Evagrius said: 'When I saw that brothers were coming to me not for the sake of virtue, but only for the sake of being taught, I stopped teaching them'."

215 **The Brothers asked:** "When the priests in the Scetis Desert would bless the Offering, an eagle would come down on the Offering. Why does the [Holy] Spirit appear over the Offering in the form of an eagle, but over the Baptism in the form of a dove?"²⁷¹

216 **The Exegete replied:** "Doves teach children. What is intended by baptism is the second spiritual birth from the divine spirit. Also,

يختصمان.¹¹²¹ فقال لهما اخوان ويصطلحان. واحسب انا ما انا هنا.

214 **قال المفسر** كان الواحد اخا لانبا بجمن. وصار له حب مع قوم خارجا عن ديره. (e117v) فلم يرض ذالك انبا بجمن. ومضى الى انبا امون وعرفه. فقال له وانت حي بعد¹¹²² يا بجمن. امض واجلس في قلايتك. واحسب (b59v) في فكرك انك في القبر (a45v) ولك سنه من حيث مت. فانبا بجمن كان له ستة اخوه طبيعيه وكانوا متوحدين مثله ساكنين معه. وانبا ايوب كبيرهم في العمر. وكان احدهم اعماله رديه. ولا يطيع انبا بجمن. فمضى وخالط اخوه محلولين فوعظه ولم يقبل. فطاش عقله في فكرة اهتمامه به فهرب الى انبا امون من ضيق نفسه. وكشف له سبب ضيقته. فقال له ذاك ما يقبل ولا يبرح. وانت تتاذى فاحسب انك ميت ولا تعلم ولا توعظ ولا تونب. فلما تقاتل مع احد اخوته مثل عادته. حسب نفسه كمثل من لم يعلم كوصية شيخه. وما كان عند انبا ايوب خبرا مما تقدم. فلما راى انبا بجمن قد توانا عن اخوته لامه. وما احتمل الوقت¹¹²³ ان يكشف له السبب كله. فاجابه بحكمة بما اقنعه. وعادة¹¹²⁴ الابا ان يقطعوا (c79r) وعظهم عن من لا يسمع منهم. فالطوباني مرقس يقول من لا يسمع من كلمة واحده لا تلزه بل الريح الذي (d116v) رذله ذاك (b60r) تجده انت لنفسك بصبرك (e118r) اكثر من استقامة ذاك. وقال انبا وغريس. لما رايت اخوه ياتون الي.¹¹²⁵ لا من اجل عمل الفضيله لكن من اجل التعليم فقط. سكت عن تعليمهم.

215 **قال الاخوه** كان الكهنه في الاسقيطي اذا قدسوا القرابين ينزل نسر على القرابين. فلماذا يترايا الروح على القرابين شبه نسر وعلى المعموديه شبه حمامه.

216 **قال المفسر** كان الحمام (a46r) يربي الاولاد. والمعموديه المقصود بها الميلاد الثاني الروحاني من الروح الالهي. وايضا

the species of the dove is known for gentleness and peace. Through baptism, enmity was transformed into peace. One of the effects of the Gospel is to transform the believers into [a state] that resembles the gentleness of boys. Moreover, since the dove does not desert its nest unless a strange creature comes to live in it, either a snake or a predatory bird, similarly, the Holy Spirit distances itself from a believer if he is inhabited by a foul spirit by his own volition. The appearance of the Spirit over the Offering in the form of an eagle points to what our Lord said: 'Where the corpse is, there the eagles will gather'.[272] Also, the saying of the Apostle: 'We will be caught up in the clouds to meet our Lord'.[273] The characteristic of eagles is to soar in the upper sky and gather where the corpse is."

217 **The Brothers inquired:** "The Fathers said: 'Whoever lives with youths, even if he is strong such that he is not set back in virtue, he will not advance in it.'"[274]

218 **The Exegete replied:** "Youths possess two things: one of them is beauty of appearance, like the beauty of women, which stirs desire. The other is that they are subordinates, like children and slaves. Authority over them stirs the usual [reaction to] subordination, namely, anger and despising others. They cause the dissolute to fall, and the cautious to struggle. Abba Abraham came to a monastery and, finding a youth, he refused to stay the night. They said to him: 'Even you are afraid, O father?' He replied: 'Truly, I do not fear to fall, but what do I benefit from vain struggle?'[275] Paphnutius, the abbot of the monastery in the Scetis Desert said: 'I will not allow as long as I live a youth to live with the monks because of the difficulty of the struggle'.[276] As for Saint Basil,[277] he explained in the *Questions*[278] how boys are to be received and prescribed how to take care of them in his letter which he wrote to his brother Gregory. He said: 'Boyhood requires caution because the intensity of the instinct found in it chases after yearnings. Just as it has the capacity to pursue evil more than the rigidity of old age, so too it is regarding the good'."[279]

219 **The Exegete also said:** "Evagrius said: 'Just as the drunk from the intensity of the wine that reaches his mind might see things and not recognize them, so too is the one who becomes perfect in the love of God. Intensity and love ignite in his soul, allowing his

فلان نوع الحمام مخصوص بالوداعه والسلامه وبالمعموديه انتقلت[1126] العداوه الى السلامه. ومن عرض البشاره انتقال المومنين الى شبه وداعة الصبيان. وايضا لان الحمام لا يهرب من عشه الا اذا تعاهده فيه الغريب اما ثعبان او وحش كاسر.[1127] وهكذى الروح القدس يبعد من[1128] المومن اذا سكنه الروح[1129] النجس باختياره. وانما ظهور الروح على القربان[1130] شبه النسر فاشارة على قول ربنا حيث تكون الجثه[1131] هناك تجتمع (b60v) النسور. وقول الرسول. ان نحن نختطف في السحب[1132] للقا ربنا. ومما يخص النسور التحليق في الجو الاعلا والاجتماع حيث[1133] الجثه.

217 **قال الاخوه** ان الابا قالوا من يسكن مع الصبيان[1134] (e118v)[1135] فان كان قويا حتى انه لا يتاخر في الفضيله فما يتقدم فيها.

218 (d117r) **قال المفسر** الصبيان فهم شيان. احدهما جمال المنظر المشبه جمال النسا[1136] المحرك الشهوه. والاخر انهم مروسون كالاولاد والعبيد. فتحرك الاستطاعه عليهم التراس المعود الحرد واحتقار الغير. فهم المنحلين سبب عثره. (c79v) والمتحذرين[1137] سبب جهاد.[1138] فانبا ابراهام وصل الى دير فوجد صبيا. فما اراد ان يقيم. فقالوا له وانت تخاف يا ابانا. فقال اما لاجل الصدق فما اخاف من السقوط. ولكن ماذا انتفع من القتال الباطل. وبننوده رييس دير برية الاسقيطي قال[1139] ما اخلي (a46v) في ايامي صبيا يسكن مع الرهبان من اجل صعوبة القتال. فاما القديس بسليوس فشرح في المسايل التي كتبها لاخيه غريغويوس.[1140] (b61r) في رسالته التي كتبها لاخيه غريغويوس. ورتب الحرص عليهم. قال الصبا يحتاج الى تحرز لان الحراره الغريزيه المتوفره فيه تقفز خلف الاوجاع. وكما انها مستعده لعمل الشر اكثر من برد الشيخوخيه كذالك[1141] هي في الخير ايضا.

219 **قال المفسر** قال وغريس كما ان السكران من حراره الخمر الذي يصعد الى دماغه قد ينظر الاشيا ولا يعرفها كذالك الذي يكمل في حب الرب (e119r) تشتعل الحراره والمحبة في نفسه

thought to rise to Heaven, his mind to unite with God's wonders, his soul to boil with the love of God, and his heart to be filled with joy. His eyes would be open but he would not perceive worldly things. This is the spiritual way of life that belongs to the Perfect, blessed are those who are worthy of it'."

220 **The Brothers asked:** "What is the attentiveness of the mind and its effort?"

221 **The Exegete replied:** "It is to drive away the thoughts of yearnings quickly so that one does not commit a sin either in thought or word, to pray without languor or distraction, and to perform good deeds at all times and in all places. One is then purified and reaches perfection."

222 **The Holy Man said:** "In the same way as the brothers come and inquire, they also take and leave, meaning if they ask for labor with care and caution, they labor. Otherwise, they do not."

223 **The Brothers inquired:** "A brother said to a holy man: 'Many thoughts accost me, and I do not know what to do'. He said to him: 'Do not fight them all, but only one: the chief thought of Satan'."[280]

224 **The Exegete replied:** "It means do not be fooled by the first thought with which Satan fights you. For he then brings forth other thoughts that you cannot bear to struggle against. Rather, struggle against the first with care and awareness so that your struggle will always be with one, which is the first, even though he might follow it with others. For this reason he called it the chief thought of Satan."

225 **The Brothers asked:** "Differentiate for us between Satan and deception, desire, sin, yearnings, and death, and how to fight and win with the help of Christ, our Lord?"

226 **The Exegete replied:** "Regarding Satan, he is the self-fallen angel. He is the chief of the demons and the Enemy who fights. Regarding deception, they are his thoughts that he stirs in our heart to remind us of sin and deceive us to commit it. Regarding desire, it is the enjoyment of the thought of deception and obeying it. Regarding sin, meaning the sin of the solitary, it is his will to fulfill desire through action, through the organs of the body. Regarding

فترتفع فكرته الى السما. ويرتبط عقله بعجايب الله. وتغلي نفسه في حب الرب. ويمتلي قلبه فرحا. فتكون عيناه (d117v) مفتوحتان وهو لا يدرك الاشيا العالميه. فهذا هو التدبير الروحاني الذي للكاملين وطوبا لمن يستحقه.

220 **قال الاخوه** ما هو حرص العقل ونشاطه.

221 **قال المفسر** طرد افكار الاوجاع عاجلا حتى لا يخطي في فكر ولا كلام. والصلاه بلا فتور ولا طياشه. وعمل البر في كل زمان وكل مكان. وحينيذ ينقى ويصل الى [1142] الكمال.

222 **قال الشيخ** الاخوه كما ياتون ويسالون كذلك [1143] ياخذون ويمضون (b61v/c80r) اي ان طلبوا بتوج وحرص ليعملوا عملوا. والا فلا.

223 **قال الاخوه** ان اخا قال لشيخ. افكار [1144] كثيره تقاتلني وما اعرف كيف اصنع. فقال له لا تقاتل الجمع. لكن واحدا الذي هو راس افكار الشيطان.

224 (a47r) **قال المفسر** اي لا تنخدع للفكره الاولى الذي يقاتلك [1145] بها الشيطان. فياتيك بافكار اخرى فلا تطيق قتالها. لكن قاتل الاولى بحرص وتيقظ. فيكون قتالك ابدا مع واحده فلانها [1146] اوله. وقد يتبعها غيرها سماها [1147] راس افكار الشيطان.

225 **قال** [1148] **الاخوه** ميز لنا بين الشيطان والخداع. والشهوه والخطيه والالام. والموت. وكيف (e119v) القتال والغلبه بعون المسيح ربنا.

226 **قال المفسر** اما الشيطان فهو الملاك الساقط بنفسه. وهو راس الشياطين. وهو العدو المقاتل. واما الخداع فهي افكره التي يحركها في قلبنا ليذكرنا الخطيه ويخدعنا لها. واما الشهوه فهي التذاذه (d118r) بفكره الخداع وطاعته لها. واما الخطيه اعني خطية المتوحد وهي ارادته تكميل الشهوه بالفعل. باعضا الجسد. واما

yearnings, it is the maintenance of this will for a long period of time. Regarding death, it is these yearnings inflicted on the solitary, because this is spiritual death from the life that comes from the connection of the mind with God through constant remembrance of Him and delighting in His love. Fulfilling this purpose through action, through the organs of the body, by the solitary or non-solitary, distances one from God. This is in accordance to what was written: 'If desire conceives, it gives birth to sin. If it is fulfilled through sin, it gives birth to death'.[281] That is, desire gives birth to sin inside the heart. If the sin is fulfilled, death becomes complete, because then the soul consorts with Satan. This resembles the consorting of a woman with a man and her consent to his deception with love and obedience, and her reception of his seed. For the devil's deception gives birth to sin within the heart with the soul's consent as the conception of the fetus in a woman's womb is by means of the man's seed and the woman's consent. If sin is established in the heart for a time, it leads to action and is fulfilled through the organs of the body. This is the complete death of the soul and its devotion, and the life of sin and its triumph and domination, as our Lord said: 'Whoever commits a sin is a slave of sin'.[282] Regarding what is expected of the combatant in this war, he needs to be in stillness, to carefully fulfill the commandments of our Lord, meditate on His love and long to see Him. If Satan envies us for this and fights us with his deception: if he fights you lightly, scold him and continue to labor. If his fighting is moderate, lift your mind's sight to Heaven and ask the Lord for help. If his fighting is intense and constant, put your mind aside and raise your body to pray, recite the Psalms of the Holy Spirit with understanding, knock the head with prostrations, rub your face on the ground before the cross of our Lord, let us beat our chests and weep with a yearning voice and flowing tears, and let us call our Lord to help us through mental cries. Satan would then withdraw deception, sin, yearnings, and death from us. We are then freed from servitude, our heart is purified, and we boil in the love of our Lord. Abba Isaiah said: 'It happens that sin might overcome the soul ten times or twenty times. Nevertheless, the soul is patient and begins to gradually overcome and defeat sin and Satan'."

227 **The Brothers asked:** "Why were demons left to fight us so that virtuous acts have become hard for us to perform?"

الالام فهو بقا هذه الاراده زمانا طويلا.¹¹⁴⁹ واما الموت فهو هذه الالام في (b62r) حق المتوحد. لان هذا هو الموت النفساني من الحياة التي هي الاتصال العقل بالله بدوام تذكاره والتنعم بحبه. وتكميل هذه الاراده ¹¹⁵⁰ بالفعل بالاعضا البدنيه في حق المتوحد وغير المتوحد تبعد من الله. وهذا كما كتب ان الشهوه اذا حبلت ولدت الخطيه. (c80v) واذا تكملت بالخطيه فتلد ¹¹⁵¹ الموت. اي الشهوه تلد داخل القلب الخطيه. واذا تكملت الخطيه كمل ¹¹⁵² الموت. لان النفس تشترك مع الشيطان. مثل اشتراك المره ¹¹⁵³ مع الرجل وقبولها خداعه بمحبه (a47v) وطاعه. مثل قبول المراه زرع الرجل. فيولد خداعه مع موافقة النفس له داخل القلب الخطيه. كما يتولد في بطن (e120r) المراه الجنين من زرع الرجل وموافقة المراه. واذا ثبتت الخطيه داخل القلب مده خرجت ¹¹⁵⁴ الى ¹¹⁵⁵ الفعل. وكملت ¹¹⁵⁶ باعضا ¹¹⁵⁷ الجسم. وهذا هو موت النفس الكامل وتعبدها. وحياة الخطيه وغلبتها وملكتها. كما قال ربنا. ان الذي يصنع الخطيه هو عبد الخطيه. واما كيفية ما ينبغي من المجاهده في هذا الحرب بان يكون (b62v) في الهدو ويحرص في عمل وصايا ربنا. ويكون في هذيذ حبه وشوقه (d118v) لنظره. فاذا حسدنا الشيطان على هذا وقاتلنا بخداعه فان قاتلك قليلا قليل ازجره ¹¹⁵⁸ واحرص في العمل. فان كان قتاله متوسطا فارفع نظر عقلك ¹¹⁵⁹ الى السما واطلب من الرب عونا. فان كان قتاله شديدا ودايما ¹¹⁶⁰ فليحير ¹¹⁶¹ ذهنك. وانهض بجسدك للصلاه. ورتل بمزامير روح القدس بفهم واضرب المطانيات ¹¹⁶² بلطم الراس. وتمريغ الوجه على الارض قدام صليب سيدنا. ولندق على صدورنا ونبكي بصوت حنين ودموع جاريه. ولنستدع ربنا لعوننا بالصراخ العقلي. وحينيذ يبعد عنا الشيطان الخداع. والخطيه. والالام. والموت. وننعتق من العبوديه. ¹¹⁶³ وينقى قلبنا. ونغلي في حب ربنا. وقد قال انبا اشعيا. يتفق ان تغلب الخطيه النفس ¹¹⁶⁴ عشرة مرات او عشرين مره. ومع ذلك ¹¹⁶⁵ تصبر النفس (e120v) وتبتدي في الغلبه اولا ¹¹⁶⁶ (a48r/c81r) فاولا فتغلب الخطيه والشيطان.

قال الاخوه (b63r) لماذا تركت الشياطين يقاتلونا ¹¹⁶⁷ حتى صعبت علينا اعمال الفضيله.

228   **The Exegete replied:** "For four reasons. The first is in order for our rational souls to be trained in learning our fear of God and our love for Him. The second is in order for our love of our God and our fear of Him to be displayed through our hate for what contradicts His will, and our escape from submitting to him who distances us from obedience to Him. The third is in order for us to recognize our weakness and that without His aid, we would not be able to fulfill His will. The fourth is in order for us to deserve grace through our labor, thus enjoying favor without shame."

229   **The Brothers asked:** "Why would some Fathers become angry and sometimes escape to their cells while at other times escape from their cells if they discerned a loss, such as when John the Less went to sell the products of his labor. The camel driver spoke to him and he became angry, took his baskets and fled to his cell.[283] But Abba Agathon built a cell with brothers who were with him. When it was finished, he saw something in the place that would cause him loss so he abandoned it?"[284]

230   **The Exegete replied:** "This is because of their love of God and hatred of sin. Just as those who face fierce waves dump heavy items off their boat so that they would not cause them to drown, so too the Fathers abandoned things when they found that attachment to them would lead to sin in order not to perish through them. For the love of the world is a sin, and sin causes enmity with God, and enmity with God is fatal."

231   **The Brothers inquired:** "A holy man said: 'If you have a friend who falls into temptation, extend your hand and lift him up'. Another said: 'If you see someone who has fallen into the water extend your staff to him, because if you extend your hand and cannot lift him out, he might pull you in, drowning you both'.[285] He meant that a person should help his brother as far as he is able, for God does not ask from a person more than their capability."

232   **The Exegete replied:** "Regarding the one who extends his hand, he must be one of the Perfect holy men, such as the holy man who did so with the monk who had rejected his baptism and monastic vow for the sake of the pagan priest's daughter.[286] Those who cannot extend their hands and extend their sticks instead are the weak brothers. This denotes that they should send the one who has fallen into temptation to the experienced holy men so that they do

228 **قال المفسر** ¹¹⁶⁸ لاربعة اسباب. الاول لتتدرب نفوسنا الناطقه بمعرفة خوفنا من الله ومحبتنا له. والثاني لتظهر محبتنا لالهنا وخوفنا منه ببغضنا لمضاد ارادته. وهربنا من طاعة من يبعدنا من طاعته. الثالث لنعرف ضعفنا. وانه لولا معونته ما قدرنا نكمل ارادته. الرابع. لنستحق النعيم (d119r) باعمالنا. فنتنعم بداله بلا حيا.

229 **قال الاخوه** لماذا بعض الابا كانوا يجردون ويهربون تاره الى قلاليهم وتاره من قلاليهم اذا راوا خساره. مثل يوحنا القصير لما مضى يبيع شغل يديه. فكلمه الجمال لجرد واخذ قففه وهرب الى قلايته. وانبا اجاتن بنا قلايه هو واخوه معه. وبعد فراغها راى بالموضع شيا فيه خساره له فتركها.¹¹⁶⁹

230 **قال المفسر** من اجل حبهم لله وبغضهم للخطيه. كما ان الذين تشتد عليهم الامواج يطرحون من سفينتهم الاشيا الثقيله ليلا تكون سببا لغرقهم معها. وهكذى الابا (b63v) تركوا الاشيا التي وجدوا التمسك بها يكون سببا للخطايا (e121r) ليلا يهلكوا بها. لان محبة العالم خطية. والخطيه عداوة الله.¹¹⁷⁰ وعداوة الله مهلكه.

231 **قال الاخوه** بعض الشيوخ قال ان كان لك صديقا وسقط في تجربه فمد يدك واطلع به. وبعضهم قال ان رايت انسان وقع في الماي¹¹⁷¹ فمد له عكازك (a48v) ليلا تمد له يدك وما تقدر تصعد به فيجذبك. وتغرقان معا.¹¹⁷² عنى انه ينبغي للانسان ان يساعد اخاه بقدر قوته. فان الله ما يطلب من احد اكثر من قدرته.

232 **قال المفسر**¹¹⁷³ اما الذي يمد يده فينبغي ان يكون من الشيوخ الكاملين كما صنع ذلك¹¹⁷⁴ (d119v) الشيخ مع (c81v) الذي كفر بمعموديته ورهبنته من اجل بنت كاهن الاصنام. والذين ما يقدرون يمدون ايديهم فيمدون عكازهم. هم الاخوة الضعفا اي يرسلون الساقط في التجربه الى الشيوخ المجربين.

not end up falling with him as happened to a certain brother when his companion was fighting demonic phantoms. He went along with him to his cell to help him, but met much fiercer fighting than his companion. The holy men went looking for him and found him not yet perfect in the struggle of his way of life. Also, he who befriends a layperson who falls into temptation should help his friend through prayer, tears and counsel, and not go to him in the city and enter houses lest his eyes and ears be filled with the worries of this world. This is what befits the solitaries."

233 **The Brothers inquired:** "The Fathers advise the brothers to proceed with fear, love and zeal to receive the divine sacraments, to the banquet of fraternity, and to ablution which is similar to what our Lord did on the eve of the Passover."[287]

234 **The Exegete replied:** "Because these three illustrate all that resembles the mystery of virtue. The holy sacraments illustrate correct faith and the perfect love of God through our Lord Jesus Christ. The banquet of fraternity illustrates the love of people which resembles the love of God. The washing of the Passover illustrates the mystery of perfect humility. Through the Sacraments we recollect and contemplate the communion that we attain with our Lord Jesus Christ in the eternal bliss of His heavenly Kingdom. Through the banquet of fraternity we contemplate the communion that we attain in the Kingdom through the bliss of our love for each other. Through the washing of humility we contemplate the humility of the serving souls, I mean the saintly angels who permanently stand in the service of glorifying the Lord. Nothing endures in the spiritual way of life at the Resurrection more than this. We only seek the love of God, the love of neighbor, and humility toward all."

235 **The Brothers asked:** "A holy man said: 'It is better for a solitary to be far from the temptation of the body, because he who is near it resembles one who stands on the edge of a deep pit, making it easy for his hater to cast him into it as he wills. He who is far from it is like one who is far from the pit, making it difficult to draw him and cast him [in], and he finds space to seek help and deliverance from God'."

236 **The Exegete replied:** "Many difficult struggles take place with those in this isolation, the most difficult of which is the struggle of

ليلا يسقطوا معه كما جرى لبعض الاخوه لما كان قتال فناطس الشياطين مع صديقه. فانه مضى¹¹⁷⁵ معه الى قلايته ليعينه. فصار عليه¹¹⁷⁶ قتال صديقه ازيد منه. والشيوخ فتشوا عن هذا فوجدوه ما كان تكمل بعد (b64r) في قتال تدبيره. وايضا فالذي له صديق علماني فيسقط في تجربه فبالصلاه والدموع والمشوره ينبغي له ان يعين صديقه. لا بان يمضي اليه في المدينه ويدخل الى البيوت (e121v) ليلا يمتلي نظره وسمعه من مقلقات هذا العالم. فهذا ما يليق بالمتوحدين.

قال الاخوه ان الابا يوصون الاخوه ان يتقدموا بخوف ومحبه ونشاط لتناول السراير الالهيه. ولمايدة الاخوه. والغسل الذي هو مثال ما عمله سيدنا ليلة الفصح. 233

قال المفسر لان هذه الثلثه¹¹⁷⁷ تصور جميع شبه سر الفضيله. والسراير المقدسه تصور الايمان الصحيح وحب الله الكامل الذي بربنا يسوع المسيح. ومايدة الاخوه (a49r) تصور حب الناس المشابه بحب الله. وغسل الفصح يتصور سر الاتضاع الكامل. فبالسراير نتذكر (d120r) ونفكر في الشركه التي تكون لنا مع ربنا يسوع المسيح في النعيم الابدي في ملكوته السماييه وبمايدة الاخوه. (b64v) نفكر في الشركه التي تكون لنا في الملكوت في نعيم حب بعضنا لبعض. وبغسل الاتضاع. نفكر في اتضاع الارواح الخادمه. اعني الملايكة القديسين في دوام الوقوف في خدمة تمجيد الرب. وليس يثبت من التدبير الروحاني في القيامه ازيد¹¹⁷⁸ ونريد الا حب الله وحب القريب والاتضاع للكل.¹¹⁷⁹ 234

قال الاخوه ان شيخا قال الاجود ان يكون المتوحد بعيد من تجربة¹¹⁸⁰ الجسد. لان القريب (e122r) منها¹¹⁸¹ (c82r) يشبه القايم على فم الجب العميق. فيسهل على باغضه ان يرميه فيه كما اراد. والبعيد¹¹⁸² منها كالبعيد¹¹⁸³ من الجب فيتعسر جذبه ورميه ويجد فسحه في طلب العون من الله والنجاة. 235

قال المفسر ان حروبا كثيره وصعبه تكون مع الذين في هذه الوحده. واصعبها قتال 236

fornication which takes place with the perfect Fathers a little time before their perfection, as happened to Abba Pachomius for twelve years.[288] During the period of this struggle, the one concerned should not enter into the towns and cities, and not look at women or talk with them. The excellent Palladius set foot in one hundred and six cities and he used to go everywhere and see the Fathers and was not tempted with fornication by the Lord's command, not even in dreams. When he was fought with it, he did not leave his cell, nor look at a woman, until it left him. He went round [visiting] the Fathers to reveal his experience to them. When this struggle became severe for Abba Pachomius we would cast his spirit naked before the cave of a hyena. The last of the Fathers was called Pachomius who would take a snake from the desert and put it on his organs.[289] He would not move about in the cities. Indeed, this is the medicament for this ailment: stillness, prayer, tears, the consolation of the Fathers, distance from women's speech, gazes, and recollection. And if this was the case for the holy men who were perfect and strong, what would the case be for the youth, the weak, and the novices?"

237 **The Brothers asked:** "Abba Poemen said: 'If you hear or see visions, do not relate them to anyone, for this would be defeat'."[290]

238 **The Exegete replied:** "At first the demons fight with the solitaries in the mind through the thoughts of all the yearnings of sin. If they are defeated then they would struggle with them outwardly. They would scare them with terrifying and ugly sounds and phantasms, and at times with blows. The meaning of Abba Poemen's statement is that if you are victorious in the struggle of thoughts and are fought with phantasms and sounds then do not mention this lest they suppose from your speech that you were victorious and so find something against you for the temptation of boasting."

239 **The Brothers asked:** "A holy man said: 'If you are tempted in a place then do not move away from it during the period of temptation. Rather, stay fixed until the temptation passes so that your move would be without suspicion and sadness'."[291]

240 **The Exegete replied:** "Because in his place he is aided by the prayer of his Fathers and brothers, through the love that is between him and them, and so both would be victorious. If he departs while

الزنا الذي يكون مع الابا الكاملين من قبل كالهم بالزمان قليل. كما كان انبا باكوم مع انبا اثني عشرة[1184] سنه. ففي زمان هذا القتال ما ينبغي لصاحبه ان يدخل الى المدن والقرى ولا يرى النسا ولا (b65r) يتحدث معهن. فان الفاضل بلاديس (d120v)[1185] وطى مايه وست مدن. وكان يدور في كل مكان ويرى الابا. ولم يجرب في الزنا بامر الرب. ولا في الحلم. ولما قوتل به (a49v) ما خرج من قلايته. ولا شاهد امراه. حتى انصرف عنه. ودار على الابا ليكشف لهم تجربته. وانبا باكوم لما اشتد عليه هذا القتال كان يرمي روحه عريان قدام مغارة الضبع. اخر من الابا اسمه باكوم. اخذ من البريه ثعبانا وضعه على اعضايه. ولم يتقلب في المدن. فهذا هو دوا هذا الداء.[1186] الهدو والصلاه والدموع والعزا من الابا والبعد من كلام النساء[1187] ونظرهن وتذكارهن. واذا كان هذا للشيوخ الاقويا الكاملين فكيف (e122v) الصبيان والضعفا والمبتديين.

237 **قال الاخوه** ان انبا بجن قال ان كنت تسمع او تنظر مناظر فلا تذكرها لغيرك. فان هذا انغلاب.

238 **قال المفسر** في الاول تتقاتل الشياطين مع المتوحدين في الذهن بافكار جميع اوجاع الخطيه. فاذا غلبوا تقاتلوا معهم في الخارج (b65v) كان يخيفوهم بالمناظر واصوات قبيحه مخيفه ودفعات بالضرب. فمعنى قول انبا بجن هو انك اذا غلبت في قتال الافكار وقوتلت[1188] بالمناظر والاصوات فلا تذكر ذلك ليلا يظنوا انك غلبت من كلامك فيجدوا عليك شيا لتجربة الافتخار.[1189]

239 **قال الاخوه** ان شيخا[1190] قال ان جرت (c82v) لك تجربه في موضع فلا تنتقل منه في زمان (d121r) التجربه. بل اثبت حتى تعبر التجربه ويكون انتقالك بغير شك ولا حزن.

240 **قال المفسر** لانه في مكانه يعان بصلاة ابايه واخوته بالمحبه التي بينهم وبينه. فيريحون (a50r) هم وهو. فان خرج وهو

in his temptation they would become suspicious of him and he would lose the aid of their prayer and the consolation of their love and would then fall."

241 **He said:** "If Abba Agathon saw a brother sinning or in ignorance and judged him in his thoughts, he would say to himself: 'Why do you accuse your brother and who made you a judge over him? Do you ask after the sins of others or does God alone ask you after your sins and ignorance?' His thought would then cease."[292]

242 **The Brothers asked:** "Abba Abraham said to Abba Sisoes: 'My father, you have grown old, therefore, approach people a little'. He replied: 'Let us go to a place where there are no women'.[293] Why, then, do holy men advanced in age fear women?"

243 **The Exegete replied:** "For their sake and for the sake of their disciples. Regarding their disciples it is for the sake of the struggle of youth. As for them, it is so that they do not grow proud, lose the aid of God, and so fall. Since, every solitary who grows proud falls into the grasp of the devil of fornication in order to disgrace him with thoughts of fornication. If he were close to a woman he would fall with her. For this reason they distanced themselves from women and lived in the deserts."

244 **The Brothers asked:** "Abba Poemen said: 'How many a brother is thought to be silent but is talking all the time when silent, and another is talking all day but is silent'."[294]

245 **The Exegete replied:** "As for the one who is thought to be silent but is talking: he is silent through his lack of speech with the brothers but also [absence of] meditation through the remembrance of God. If the demons stir in his heart the recollection of a person who upset him or cursed him or quarreled with him, or of one who does not struggle as far as he is able from among the brothers, and does not chase away from his mind the thought of indignation and blame through prayer and tears and suffering, but rather accepts and consents to it, then he fights his brothers in his heart and blames them in case he reconciles with them, to such an extent that if he met with them he would fight and reproach them with his words. He wonders all day in his mind concerning the economy of the monastery, and blames the head of the monastery and his assistant, not ceasing from these thoughts by

في تجربته فهم يشكون في امره وهو يعدم عون صلاتهم وتعزية محبتهم فيسقط.

241 **وقال** ان انبا اجاث ⁱ¹⁹¹ كان اذا راى اخا¹¹⁹² يخطي او يجهل دانه في فكره يقول في نفسه لماذا تلوم اخاك ومن جعلك ديانا له. هل انت تطالب بخطايا غيرك او انا (e123r) يطالبك الله بخطاياك وجهلك فقط. فتسكن فكرته.

242 **قال الاخوه** ان ¹¹⁹³ انبا ابراهم ¹¹⁹⁴ (b66r) قال لانبا شيشاي. يا ابي قد كبرت فتقدم الى قرب الناس ¹¹⁹⁵ قليلا. فقال نمضي موضعا لا يكون فيه امراه. فلمذا الشيوخ الكبار يخافون من النسا.

243 **قال المفسر** لاجلهم ولاجل تلاميذهم. اما تلاميذهم من اجل حرب الصبى ¹¹⁹⁶ واما هم فليلا يتكبروا فتتخلا عنهم معونة الله فيسقطوا. لان كل متوحدا يتكبر يقع في يد شيطان الزنا ليفضحه بافكار ¹¹⁹⁷ الزنا. وان كان قريبا¹¹⁹⁸ من امراه¹¹⁹⁹ وقع معها. فلهذا بعدوا من¹²⁰⁰ النسا وسكنوا البراري.

244 **قال الاخوه** قال انبا بيمن كم من اخ يظن به انه ساكت وهو في كل ساعه يتكلم فهو الساكت (d121v) واخر يتكلم النهار كله وهو ساكت.

245 **قال المفسر** اما الذي يظن انه ساكت وهو يتكلم فهو الساكت في هدوه من الكلام مع الاخوه ومن الهذيان بتذكار الله ايضا. فاذا حركت الشياطين في قلبه تذكار من احزنه او شتمه او خاصمه او من لا يجاهد قدر قوته من الاخوه فليس (b66v) يطرد من ذهنه فكر الحرد والملامه بالصلاة والدموع والتوجع بل يقبله ويوافقه فيقاتل اخوته في قلبه ويلومهم (a50v) في حال صلحه معهم. (e123v) حتى انه لو اجتمع بهم لقاتلهم وبكتم (c83r) بلفظه. وطول النهار يدور بعقله في تدبير الدير. ويلوم راس الدير وخدمه ولا يقطع هذه الافكار

recalling death, the Resurrection, the Last Judgment, and requital, and not invoking the aid of the Lord through prayer, and tears and anointing oneself with oil. As for the one who talks but is silent: he is the one who in the stillness of his solitude does not speak except out of necessity in order to benefit from the Fathers and to benefit the brothers. The Fathers did not allow even the Perfect to leave their stillness for the purpose of profitable counsel rather to remain in their stillness until death because the solitary should not speak in the economy of the mind alone but also in visions. Since, after becoming perfect in keeping the Commandments and in the love of the Lord, the divine graces are renewed for him as long as he remains in stillness which enriches him until the hour of his death. If he leaves his cell and his stillness resembles that of the Perfect who does not require the stillness of solitude, then he not only loses these graces which are always renewed in stillness but he may also lose that which he possessed and his perfection would be diminished. On a similar subject the wise Evagrius said: 'It would have been better for him had he not entered into the struggle'.[295] Saint John of Thebaïs said: 'If the solitary becomes perfect in love he attains the vision of Christ. He must then remain in his stillness in order to rise through this vision to the elevated degrees which belong to the perfection of this vision'."[296]

246 **The Brothers asked:** "A brother asked a holy man: 'How can someone not blame his brother in his heart?' He replied: 'He is unable to do so unless he considers in his heart that he has been in the grave for three years'.[297] Abba Ammon reminded Abba Poemen because of his brother of one year [in the grave]."[298]

247 **The Exegete replied:** "This is because after three years the flesh and muscle of the dead disappears, and nothing remains of the heart and bodily senses with which he judges his brothers and accuses, quarrels, and reproaches them. When this one asked about the person he accused and reproached unjustly and without benefit, the holy man mentioned three years to him. And when that one was preaching to his brother in order to benefit him Abba Ammon mentioned one year."

248 **The Brothers asked:** "A certain brother said to a holy man: 'I do not find that I have a single struggle'. The holy man said to him: 'You are a *dathīr abālin* with no door for you to close, and anyone

بتذكار الموت والقيامه والدينونه والمجازاه. ولا يستدعي معونة الرب بالصلاه والدموع والتمرغ. واما المتكلم الساكت فهو الذي في[1201] هدو وحدته لا يتكلم الا لضروره الانتفاع من الابا والنفع للاخوه. والابا لم يفسحوا ولا للكاملين[1202] ان يخرجوا من هدوهم للكلام النافع. بل يمكثوا في هدوهم الى الموت. لان المتوحد ليس ينبغي ان يتكلم في تدبير الذهن فقط بل في المناظر. لانه بعد ان يكون كاملا في عمل الوصايا وفي حب الرب يتجدد له ما دام في الهدو من المواهب الالهيه ما يزيد في غناه الى ساعة[1203] موته. فان خرج[1204] من قلايته وهدوه (d122r) مثل كامل لا يحتاج الى هدو الوحده فليس انه يعدم هذه المواهب المتجدده دايما في الهدو بل وقد (b67r) يعدم مما كان بيده شيا وينقص كلاه. وعن مثل هذا قال الحكيم وغريس. كان الاجود له لو لم يدخل القتال. والقديس يحَنا التبايسي قال اذا كمل المتوحد في الحب وصل الى نظر المسيح. فينبغي له ان يثبت في هدوه ليصعد في هذا المنظر الى (e124r) الدرجات العاليات التي لكمال هذا النظر.[1205]

246 **قال الاخوه** ان اخا سال شيخا (a51r) كيف يقدر الانسان ان لا يلوم اخاه في قلبه. فاجابه ان كان ما يحسب في قلبه ان له ثلث[1206] سنين في القبر فما يقدر. وانبا امون ذكر انبا بجمن من اجل اخيه سنه واحده.

247 **قال المفسر** لان في ثلث سنين يعدم اللحم والعصب من الميت. ولا يبقا من القلب وحواس الجسد شي[1207] من هذه التي بها يدين اخوته ويلومهم ويخاصمهم ويبكتهم. فهذا لما سال عن من يلوم ويبكت بغير حق وبغير فايده ذكر له الشيخ ثلثة[1208] (c83v) سنين. وذاك لما كان يعظ اخاه لينفعه ذكر له انبا امون سنة واحده.

248 **قال الاخوه** بعض الاخوه قال لشيخ ليس اجد معي ولا حربا واحدا. فقال له الشيخ انت دثير ابالن وليس باب تغلقه وكل

who wants enters and leaves without your knowledge. Were you to make doors for yourself you would know'."[299]

249 **The Exegete replied:** "*Dathīr abālīn* is a hut by the road in which those who wish to shelter from the heat of the sun in the summer rest, and it does not have any doors. The holy man means that his senses, which are the doors of his soul, are open and neglectful of the many who enter and exit. Neglecting their discernment he does not know the evil among them. He who controls his senses in the stillness of solitude discerns the thoughts of his heart in order to cast out what is foul. All that was said by the Fathers is true regarding the difficulty of the struggle of the solitaries in their inner thoughts firstly and in their outer senses secondly which come upon them because of the envy of the demons."

250 **He said:** "As for Abba Pambo's statement: 'Every person who loves another should not say anything bad about him, and if he said anything bad about him then he hates him'.[300] That is, if he submits to lustful thoughts, obeys them and takes pleasure in them, and does not suffer from them and complain about them then he is a lover of lust. If he struggles against its thoughts and suffers and complains about them then he is not a lover of lust. If he struggles against its thoughts and suffers and complains about them then he hates it."

251 **Concerning Love and Mercy.**

252 **The Brothers asked:** "Why was the eye of that holy man's disciple plucked out through the devil's action?"[301]

253 **The Exegete replied:** "The demons tempt people in two ways: the first for the purpose of sin and the other for the purpose of good. For the purpose of sin: this resembles the trial of Saul when he submitted to the devil's deception and sinned and did not feel remorse and repent, and so God abandoned him and he died a grim death with his children. Regarding the purpose of good: it resembles the trial of Job when his goodness increased and the devil became envious of him and God allowed him to test him in order to reveal his goodness. He was overcome by great hardships. The blessed Mark stated that if the solitary sins and does not repent then the demons would torment him as with Saul, and if he repented from his sin like David then it is necessary that he be

من يشا يدخل ويخرج وانت لا تعلم. فلو اعملت لك ابوابا (d122v) علمت.

249 **قال المفسر** دثير ابالن هو عريش على الطريق يستريح فيه الذين يعبرون من حر الشمس في الصيف وليس له ابواب. (b67v) فالشيخ يعني ان حواسه التي هي ابواب نفسه مفتوحه محمله بكثرة الداخلين والخارجين وترك التميز لهم لا يدري بالاشرار منهم. فمن ضبط حواسه في هدو الوحده وميز افكار قلبه (e124v) ليطرد الردي منها.[1209] صدق كلما قيل من الابا على صعوبة القتال الذي للمتوحدين في افكارهم الباطنه اولا وحواسهم الظاهره ثانيا التي تاتي (a51v) عليهم من حسد الشياطين.

250 **وقال** اما قول ببنوده. ان كل انسانا يحب انسانا فما يقول من اجله شرا. وان قال فيه شرا فهو يبغضه. اي ان كان ينخدع لافكار الشهوات ويطيعها ويلتذ بها ولا يتالم منها[1210] ويشكوا بسببها فهو المحب الشهوات. وان كان يقاتل افكارها ويتوجع ويشكوا منها فهو لا محب[1211] الشهوات. وان كان يقاتل افكارها ويتوجع ويشكوا منها فهو يبغضها.[1212]

251 **عن الحب والرحمه.**

252 **قال الاخوه**[1213] لماذا قلعت عين تلميذ ذلك الشيخ بفعل الشيطان.

253 **قال المفسر** بنوعين تجرب الشياطين الناس. الواحد من اجل الخطيه. والاخر من اجل البر. اما من اجل[1214] الخطيه مثل محنة شاوول لما اطاع خداع الشيطان واخطا وما ندم وتاب فتخلا الله عنه (d123r) ومات هو واولاده موتا صعبا. واما من اجل البر كامتحان ايوب لما زاد بره وحسده الشيطان وخلاه الله يمتحنه ليظهر بره. فغلب عليه شدايد عظيمه. وقد ذكر الطوباني مرقس ان المتوحد اذا اخطا ولم يتوب عذب (e125r) من الشياطين (c84r) كشاوول وان (b68r) تاب من خطيته كداوود فلا بد ان يقع في

tested by the demons regarding the aforementioned sin until he becomes good through actions. For this reason it was said that if you do not want evil to happen to you then you should not wish to commit evil because that which a person sows is what he reaps. He also said that if the devil sees the righteous person in his goodness and praying in his heart, he becomes envious of him and exhausts him with severe temptations. Two types are cited in books. He said that it is written that the sinners and hypocrites oppress and it is also written that those who wish to live in the fear of God which is through Jesus Christ are oppressed. The disciple of that holy man, because his teacher toiled with him for three years was overcome by the devil the result of his sin and he plucked out his eye. He then confessed to his Father saying: 'Do not be afflicted, my Father, for I am the cause of this trial because of the strenuous fatigue that I brought upon you when you used to come and go to me. The devil caused this trial because of the sin'. When the devil saw the patience and love of the holy man and the humility of the disciple and his confession he showed his envy towards them by plucking out his other eye. This greatly afflicted them both. The cause of this trial is goodness, and God the Wise and Merciful who chastises the sinful in order to make them upright, who tests the good in order to reveal their love and courage, and in the end rewards generously and gloriously, granted this holy man favor with Him not only in this life but also after he died and passed away to Heaven. For he asked God about his disciple and God heard him, his penance was accepted and the disciple felt remorse, repented, and became good. His eyes were opened and he saw, and he became an abbot and a director for his brothers. God was praised through him and through his holy man, and the devil tempter was exposed and defeated."

254 **The Brothers asked:** "Three brothers went to a holy man and the reputation of one of them was bad. Two of them asked him to make a net for them, but he did not, then the one of reprehensible action asked him to make a net for him and he did. The other two asked him in private: 'Why did you accept with him and not with us?' He replied: 'Had I not made one for him he would have said: "The holy man has heard bad things about me and thus did not accept with me" and the love between us would have been cut'.[302] In another copy he states: 'And the rope would have been cut'.

تجربة الشياطين عن الخطية المتقدمه حتى يتبرر بالاعمال. ولذلك^{1215} قيل ان اردت ان لا يكون لك شر فلا ترد ان تصنع^{1216} شرا لان الذي يزرعه الانسان هو الذي يحصده. وذكر ايضا ان البار اذا اراه الشيطان في بره^{1217} وصلاته (a52r) القلبيه حينيذ يحسده وياتي عليه بتجارب شديده. واستشهد على النوعين بالكتب. فقال مكتوب ان الاثمه والمنافقين يضطهدون. ومكتوب ايضا ان الذين يريدون يعيشون في مخافة الله التي بيسوع المسيح يضطهدون. فتلميذ ذلك الشيخ من اجل ان معلمه تعب معه ثلث سنين تسلط عليه الشيطان بسبب خطيته وقلع عينه. واعترف لابيه حينيذ قايلا لا يصعب عليك يا ابي. فانا سبب هذه التجربه من اجل (d123v) التعب الصعب الذي جلبته عليك لما كنت تروح وتاتي الي. فهذه التجربه صنعها الشيطان من اجل الخطيه. ولما راى الشيطان صبر الشيخ ومحبته. واتضاع التلميذ واعترافه حسدها بقلع عينه الاخرى. فصعب^{1218} عليها جدا. وهذه تجربه سببها (e125v) البر. والله الحكيم الرحيم الذي يودب الخطاه^{1219} من اجل استقامتهم. ويمتحن الابرار لاظهار حبهم وشجاعتهم. ويجازي بالكرامه (b68v) والمجد اخيرا. منح هذا الشيخ عنده داله. وليس في هذه الحياة^{1220} فقط بل وبعد ان تنيح ومضى^{1221} الى الفردوس. فانه سال الله عن تلميذه وسمع له. وقبلت توبته فندم التلميذ وتاب وتبرر وانفتحت عيناه وابصر وصار ريسا ومدبرا لاخوته. وتمجد الله فيه وفي شيخه. وافتضح الشيطان المجرب وغلب.

254 **قال الاخوه** مضت ثلثة^{1222} اخوه الى شيخ وكانت سمعت احدهم رديه (c84v) فطلبا الاثنان منه ان يعمل لها شبكه (a52v) فما فعل وساله المذموم الفعل^{1223} ان يعمل له شبكه ففعل. فقالا^{1224} له بينها وبينه لماذا قبلت منه ولم تقبل منا. فقال لو لم اعمل له كان يقول ان الشيخ سمع عني الردي ولم يقبل مني وينقطع الحب بيننا.^{1225} وفي نسخة اخرى ينقطع الحبل

Therefore, which of these is more correct: the love would have been cut or the rope would have been cut?"

255 **The Exegete replied:** "The rope would have been cut is more correct because it is representative of hope, for it is written: 'Let us be firm in hope which is for us like an anchor'.[303] It is also written that hope is a spiritual rope which raises the mind from the ground and ties it to Heaven, to our Lord the Anchor, in order for the waves not to move the ship far away which are the divisions of thoughts and the cutting off of hope."

256 **The Brothers asked:** "Why did Abba Sisoes during the first days of the fast give food and drink early to the bishop of Nablus [Neapolis] and the brothers who were with him?"[304]

257 **The Exegete replied:** "The holy Fathers are above the law as is written. The good are not subject to a law, and they teach us that love is the master of every action, better than all virtues, and more sublime than all graces as Paul the Apostle wrote.[305] And because of his eminence in fasting and asceticism and the other labors, he is found in the Kingdom without these. I mean that the love of God and the love of neighbor is perfected there by the angels and saints without fasting and asceticism, and the holy man wished to reveal the excellence of love over fasting. He therefore compelled the bishop and those with him to eat early during the first week of the fast, and before leaving him. Mark had explained the words of our Lord that the last shall be first[306] through a spiritual explanation that is consistent with his life. He stated that the last is love because you reach it and perfect it at the end of virtuous actions. When you reach it you find that it is first and all those virtues come after it, as is written: 'He who loves his neighbor has fulfilled the law',[307] and the law and prophecies are connected to the love of God and love of neighbor. This is permissible for the perfect Fathers who have overcome and crossed over from restraint to the harbor of love, but not for the weak and the novices since weakness and youth require restraint."

258 **The Brothers asked:** "A solitary was in an exalted way of life which coincided with the arrival of strangers to the monastery who forced him to eat with them against his habit. After this the brothers said to him: 'How difficult this was for you O father'. He replied: 'My difficulty is not to cut off my desire'."[308]

فاي ما اصح ينقطع الحب او ينقطع (d124r) الجبل.

255 **قال المفسر** ينقطع الجبل اصح لانه ممثل بالرجا فقد كتب لنثبت بالرجا الذي هو لنا مثل المرسا ومكتوب ايضا ان الرجا هو حبل روحاني يرفع الذهن من الارض ويعقده في السما (e126r) بربنا المرسا.[1226] ليلا تبعد الامواج السفينه التي هي تقسيم الافكار[1227] وقطع الرجا.

256 **قال الاخوه** لماذا انبا شيشاي في الايام الاوله التي للصوم[1228] اطعم وسقا باكرا اسقف نابلس هو والاخوه الذين معه.

257 (b69r) **قال المفسر** ان الابا القديسين هم فوق الناموس كما[1229] كتب. ان الصالحين ليس عليم ناموس. وهم يعلمونا ان الحب هو سيد كل عمل. وافضل من كل فضيله. واجل من جميع المواهب. كما كتب بولص الرسول. ولشرفه على الصوم والنسك وباقي الاعمال يوجد في الملكوت دون هذه. اعني يتكمل هناك حب الله وحب القريب من الملايكه والقديسين دون الصوم والنسك. والشيخ اراد ان يظهر فضيله الحب على الصوم. فالزم الاسقف ومن معه ياكلوا باكرا في الجمعه الاولى من الصوم. فقبل ان يمضوا (a53r) من عنده. وقد فسر مرقس قول ربنا الاخرون يصيرون اولين تفسيرا روحانيا يلايم سيرته. فقال ان الاخير هو الحب لانك في اخر عمل الفضايل تصل اليه وتكمله. فاذا (c85r/d124v) وصلت اليه وجدته هو الاول وتلك الفضايل كلها تتبعه كما كتب ان من احب قريبه فقد اكمل الناموس. وان الناموس والنبوات متعلقه بحب (e126v) الله وحب القريب وهذا انما يجوز للابا الكاملين الذين غلبوا وعبروا من التحفظ الى مينا الحب. فاما الضعفا والمبتديون[1230] فلا. لان الضعف والصبا محتاج الى التحفظ.

258 **قال الاخوه** كان متوحد في تدبير عظيم. فاتفق مجي غربا الى الدير وغصبوه (b69v) ان ياكل معهم بغير عادته. وبعد ذلك[1231] قال له الاخوه ما صعب عليك ايها الاب. فقال صعوبتي ان لا اقطع[1232] هواي.

259   **The Exegete replied:** "That is: 'During the period of fasting I cut off my desire which tricks me into eating, and during the period of love I cut off my desire which tricks me into fasting and prohibits me from loving the brothers'."

260   **The Brothers asked:** "Abba Isidore used to say at all times the following: 'It is written: forgive your brother that you may be forgiven'.[309] Why did he only say this?"

261   **The Exegete replied:** "Because all goodness is perfected through two commandments: the love of God and the love of neighbor; and all sins consist of two parts: hypocrisy towards God and sinfulness towards one's neighbor. If we forgive our brothers it is for the sake of God who said: 'Forgive and you will be forgiven. And if you do not forgive your brothers as your Father who is in Heaven forgives you, you will not be forgiven'.[310] We are purified from sin, and love has perfected us and we will be saved from Hell and attain Paradise."

262   **The Brothers asked:** "The early Fathers used to go to the cells of the new brothers living in solitude and those of them they found harmed they brought to the community and prepared a wash-basin for them containing water and prayed over it. All the brothers washed their feet in it and they poured [the water] from it onto the brother who was immediately cleansed."[311]

263   **The Exegete replied:** "This is because the novices in solitude grow very weary through labors, and become proud. Therefore, the Fathers carry out for them what resembles the washing of humility. All the brothers wash their feet in it [wash basin] and pour [water] from it onto the brother who was harmed by proud thoughts if he considered that he was superior to them. They then return him to his cell to labor in accordance with his initial service and he becomes calm and puts the devil to shame. A brother used to treat his brother haughtily. Saint Isaac instructed him to wash the straps of his shoes with water and to drink from it. As a result of his obedience and humility the struggle with pride left him and he thanked God."

264   **The Brothers asked:** "It is said that a holy man who was ill in Scete had the appetite for a little soft bread. When one of the brothers heard this he went to Egypt and brought him some. He,

259 **قال المفسر** اي في زمان الصوم قطعت هواي الذي يخدعني للاكل. وفي[1233] زمان الحب قطعت هواي[1234] الذي يخدعني بالصوم ويمنعني من حب الاخوه.

260 **قال الاخوه** ان انبا ايسيدرس كان في كل وقت يقول هذه الكلمه. مكتوب اغفر لاخيك حتى يغفر لك. فلماذا كان يقول هذه الكلمه فقط.

261 **قال المفسر** لان جميع البر يكمل بوصيتين.[1235] حب الله وحب القريب. وكل الخطايا على قسمين. النفاق على الله. والاثم في القريب. فان غفرنا لاخوتنا من اجل الله القايل اغفروا يغفر لكم. وان لم تغفروا لاخوتكم (a53v) كما يغفر لكم ابوكم الذي في[1236] السما.[1237] لم يغفر لكم.[1238] نقينا من الخطايا وكملنا الحب (d125r) ونخلص من الجحيم وننال النعيم.

262 **قال الاخوه** ان الابا الاولين[1239] كانوا يمضوا (e127r) الى قلالي الاخوه الجدد في الوحده ومن وجدوه تاذى احضروه الى المجمع وعملوا له قصريه فيها ما وصلوا عليه. وغسلت الاخوه جميعهم ارجلهم فيه. وسكبوا منه على الاخ فيخلص لوقته.

263 **قال المفسر** (b70r) لان المبتدين في الوحده يتعبون في الاعمال كثيرا. فيتكبرون. فتعمل لهم الابا مثل[1240] (c85v) غسل الاتضاع. وتغسل فيه جميع الاخوه ارجلهم. ويسكبون منه على الاخ الذي قد تاذى من فكر الكبريا اذا ظن انه افضل منهم. ويردونه الى قلايته يعمل في خدمته الاولى فيستريح ويخزى الشيطان. وقد كان اخ يتكبر على اخيه. فامره مار اسحاق ان يغسل سيور حذايه بماء[1241] ويشرب منه. ومن اجل طاعته واتضاعه بعد عنه قتال الكبريا وشكر الله.

264 **قال الاخوه** قيل عن[1242] شيخ انه مريض في الاسقيطي فاشتهى[1243] قليل خبز لين. ولما سمع بعض الاخوه مضى[1244] الى مصر واحضر له.

however, refused to eat it saying: 'This is blood, my brother'. They asked him not to reject the will of his brother, he then put his will to rest and ate."[312]

265 **The Exegete replied:** "He imitated the joyful David when the inhabitants of Palestine were ready to fight the Israelites. A little before drawing up battle lines with them he desired water and said: 'Who will give me a drink of water from the big well in Bethlehem?'[313] When they heard him, three men set off and took with them three waterskins. They broke through the Philistine army and brought him the water. When he saw this he was amazed and said: 'They risked shedding their blood', meaning: 'Because of their love for me they disregarded their lives'. As a result, he did not drink but poured out the waterskins before God like burnt offerings because they were saved from death. Similarly, when this holy man witnessed the love of the brother and his act he thought to himself saying: 'Perhaps my brother would have fallen into temptation while on his way because of me'. He, therefore, did not eat. When the Fathers saw the love of these two and their humility, they asked the holy man to eat so that the effort of the brother would not go to waste and he would then become sorrowful. He ate, therefore, in order to obey them and relieve the thought of the brother."

266 **He said:** "Abba Poemen used say while sighing: 'All virtues have entered this house except for one, which is that a person despise and blame himself'.[314] Meaning that suffering, regret and tears wash the heart from filthy thoughts, however, pride follows on tears. By 'house' and 'monastery' the Fathers might mean the solitary way of life as Antony said: 'If there was to be patience in this monastery then it ascends over everyone'.[315] Meaning that the forbearance of the solitary towards the temptations and struggles that come upon him defeats the demons and he is liberated from yearnings."

267 **The Brothers asked:** "When the good king Theodosius the Less entered the cell of that solitary he said: 'I was brought up in royalty and have never been satisfied with bread and water except on this day'."[316]

268 **The Exegete replied:** "He used to be satisfied with sumptuous food but which was mixed with worldly yearnings. For this reason he said: 'Blessed are you because you are free of the concerns of

فما رضى ياكله. وقال هذا هو دم اخي. فسالوه ان لا يذل ارادة اخيه. فنبح ارادته واكل.

265 **قال المفسر** انه تشبه بداوود المغبوط لما كان اهل فلسطين مستعدين لقتال الاسراييليين. فن قبل مصافتهم (d125v) بقليل اشتهى ماء[1245] وقال من (e127v) يعطيني شربة ماء[1246] (a54r) من الجب الكبير الذي في بيت لحم. فلما سمعوه مضى ثلثة[1247] رجال واخذوا معهم ثلثة[1248] قرب وشقوا العسكر الفلسطيني واحضروا له الماي.[1249] فلما راه تعجب وقال جسروا على اهراق دمهم. اي من اجل (b70v) حبهم لي تهاونوا بحياتهم. فلم يشرب بل سكب القرب قدام الله مثل قربان ومحرقه من اجل انهم خلصوا من الموت. وهكذى هذا الشيخ لما راى حب الاخ وفعله افتكر قايلا لعل اخي كان يسقط بسببي في تجربة فامتنع من الاكل. والابا لما راوا حبها واتضاعها سالوا الشيخ ان ياكل لكيلا[1250] يضيع تعب الاخ فيحزن.[1251] فاكل من اجل طاعتهم ونيح فكرة الاخ.

266 **وقال** ان انبا بجن كان يقول وهو يتنهد. جميع الفضايل دخلت الى هذا البيت ما خلا واحده. وهو ان يحتقر الانسان نفسه (c86r) ويلومها. يعني ان الالم والندم والدموع تغسل القلب من الافكار الوسخه. لكن الكبريا تتبع الدموع. والابا قد يعنون بالبيت والدير تدبير الوحده. كما قال انطونيوس. ان كان يكون في هذا الدير طول روح فهو يرتفع على الكل. اي ان صبر المتوحد على ما ياتي عليه من التجارب والحروب فهو يغلب (e128r) الشياطين. وينعتق من الاوجاع.

267 **قال الاخوه** الملك البار تاودسيوس (d126r) الصغير لما دخل قلاية ذلك[1252] المتوحد قال اني تربيت في (b71r) الملك وما شبعت خبزا ولا ماء (a54v)[1253] سوا هذا اليوم.

268 **قال المفسر** هو كان يشبع من الاطعمة الفاخره. لكن مخلوطه بالام العالميه. ولهذا قال طوباكم لانكم معتوقون من اهتام

this world, and we are troubled with its care'. And because he had grown tired and hungry in the wilderness, then entered upon the solitary to find him in stillness, fasting and prayer, grace came upon him. When he offered him dry bread moistened with water, and with oil and salt on it, he found it to be delicious because of his weariness, hunger, elevated thoughts relating to love of virtue and his having been awoken by grace."

269 **The Brothers asked:** "The brother wearing a mat[317] said to Abba Ammon: 'I would like to be either a wanderer, or an itinerant, or secluded in a cell for two days [at a time without eating]'. He advised him to sit in a cell and not leave it except on Sunday, to fast only until evening, and that he should keep in his heart at all times the words of the tax collector: 'God, have mercy on me a sinner and pity me'."[318]

270 **The Exegete replied:** "This brother was excellent in his labors but lacked humility. He therefore advised him how to gain humility, for the Fathers advise each person how to remove their ailment and protect their health."

271 **The Brothers asked:** "Abba Ammon set off to Antony but lost his way. He opened his hands towards Heaven and prayed saying: 'O Lord do not destroy that which you have fashioned'. Then a hand appeared to him which showed him the way and he reached him safely.[319] Two brothers also set off to him, they lost their way and one of them died of thirst while the other revealed to the saint that it was because of him. He sent some brothers who carried him and brought him, and he did not die [after all]."

272 **The Exegete replied:** "We stated earlier that these are the actions of God which a person in this world does not recognize. However, we know that God guides people to two ways of life: he guides the good and perfect to a way of life that is particular to them; and he guides all people to a general way of life for them. Regarding his close followers he said: 'He who loves me keeps my words and my Father will love him, and my father and I will come and make him our place of abode'.[320] Such a person would be in a great [state of] observance. Abba Ammon, the disciple of Antony was the abbot of a monastery and became a bishop. He was perfect in the solitary way of life and God guided him to a way of life which was particular to him. The two brothers were at a minor stage in the

هذا العالم. ونحن اهتمامه يعذبنا. ولانه كان قد تعب في البريه وجاع. فدخل الى المتوحد فوجده هاديا صايما مصليا. فزارته النعمه. ولما قدم له خبزا يابسا مبلولا[1254] بماي[1255] وعليه زيت وملح. طاب له من اجل[1256] تعبه وجوعه وعلو فكرته في حب الفضيله وتنبيه النعمه له.

269 **قال الاخوه** ان الاخ اللابس الحصير قال لانبا امون اريد ان اكون اما سايحا واما منتقلا واما منحبسا في قلايه واطوي يومين. فاشار عليه بان يجلس في القلايه ولا يخرج منها الى يوم الاحد. ويصوم الى عشيه فقط. ويكون في قلبه كل ساعه كلمة العشار. اللهم اغفر لي انا الخاطي وتحنن علي.

270 **قال المفسر** ان هذا الاخ كان فاضلا في اعماله وناقصا في اتضاعه. فاشار عليه بما يقتني به الاتضاع. فان الابا يشيرون على كل واحد بما يزيل مرضه ويحفظ صحته.

271 (e128v) **قال الاخوه** ان انبا امون مضى الى انطونيوس. فضل في الطريق. فبسط يديه الى السما وصلى قايلا يا رب لا تهلك جبلتك (c86v/d126v) فترات (b71v)[1257] له يد تريه الطريق ووصل سالما اليه. واخوان مضيا اليه ايضا. فضلا في الطريق ومات احدها بالعطش. والاخر كشف للقديس (a55r)[1258] بسببه. فنفذ اخوه حملوه واتوا به ولم يمت.

272 **قال المفسر** قد قلنا فيما[1259] تقدم ان هذه اعمال الله التي لا يدركها انسان في هذا العالم. لكنا نعرف ان الله يدبر الناس بنوعين. فيدبر الابرار الكاملين تدبيرا خاصا بهم. ويدبر كل الناس تدبيرا عاما لهم. وعن خواصه قال. من يحبني يحفظ قولي وابي يحبه. وانا وابي ناتي ونتخذه لنا مسكنا. فهذا يكون في حفظ عظيم. فانبا امون تلميذ انطونيوس كان ريس دير وصار اسقفا. وكان في تدبير الوحده كاملا. وكان الله يدبره تدبيرا يخصه. والاخوان كانا في درجة صغيره في

community of general communion. When they lost their way they were struck by that which strikes many people."

273 **The Holy Man replied:** "The brothers lose their way through each other for two reasons: the first is if the person does not become perfect in love and humility and is purified of all yearnings and becomes perfect in love for all people and considers everyone to be pure like him, as is written: 'For the pure everything is pure'.[321] If a brother enters [his cell] even if he has not yet become perfect, nevertheless, in the stillness of the cell he is in sadness, suffering, tears and remorse, and his mind is vigilant in the observation of his sins and the recognition of his yearnings, and his only desire is to perfect himself, then too, if a brother entered [the cell] of such [a solitary] he would not lose his way through him, even if he was dissolute and neglectful, because of the vigilance of his mind and the recollection of his sins and his concern with his own uprightness. For this reason he does not see the shortcomings of the brother. As for the one whose heart is empty of the pain of remorse and sadness for his sins, he sees the shortcomings of him who enters [his cell] and is suspicious of him and blames him in his thoughts. Sometimes he reproaches him to his face because of what he sees or hears from him in terms of a slight shortcoming or a rude word. After he departs he remembers his shortcomings and accuses him in his thoughts, then complains about him in his heart, meaning that his entry into [his cell] caused him a great loss. As for Abba Poemen, he urges us to always lamentingly recall our sins, and to sigh, in order not to look at the shortcomings of our brothers that we may become worthy of the perfection of humility and love."

274 **The Brothers asked:** "Saint Antony said: 'I saw all the snares of the devil set in the ground. I sighed and said: Woe unto us, who can escape from these? I was then told that humility is what rescues [us] from them'. Did he see them with his eyes or in his mind, and how does humility rescue [us] from them?"[322]

275 **The Exegete replied:** "Abba Macarius also saw in the inner desert all the snares of the devil. He saw the image of two men, one of whom was wearing a perforated robe which was covered with colored things; and the other was wearing a damp cloak on his entire body, and many glass bottles were strung to it. Each of them

مجمع الشركة العامة. فلما ضلا اصابها[1260] ما يصيب كثيرا من الناس.

273 **وقال الشيخ** لسببين ما تخسر الاخوه بعضهم من بعض. احدهما اذا ما كل الانسان في الحب والاتضاع وتنقى من جميع الاوجاع وتكمل في الحب لكل انسان[1261] فحسب[1262] الكل مثله انقيا. (e129r) كما هو مكتوب ان كل شيا طاهر للاطهار. فاذا دخل اليه اخ ولو كان الذي لم يكمل بعد لكنه في سكنة القلايه يكون في حزن والم ودموع وندامه. وعقله متيقظا لنظر خطاياه وفهم (b72r) اوجاعه. وليس له حرص الا (d127r) تكميل ذاته. فهذا ايضا اذا دخل اليه اخ ما يخسر منه لو كان منحلا ومتوانيا من اجل تيقظ ذهنه وتذكر خطاياه واهتمامه باستقامة ذاته. فلهذا ما يرى نقص الاخ. فاما من قلبه فارغ من الم الندم والحزن على (a55v) خطاياه فهو ينظر نقص من يدخل اليه فيشكك فيه ويلومه في فكره. في بعض الاوقات يبكته (c87r) في وجهه بسبب ما يراه. او يسمع منه من نقص يسير او كلمه بغير ادب. وهو بعد خروجه يتذكر نقصه ويلومه في فكره. ثم يتذمر عليه في قلبه. بمعنى[1263] ان دخوله اليه قد سبب له خسرانا كثيرا. فاما انبا بمن يحرصنا[1264] على ان نتذكر خطايانا دايما بتوجع. ونتهد لكيلا ننظر الى نقص[1265] اخوتنا حتى نستحق كمال الاتضاع والحب.[1266]

274 **قال الاخوه** ان القديس انطونيوس قال. اني رايت جميع فخاخ الشيطان منصوبه على الارض. فتنهدت وقلت الويل لنا من الذي يخلص من هذه. فقيل لي الاتضاع يخلص منها. فهل راها بنظره (e129v) او بعقله. وكيف يخلص منها الاتضاع.

275 **قال المفسر** ان انبا مقار ايضا راى في البريه الداخله جميع فخاخ الشيطان. فراى شبه رجلين احدهما كان عليه ثوب مثقبا وفيه اشياء[1267] ملونه والاخر كان لابسا ثوبا باليا على جسده (b72v/d127v) جميعه. وقد شال فيه قواوير كثيره. ولكل منها

had wings that resembled covers, and he was wrapped in it.[323] This he saw with his bodily eyes. As for Antony, he saw with the eye of the mind the snares which the devil set for the solitaries through which he obstructs, fetters and hinders them from proceeding along the path of virtue as is written: 'Along the path of my course they buried a trap for me and the cords of their nets they have spread along my routes'.[324] When he saw them he was astonished and bewildered because of the number of nooses and the mesh knotted into them and the wild beasts which were falling into their small openings and not escaping from them. He saw all the yearnings of the body and the soul with which the demons fight all the solitaries, and the angels showed them and made them known to him, each by its name, I mean: gluttony, fornication, love of silver, vainglory, pride and the rest. When he became bewildered he sighed and cried and said: 'Woe unto us, how will we escape?' The angels then said to him: 'Through humility and those actions it necessitates'. Just as actions without humility corrupt like fatty meat without salt, so too humility alone without works is of no benefit like salt on its own."

276 **He also said:** "It is necessary for the solitary to imitate the blind man whose story is written in the Gospel. His cry: 'O son of David, have mercy on me!'[325] is the fervent prayer of the solitary through which he cries in his mind saying: 'O son of God, have mercy on me!' And the cry of the throngs for him to be silent is his hindrance by the demons through their thoughts and fright in order that his prayer cease. Our Lord stopping and summoning him is the aid of our Lord which comes to the solitary during the time of his temptation. Those who said to him: 'Rise, for He is calling you'[326] are the angels who render to him the aid of God. The casting away of his garment and his rising to the Lord is the leaving aside of everything that prevents his mind from communicating with God, and his entreating the Lord with increased effort is when His aid and the hope of His salvation came to him and his eyes were opened. His praise of God is the light of the solitary's heart after the completion of [spiritual] exertion and seeing the light of Christ and his praise of the Father and of the Son and of the Holy Spirit, the one God. He who wishes to achieve this must weary himself through stillness and bodily labor, and must undertake a great battle with all base thoughts which stir in

اجنحه شبه غطا. وهو ملتف به. وهذا[1268] راه بعين الجسد. واما انطونيوس فراى بعين العقل مناصب الشيطان للمتوحدين[1269] التي بها يعرقلهم ويكتفهم ويعوقهم من السير في طريق الفضيله. كما كتب ان في طريق مسيري دفنوا لي فخا وحبال شباكهم بسطوا على مسالكي. ولما راها تعجب وتحير (a56r) من كثرة الشرك والزرد المعقوده فيها والوحوش التي تقع في عيونها وما تتخلص منها. فراى جميع اوجاع الجسد والنفس التي بها تقاتل الشياطين كل المتوحدين. والملايكه اروها له وعرفوه بها. كل واحد باسمه. اعني محبة البطنه والزنا ومحبة الفضه والمجد الفارغ والكبريا والباقي. ولما تحير تنهد وبكا وقال الويل لنا كيف نخلص. فقالت له الملايكه بالاتضاع وما يلزمه من الاعمال. (c87v) فكما ان الاعمال بغير اتضاع تفسد كلحم سمين بغير ملح. كذلك[1270] الاتضاع وحده بغير الاعمال[1271] (e130r) ما ينفع كالملح وحده.

وقال ايضا ينبغي للمتوحد ان يتشبه بالاعمى المكتوب خبره في الانجيل.[1272] فصراخه يا ابن داوود[1273] ارحمني. هي صلاة المتوحد بلا فتور التي فيها يصرح بعقله قايلا. يا ابن الله ارحمني. وصياح الجموع (b73r) عليه ليسكت هو تعويق الشياطين له بافكارهم وتخوفهم (d128r) لتنقطع صلاته. ووقوف ربنا واستدعاه اليه هو عون ربنا الذي ياتي للمتوحد في زمان تجربته. والذين قالوا له قم فها هو يدعوك. هم الملايكه الذين يخدمون عون الله له. وتعريه ونهوضه الى الرب هو ترك كل ما يعوقه عن اتصال[1274] عقله بالله وطلبه الى الرب بزيادة اجتهاد عندما اتته معونته ورجا خلاصه وانفتاح عينيه. وتمجده لله هو نور (a56v) قلب المتوحد بعد كمال الجهاد. ونظر نور المسيح وتمجيده للاب والابن والروح[1275] القدس الاله الواحد. فالذي يريد يصل الى هذا يتعب في الهدو وفي اعمال الجسد. ويصنع حربا عظيما[1276] مع جميع الافكار الرديه التي تتحرك في

276

his heart from the recollections of wicked demons, and all the more with thoughts which glorify him and blame others, and magnify him while despising others. His heart becomes filled with anger, struggle, envy, boasting and pride. These things prevent him from purifying the heart of yearnings, thus depriving him from the divine light which illuminates the heart during the time of prayer as the Fathers stated."

277 **He also said:** "We must be humble at all times. During the period of struggle with yearnings and demons let us undertake labor and become strong through forebearance. During the period of peace and relief from yearnings let us keep from falling into pride. For our Lord does not wish that we should be in strife at all times and so he overshadows us with His power. We must, therefore, be humble and know that our rest from the difficulty of struggle is because of His care, therefore, there is no time in which the solitary does not require humility, nor also a place or action, but rather he requires it necessarily in all things."

278 **The Brothers asked:** "Abba Poemen said: 'Humility is seasoned with salt'. What is the salt of humility?"[327]

279 **The Exegete replied:** "It is the discernment by which a person knows to whom he should be humble, for what reason and when, and towards whom he should be haughty, why and when, as our Lord, in addition to his Apostles and the other most excellent leaders, acted at certain times, when they would demonstrate a dryness and would reproach and act justly for the sake of stature. The purpose behind the humility and the demonstration of haughtiness is one, namely, the success of the head and the benefit of those who are under his authority."

280 **The Brothers asked:** "Macarius the Egyptian's direction of all the brothers was without wickedness. People used to say to him: 'Why do you humble yourself in this way?' He replied: 'For twelve years I have been asking the Lord to grant me this gift, and you are advising me that I should abandon it? If a brother sins in front of one who is not wicked then he should not carry the pain of him who has fallen into wickedness'."[328]

281 **The Exegete replied:** "If the solitary enters into stillness then he is first deceived by the demons through thoughts and yearnings.

قلبه من تذكارات الشياطين الاشرار. وبالاكثر الافكار التي تمجده وتلوم غيره وتعظمه وتحتقر غيره. وتملا قلبه غضبا وحربا وحسدا وافتخارا (e130v)[1277] وكبريا. فان هذه تعدمه نقا القلب من الاوجاع. فيعدم النور الالهي الذي يضي في وقت الصلاه في القلب كما قالت الابا.

277 **قال ايضا** ينبغي لنا نتضع[1278] في كل زمان. في زمان قتال الاوجاع والشياطين لنعان على العمل ونقوى على الصبر. وفي زمان (b73v) السلامه (d128v) والراحه من الاوجاع لنتحفظ من سقطة الكبريا. فربنا ما يشا ان نكون في الضيق كل حين. فيظللنا بقوته فيجب ان نتضع ونعلم ان (c88r) راحتنا من ضيق القتال. انما هي من عنايته. فاذن ليست وقت لا يحتاج المتوحد فيه الى الاتضاع. ولا مكان ايضا ولا فعل. بل هو محتاج اليه في كل شي بالضروره.

278 **قال الاخوه** ان انبا بيمن قال ان[1279] الاتضاع متبل بالملح فما هو ملح الاتضاع.

279 **قال المفسر** هو الافراز الذي به يعرف الانسان لمن يتضع ولاي سبب ومتى وعلى من يتكبر ولماذا ومتى كما فعل ربنا ورسله وباقي المدبرين الافضال في بعض (a57r) الاوقات. اذا كانوا يظهرون الجفا. ويبكتون ويعدلون من اجل البنيان. فيكون القصد بالاتضاع وبالاظهار الترفع واحدا. وهو ربح المدبر وانتفاع المدبرين.

280 **قال الاخوه** ان مقاريوس المصري كان تدبيره مع (e131r) جميع الاخوه بغير شر.[1280] وكان قوم يقولون له لماذا تتضع هكذى. فقال لهم هذه اثنيعشره[1281] سنه وانا اسال[1282] الرب ان يعطيني هذه العطيه. وانتم تشيرون علي ان اتركها. فان كان اخ يخطي. قدام من ليس له شر فما ينبغي له ان يحمل معه الم (d129r) الذي سقط في الشر.

281 **قال المفسر** (b74r) اذا دخل المتوحد الى الهدو فانه يخدع من الشياطين اولا فاولا في الافكار والاوجاع.

The struggle increases little by little. If he achieves purity of heart then difficult struggles come upon him which are above his strength. As Abba Evagrius said: '[These] actions include the fury of the demons towards us. When the evils which are within us depart from the soul due its continuous expulsion and distancing of them, then they [demons] resist the soul to the point of drawing blood until the soul is weakened and reaches the point of loss of hope. Then love appears through God and the effort in struggling to obey Him, and blessed is the soul which was worthy of these struggles for the sake of Christ. If it transcends these struggles then the solitary is worthy of purity of heart and seeing the light of his mind and he becomes disposed to it. Then he sees wickedness and hears it as though he does not see or hear it', as is stated in this report.[329] The words of the Apostle complete it: 'All things are pure for the pure'.[330] He no longer recognizes a sinful or wretched person as he used to and he does not rage against or hate in his heart the one who behaves ignorantly towards or trespasses against him. As the good God when he demonstrates ardor, then chastisement and benefit like a wise father with his beloved son. And God made people pray to Him through the toils of labor so that they attain through action the resemblance of God's goodness and mercy. As is written: 'The Creator knows His creation'.[331] Because of this resemblance the Fathers said that Abba Macarius became an earthly god. In some of his sayings it was written that he who knows the Truth does not judge anyone: neither sinners, nor Jews, nor Pagans, nor their wicked acts. He whose mind's eye is pure does not see darkness in it."

282 **He also said:** "There is no person in whom a foul thought, which comes from the deception of the demons, does not stir, because if they could stir in people the thought of blasphemy against God then how much the more blasphemy against people. I mean cursing, disdaining, blaming and belittling them. However, it was said of Abba Poemen that such a thought never lingered in his heart, rather, he would expel it as soon as it occurred in his mind. His mind was alert and had foresight, as he used to say: 'A person does not need anything other than an alert mind that is zealous in discerning thoughts and active in expelling from it what is foul with natural indignation and keen prayer'."[332]

ويتزايد الحرب قليلا قليلا. فاذا وصل الى نقاوة القلب تاتي عليه الحروب الصعبه فوق قوته. كما قال انبا وغريس. ان من الاعمال تخنق الشياطين علينا. والشرور التي فينا عندما تنتقل من النفس لاستمرار طردها لها وابعادها[1283] اياها. فتقف في مقاومة النفس الى الدم حتى تضعف النفس وتصل الى قطع الرجا. وحينيذ تظهر الحب في الله والنشاط في جهاد طاعته وطوبى للنفس التي استحقت (c88v) هذه الحروب من اجل المسيح. فاذا عبرت هذه الحروب[1284] استحق المتوحد نقاوة القلب ونظر نور ذهنه. ويصير لها ارضيا. وحينيذ يبصر الشر ويسمعه. وكانه لم يبصره ولم يسمعه. كما (a57v) قيل في هذا الخبر. ويكمل عليه قول الرسول (e131v) ان كلشي[1285] طاهر للاطهار. ولا يرجع يعرف انسانا خاطيا ولا حقيرا كما كان. ولا يحرد ولا يحقد بقلبه على من يجهل او من يسى[1286] اليه. كشبه الله الصالح ان اظهر حررا[1287] فالتاديب والنفع كالاب الحكيم مع ولده المحبوب. (b74v) وهذا جعل الله البشر يصلون (d129v) اليه باتعاب الاعمال. فيصلون بالفعل الى التشبه بجود الله ورحمته. كما هو مكتوب ان الصانع يعرف صنعته فلهذا التشبه قال الابا ان الاب مقاريوس صار الها[1288] ارضيا. وقد كتب في بعض اقواله ان الذي يعرف الحق لا يدين انسانا لا الخطاه ولا اليهود ولا الحنفا ولا باعمالهم الرديه. والذي عين ذهنه نقيه ليس يرى[1289] فيه ظلمه.

282 **وقال ايضا** ليس احد من الناس لا يتحرك فيه الفكرة الرديه الذي من خداع الشياطين. لانهم اذا كانوا يقدرون يحركون في الناس فكرة التجديف على الله. فكم بالحري النجديف على الناس. اعني شتمهم واحتقارهم[1290] وملامتهم[1291] وتنقيصهم[1292]. لكن قيل عن انبا بجمن ان هذه الفكره ما كانت تبطي في قلبه البته. لكنه يطردها من ابتدا خطورها بباله.[1293] وانه كان عقله مستيقظا وينظر الى ما ياتي. كما كان يقول ليس يحتاج انسان الى شي اخر غير عقل (e132r) متيقظ حريص على تمييز[1294] الافكار نشيطا[1295] الى طرد الردي منها بغضب[1296] طبيعي وصلاه حاده.

283 **The Brothers asked:** "When the devil struggled with Abba Isidore mouth to mouth [face to face],³³³ he said: 'There is no one like you among the Fathers'. He replied: 'I am not like Saint Antony nor like Abba Agathon'. Why did he only mention these two from among the Fathers?"

284 **The Exegete replied:** "This is because in his day Antony was more elevated than all the holy men and Agathon was more elevated than all the brothers. He, therefore, replied to him: 'How is it you said "There is no one like you among the Fathers" and I am not glorified among the early Fathers as Saint Antony is nor known among the later Fathers as Abba Agathon is?'"

285 **The Brothers asked:** "Theophilus, the Patriarch of Alexandria said to the abbot of the monastery of Barbūnij: 'What additional matter did you encounter on the path of the solitary life?' He replied: 'I used to blame myself at all times'."³³⁴

286 **The Exegete replied:** "This is because this is the perfection of the solitary and not as some people think – that their perfection is only through spiritual visions. Rather, it is through perfect humility by means of excellence in knowledge, work, struggle with forebearance and overcoming, and in the spiritual gifts [that come] with this for a long period of time until old age. Despite this he would consider himself to be a sinner and base."

287 **He said:** "He who knows before his time remains rude for the rest of his time and wrongs those he teaches like a blind man leading the blind so that they all fall into the ditch."³³⁵

288 **The Brothers said:** "Abba Agathon said: 'Do not believe the man filled with hate [even] if he raises the dead'.³³⁶ The solitaries are angered in three ways: pride, actions and temper. The youth become angry because of the acuteness of their temper. The holy men become angry because of the harshness of their labors and the difficulty of the struggle they endure with the demons and with yearnings. The proud become angry because of their haughtiness. This is what Abba Agathon meant by: 'Even if he was perfect in talents such that he raises the dead yet becomes angry from wonder and pride like the supercilious, then he is the basest of people and wicked before God'."

283 **قال الاخوه** ان انبا ايسيدرس (c89r) لما قاتله الشيطان (b75r) فما (a58r) [1297] لفم قايلا ليس مثلك في الابا. اجابه ليس انا مثل القديس انطونيوس ولا انبا اجاث فكيف لم يذكر من الابا غير (d130r) هذين.

284 **قال المفسر** لان في زمانه كان انطونيوس اعلا من جميع الشيوخ وكان اجاث اعلا من جميع الاخوه فقال له كيف قلت ليس مثلك في الابا ولست ممجدا في الابا الاولين مثل القديس انطونيوس ولا معروفا في الابا الاخريين مثل انبا اجاث.

285 **قال الاخوه** ان ثاوفيلوس بطريرك الاسكندريه قال لريس دير بربونج ماذا وجدت في طريق الوحده زايدا قال كنت الوم ذاتي في كل حين. [1298]

286 **قال المفسر** لان هذا هو كمال المتوحد وليس كما يظن قوم ان كمالهم بالمناظر الروحانيه فقط لكن وبالاتضاع الكامل وذلك بان [1299] يتفاضل في المعرفه والعمل والجهاد بالصبر والغلبه وفي العطايا الروحانيه مع ذلك زمانا طويلا الى الشيخوخه. ومع ذلك يكون عند نفسه خاطيا حقيرا.

287 **وقال** ان من يعلم قبل زمانه يبقا بقية زمانه قليل الادب. ويظلم الذي يعلمهم (e132v) كاعمى يقود عميانا فيقعون جميعا في الحفره. [1300]

288 **قال الاخوه** (b75v) قال انبا اجاث الرجل الحقود اذا اقام الموتى لا تصدقه. لثلثة [1301] انواع تجرد المتوحدين الكبريا والاعمال والمزاج والفتيان يجردون بسبب حدة مزاجهم (d130v) والشيوخ يجردون من مشقة اعمالهم وصعوبة القتال الذي، يكون معهم من الشياطين والاوجاع، والمتكبرون (a58v) يجردون من اجل افتخارهم. والى هذا الحد اشا[ر] انبا اجاث يعني (c89v) لو كان كاملا في المواهب حتى انه يقيم الموتى. وهو يجرد من العجب والافتخار مثل المتكبرين. فهو حقير من [1302] الناس ومرذول قدام الله.

289 **The Brothers asked:** "A certain brother committed wrong and was expelled by the abbot of the monastery. Abba Isirine got up and went out with him saying: 'If you judged that this man, who committed a single fault, does not deserve to praise and prostrate before God here, then how much the more myself who have committed many sins, and woe to those who are outside over those who are inside'."[337]

290 **The Exegete replied:** "The holy man did not reply so as to equate the ignorance of the brothers with the heads of the monasteries in terms of morals, reprimand, decorum, patience, and learning according to the prescription of the Apostle. Rather, he wanted that if a brother falls into certain sins especially fornication then he should rise again through kindness, compassion and with discretion, not through harshness, disclosure and with abuse and expulsion from the monastery, so that those outside do not hear and doubt our habit and thus fail, while we would be reviled and moral excellence would be cursed."

291 **Commentary:** "It is valid to say: 'Woe to those who are inside over those who are outside'.[338] Meaning that if he who passed judgment on him because of one sin then those who remain inside are also subject to the judgment because of their [many] sins, meaning that as they judge they too will be judged."[339]

292 **The Brothers asked:** "A brother said to a holy man: 'I see my thought is always with God'. He replied: 'What is greater than this is for you to see your thought beneath all creation'."

293 **The Exegete replied:** "The solitary does not possess a higher virtue than that he should have the remembrance of God always in his heart as the wise Evagrius said: 'This is perfection: that you should not cease from the remembrance of God in your thought. Whenever you cease, you should resume it. Yet he will possess this merit after he transcends all the struggles and impediments which come from the devil and from wicked brothers and from the yearnings of habit and nature. For the demons may raise the novices to the heights of the remembrance of God before the perfection [brought about] by labors and struggle, and in the end they cast them down to the pit of perdition which is the fall of pride. The novices should at first opt to meditate on all the commandments of our Lord and on virtues, and not cease from

289 **قال الاخوه** ان اخا اخطا فطرده ريس الدير. فقام انبا ايسيرين وخرج معه وقال اذا كان هذا عمل[1303] نقصا واحدا حكمتم انه ما يستحق ان يمجد الله ويسجد له هنا فكم بالحرى[1304] انا الذي صنعت خطايا كثيره والويل للذين هم خارج من الذين هم داخل.

290 **قال المفسر** لم يرد الشيخ من ان يعدل جمل الاخوه من مدبري الاديره بالعظة والتوبيخ والادب بطول الروح وشفقه وكوصية الرسول. وانما[1305] اراد ان اخ[1306] اذا سقط في بعض الخطايا (e133r) لا سيما الزنا فبرفق وشفقه وفي خفيه ينبغي ان يقوم. لا بقساوة وشهره وشتيمه وطرد من الدير لكيلا يسمعون (b76r) البرانيون فيشكون في اسكيمنا فيخسرون هم ونشتم نحن. ويجدف على الفضيله.

291 **حاشيه** ويجوز ان يقال الويل للذين هم (d131r) داخل[1307] من الذين هم خارجا. يعني انه اذا كان الذي اخرج حكم عليه بسبب خطيه فالذين بقيوا داخلا الحكم يجب عليهم بسبب خطاياهم. وبمعنى انهم كما حكموا يحكم عليهم.

292 **قال الاخوه** ان اخا قال لشيخ اري فكرتي مع الله في كل حين. فقال له اعظم من هذا ان ترى فكرتك اسفل كل الخليقه.

293 (a59r) **قال المفسر** ليس للمتوحد[1308] فضيله اعلا من ان يكون ذكر الله في قلبه دايما كما قال الحكيم وغريس ان هذا هو الكمال. وهو ان لا[1309] تقطع تذكار الله من فكرك[1310]. وكلما انقطع اوصله. لكن انا تكون له هذه فضيله من بعد ان يعبر جميع الحروب والمعاوق التي تكون من الشيطان ومن (c90r) الاخوة الاشرار ومن اوجاع العاده والطبع. فان الشياطين قد ترفع المبتديين لعلو تذكار الله من قبل كمال الاعمال والجهاد. وفي الاخر يحطونهم الى عمق الهلاك الذي هو (e133v) سقطة[1311] الكبريا. فينبغي المبتديين ان يختاروا الهذيذ اولا في جميع وصايا ربنا. وفي الفضايل ولا يتركوا

the recollection of their sins and the cognition of their yearnings, and to fix their minds on the remembrance of God without lassitude lest they become unable to cast off difficult wars that would oppose this remembrance'.[340] This is what this holy man advised. Another holy man said: 'Some people say that they can see a vision of angels. Blessed is he who sees his sins [before him] at all times'.[341] For also, seeing a vision of angels does not diminish from seeing sins but is rather a warning of the leading astray of the demons when they imitate the angels in order to lead the novices astray."

294 **He said:** "A brother was assiduous in completing his canon of work, prayer, sorrow and suffering. Because of his humility, he was not satisfied with accepting consolation from his conscience but would wait for the grace of God's dispensation. When he revealed this to the holy man, he said to him: 'Given that you did not accept consolation from your works is an indication of your humility before the Lord and your love for Him, because he who truly loves God does not see that he has undertaken anything which merits God's love'. For this reason the joyful David said: 'What can I give back to God?'[342] He who is humble also looks at himself and his actions with contempt."

295 **The Brothers asked:** "Arsenius said to his disciples: 'Do not create a memorial for me other than an Offering'. What is the difference between a memorial and an Offering?"

296 **The Exegete replied:** "By memorial he means: 'Do not build a church for my body through which my commemoration would spread'. Just as he said upon his death: 'I stand with you before the pulpit of Christ if you give my bones to anyone'. Meaning: 'I stand with you in trial if you give my bones to him who will make of them a cause in the spread of my commemoration'. He means by an Offering the commemoration of his name at the altar during the consecration of the Offering, because this Offering is the commemoration of the death of Christ for the sake of the forgiveness of our sins, and he depicts for our visualization the meaning of the saying which we heard with our ears: 'This is the Lamb of God who takes away the sins of the world';[343] and: 'This is my Body which will be broken for you';[344] and: 'This is my Blood which will be shed for the forgiveness of your sins'."[345]

تذكار (b76v) خطاياهم ومعرفة¹³¹² اوجاعهم ويوصلوا¹³¹³ عقولهم بتذكار الله بغير فتور ليلا ما يقدروا ان يلقوا الحروب الصعبه التي (d131v) تضادد هذا التذكار. فالى هذا اشار هذا الشيخ. وقد قال شيخ اخر ثم قوم يقولون اننا ننظر الملايكه. فطوبا لمن يبصر خطاياه في كل حين. فليس ايضا نظر الملايكه ينقص نظر الخطايا. وانما حذر¹³¹⁴ من طغيان الشياطين اذا يتشبهون بالملايكه ليطغوا المبتدين.

294 **وقال** ان اخا كان مجتهدا في كمال قانونه في العمل والصلاه والحزن والالم. ولاتضاعه¹³¹⁵ ما رضي ان يقبل العزا من سريرته بل كان ينتظر نعمة تدبير الله. ولما كشف هذا للشيخ¹³¹⁶ قال له كونك لم تقبل (a59v) العزا من اعمالك يدل على اتضاعك قدام الرب وحبك له. لان الذي يحب الله بالحقيقه ما يرى انه صنع شيا يستحق حب الله. ولهذا قال داوود المغبوط بماذا اجازي الرب. والمتضع ايضا يرى ذاته واعماله بالاحتقار.

295 **قال الاخوه** ان ارسانيوس قال لتلاميذه لا تصنعوا لي تذكارا (e134r) ما خلا قربانا لا غير. فما الفرق بين التذكار والقربان.

296 **قال المفسر** يعني بالتذكار لا تبنوا لجسدي كنيسه (b77r) يشيع بها ذكري كما قال عند¹³¹⁷ موته انا اقف معكم قدام منبر المسيح. ان دفعتم عظامي لانسان. اي انا اقف معكم في (d132r) المحاكمه ان دفعتم عظامي لمن يجعلها سببا¹³¹⁸ في اشاعة (c90v) ذكري. ويعني بالقربان ذكر اسمه على المذبح في اوقات تقديس القربان. لان القربان هذا تذكار موت المسيح من اجل مغفرة خطابانا. وهو يرسم لابصارنا معنى القول الذي سمعناه باذاننا هذا حمل الله الذي يرفع خطايا العالم.¹³¹⁹ وهذا جسدي الذي يكسر بسببكم. وهذا دمي يهرق من اجل مغفرة خطاياكم.

297 **He also said:** "That which is said in fifty prayers and five hundred prayers are the prostrations and the repetition of prayer by which I mean that which our Lord carried out for us."

298 **The Brothers asked:** "Abba Muthues said: 'In my youth I used to think that I might perhaps do something good. But when I grew old I saw that I had not done a single good work'.[346] Is this correct or did he say it out of the decorum of humility?"

299 **The Exegete replied:** "It is correct because the more the Perfect approach God and become worthy of seeing Him in the vision of light the more they see their own shortcomings."

300 **He said:** "The Fathers named and depicted humility using fine words and excellent depictions, and Saint Antony said: 'It is the banisher of and the salvation from the snares of the devil'. Abba Macarius said: 'It is the seal of military service of Christ'. Abba Ammon called it the sublimity of a human being. Arsenius said it is the earth which does not fall. Abba Timath said it is superior to all virtues. Abba Theodore called it the frightener of the demons. Tebansis called it the instrument of the solitary life. Sisoes of the Rock alluded to it as the wall of virtues. Pachomius the Great called it the perfection of the solitaries. The Kalmiran called it the door of the Kingdom of Heaven. Abba Pior depicted it as an icon which sees shortcomings. John the Prophet called it the anchor of souls. Serapion said it is the perfection of goodness. John the Less said it is the first of the joyful commandments. He points to the opening words of our Lord saying: 'Blessed are the humble in spirit for theirs is the Kingdom of Heaven'.[347] Abba Evagrius said it is the Tree of Life which rises up to the heights. Abba Patra said it is the basis of virtue. Abba Isaiah called it the safeguard of virtue. The blessed David called the humble souls the sacrifices of God. He who rises will fall like the devil, and he who is humble rises with our Lord Jesus Christ to Him be glory."

301 **Commentary:** "Christ decreed for the humble dominion over heaven and earth with the words: 'Blessed are the humble in spirit and blessed are the meek', and the rest."[348]

302 **Concerning the Struggle with Fornication.**

303 **The Brothers asked:** "The struggle with fornication became like a burning fire, day and night, in one of the solitaries. He would

297 **قال ايضا** ان الذي قيل في خمسين صلاه وخمسماية صلاه هو المطانيات[1320] وتكرار الصلاه. اعني التي عملها لنا ربنا.

298 **قال الاخوه** قال انبا ماطيس في صباي كنت اظن لعل شي حسنا كنت اصنع. ولما شخت نظرت[1321] انني ولا فعلا واحدا (a60r) صنعت حسنا. فهل هذا صحيحا او قال هذا من اجل ادب الاتضاع.

299 **قال المفسر** هو صحيح لان الكاملين كلما تقدموا الى الله واستحقوا نظره (e134v) في رويا النور راوا نقصهم.

300 **وقال** ان الابا قد سموا ورسموا الاتضاع باسما[1322] حسنه. ورسم فاضله.[1323] والقديس انطونيوس قال انه المبعد والمخلص (b77v) من فخاخ الشيطان. وانبا مقار قال هو ختم جندية المسيح. وانبا امون سماه عظمة الانسان. وارسانيوس (d132v) قال هو ارض التي لا تسقط. انبا تماويا قال هو[1324] اعلا من جميع الفضايل. وانبا ثادري دعاه مخيف الشياطين. والتبايسي سماه عدة الوحده. وصاحب الصخره كناه بسور الفضايل. وبكوميوس الكبير سماه كمال المتوحدين. والقلزمي[1325] دعاه باب ملكوت السما. وانبا بيور[1326] رسمه بانه القونة التي ترى النقص. ويوحنا النبي سماه مرسى النفوس. وسرافيون قال هو كمال البر. ويوحنا القصير قال هو اول الوصايا المغبوطة. يشير الى استفتاح ربنا بقوله طوبا للمساكين بالروح فان لهم ملكوت السماوات. وانبا وغريس (c91r) قال هو شجرة الحياة[1327] التي ترتفع الى العلا. وانبا بطرا قال هو اساس الفضيله. وانبا شعيا[1328] سماه امان الفضيله. والطوباني داوود دعا النفوس المتضعه ذبايح (a60v) الله. فمن يرتفع (e135r) يسقط كالشيطان. ومن يتضع يرتفع مع ربنا يسوع المسيح له المجد.

301 **حاشيه** المسيح قد قرر للمتضع ملك السما[1329] وملك الارض بقوله طوبا للمساكين بالروح وطوبا للمتواضعين وته.

302 (b78r) **على قتال الزنا.**

303 **قال الاخوه** صار (d133r) قتال الزنا في واحد من المتوحدين مثل النار المشتعله في الليل والنهار. وكان

persevere without descending to it in his thoughts and after a long period of time the struggle left him and light shone in his mind."[349]

304 **The Exegete replied:** "His saying that his thought did not descend means that he did not cease from the remembrance of God, may He be exalted, and from inner prayer and descending to the rumination of thought about fornication. Rather, he would compel himself to cut off his desires through the desire of the love of God. He would compare the desire of the body with the desire of the spirit and the love of [this] yearning with the love of God. His saying, upon overcoming the yearning, that light rose in his mind is because this [is] specific to purity and humility. For this reason Abba Evagrius calls it the holy light. The Fathers said that if the solitary defeats vainglory and rises to the heights of humility then divine light descends upon his mind during the time of prayer, and he becomes worthy of seeing the light of Christ our Lord."

305 **The Brothers asked:** "The struggle with fornication occurred to another brother who bore it through a great deal of asceticism for fourteen years. He would guard his mind from descending to the desire. Finally he came to the church and revealed his struggle to all the community of the monastery. They all suffered with him and prayed to God for him. As a result the struggle [he was experiencing] ceased."[350]

306 **The Exegete replied:** "The struggle became fixed within him because he was at first reliant upon his own labor, and he was liberated from it when he confessed it to the community and they prayed for him because he applied a great deal of humility."

307 **He also said:** "A brother was experiencing the struggle with fornication. He came and went to his holy man eleven times during one night. Every time he came to him a demon would flee from him and his struggle would cease because of the power of the holy man's prayer and his conversation with him. When he sent the brother back to his cell his struggle would return. This is because the holy man was only toiling with him when the brother came to him. When he departed from him the holy man became concerned with himself. When the brother informed the holy man he understood that he was the cause and he said: 'I am the one who was negligent because I did not assist you, and I suffered and prayed for your sake [only] if you were present'. When the holy

يصبر ولا ينزل بفكرته اليه. وبعد زمان كثير عبر عنه القتال فاضا النور في ذهنه.

304 **قال المفسر** قوله ماكانت فكرته تنزل. اي ماكان يترك تذكار الله تعالى والصلاة الخفيه الى الهذيذ في فكر الزنا. بل كان يغصب نفسه بقطع شهواته بشهوة حب الله. ويقايس شهوة الجسد بشهوة[1330] الروح ومحبة الوجع بمحبة الله. وقوله لما غلب الوجع اشرق النور في ذهنه لان هذه خاصة الطهاره والاتضاع. ولهذا يدعوه انبا وغريس النور المقدس. وقال الابا اذا غلب المتوحد المجد الفارغ وارتفع الى علو الاتضاع هبط الى عقله نور الاهي في وقت الصلاه. ويستحق ان ينظر نور المسيح ربنا.

305 **قال الاخوه** (e135v) صار[1332] قتال الزنا مع اخ اخر وصبر له بنسك كثير اربعة عشر سنه. وكان يحرس فكرته لا تنزل الى الشهوه. وفي الاخر جا الى الكنيسه وكشف قتاله لجميع (a61r) جمع الدير. فتالموا معه جمعه.[1333] وكانوا يصلون عنه. فبطل القتال عنه.

306 (d133v) **قال المفسر** (b78v) ثبت القتال معه لانه كان في الاول متكلا[1334] على عمله. وتخلص منه لما اعترف به للجماعه وصلوا[1335] عنه لانه استعمل الاتضاع (c91v) الكثير.

307 **وقال ايضا** ان اخاكان معه قتال الزنا. فتردد الى شيخه في ليلة واحده احدعشر دفعه. وفي كل دفعه ياتيه كان شيطان يهرب عنه ويبطل القتال منه[1336] من قوة صلاة الشيخ وكلامه معه. واذا ارجع[1337] الاخ الى قلايته رجع اليه القتال. وهذا لان الشيخ كان يتعب معه اذا اتا اليه الاخ فقط. واذا مضى[1338] من عنده يهتم الشيخ بنفسه. فلما عرف الاخ الشيخ فهم ان السبب من عنده فقال انا الذي توانيت لاني ماكنت اهتم بك. واتالم واصلي من اجلك اذا حضرت. فلما

man humbled himself and blamed himself, God in His mercy removed the struggle from the brother and he praised God."[351]

308 **He also said:** "The demon of fornication is released on every person according to the measure of their way of life. He who struggles for a long time with thoughts, if he struggles through action and prayer and overcomes the struggle of thoughts, then the demons fight him openly through touching and groping of organs against his will. They set up phantasms in front of him of male and female beasts and people as though having intercourse. They may deceive him forcefully to have a predilection for the yearning. If they become this intense then it is unlikely that he will persevere. For Abba Moses saw disgusting phantoms and his struggle grew intense. As a result he was not able to persevere in his cell and he went to Abba Isidore who took him up to the roof and showed him an army of warring demons to the west and an army of supporting angels from the east, as a result of which he was consoled and encouraged and returned to his cell and struggled joyfully and eagerly."[352]

309 **The Brothers asked:** "The holy men said that if thoughts of fornication remain in the heart of a person and are not realized through action then it is like one who sees grapevines and longs to eat from its grapes but does not enter the vineyard nor eat from the grapes. Such a one deserves a beating not death."[353]

310 **The Exegete replied:** "The Fathers consider that the fornication which occurs in thoughts and lingers in them and is accepted by them with delight but is not acted out, [in this case] the soul does not die from its life in God because of it and is not oppressed through perfection, rather, it hinders the purity of the heart and cuts off the remembrance of God, and this is what they meant by 'a beating without death'. As for fornication through bodily action, the Fathers consider this to be a natural death for the soul because a person through his action harms his mind, forgets God, becomes base in his heart, and loses the favor which he has with God, and he sees that his defeat is complete and that his hope may be cut, and this is death not a beating."

311 **The Brothers asked:** "What is the meaning of Mother Sarah's statement: 'When I put my foot on the ladder and want to go up to the roof, I set my death before my eyes before I remove it'.[354]

اتضع الشيخ ولام ذاته بطل الله القتال عن الاخ برحمته ومجد الله.

308 **وقال ايضا** ان كل انسان على قدر (e136r) قياس تدبيره يخلا عليه شيطان الزنا. فالذي يكون معه القتال في الافكار زمانا طويلا ان كان يجاهد بالعمل والصلاه ويغلب قتال الافكار فالشياطين حينيذ تقاتله ظاهرا[1339] في الجس وتلمس الاعضا[1340] بغير ارادته. ويركبون قدامه خيالات ذكور (d134r) واناث من البهايم (b79r) والناس كانهم يتجامعون. وقد يخدعونه[1341] غصبا[1342] الى الميل الوجع. واذا اشتدوا هكذى فبعيد (a61v) ان يصبر. فانبا موسى راا[1343] الخيالات القبيحه واشتد عليه القتال. فلم يقدر يصبر في قلايته. فمضى الى عند انبا ايسيدرس. فطلع به الى السطح واراه عسكر الشياطين في الغرب يقاتلون. وعسكر الملايكه من الشرق يساعدون. فتعزا وتشجع ورجع الى قلايته وجاهد بفرح ونشاط.

309 **قال الاخوه** ان الشيوخ قالوا ان افكار الزنا اذا كانت في قلب الانسان ولم يكملها بالفعل[1344] فهو مثل الذي يرى الكرم ويشتهي ان ياكل من عنبه ولم يدخل الكرم ولا اكل من العنب فهو يستحق الضرب لا الموت.

310 **قال المفسر** ان الابا يرون ان[1345] الزنا الذي يدور في الافكار ويبطي فيها وتقبله (c92r) بلذه وما ياتي الى الفعل ما تموت (e136v) النفس به من الحيات التي بالله ولا تظلم بالكمال. لكنه يبعد من نقاوة[1346] القلب ويقطع عن ذكر الله وهذا هو الذي اشاروا اليه بالضرب دون الموت. فاما الزنا بالفعل الجسداني يعدوه الابا موتا طبيعيا للنفس لان الانسان (b79v) بفعله يظلم (d134v) عقله[1347] وينسى الله ويخزي في سريرته ويعدم الداله التي[1348] له عند الله ويرى انه كل[1349] انغلابه وقد ينقطع رجاه. وهذا هو الموت لا الضرب.

311 **قال الاخوه** ما معنى قول الام ساره انى احط رجلي على السلم اريد ان اصعد الى السطح.[1350] فاهي موتي بين عيني قبل ان اشيلها.

Another father said: 'When I am plaiting a basket whenever I pass the needle I set my death before my eyes before I work the second [stitch]'.³⁵⁵ What is the way of life in which a person upholds the remembrance of death at all times?"

312 **The Exegete replied:** "Through a gift after exertion. For the Fathers toil first and coerce themselves into recollecting the fear of God by always remembering death and the Last Judgment to come, and the punishment in Hell. Then they will receive the aid of power through the gift of Christ our Lord as the blessed Mark said: 'The fear of Hell and the love of Paradise grant perseverance during difficulties and this does not come from it but from He who knows thoughts'. Meaning that it is not from recalling Hell alone that a person refrains from sins nor from recollecting the Kingdom of Heaven that he boils with good works, for everyone can recollect this, however, not everyone possesses the thinking which accompanies the power of aid through the gift of our Lord."

313 **He also said:** "A brother went to Abba Poemen and said to him: 'At first I was fearful of illnesses and natural yearnings and so I was neglectful of [good] works, despite this I was beset by what I feared and I fell into those illnesses for the sake of which I had been neglectful of works'. He replied to him: 'Had you become weary for the sake of virtue you would have been freed of the natural yearnings and the yearnings of sin like many of the Fathers; and had you fallen into natural illnesses for the sake of your works, undertaken for the love of God, like certain solitary Fathers, they would have been counted as a testimony of your work and your overcoming of yearnings and sin and a testimony of your perseverance and gratitude for natural illnesses'."

314 **The Brothers asked:** "A brother asked Abba Poemen about fornication. He replied: 'Guard your tongue, and belly, and estrangement'.³⁵⁶ What is 'estrangement'?"

315 **The Exegete replied:** "It is not to be known or to know anyone in the place one is in, like a stranger, in order to protect one's mind from pride and from being judgmental. Because of these two things many have fallen into fornication so as to be humbled and absolved."

واب اخر قال اذا خيطت القفه فكما عبرت بالمسله قدام عيني (a62r) اهىي موتي قدام عيني قبل ان اعمل الثانيه. فباي تدبير ينقام ذكر الموت دايما في الانسان.

312 **قال المفسر** بالموهبه بعد العمل. فالابا يتعبون اولا[1351] ويغصبون نفوسهم في تذكار مخافة الله بذكر الموت دايما والدينونه التي ستكون والعقوبه في جهنم. وحينيذ ينالون عون القوه من موهبة المسيح ربنا كما قال الطوباني مرقس. ان مخافة جهنم ومحبة الفردوس يعطيان[1352] الصبر في الشدايد وليس هذا منها لكن من الذي (e137r) يعرف الافكار. يعني ليس من تذكار جهنم بمفرده يمتنع الانسان من الخطايا ولا من تذكار ملكوت السما يغلي في اعمال البر. فان[1353] كل احد له هذا التذكار. لكن ليس لكل احد[1354] الافتكار الذي يستصحب قوة العون من (c92v) موهبه (b80r) ربنا.

313 **وقال ايضا** ان اخا مضى الى (d135r) انبا بهمن وقال له في الاول خفت من الامراض والاوجاع الطبيعيه فتوانيت في الاعمال والا قد اتي[1355] علي[1356] ما خفت منه فوقعت في الامراض التي من اجلها توانيت في الاعمال. فقال له لو كنت تعبت من اجل الفضيله كنت تخلص من الامراض الطبيعيه واوجاع الخطيه مثل كثير من الابا. ولو وقعت في امراض طبيعيه من اجل اعمالك التي في حب (a62v) الله. مثل بعض الابا المتوحدين كانت تحسب لك شهاده من اجل[1357] اعمالك وغلبتك الاوجاع والخطيه وشهاده من اجل صبرك وشكرك في الامراض الطبيعيه.

314 **قال الاخوه** سال اخ انبا بهمن من اجل الزنا. فقال له احرس لسانك وبطنك وغربتك فما هي الغربا.

315 **قال المفسر** هي ان لا يكون معروفا ولا عارفا باحد في الموضع الذي يكون فيه كمثل الغريب ليحفظ ذهنه من الكبريا والمداينه فبسبب هذين سقط كثير في الزنا ليذلوا ويعذروا.

316 **He said:** "Were we required to be pure of body alone then thoughts relating to fornication would not have harmed us nor would we have sought purity of heart through which we see God. We must also concern ourselves with repelling the deceptions of thoughts."

317 **The Brothers asked:** "Some Fathers advised that if the demons stir within us the yearnings of fornication then we should pray that they be nullified. Others prescribed that we should firstly be indignant with the thoughts and scold the demons, then pray. One said: 'If the thought of fornication occurs in your mind then quickly lift your thinking to God through prayer and do not delay'.357 Abba Evagrius said: 'Do not pray at the beginning of your temptation until you have spoken an indignant speech against the demon who is pressuring you because if your soul is steeped in thoughts then your prayer will not be pure, and through your indignation at the enemies you dismiss their thoughts'."

318 **The Exegete replied:** "The Fathers instruct the brother according to his way of life. He who leads a way of life struggling against thoughts and who continuously prays mentally should dismiss the impure thought through prayer upon its [first] stirring. And it would be better for the novice who has not yet reached continuous mental prayer to at first be indignant with and scold the Enemy then to pray. As for scolding, it is to say: 'May the Lord drive you away'. As for this prayer, he says: 'O our Lord, through you we humiliate our foes and by the power of your cross we tread underfoot our haters. We do not rely upon our strength and way of life for our salvation, rather, you are the one who saved us and exposed our enemies, the demons. You granted that we might praise you and confess your power and redemption'."

319 **The Brothers asked:** "A holy man said: the Enemy said to the Lord, 'I send my own against yours in order to drive them back. If they are unable to do so then I, in a nighttime dream, will overcome them'. The Lord replied to him saying 'If an abortion can inherit his father then this [also] is counted as sin for my companions'."358

320 **The Exegete replied:** "The devil did not say this to our Lord nor did our Lord reply to him in this way but rather this holy man wanted to make their will known to us in this way. The demons

316 (e137v) **وقال** لو كنا مطلوبين بطهارة^{1358} الجسد فقط لم كان افكار الزنا توذينا ولما كنا نطلب بنقاوة^{1359} قلب التي بها نعاين الله. وجب ان نهتم بطرد خداع الافكار ايضا.

317 **قال الاخوه** ان بعض الابا وصوا اذا (b80v) حركت الشياطين فينا اوجاع الزنا ان نصلي على ابطالها وبعضهم (d135v) وصوا ان نغضب اولا^{1360} على الافكار ونشتم الشياطين. وحينيذ نصلي. فواحد قال اذا خطرت فكرة^{1361} الزنا ببالك فارفع فكرك عاجلا الى الله في الصلاه ولا تتاخر. وانبا وغريس قال لا تصلي في الاول تجربتك حتى تقول كلام غضب على الشيطان الذي يضغطك^{1362} لانك اذا انغمست نفسك في الافكار تكون صلاتك غير نقيه. وبغضبك على الاعدا تصرف (c93r) افكارهم.

318 **قال المفسر** ان الابا على تدبير الاخ يعلمونه. فالمتدبر في (a63r) قتال الافكار المداوم الصلاة الذهنيه ينبغي له ان يصرف الفكرة الدنسه بالصلاه من حركها. والمبتدي الذي ما وصل بعد الى الصلاة الذهنيه^{1363} الدايمه فالاجود له تقدم الغضب والشتيمه للعدو^{1364} وحينيذ يصلي. اما شتيمته فبان يقول الرب يزجرك. واما هذه الصلاه فيقول يا ربنا بك نذل اعدانا^{1365} وبقوة صليبك ندوس مبغضينا. فليس اتكالنا على قوتنا وتدبيرنا في خلاصنا بل انت (e138r) الذي خلصتنا وافضحت الشياطين اعدانا. ومنحتنا^{1366} ان نمجدك ونعترف على قوتك وخلاصك.

319 **قال الاخوه** ان شيخا قال ان العدو قال للرب انتي ارسل الذي لي على الذين لك فيردوهم. وان لم يقدروا^{1367} فاني في حلم الليل اطغمهم فقال له الرب ان كان السقط يرث اباه^{1368} (b81r) فهذه تحسب خطية لاصحابي.

320 **قال المفسر** لا الشيطان قال هذه لربنا ولا ربنا اجابه بهذا وانما هذا الشيخ اراد ان يعرفنا ارادتها في هذا الوجه.

fight the solitary at the outset of his struggle during the day through wicked thoughts, and during the night through shameful dreams. If his heart becomes purified through struggle and his mind becomes illuminated with the light of grace then he becomes worthy to receive thoughts during the day that are rightly guided and pure, and during the night sinless and pure dreams. As the sage Evagrius said: 'If you want to know that you have come near to transcending yearnings then understand this from your thoughts during the day and dreams during the night. The novice who comes from the world and does not weary himself with repentance and does not ask forgiveness from God for his initial ignorance then his sordid dreams would be counted as a sin against him. He who is dissolute among the brothers who accepts the deception of lust in his heart during the day and does not fight against it then his carnal dreams are counted as a sin against him. He who struggles against the thoughts which the devil stirs in his heart during the day then his sordid and impure dreams of fantasy are not counted as a sin against him because God, who is just and merciful, knows that during the time of his own volition and control he was not deceived by the sensual delight of lust but rather he fought it and cast it out. If it comes upon him during his sleep He does not count it a sin against him because he did not accept it of his own volition and he was not able to struggle against it and to drive it away and banish it'. Abba Isaiah said: 'If a fantasy comes upon you during the night – a wedding fantasy – do not recall it during the day so that your thought does not take pleasure in it and your heart is deceived by it and draws you to consummate it in action, rather, stop quickly and cast yourself before the holy cross and ask for mercy and redemption from God, and God through His grace towards the weakness of human beings will help you'. His saying: 'Just as an abortion does not inherit his father', means it does not inherit because it is incomplete in terms of life and existence. Similarly, the impurity of the dream is incomplete because it does not take place willingly."

321 **The Brothers asked:** "A brother said to Abba Poemen: 'What do I do my Father since I am beset by thoughts of fornication'. He replied to him: 'Flee the first time [they come upon you], flee the second time, and the third time set yourself against them like a sharp sword'."[359]

فان المتوحد في اول جهاده يقاتلوه الشياطين في النهار بالافكار الشريره وفي الليل بالاحلام القبيحه. فاذا تنقى قلبه في الحرب ونار ذهنه بنور النعمه حينيذ يستحق ان ينال في النهار افكار مهتديه طاهره. وفي الليل احلاما ذكيه نقيه. كما قال الحكيم وغريس. اذا اردت تعرف انك قد قربت (a63v) من ان تعبر الاوجاع فافهم ذلك[1369] من افكارك في النهار واحلامك في الليل. فالمبتدي الذي ياتي من العالم ولا يتعب في التوبه ولا يطلب من الله غفرانا لجهالته الاولى فهذا احلامه المرذوله تحسب له خطيه. والمحلول بين الاخوه الذي يقبل بالنهار خداع الشهوه في قلبه ولا يجاهدها فهذا احلامه شهوانيه تحسب له خطيه. والذي (c93v) يجاهد الافكار التي يحركها الشيطان في قلبه في النهار فهذا احلامه المرذوله بالفناطس[1370] النجسه ما تحسب له (b81v) خطيه. لان الله عادل رحيم يعلم انه في وقت اختياره وتمكنه لم ينخدع للذة الشهوه بل قاتلها وطردها. فاذا وردت عليه وقت نومه لا يحسبها عليه خطيه لانه لم يقبلها باختياره ولا كان متمكنا من جهادها وطردها وابعادها. وقد قال انبا اشعيا ان وردت عليك في الليل فنطسة الزيجه فلا تذكرها بالنهار ليلا تلتذ بها فكرتك وينخدع لها قلبك ويجتذبك الى تكميلها بالفعل. بل قف[1371] عاجلا والق نفسك امام الصليب المقدس واطلب من الله رحمة وخلاصا. والله بتحننه على ضعف البشر يعينك. وقوله كما[1372] ان السقط لا يرث والده يعني لكونه غير كامل الحياة[1373] والوجود لا يرث. كذالك نجاسة الحلم هي غير كامله لانها لا تتم (a64r) بالاراده.

321 **قال الاخوه** ان اخا قال لانبا بيمن ماذا افعل يا ابي اذ[1374] تقوم علي[1375] افكار الزنا. فقال له في الدفعة الاولى اهرب والثانيه اهرب والثالثه قم[1376] في مضاددتها مثل السيف الحاد.

322   **The Exegete replied:** "This means that if grace visits you and you were joyful with love for our Lord or yearning for the blessings to come, or in fear for the coming punishment, or in repentance for your sins and suffering because of them, and the devil of fornication stirs in you base thoughts during such a time then do not stop your soul from these matters by struggling with him but rather turn away from him in your mind and concern yourself with your profit. This is the meaning of his statement: 'Flee the first time', and if he stirs base thoughts in you again then do this again, and this is 'The second time', and if your thought grows cold and becomes unbound from such matters and the stirring of foul thoughts does not cease, then make a stand in repelling them and prostrate before the holy cross and beat your head with indignation before the Lord. Stir yourself with supplications, sighs, tears and weeping. Chant the Psalms with knowledge and understanding and select from them Psalms of courage and victory such as: 'The Lord is my light and salvation – whom shall I fear?'[360] And: 'To you Lord I lifted up my soul. O my God, upon you I have relied: I will not be ashamed'.[361] And: 'O God, be my aid; make haste to help me, O Lord'.[362] And other similar Psalms such as: 'How long will you forget me O Lord, forever?'[363] And: 'May God arise, may all His enemies be scattered'.[364] And: 'O Lord do not rebuke me in your anger, nor reprimand me in your wrath'[365] and other similar Psalms. Undertake this with understanding regarding what you are saying and with a spirited soul, for you will defeat the devil and receive the grace of purity and the sacred light will be illuminated for you and you will be joyful in Christ your hope, glory be to Him forever, amen."

323   **Concerning Repentance.**

324   **The Brothers asked:** "Two brothers returned to the world and got married, after which they felt remorse and repented. When they completed their penance and they left their hermitage one of them had a gloomy face whose color had changed while the other was joyful and his appearance was fine because the first was reflecting upon his sins and the fire of Hell while the second was thinking about the grace of God and hoping for His mercy. The Fathers said that their repentance is equal before God."[366]

325   **The Exegete replied:** "Just as fire has two characteristics: heat and light, and the first is suitable for suffering while the other is suitable for

322 **قال المفسر** يعني اذا زارتك النعمه او كنت في الفرح بمحبة ربنا او الشوق الى الخيرات الاتيه او في الخوف من العقوبة الاتيه (b82r) او في الندم على خطاياك والتوجع بسببها. ويحرك فيك شيطان الزنا افكار قبيحه في وقت من هذه الاوقات فلا تبطل نفسك من هذه الامور في القتال معه بل التفت بذهنك عنه واهتم بربحك. فهذا معنى قوله اهرب في الدفعة الاولى.[1377] فان حرك فيك افكار القبيحه ايضا فاصنع كذلك[1378] ايضا وهذه هي الدفعة الثانيه. فاذا بردت فكرتك وانحلت من تلك الامور ولم يطل تحريكة الافكار (c94r) القبيحه قف في صدها واسجد قدام الصليب المقدس والطم راسك بغضبك قدام الرب. وحرك نفسك بالطلبه والتنهد والدموع والنوح. ورتل بالمزامير بمعرفه وفهم. وانتخب منها مزامير الشجاعه والاستنصار.[1379] مثل الرب نوري ومخلصي ممن اخاف. واليك يا رب رفعت نفسي الهي[1380] عليك توكلت فلا اخزى. ويا الله كن لي معينا انصرني[1381] يا رب عاجلا. وما يشبه ذلك.[1382] مثل حتى متى تنساني يا رب دايما.[1383] ويقوم الله (a64v)[1384] وجميع اعدايه يتفرقون. ويا رب لا بغضبك تبكتني ولا بسخطك توبخني وما يشبه ذلك. واعمل هذا بتفهم لما تقوله وبحرارة نفس. فانك تغلب الشيطان[1385] وتقتني نعمة الطهاره[1386] ويضي لك النور (b82v) المقدس وتفرح بالمسيح رجاك له المجد الى الابد[1387] امين.

323 **على التوبه.**

324 **قال الاخوه** ان اخوين رجعا الى العالم وتزوجا. وبعد ذالك ندما وتابا.[1388] ولما كملا قانون توبتها وخرجا من حبسها كان الواحد وجهه معبسا ولونه متغيرا وكان الاخر فرحا ومنظره حسنا لان الاول كان يفتكر في خطاياه وفي نار جهنم والثاني كان يفكر في تحنن الله ويرجو رحمته. والابا قالوا ان توبتها متساويه عند الله.

325 **قال المفسر** كما ان النار لها خاصتان الحراره والنور. والاولى تصلح للعذاب والاخرى[1389] تصلح للنياح. هكذى التوبه لها قوتان فتتم بمخافة الله وبمحبته. وتذكار مخافة الله يحزن. وتذكار رجا

rest, similarly repentance has two forces and is achieved through fear of God and His love. The recollection of the fear of God saddens while the recollection of the hope of His love gladdens. Abba Evagrius said: 'I act with love towards God because he is a Father and is good, and with fear because He is a lord, and a judge, and just'."

326 **The Brothers asked:** "Why is the one who flees from sin, leaves the world, and comes to the yoke of monasticism accompanied by joy, and the comfort of perseverance, while the solitary who slips and falls into sin and wishes to repent grows sad and finds it unbearable?"

327 **The Exegete replied:** "This is because leaving the world for the sake of God does not take place except by the grace of God, just as he who is baptized is accompanied by the joy of the grace of the Holy Spirit and does not remember his first sins. If he sins again then repents, he repents with sadness because of the absence of that grace. Similarly, he who departs from the world for the sake of God is accompanied by a sacred ebullience as a result of which he does not remember his earlier sins in the world. If he becomes a solitary and falls into sin afterwards then repents, he repents with sadness. This through God's dispensation so that he does not easily fall once more and is obstructed from his course along the path of virtue. The solitaries state that he who slips, falls and quickly rises to repent becomes perfect in knowledge and way of life more than he who began in the labor of the virtue of solitude. This is because the first resembles the one who built a house which collapsed or sailed in a ship which sank. If he returns to the building or course he knows the causes of the collapse and of the sinking and he guards against them, constructing better than the first building. The second resembles the one who begins the building and the journey not knowing the causes of the collapse nor of the sinking. For this reason he deserves that aid accompanies him during the labor and that his struggle is reduced."

328 **The Brothers asked:** "A brother said to Abba Sisoes: 'What shall I do my Father?' He replied: 'If you fall, then rise'. He said: 'I have fallen many times and risen. How much longer must I fall and rise?' He replied: 'Until you advance either in rising or in falling. For the action in which a person is to be found is the one he continues in'."[367]

329 **The Exegete replied:** "He is pointing to the statement by God on the tongue of Ezekiel: 'The day on which the righteous person turns away from his righteousness, I will not remember his

محبته يفرح. وقد قال انبا وغريس اعمل مع الله في الحب من اجل انه اب وصالح. وفي المخافه لانه رب وديان وعادل.

326 **قال الاخوه** لماذا الذي يهرب من الخطيه ويخرج من العالم وياتي الى نير[1390] الرهبنه يصحبه الفرح ونياح الصبر. (c94v) والمتوحد الذي يزل ويسقط في خطيه ويريد ان يتوب يحزن (a65r) ويستثقل.

327 **قال المفسر** لان خروج من العالم من اجل الله لا يكون الا بنعمة الله. كما ان الذي يتعمد يصحبه (b83r) فرح نعمة روح القدس. فلا يفتكر خطاياه الاولى. فاذا رجع اخطا ثم تاب. يتوب بحزن لعدم تلك النعمه. كذلك[1391] الذي يخرج من العالم من اجل الله يصحبه غلوة مقدسه فلا يذكر خطاياه المتقدمه في العالم. فاذا توحد وسقط في خطيه بعد ذلك ثم تاب فانه يتوب بحزن. وذلك بتدبير الله ليلا يعود يسقط بسهوله وينعاق عن مسيره في طريق الفضيله. والمتوحدين يقولون ان الذي يزل ويسقط وينهض للتوبه سريعا فانه يتكمل بالمعرفة والتدبير اكثر من الذي ابتدى في عمل فضيلة الوحده. لان الاول يشبه الذي بنا بيتا وانهدم او سار في مركب وغرق. فانه اذا عاد للبنايه او المسير يعرف اسباب الهدم والغرق ويحترز منها. ويبني افضل من البناية الاوله.[1392] والثاني يشبه الذي يبتدي بالبنايه والسفر. فيكون غير عارف باسباب الهدم والغرق. ولهذا يستحق ان تصحبه معونة في العمل. وان يخفف عنه القتال.

328 **قال الاخوه** ان اخا قال لانبا شيشاي ماذا اصنع يا ابي. فان سقطت. قال قم.[1393] قال دفعات كثيره سقطت وقمت.[1394] فالى متى اسقط (a65v) واقوم. قال حتى تسبق اما في القيام او في السقوط. فان (b83v) الفعل الذي فيه يوجد الانسان فيه يمضي.

329 **قال المفسر** هو يشير الى قول الله على لسان حزقيال ان في اليوم الذي يرجع فيه البار عن بره ويصنع اثما. لا اذكر له

righteousness rather he will die in iniquities. Similarly if the iniquitous person turns away from his iniquity and does good, I will not recall his iniquity rather he will die in his righteousness'.[368] For this reason we should see to it that we repent quickly when we fall so that we do not die while we are fallen and have not repented and so leave the world and are handed over to the punishment."

330 **The Brothers asked:** "This appears to contradict the words of Abba Mark that upon our departure from the world our profits and losses are weighed and we are judged accordingly."

331 **The Exegete replied:** "There is no contradiction between them because Abba Mark intended those who win and lose during struggle while in a willing state of repentance and righteousness. Abba Sisoes intended those who die in those sins to which they were fixed by their own desire and will until death, because they suppressed the grace of God for whose sake He became incarnate. For Christ said: 'I have not come to call the righteous but sinners to repentance'.[369] There is no hindrance from Him to forgive sins, rather he who is slow to repent until he dies will be judged as a wicked person who does not believe because he deprived himself of the grace which Christ came to grant to the faithful. I mean repentance which is the righteous gift of the sinners among the believers."

332 **The Brothers asked:** "What is the difference between repentance and righteousness?"

333 **The Exegete replied:** "Repentance is righteousness with humility. For pride is alien to the repentant. As for the one who performs righteous virtue then he is not far from pride because pride follows virtue as was written regarding the humility of the tax collector and the righteousness of the Pharisee."

334 **The Brothers asked:** "A brother asked Abba Poemen about a matter saying: 'There was a solitary and a lay man. The solitary thought during the evening that he would cast off his monastic garb in the morning, and the lay man thought in the evening that in the morning he would put on the monastic garb, but they both died on that night. What then is their lot?' The holy man replied: 'The monk died a monk and the lay man died as a lay man, for they

بره بل يموت بالخطايا. وكذلك 1395 اذا رجع الاثيم عن اثمه ويصنع برا لا اذكر له اثمه بل يموت في بره. فلهذا يجب (c95r) ان نحرس على سرعة التوبه متى سقطنا ليلا يدركنا الموت في السقوط بلا توبه ونخرج من العالم فنسلم للعقوبه.

330 **قال الاخوه** فيظهر ان هذا يضادد قول انبا مرقس ان عند خروجنا من العالم يوازن ربحنا بخسارتنا وندان.

331 **قال المفسر** لا مضاددة 1396 بينها لان انبا مرقس عنى عن الذين يخسرون في اثنا المجاهده ويربحون وهم في ارادة التوبه والبر قايمون. وانبا شيشاي اعنى عن الذين يموتون في خطاياهم التي ثبتوا فيها الى الموت بشهوتهم وارادتهم. لانهم ظلموا نعمة الله التي من اجلها تانس. فان المسيح قال ما اتيت لادعو الابرار لكن الخطاه الى التوبه. فليس من عنده عايق لمغفرة 1397 الخطايا. 1398 فالذي يتوانا في التوبه حتى يموت مثل غير بار وغير مومن لانه اعدم ذاته النعمه التي اتى المسيح لينعم بها على المومنين. (a66r) اعني التوبه التي هي الموهبة (b84r) المبررة الخطاه من المومنين.

332 **قال الاخوه** ما الفرق بين التوبه والبر.

333 **قال المفسر** التوبه هي بر باتضاع. فان التايب الكبريا غريبه منه. واما الذي يصنع بر الفضيله فليست الكبريا بعيده عنه لان الكبريا تتبع الفضيله كما كتب عن اتضاع العشار وبر الفريسي.

334 **قال الاخوه** 1399 ان اخا سال انبا بجن مساله. فقال ان رجلا متوحدا. وعلمانيا. المتوحد فكر عشيه انه بكره يطرح عنه اسكيم الرهبنه والعلماني فكر عشيه انه بكره يلبس اسكيم الرهبنه. فاتفق موتهما في تلك الليله. فماذا يحسب لها. فقال له الشيخ ان الراهب مات راهبا والعلماني مات وهو علماني. 1400

were taken just as they were found'. Is recompense according to action or according to intention?"³⁷⁰

335 **The Exegete replied:** "We do not understand the actions of God in this world because it is written that the judgments of God cannot be examined and God's judgments of you are like a great deep.³⁷¹ He gave us to search what is apparent and near as was written: 'The secret things belong to the Lord our God',³⁷² and that which we discerned from this is that Abba Poemen used to know the thoughts of many of the solitaries and that the struggle with the demons would grow strong with some of them during the night especially the demon of fornication such that they think about returning to the world the next day. Most of them, rather, all of them except a very rare few are directed away from the distress of struggle and they adhere to monasticism until death, especially those who are visited by the grace of aid during difficult struggles and they are in the majority. Similarly, many lay people contemplate leaving the world [to join] the monastic order but are impeded for many hindering reasons, and their thought disappears. This is the reason why he said that the monk died a monk and the lay man died a lay man. As for knowing the recompense then this belongs to God alone."

336 **The Brothers asked:** "That brother who went into the world and married a woman, and when his master the holy man heard about this he prayed for him and supplicated our Lord saying: 'O Lord do not let your servant become defiled'. When he cohabited with the bride he died at once.³⁷³ Did he then die as a solitary or as a lay man?"

337 **The Exegete replied:** "Knowledge of this is also difficult for people, however, according to human inquiry we say this latter also died a monk like that other. However, he exceeded him in that his volition took lust further, but they both attained the blessings of God which stopped them from actually completing the break with monasticism. Other Fathers had supplicated God in this way concerning their disciples, however, He did not heed them and their disciples died in their fallen state. When the blessings of God touched him, however for the sake of the holy man, his master, then his intention behind his supplication was that his disciple should be considered among the solitaries that he might be

فكما وجدا اخذا. فهل المجازه على قدر العمل ام على قدر النيه.

335 **قال المفسر** لسنا ندرك اعمال الله في هذا العالم لانه مكتوب احكام الله لا تفحص واحكامك لله مثل العمق العظيم. ونحن جعل لنا تفتيش الظاهر والقريب كما كتب ان الخفايا هي للرب الاهنا (c95v) والذي ادركناه من هذا ان ابنا بجمن كان يعرف افكار كثيرين من المتوحدين وان منهم من يشتد عليه قتال الشياطين في الليل لان[1401] سيما شيطان الزنا (a66v) حتى يفكر انه في الغد (b84v) يرجع الى العالم. واكثرهم بل كلهم الا النادر جدا يبتدي عنهم هم القتال. ويثبتون في الرهبنه الى الموت لا سيما الذين تزورهم نعمة المعونه في القتال الصعب وهم الاكثرون. وكذلك[1402] كثيرين من العلمانيين يتفكرون في خروج من العالم الى[1403] الرهبنه فينعاقون من الاسباب الكثيره المعوقه. وتنحل فكرتهم. فلهذا قال ان الراهب مات راهبا والعلماني مات علمانيا. فاما معرفة المجازه بتحرير فلله وحده.

336 **قال الاخوه** فذلك الاخ الذي مضى الى العالم وتزوج امراه ولما سمع معلمه الشيخ صلى من اجله وطلب من ربنا قايلا يا رب لا تدع عبدك يتنجس. ولما دخل الى العروسه اسلم روحه لوقته. فهل مات متوحدا او علمانيا.

337 **قال المفسر** وهذه ايضا معرفتها عسره على الناس لكن بقدر التفتيش الانساني نقول مات هذا الاخر ايضا مثل ذلك راهبا. فانما زاد عليه بان ابطت ارادته في الشهوه اكثر وكلاهما ادركتها خيرة الله. وقطعتها عن تكميل فسخ الرهبنه بالفعل. واما اخر قد سالوا الله في تلاميذه هكذى فما سمع منهم وكملت تلاميذهم وفاتهم في سقوطهم. فلما ادركت هذا خيرة الله. (a67r) اما لاجل الشيخ معلمه.[1404] فان مقصوده في ساله ان يكون تلميذه محسوبا (b85r) في المتوحدين

requited as a solitary, or because God knew from his intention that he deserved this and that he subordinated himself either because of his youth, or because of the triumph of the demon who was struggling with him, or because of the weakness of his nature and knowledge, or because God knew the goodness of his earlier service and obedience to his master for the sake of God. He therefore responded to the supplication of his master for his sake. This was recounted to us by a monk upon his death. As for why the prayer of the holy man was heard so that his disciple would not get married, how else would he have lived and returned to him to become established in the solitary life through volition and action? Knowledge of this belongs to God and not to human beings in this world."

338 **The Brothers asked:** "Abba Poemen said: 'Every time a person falls into any shortcoming or ignorance and immediately says: "I have sinned", then God will receive him'."[374]

339 **The Exegete replied:** "The sins which are [committed] before baptism are forgiven because it is written: 'Repent, and let every one of you be baptized in the name of our Lord Jesus Christ for the remission of sins'.[375] And the sins [committed] after baptism are forgiven through the holy sacraments because Jesus said: 'This is my body and my blood which is broken and shed for you for the forgiveness of sins'. If the sins were cardinal such as those which the Apostle said excludes one from the Kingdom then if the sinner completes his penances which he accepts from his director then receives the divine Sacraments while his soul is filled with suffering and remorse for his sins then they will be forgiven. If, moreover, a person behaves ignorantly towards his brother in any way and then makes a prostration to him with a humble heart saying: 'I have sinned', and immediately asks for forgiveness with remorse for his ignorance then he will be forgiven because the Lord said: 'Forgive, and you shall be forgiven',[376] and: 'First go and be reconciled with your brother'.[377] The one sitting in his cell who slips because of struggling with the devil and the pain of yearnings, if he immediately repents and suffers and prays Gospel prayers and the Psalms, and prepares himself to receive the Sacraments, and believes without any doubt that his sins will be forgiven in this way, then his omission will be forgiven. If, however, the yearning remained with him for a long period of time until it overcame

ليجازى كمتوحد او لان ⁱ⁴⁰⁵ الله عرف من نيته انه كان يستحق هذا وانه قهر على ذاته. اما من اجل حداثته او من غلبة ⁱ⁴⁰⁶ الشيطان الذي (c96r) يجاهده او من ضعف طبعه ومعرفته. او لان الله عرف جودة من تقدم من خدمته وطاعته لمعلمه من اجل الله. فاجاب سال معلمه من اجلي. ⁱ⁴⁰⁷ فذلك حدسنا على موته راها. فاما لماذا قبلت صلاة ⁱ⁴⁰⁸ الشيخ حتى ان تلميذه لم يتزوج فكيف لم يعيش ويرجع اليه ويثبت في الوحده بالاراده والفعل. فمعرفة هذا لله لا للبشر في هذا العالم.

338 **قال الاخوه** ان انبا بجمن قال كل وقت يسقط الانسان باي نقص او جهل كان ويقول في ساعته اخطيت يقبله ⁱ⁴⁰⁹ الله.

339 **قال المفسر** اما الخطايا التي قبل المعموديه تغفر لانه مكتوب توبوا وليتعمد ⁱ⁴¹⁰ كل امر[ا] منكم باسم ربنا يسوع المسيح لغفران الخطايا والخطايا التي بعد المعموديه تغفر بالسراير المقدسه لان المسيح قال هذا هو جسدي ودمي الذي من اجلكم يقسم ويهرق لمغفرة ⁱ⁴¹¹ الخطايا. فان كانت الخطايا كباير ⁱ⁴¹² مثل التي قال الرسول عنها انها تبعد من الملكوت فهذه اذا تم (b85v) الخاطي قوانينه ⁱ⁴¹³ التي يقبلها (a67v) من مدبره. ثم تناول السراير الالهيه ونفسه مملوه الم وندما على خطاياه فانها تغفر له. واما اذا جهل انسان على اخيه باي جهل كان ويضرب له مطانيه باتضاع قلبه ويقول اخطيت. ويطلب الغفران من ساعته بندامه على جهله. فانه يغفر له. لان الرب قال اغفروا يغفر لكم. وامض اولا ⁱ⁴¹⁴ وصالح ⁱ⁴¹⁵ اخاك. واما الجالس في قلايته ومن حرب الشيطان والم الاوجاع يزل فاذا ندم وتالم لوقته وصلى بالصلاة الانجيليه والمزامير وهيا نفسه لاخذ السراير وامن بلا شك انه بذلك ⁱ⁴¹⁶ يغفر له خطاياه. غفرت له زلته فان ابطيا الوجع معه زمانا كثيرا حتى تسلط على

successful volition, then this requires many exertions, both labors of the body and of the mind, and remorse, and suffering, and constant prayers with a fervent soul. He would then be able to overcome it by receiving the Body and Blood of our Savior to whom glory, power and victory belong forever."

340 **Concerning the Performance of Miracles.**

341 **The Brothers asked:** "Why did Abba Macarius and Abba Sisoes and their like raise the dead but did not allow them to remain in this life, rather, they said to them: 'Rest until the time of the Resurrection'."[378]

342 **The Exegete replied:** "This is because there is no gain in their remaining [alive], neither for the dead nor for those who raised them and maybe not for others according to God's teaching, whose dispensation is that this matter should be thus, and for what used to appear to the Fathers in visions. Regarding the dead, this is because when one of the saints raised one of them he asked him: 'Do you wish to remain in this life?' He replied: 'The repose of death is better for us than toil in this life'. Regarding the ones they raised, this is so that the appearance of the traces of their miracles do not remain as a result of which their reputation would become great and they would be attacked by pride and vainglory and more generally. Were it not for the knowledge of God who gave them the power to raise them there would be no harm in their being raised, and some benefit from their return to their death when He commanded them to return them to death. Through this it becomes known that death is not an evil and that it does not take place without God's volition and dispensation, as is written: 'The hairs on your head are numbered'.[379] If God did not create Man in vain as the Prophet said[380] then he would not put him to death in vain without benefit. The death of many is the result of general causes either through nature as David said: 'When his day comes he dies', or through volition as Saul who slew himself by his own hand, or through the rage of the wicked be they demons, or people, or beasts, or venomous reptiles, or through Divine wrath such as the people of Noah by drowning in water, or the people of Lot by burning in fire, or the sons of Korah by being swallowed up, or the people of David at the hand of the angel, or through coincidence such as falling from high places, and heavy things falling, and

الاراده المفلحه. ^{1417} (c96v) فهذا يحتاج الى اعمال كثيره اعمال الجسد والذهن والى تندم وتالم. والى صلوات دايمه بحراره نفس. وحينيذ ياخذ الغلبه عليه بتناول جسد ^{1418} ودم مخلصنا الذي له المجد والعز والغلبه الى الابد.

على عمل الايات. 340

341 **قال الاخوه** لماذا انبا مقاريوس وانبا شيشاي وامثالها قاموا موتى وما ^{1419} خلوهم يبقوا في هذه الحياة ^{1420} بل قالوا لها ارقدوا الى زمان القيامه.

342 **قال المفسر** لانه لا ^{1421} ربح في بقاهم لا للموتى ولا للذين اقاموهم وعسى ولا ^{1422} لغيرهم حسب (b86r) ما يعلم الله الذي دبر (a68r) ان يكون هذا الامر هكذى وعلى ماكان يظهر للابا في الرويا. ^{1423} اما الموتى فلان بعض القديسين لما اقام بعضهم ساله هل تريد ان تبقا في هذه الحياة. فقال نياح الموت اخير لنا من عمل ^{1424} هذه الحياة. ^{1425} واما الذين اقاموهم ^{1426} فليلا يستمر ظهور اثار اياتهم فيعظم سيطهم ويقاتلوا بالكبريا والمجد الباطل وبالجمله فلولا علم الله الذي اقدرهم على اقامتهم ما في بقايهم من المضره. وفي عادتهم الى موتهم من المنفعه لما امرهم بعادتهم الى الموت. وبهذا يعرف ان الموت ليس هو شرا وانه لا يكون بغير اراده الله وتدبيره. كما كتب ان شعور روسكم ^{1427} محصاه. واذا كان الله لم يخلق الانسان باطلا كما قال النبي. فذلك ولا يميته باطلا بغير منفعه. وموت الكثيرين انما يكون بالاسباب العامه اما بالطبع كما قال داوود ان يصل يومه يموت. واما بالاراده فكما قتل شاوول نفسه بيده اما ^{1428} بالغضب من الاشرار اما الشياطين او الناس او الوحوش او الهوام واما بسخط اللهي ^{1429} فمثل قوم نوح التغريق في الماء ^{1430} وقوم لوط بالاحراق بالنار. وبني قورح (b86v) بالخسف. وقوم داوود بيد الملاك. واما بالاتفاق فمثل السقوط من المواضع العاليه وسقوط الاشيا الثقيله

drowning, and burning. All of this is by the will of God, may He be exalted, and His hidden dispensation which no creature in this world can discern and which will be known by all rational beings in the next world who will thank God for it. This hidden dispensation by Him, may He be exalted, towards people is not only at the time of their death but also during all the days of their lives and after their death alone and at their resurrection and forever without end, in the womb and out of the womb, in this world and in the coming world, in Paradise and in the Kingdom and in Hell. As for those whom the Lord and His Apostles raised at the outset of the Gospel and who remained in this life for a period after having died, then this was to establish the belief in the Resurrection, such as Lazarus and the son of the widow and the daughter of Jairus, and such as Tabitha whom the Apostle Peter raised."

343 **The Brothers asked:** "Why did Palladius in the book of *The Paradise* not write the accounts of the saint Mar Eugenius?"

344 **The Exegete replied:** "Because he lived before his time, and in the days of King Constantine he went to the land of the Persians in the days of King Shapur. He lived near Nisibis in the Ma'ara mountain and Mardin and he performed many miracles in the land of the Byzantines and the Persians. Through his prayers he raised the young man who had been killed by a lion when he was gathering firewood in the wilderness. He called him Lazarus and clothed him in a holy [monastic] garb and made him a solitary, and he became his servant. On another occasion he entered into the middle of a crematory fire and made a prostration in prayer. In the land of the Persians he exorcised the son of Shapur and debated with the Magians before the king and defeated them. In order to verify his faith they made a great fire in the house of the king and he made the sign of the cross on one of his ten disciples and ordered him to enter and stand in the middle of the blaze. He entered until he summoned him back as a result of which the Magians were disgraced and everyone praised God. King Shapur gave him authority and he built many churches and monasteries in all the land of Ahwaz [Khuzestan]. His biography was written by one of his disciples accompanied by a long commentary. For this reason Palladius did not mention it."

والغرق والحريق. وكل (a68v) ذلك[1431] بارادة[1432] الله تعالى وتدبيره الخفي الذي لا (c97r) يدركه مخلوق في هذا العالم وسيعرفه جميع الناطقين في العالم المزمع ويشكرون[1433] الله من اجله. وليس هذا التدبير الخفي يكون منه تعالى للناس في زمان موتهم فقط بل وفي جميع ايام حياتهم وفيما بعد موتهم فقط[1434] وفي قيامتهم والى الابد بلا انقضا. في البطن وخارج البطن في هذا العالم وفي العالم الاتي وفي الفردوس وفي الملكوت وفي الجحيم. واما الذين اقامهم الرب ورسله في مبادي البشاره وبقيوا في هذه الحياة[1435] مده بعد موتهم. فذلك[1436] كان لاثبات[1437] اعتقاد القيامه. مثل العازار[1438] وابن الارمله وبنت يايرس. ومثل طابيثا[1439] التي اقامها بطرس الرسول.

343 **قال الاخوه** لماذا لم يكتب بلاديس في كتاب الفردوس[1440] اخبار القديس مار اوجين.

344 **قال المفسر** لانه كان قبل زمانه وفي ايام قوسطنطين الملك جا الى بلاد الفرس في ايام[1441] سابور الملك. وسكن قريب من نصيبين في جبل المعره وماردين وصنع عجايب كثيره (b87r) في بلاد الروم والفرس. واقام بصلاته الشاب الذي افترسه السبع عندما كان يحطب في البريه وسماه لعازار ولبسه الاسكيم المقدس وجعله متوحد وصار له خديما. وفي زمان اخر (a69r) دخل وسط النار المحرقه وضرب المطانيه في الصلاه. وفي ارض الفرس اخرج الشيطان[1442] من ابن سابور وتجادل مع المجوس قدام الملك وغلبهم. ولتحقيق ايمانه[1443] عملوا نارا[1444] عظيمه في دار الملك. ورسم على واحد من تلاميذه العشره وامره ان يدخل ويقف وسط اللهيب. فدخل حتى استدعاه وافتضح المجوس وسبح الله[1445] كل احد. واعطاه الملك سابور سلطانا فبنى كنايس واديرة كثيره في جميع بلاد (c97v) الاهواز وسيرته وضعها احد تلاميذه بشرح طويل. ولهذا ترك بلاديس ذكرها.

345 **Concerning Divine Visions.**

346 **The Brothers asked:** "Saint Antony said: 'The power that I saw in baptism I have seen on the apparel of the solitary when he puts on the monastic garb'."[381]

347 **The Exegete replied:** "If the faithful is baptized he receives the token of filiation by the grace of the Holy Spirit. Through it he is able to fulfill the commandments of Christ. If the solitary puts on the monastic garb he acquires spiritual fervor by the grace of the Spirit. Through it he is able to reach perfection and then he will be worthy of divine visions. The action of these two powers is hidden in the solitaries and monks. It does not appear except to saints through visions. He who attains these two powers and strives through actions and prays constantly to the point of purity of heart then attains the third power by the grace of the Spirit which is called the spirit of visions about which the blessed Evagrius said: 'We do not give rest to our souls until a power from on high descends upon us'. The Commentator Saint[382] called it, 'The communion of the Spirit' in his commentary on 'May your Kingdom come',[383] and he described it as being the action of the Spirit through which the pure-hearted acquire the vision from God in the commentary on 'Blessed are the pure in heart for they shall see God'.[384] The gifts of the Spirit are many and the Spirit is one working in every person according to benefit and merit."

348 **The Brothers asked:** "It is written that a holy man used to look up to Heaven and see everything in it and look down to the earth and see the depths and what they contained."[385]

349 **The Exegete replied:** "The holy angels see all creatures at all times, both the perceptible and imperceptible. As for our Lord, they see him in this world according to their degrees of vision, and at the Resurrection they will all see Him through their natural vision. Each one according to his level will enjoy seeing the Lord face to face and seek enlightenment from His light. As for what lies outside of the whole created world, both the rational and the sensible, they do not see it, neither through a vision in this world nor through their natural vision in the next world because that which is not cannot be seen. Just as they are unable in their selves to be outside of the created world in nothingness, so too they are unable to see nothingness. And just as they are limited within time,

345 على المناظر الالهيه.

346 **قال الاخوه** قال القديس انطونيوس ان القوه التي رايتها الى المعموديه رايتها على لباس المتوحد عندما يلبس الاسكيم.

347 **قال المفسر** اذا تعمد المومن ياخذ اربون البنوه من نعمة روح القدس. وبها يقدر يكمل وصايا المسيح. واذا لبس المتوحد الاسكيم ياخذ من نعمة الروح (b87v) الغلوة الروحانيه. وبها يقدر يصل الى الكمال وحينيذ يستحق المناظر الالهيه. هاتان القوتان فعلها خفي في المتوحدين والرهبان. فلا يظهر الا للقديسين 1446 في الرويا. ومن وصل بهاتين القوتين وجاهد الاعمال وداوم الصلاه الى 1447 نقاوة القلب نال من نعمة الروح القوة الثالثه التي (a69v) تدعى روح المناظر عنها 1448 قال الطوباني وغريس لا نعط راحة لنفوسنا حتى ينزل علينا قوة من العلا. والمفسر القديس دعاها شركة الروح في تفسيره لتاتي 1449 ملكوتك ووصفها بانها فعل الروح الذي به ياخد الاتقيا القلوب الرويا من الله في تفسير طوبا النقية قلويهم. فانهم يعاينون الله. فمواهب الروح كثيره والروح واحد هو يعمل في كل انسان على قدر المنفعة والاستحقاق.

348 **قال الاخوه** مكتوب بان شيخا كان يرفع نظره الى السما فيرى كلما فيها ويحط نظره الى الارض فيرى الاعماق وما فيها.

349 **قال المفسر** الملايكة القديسين يرون جميع المخلوقات كل حين 1450 المحسوسه وغير المحسوسه. فاما ربنا فانما يرونه في هذا العالم بقدر درجاتهم في الرويا (c98r) وفي القيامه يراه جميعهم بالنظر الطبيعي لهم. وكل واحد على قدر رتبته يتنعم بنظر الرب (b88r) مواجهه ويستنير من نوره. اما ما هو خارج عن جميع العالم المخلوق المعقول منه والمحسوس فليس يرونه لا في الرويا في هذا العالم ولا في النظر الطبيعي لهم في العالم الاخر لان المعدم لا يرى. وكما لا يقدرون ان يكونوا خارجا بذواتهم عن العالم المخلوق في لا شي هكذى 1451 لا يقدرون يرون لا شي. وكما انهم داخلون تحت حدود 1452 الزمان

so too they are limited in their person and vision within created things. The perfect saints have through their vision, as we mentioned, the sight of the holy angels and this even though they do not equal the angels in purity of mind. Therefore, this holy saint's heart was purified through toil and the vision of his mind was illuminated by the light of grace. He was then able to see the high and low, heavenly and earthly created things through the vision of his mind."

350 **The Brothers asked:** "A certain holy man had light in his cell during the night resembling the light of day. He would read during the night and toil as much as he could during the day. Was this sensible or intelligible?"[386]

351 **The Exegete replied:** "It was sensible and is called the light of grace because it is one of the gifts of God which is granted to him whose heart is purified and whose love becomes perfect to the greatest extent. No one sees it except those who are granted it."

352 **The Brothers asked:** "What is the intelligible light which rises in the hearts of the righteous?"

353 **The Exegete replied:** "The intelligible light is called divine light and the light of the mind. If the heart becomes pure through toil and prayer, as the Fathers say, then a person sees the intelligible light, the hidden light which belongs to his mind. If he becomes perfect in [his] way of life and vision then he would merit seeing the light of our Lord: 'He who loves me keeps my commandments and I will love him and show myself to him'.[387] This is what is called the light of Christ and is what dawns in the minds of the righteous. As for the divine nature which is the Holy Trinity that is united in our Lord, no creature can see it or approach it, or also see the light of its glory that resides in it as Paul the Apostle said.[388] Since what is created cannot perceive what is uncreated, and the essence of God is uncreated, so too the light of His glory which resides in Him. The angels and the righteous no longer have any desire upon their resurrection other than the desire to see their Lord."

354 **The Brothers asked:** "Abba Theodore was staying in Scete when he was approached by three demons who wanted to enter his [cell]. He found out about them and fettered them outside his cell. They

هكذى هم داخلون باقنومهم (a70r) ونظرهم في حدود المخلوقات. والقديسين الكاملون هم بنظرهم كما ذكرنا في نظر الملايكه القديسين وذلك اذا ما ساووا الملايكه في نقا العقل. فهذا الشيخ القديس تطهر قلبه في الجهاد واستنار نظر ذهنه بنور النعمه فراى¹⁴⁵³ المخلوقات العاليه والسافله السمايه والارضيه بنظر ذهنه.

350 **قال الاخوه** بعض الشيوخ كان له نور في قلايته في الليل كنور النهار فيقرا في الليل ويعمل ما يمكنه ان يعمله بالنهار. فهل كان محسوسا ام معقولا.

351 **قال المفسر** كان محسوسا وهو يدعى نور النعمه لانه من موهبة الله يدفع لمن قد تنقى قلبه. وتكمل حبه على الاكثر لا يراه الا الذي وهب له.

352 **قال الاخوه** (b88v) ما هو النور المعقول الذي يشرق في قلوب الصديقين.

353 **قال المفسر** النور المعقول يسمى النور الالهي ونور الذهن. فاذا تنقى القلب في الجهاده والصلاه كما يقول الابا حينيذ يرى الانسان النور المعقول. النور الخفي الذي لذهنه. واذا تكمل في التدبير والنظر حينيذ يستحق نظر نور (c98v) ربنا الذي يجبني يحفظ وصاياي وانا احبه واريه نفسي. وهذا يدعى نور المسيح وهو الذي يشرق في عقول الصديقين. فاما الطبع الالهي¹⁴⁵⁴ الذي الثالوث المقدس المتحد¹⁴⁵⁵ بربنا. فليس يقدر مخلوق ان يراه ولا يدنوا منه. ولا يرى ايضا نور مجده الساكن فيه (a70v) كما قال بولس¹⁴⁵⁶ الرسول لان المخلوق لا يقدر يدرك غير المخلوق وجوهر الله غير مخلوق. وكذلك نور مجده الساكن فيه.¹⁴⁵⁷ وليس يبقا للملايكه والابرار شهوه في القيامه غير شهوة النظر الى ربهم.

354 **قال الاخوه** انبا تاودري كان جالسا في الاسقيطي فاتى اليه ثلث شياطين وارادوا ان يدخلوا اليه. فعلم بهم وربطهم خارج قلايته

feared his prayers and asked him to unfetter them and they departed in shame.³⁸⁹ Did he see them sensibly or intelligibly?"

355 **The Exegete replied:** "If the hearts of the saints become purified from the yearnings of sins and their minds become illuminated with the light of grace, the angels, and demons, and souls become at times sensible but without body, and at times intelligible through the deliberation of the mind, and at times near and at others far. However, not all of them have this at all times. Most of them have this if it is remitted to them at certain times. A few of them speak a great deal and so this gift becomes theirs whenever they wish. Sensible things do not hinder the vision of their mind. When they wished to enter this saint's [cell] and trouble him, he was granted the gift and saw them before they entered and fettered them with his prayers outside his cell until they sensed each other and were put to shame. A certain demon in the form of a man came to Abba Sisoes of Thebaïs and wanted to enter his cell and corrupt him with conversation. The holy man sensed him and said to his disciple: 'Go out and say to the one knocking that Sisoes is here'. When he heard this he went away ashamed because he knew that he had learnt of his coming and that he could not be able to overcome him."

356 **He also said:** "Those who act virtuously with their bodies alone and do not engage their souls in the struggle with wicked thoughts until they overcome all the yearnings do not merit reaching the land of safety, that is, as the Fathers say, the perfect love of God that is through our Lord Jesus Christ and seeing His mysteries through visions. Then there is the one who is in this world and deserves spiritual light from our Lord once or twice or three times or more. Then there is the one whose labors are many and is free from yearnings and has attained purity of heart: he is not granted the vision of our Lord in this life so as not to fall into pride and for another reason hidden from people. He may be granted this vision at the time of his death just as Abba Moses the Black saw it upon his death. He said to his disciple: 'Be happy and glad my son Zechariah for the doors of the Kingdom of Heaven have opened'.³⁹⁰ Then there is the one who only sees our Lord in Paradise as a token of his vision when He comes in His glory."

فخافوا من (b89r) صلاته وسالوه حتى يحلهم ومضوا مخزيين فهل راهم محسوسا ام معقولا.

355 **قال المفسر** اذا تنقت قلوب القديسين من اوجاع الخطايا واستنارت[1458] اذهانهم بنور النعمه والملايكه والشياطين والنفوس اوقاتا محسوسا بغير الجسد واوقاتا معقولا برويه العقل واوقاتا قريبا واوقاتا[1459] بعيدا. لكن ليس كلهم يكون هذا لهم في كل وقت. فان اكثرهم انما يكون هذا لهم اذا دفع لهم في بعض الاوقات. وقليلا منهم يتكلمون كثيرا فتكون هذه الموهبه لهم كلما ارادوا. ولا تعوق الاشيا المحسوسه نظر ذهنهم. فهذا القديس لما اردوا ان يدخلون اليه ويشغلوه[1460] اعط الموهبه فراهم من قبل دخولهم فريطهم بصلاته خارج قلايته حتى حسوا في بعضهم وخزيوا. انبا شيشاي التباييسي جا اليه بعض الشياطين شبه رجل واراد يدخل اليه ويطه بالحديث. (a71r) فاحس[1461] به الشيخ فقال لتلميذه اخرج وقل للذي[1462] يدق شيشاي (c99r) هنا. فلما سمع مضا مخزيا لانه علم انه قد علم بمجيه ولا يقدر (b89v) ان يطغيه.

356 **وقال ايضا** الذين[1463] يعملون الفضيله بجسادهم فقط ولا يلزمون[1464] انفسهم في الجهاد مع الافكار الشريره حتى يغلبوا جميع الاوجاع ما يستحقوا يصلوا الى بلد الامن. الذي هو كما تقول الابا حب الله الكامل. الذي ربنا يسوع المسيح ونظر اسراره في الرويا. وثم من هو في هذا[1465] العالم يستحق من ربنا النور الروحاني دفعه او دفعتين او ثلثه[1466] او[1467] اكثر. وثم من اعماله كثيره وهو معتوق من الاوجاع ووصل الى طهاره القلب لم يدفع له نظر ربنا في هذه الحياه[1468] ليلا يسقط في الكبريا ولسبب اخر خفي عن الناس. وهذا قد يوهب هذا النظر وقت موته كما راى انبا موسى الاسود عند نياحته. قال لتلميذه افرح وابتهج يا ابني زكريا قد انفتحت ابواب ملكوت السما. وثم من لا يرى سيدنا الا في الفردوس اربونا لنظره اذا جا في مجده.

357 **The Brothers asked:** "There were two brothers each of whom saw the power of the Spirit over the head of his companion. Then one of them accused the community of eating on Friday in the morning as a result of which the power departed from him until he felt remorse, suffered, and repented."[391]

358 **The Exegete replied:** "Because the power of the Spirit after a great deal of control over the senses and movements is given to him who merits it. Only those who do not reproach anyone with their tongue and who do not accuse anyone in their thoughts deserve it. When this brother slackened his guard, accused in his heart and reproached with his tongue, the power departed from him, and when he found out he righted himself."

359 **The Brothers asked:** "Why did a certain holy man say: 'He who adapts to wild beasts and fire is not hurt by them. If you want to find out if you are perfect then go to the community of brothers and those with them'. What is more difficult: living with wild beasts and entering into fire or joining the community and living with the brothers?"

360 **The Exegete replied:** "It is much more difficult for the Perfect to live with many brothers because of the dissolute among them, since it is through them that the demons fight them. Abba Evagrius said that they hinder them from their perfection. In the same way that men are hindered from running were they to run with children, so the perfect solitaries are hindered from their striving, exertion, and constant prayer by living with many brothers. The solitary is freed from three things: anger, censure, and complaint. The reason behind the difficulty of living with many brothers is that if a perfect person asked for aid from God to overcome wild beasts, reptiles, and fire, God would compel them to become obedient to him and make them submissive to him. Similarly, if he prays with indignation against the demons God would expel and banish them from him. As for wicked people, he cannot pray to God to force them into submission as with the wild beasts nor come against them with duress and drive them from him like demons. Even if he prayed, God would not heed his entreaty and oppress his freedom. The brothers fight them openly and curse them and in their dissoluteness, they commit what would necessitate their becoming angry at them on account of God's jealousy, and their volition is

357 **قال الاخوه** اخوان كان كل واحد منها يرى قوة روح على راس صاحبه. فلام احدهما[1469] الجمع على اكلهم يوم الجمعه من باكر فارتفعت عنه القوه حتى (b90r) ندم وتالم وتاب.

358 **قال المفسر** لان قوة الروح (a71v) بعد حراسة كثيره للحواس والحركات تعطى لمستحقها. ولا يستحقها الا الذين[1470] لا يبكتون احدا بلسانه ولا يلومون احد في افكارهم فهذا الاخ لما انحل من حرصه[1471] فلام بقلبه وبكت بلسانه[1472] ارتفعت عنه القوه. ولما علم اعتدل.

359 **قال الاخوه** لماذا بعض الابا قال الذي اصطلحت معه الوحوش والنار فلا توذيه. ان اردت ان تعرف انك كامل امض الى مجمع الاخوه من معهم. فايما اصعب السكن مع الوحوش والدخول في النار او الدخول في المجمع والسكن مع الاخوه.

360 **قال المفسر** اصعب جدا السكن مع اخوة كثيرين[1473] على الكاملين بسبب المنحلين منهم. لان الشياطين تقاتلهم بوساطتهم. وقال انبا وغريس انهم يعوقونهم عن كمالهم. وكما ان الرجال ينعاقون عن جريهم اذا جروا مع صغار كذلك[1474] المتوحدين (c99v) الكاملين ينعاقون بمساكنة الاخوة الكثيرة عن حرصهم وجهادهم وصلاتهم الدايمه. والمتوحد (b90v) ينعتق من ثلثه[1475] الغيظ والملامه والقمقمه. وسبب كون مساكنة اخوة كثيرة صعبه هو ان الوحوش والدبيب والنار اذا طلب الانسان الكامل المعونه من الله على غلبتهم قهرهم الله لطاعته واخضعهم[1476] له. وكذلك[1477] اذا صلى بغضب على الشياطين طردهم الله وابعدهم عنه. (a72r) واما الناس الاشرار فلا يقدر يصلى الله ان يجبرهم على الخدوع كالوحوش ولا ان ياتى عليهم بصعوبه ويطردهم عنه كالشياطين. ولو صلى لم يعمل الله له بطلبته ويظلم حريته. والاخوه يقاتلونهم ظاهرا او يشتمونهم ويفعلون في انحلالهم ما يوجب حردهم عليهم من اجل غيرة الله وارادتهم.

extensive and varied. They are unable to harm them on account of God or to be indignant or to fulfill their volition because of its disparity. As for the devil, he does not struggle openly with them, except rarely, and they are able to be indignant towards him. Furthermore, the monk in the community is under the authority of the heads of the monastery whereas in the solitude of the desert the wild beasts are under his authority. Being under authority is more difficult than being a head especially if opinions were to differ."

361 **The Sayings of the Fathers on All the Types of Virtue.**

362 **The Brothers asked:** "Abba Elijah said: 'I fear these three things: the departure of the soul from the body; meeting the Lord; and the handing down of the Judgment'."[392]

363 **The Exegete replied:** "This is because these three are very frightening. The Fathers prescribed that we should always remember the hour of death and the hour of Resurrection and the hour of Judgment, and Hell the most. Remembering these matters curbs us from committing sin and spurs us on to do good. At the hour of death there will be remorse for negligence and excessive sadness. At the hour of the Resurrection there will be great anxiety and tremendous fear. At the hour of standing before the Judge there will be the greatest fear concerning the judgment that He will hand down, and upon the handing down of the judgment the sinner will be in a state of shame and hopelessness. In Hell he will be in eternal torment."

364 **The Brothers asked:** "Why did God send Antony and another father to the lay men and women who saw their virtues and praised them?"

365 **The Exegete replied:** "For the benefit of the Fathers and the lay people because the Fathers were perfect in their exertions and labors but in need of humility, and the virtuous lay people were rich in humility and lacking in strength and courage through the power of hope. By sending them to them the Fathers' need for humility and the virtuous lay people's need for strength and hope was fulfilled."

366 **Marginal note:** "This he took from the words of the Apostle to the rich and the poor so that the best that you have may fill their

كثيره ومختلفه. ومن اجل الله لا يقدرون ان يوذوهم والا[1478] ان يغضبوا ولا ان يكملوا ارادتهم لاختلافها. فاما الشيطان لا يقاتلهم ظاهرا الا نادرا وتمكنون من الغضب عليه. وايضا فالراهب في المجمع يكون تحت طاعة[1479] رووسا[1480] الدير. وفي وحدة البريه تكون الوحوش تحت طاعته. وكونه مروسا[1481] اصعب من كونه ريسا لا سيما اذا تخالفت الارا.

361 **اقوال الابا** (b91r) **جميع اصناف الفضيله.**

362 **قال الاخوه** قال انبا اليا انا اخاف من هذه الثلثه.[1482] خروج النفس من الجسد. ولقا الرب. وخروج الحكم.

363 **قال المفسر** لكون هذه الثلثه[1483] مخيفه جدا. وصت الابا ان نتذكر دايما ساعة الموت وساعة القيامه وساعة الحكم وجهنم بالاكثر. ان[1484] تذكار هذه الامور تلجمنا عن فعل الخطيه وتنشطنا في عمل البر. وفي ساعة الموت يكون الندم على التفريط والحزن المفروط. وفي وقت القيامه يكون الاضطراب[1485] العظيم والخوف الشديد. وفي وقت الوقوف (a72v) بين يدي الديان يكون الخوف الاشد مما يخرج به الحكم. وفي خروج الحكم[1486] يكون الخاطي في الخجل وقطع الرجا. وفي جهنم يكون في[1487] العذاب الذي لا يبيد.

364 **قال الاخوه** لماذا انفد الله انطونيوس وابا اخر الى علمانيين رجال ونسا فنظروا فضايلهم ومدحوهم.

365 **قال المفسر** لرجح الابا والعلمانيين[1488] لان الابا كانوا كاملين في جهاد الاعمال محتاجين الاتضاع. وفضلا العلمانيين كانوا اغنيا في الاتضاع عاجزين العزا والشجاعه بقوة الرجا. فكل (c100r) بارسالهم اليهم عوز الابا من الاتضاع وعوز العلمانيين الفضلا من العزا والرجا.

366 **حاشيه** (b91v) هذا اخذه من قول الرسول للاغنيا والفقرا ليكون ما افضل عندكم سداد

shortcomings and so that what is best in them may fill your deficiencies."

367 **The Brothers asked:** "Why did some of them bring him with them by God's command to the desert and others leave him in the world?"

368 **The Exegete replied:** "Some came by God's command on account of the superior excellence of the solitary way of life over the lay way of life, and they left others behind to reproach the erring through them and to benefit the imitators with their actions, since there were people who rejected marriage and food and others who thought that virtuous action was unfeasible for all lay people."

369 **The Brothers asked:** "The Fathers went to Achristos the virtuous shepherd who said to them: 'Whatsoever God grants us from these few sheep that I have I will divide into three parts: a part for love, and a part for strangers, and a part for our needs'."

370 **The Exegete replied:** "By the part of love he signified his poor relations since Paul's command was to give to them, and by the part for strangers he signified the poor who are not of his own kind such as orphans, widows, and strangers. By the part of his needs he meant what concerns him and his wife that virtuous virgin."

371 **The Brothers asked:** "What is [the meaning of] the statement of the Fathers that this generation did not take wings and if they did take them they are not powerful and fiery."

372 **The Exegete replied:** "The wings are pure prayer. As for 'the powerful and fiery', this is the spiritual prayer which is the perfection of the solitaries in this life and he who merits it boils in his mind with the love of God and flies with it to sublimity until he unites with our Lord Jesus the Christ and enjoys His love and the joy of His remembrance and speech and miracles. Those who only act virtuously with their bodies and do not compel their souls to struggle with thoughts will not attain purity of heart and pure prayer which is free from distraction. Those who acquire purity of heart and prayer and do not remain in stillness until death but rather become neglectful and depend on what they have acquired lose the glorious gift which is the wreath of perfection of spiritual prayer."

367 **قال الاخوه** لماذا بعضهم جاوا[1490] به معهم[1491] بامر الله الى البريه وبعضهم تركوه في العالم.

368 **قال المفسر** احضروا البعض بامر الله لفضل تدبير الوحده على تدبير العلمانيه وتركوا البعض التبكيت الضالين بهم. ونفع المتشبهين باعمالهم لان من الناس من كان يرذل الزيجه والاطعمه ومنهم من كان يظن ان عمل الفضيله متعذر[1492] على جميع العلمانيين.

369 **قال الاخوه** ان الابا مضوا الى اكرسطس الراعي الفاضل فقال لهم مهما فتح الله لنا من هذه الاغنام القلايل التي لي[1493] (a73r) اقسم عليهم ثلثة[1494] اجزاء.[1495] جزو للحب وجزو للغربا وجزو لحوايجنا.

370 **قال المفسر** جزو الحب اشار به الى اقاربه الفقرا كوصية بولس بتقديمهم. وجزو الغربا اشار به الى المساكين الخارجين عن جنسه كالايتام والارامل والغربا. وجزو حوايجه يعني ما يخصه هو وزوجته تلك العذرى الفاضله.

371 **قال الاخوه** ما هو قول الابا ان هذا الجيل ما اخذوا اجنحة وان اخذوها (b92r) ما هي قويه ناريه.

372 **قال المفسر** الاجنحه هي الصلاة النقيه. واما القويه الناريه فهي الصلاه الروحانيه التي هي كمال المتوحدين في[1496] هذه الحياة والتي من استحقها يغلي في العقل بمحبة الله ويطير به الى العلو حتى يتحد مع ربنا يسوع المسيح ويتنعم في حبه ولذة[1498] ذكره وخطابه ومجاياه فالذين يعملون الفضيله في اجسادهم فقط وما (c100v) يلزمون نفوسهم في جهاد[1499] الافكار ما يصلون الى طهارة القلب والصلاة النقيه المعتوقه من الطياشه. والذين اقتنوا نقا القلب والصلاه ولا يثبتوا في الهدو الى الموت بل يتوانون ويتوكلون الى ما اقتنوه يعدمون المنحة[1500] المجهده التي للصلاة الروحانيه اكليل الكمال.

373 **Abba Poemen said:** "An evil nature is a wall of brass between God and people and he who leaves it aside says: 'By my God I will cross over the wall'.³⁹³ God whose path is without blemish'."³⁹⁴

374 **He said:** "If we undertake the part of labor which is for ourselves then we do not find impurity in us because he who is in a state of stillness when fasting or stays up laboring overcomes the volition of the body. He who is meek, humble and wretched in himself defeats the demons, and he who prays at all times rejoices in God at all times."

375 **The Brothers asked:** "The brother artisans went to a holy man who blessed some of them and said to the hermit: 'A hermit should be humble in his heart because his craft carries with it the pride of spirit'."

376 **The Exegete said:** "This is because baskets, mats and sieves can be learnt and known by all those who wish and are intent on it. Copying books is good but not everyone who wishes is capable of it and it is the most noble of crafts which exists among the brothers. For this reason the holy man said that he who is involved in it needs to be humble in his heart. He said to the one who weaves wreaths: 'May the Lord bless you and weave a garland for you my son', and to the one who made mats he said: 'May God give you strength'. He said to the one who makes sieves: 'May the Lord keep you', meaning from being sieved by the devil just as he determined to sieve the Apostles, because he used to sell the sieves to men and women. He said to the hermit: 'You know', meaning that the knower becomes proud through his knowledge and should therefore be humble."

377 **The Brothers asked:** "A brother went to Abba Poemen and said to him: 'I sow a field, I reap, and give alms from it'. He said to him: 'Well done'. His brother Abba Job said to him: 'You did not speak to him with the fear of God'. And in the end he prostrated before him and asked for his forgiveness."³⁹⁵

378 **The Exegete replied:** "This is because Abba Poemen used to say that the way of life of the brothers is divided into three parts. One is outstanding stillness, and another a sick person who perseveres and gives thanks, and another one who serves with good intent. The conscience of the three lies in worship and their recompense

373 **وقال انبا بجمن** الخلق الشرير هو سور من نحاس بين الله والناس والذي يتركه يقول بالهي اعبر السور الله الذي طريقه بلا عيب.

374 (a73v) **وقال** ان اقنا جزو العمل الذي لانفسنا فلا[1501] نوجد النجاسه فينا لان الذي في الهدو في الصوم او في السهر يعمل يغلب ارادة الجسد والذي هو وديع ومتضع وحقير عند نفسه يغلب الشياطين والذي يصلي في كل حين يفرح بالله في كل وقت.

375 (b92v) **قال الاخوه** ان اخوه ارباب صنايع مضوا الى شيخ فبارك لبعضهم وقال للناسك ينبغي للناسك ان يكون متضعا في قلبه لان صنعته فيها كبريا[1502] الروح.

376 **قال المفسر** لان القفف والحصر والغرابيل كل من يريد ويحرص يقدر ان يتعلمها ويعلمها ونسخ الكتب حسنا لا يقدر عليه كلمن اراده وهي اشرف الصنايع التي تكون بين الاخوه. فلهذا قال الشيخ ان صاحبها يحتاج الى ان يكون متضعا بقلبه. وقال للذي كان يضفر الضفيره الرب يباركك ويضفر لك اكليلا يا ولدي والذي كان يصنع الحصر الله يقويك. وقال للذي يصنع الغرابيل الله يحرصك اي من ان يغربلك الشيطان كما ازمع ان يغربل الرسل. لان[1503] كان يبيع الغرابيل للنساء[1504] والرجال. وقال للناسك انت عارف اي العارف يتكبر بمعرفته فينبغي ان يتضع.

377 **قال الاخوه** ان اخا مضى[1505] الى انبا بجمن وقال له انا ازرع حقلا واحصد واتصدق منه. فقال له جيد تصنع. فقال له انبا ايوب اخوه لم تقل له (a74r) بخوف الله وفي (c101r) الاخر ضرب له مطانيه ان يغفر له.

378 **قال المفسر** (b93r) لان انبا بجمن[1506] كان يقول ان تدبير الاخوه ينقسم ثلثة[1507] اجزا. واحد في هدو جيد واخر مريض يصبر ويشكر واخر يخدم بنية جيده. فضمير الثلاثه في العباده وجزاهم عنها

for it will be equal. This brother was a farmer from the countryside and was incapable of knowing the struggle with thoughts through stillness or fasting or constant prayer. In addition, his body was not weak in order to receive the reward of the one who perseveres and gives thanks. What he was able to do was to serve the needy which was allowed to him through his work. Abba Poemen did not know the way of life of the brother from the outset as his brother knew from him. He, therefore, reproached him since he did not instruct him concerning the best solitary life. When he finally found out he praised God who had given his brother wisdom with which to direct each one according to what is profitable for them. He, therefore, prostrated before his brother."

379 **The Brothers asked:** "What is the [meaning of the] statement of Abba Poemen to that hermit: 'Understand the origin of the first betrayal then you will understand the second betrayal. Were it not for the first the second would not have happened'."[396]

380 **The Exegete replied:** "Thieves came upon him and he handed them over to the governor. The first betrayal is his acceptance of the counsel of the devil, and the second is his handing them over to the governor. He said: 'When they came and you cried out and they seized them you should have treated them as the Prophet Elisha did with those who came to slay him: he gave them to eat and drink then sent them back to their countries unhurt. Perhaps they would have been put to shame as a result of the benefaction and both you and they would have profited by fulfilling the commandment of our Lord: "Do good to those who drive you away and make you grieve."[397] Your brothers in humanity have received nothing more than shackling, striking, prison, and punishment perhaps as far as execution'."

381 **The Brothers asked:** "Why did Abba Poemen and his brothers not allow their mothers into their cells when they came to them nor did they speak with them?"[398]

382 **The Exegete replied:** "In order to fulfill the commandment of our Lord concerning estrangement: 'He who loves father or mother more than me is not worthy of me',[399] and, 'He who does not hate his father and mother and carries his cross and follows me is not worthy of me'.[400] Meaning, that if he does not distance himself from them and keeps from assisting them, talking to them,

يكون متساويا.^1508 وهذا الاخ كان فلاح من الريف. فما كان يقدر على معرفة^1509 مجاهدة الافكار في الهدو ولا على الصوم والصلاه الدايمه. وايضا لجسده ما كان ضعيفا ينال اجر الصابر الشاكر. فالذي كان يقدر يصنع وهو الخدمه للمحتاجين فسح^1510 له في عمله. وانبا بجمن^1511 ما كان يعرف تدبير الاخ من بدايته كما كان اخوه يعرف منه. فلامه اذ لم يامره بالتوحد الافضل. ولما عرف اخيرا مجد الله الذي اعطا لاخيه حكمه يدبر بها كل واحد كما له فيه الربح^1512 وضرب لاخيه المطانيه.

379 **قال الاخوه** ما هو قول انبا بجمن لذلك الحبيس افهم التسليم الاول من اين هو وحينيذ تفهم التسليم الثاني. فلولا الاول لم تصنع الثاني.

380 **قال المفسر** ان لصوصا اتوه فسلمهم للوالي. فالتسليم^1513 الاول هو قبوله من مشورة الشيطان والثاني (b93v) هو تسليمهم للوالي.^1514 قال كان ينبغي لما اتوا وصرخت وامسكوهم ان تعمل معهم كما صنع اليشع النبي مع الذين اتوه ليقتلوه. اذ اطعمهم^1515 وسقاهم ونفذهم الى^1516 بلادهم سالمين^1517 ولعلهم (a74v) كانوا يحتشمون من النعمه فيرجعون^1518 وتربح انت كمال وصية ربنا احسنوا الى من يطردكم ويحزنكم. وما تسلم اخوتك في البشريه الى الربط والضرب والحبس والعقاب وربما للقتل.

381 **قال الاخوه** لماذا لم يدخل انبا بجمن واخوته بامهم الى قلاليهم لما مضت اليهم ولا تكلموا معها.

382 **قال المفسر** ليكملوا وصية ربنا على الغريه من يحب ابا او اما اكثر مني فما يستحقني. ومن لا يبغض (c101v) اباه وامه ويحمل صليبه ويتبعني ما يستحقني. اي اذ لم يبعد من قربهم ونصرهم ومخاطبتهم

and concerning himself with them, 'He cannot love Me spiritually', nor can he struggle against the demons and spiritual yearnings, nor can he fulfill the military service of Christ and follow the King. Just as he who wants to follow an earthly king cannot stay with his father. This is in order for the dissolute brothers to know how to imitate them. During that time the barbarians had come to Scete and all the community of monks fled to the vicinity of the villages and they were vigilant and preserving their state of estrangement."

383 **The Brothers asked:** "A lay man was serving a saintly man. He came to visit him and found him dead and eaten by hyenas. He wept and asked from the Lord to inform him why this happened to the saint. The angel of the Lord came and said to him: 'This saint had a little shortcoming which was recompensed here so that he might be perfect there'."[401]

384 **The Exegete said:** "The trials of the righteous are for two reasons: either in order to reveal their goodness that is hidden from the knowledge of people like Job who was told by God: 'I tested you so that your goodness would be revealed', or for the sake of a little shortcoming such that they receive their recompense here and would then be perfect and would be glorified and live in delight with the Perfect such as David and Hezekiah. The causes of tribulations are many and hidden from people in this world. When the Prophet Jeremiah wished to know them God said to him: 'Behold, if racing against men has tired you, how do you hope to race against horsemen?'[402] It was said to Antony: 'Take care of yourself and leave off from petitioning for this'. These are the judgments of God. When the Apostles asked our Lord about the blind man saying, 'O Lord, did this man sin or his parents that he was born blind?'[403] the Lord informed them that there are many causes and these are not limited to what they know, saying: 'Neither this man nor his parents but that the works of God might appear in him'."[404]

385 **The Brothers asked:** "[God] sent Gabriel and Michael to a solitary upon his death and they asked his soul to come out to Him but it did not wish to. Our God sent to him David and those who sing with him who chanted the Psalms which made it come out joyfully into the embrace of the two angels and it ascended gladly.[405] Furthermore, some brothers asked Antony concerning a

والاهتمام بهم فما يقدر يحبني روحانيا ولا يجاهد الشياطين والاوجاع النفسانيه ولا يقدر ان يكمل جندية المسيح ويتبع الملك. كما من اراد ان[1519] يتبع ملكا ارضيا لا يقدر ان يقيم عند ابايه. وليعلموا الاخوة المنحلين التشبه[1520] بهم. ففي ذالك[1521] الوقت كانت البرير قد اتوا الى الاسقيطي. فهربت جماعة الرهبان قريبا من الضياع وكانوا (b94r) في تيقظ وحفظ الغربه.

383 **قال الاخوه** ان رجلا علمانيا كان يخدم رجلا قديسا لجا يفتقده فوجده مات واكلته الضباع[1522] فبكا وطلب من الرب ان يعرفه لماذا جرى للقديس[1523] هذا لجا ملاك الرب وقال له هذا القديس كان له نقص قليل واخذ جزاه هنا حتى يكون هناك كاملا.

384 **قال المفسر** ان تجارب الصديقين لامرين. اما من اجل ظهور برهم (a75r) الخفني عن معرفة الناس مثل ايوب الذي قال الله له لهذا جربتك[1524] حتى يبان صلاحك. او من اجل نقص قليل لياخذوا جزاهم هاهنا ويكونوا كاملين ثم يتمجدوا ويتنعموا مع الكاملين مثل داوود وحزقيا. واسباب التجارب كثيره مخفيه عن الناس في هذا العالم. فارميا النبي لما اراد معرفتها قال الله له ها مع الرجاله جريت وتعبت فكيف ترجوا ان تجري اصحاب الخيل. وانطونيوس قيل له اهتم بنفسك واترك الطلب من اجل هذا. فهذه هي احكام الله. والرسل لما سالوا ربنا عن الاعمى قايلين يا رب هذا اخطا ام ابواه حتى ولد اعمي. فعرفهم الرب ان الاسباب كثيره وليست محصوره فيما تعرفونه. كقوله لا هذا اخطا ولا ابواه بل ليظهر فيه (b94v) اعمال الله.

385 **قال الاخوه** ان متوحدا عند موته ارسل اليه جبرايل وميخايل. وكانوا يسالون[1525] نفسه ان تخرج اليه[1526] وما ترضى[1527] فارسل اليه الهنا[1528] داوود والمرتلين معه. ورتلوا بمزامير. فخرجت بفرح في حضن الملاكين وصعدت بفرح. وايضا اخوه سالوا انطونيوس على

word in the Book of the Levites. He went out into the desert and cried out in a loud voice saying: 'O God, send me Moses to explain this word to me'.⁴⁰⁶ Is this correct, and did David and Moses appear or an angel who resembles them?"

386 **The Exegete replied:** "There are those who say that the prophets, apostles and perfect saints are sometimes sent from Paradise to the saints out of esteem for them and joyful hope at the time of their death. Similarly, the angels are sent to those who deserve to inherit the Life [to come] as the Apostle wrote and as the Blessed Paul the Exegete stated. So too, the saints in this life are sent by the will of the Savior of all to save the sinners and likewise after their departure from here [this world]. Likewise, the saints are very often carried away to Paradise in their minds while still in the body and in this [same] manner they are very often sent from Paradise through their souls to the saints here [out of] esteem and [for their] benefit. David and Moses were sent as was written in the stories of the saints from among the wise and good. Had Moses not been the one who was sent in person, then why did the virtuous Saint Antony request his presence and not the presence of an angel to explain to him? The Gospel witnessed that Moses and Elijah appeared to the Apostles and it did not state their two angels, and there is no doubt that spiritual states belong to the spiritual. Not everyone is spiritual for not everyone can understand and accept these spiritual states. The spiritual in his thought attributes these apparitions of angels to a resemblance of the saints."

387 **The Brothers asked:** "With what chant did David and his companions sing the Psalms so that the soul of the solitary came out of his body eagerly and joyfully?"

388 **The Exegete replied:** "In the attire of the spiritual which is higher than the corporeal senses, resembling the chant of the angels to the saints as Abba Isaiah said concerning one of the twelve wanderers meaning those who wander as a work of supererogation. He said: 'If you become weary and lazy then depart [in your mind] to heaven and consider the wonderful beauty of the angels and their fervent praise of God, and enjoy their singing and voices and through this delight then consider all earthly matters to be ashes and dung'. By God's command the two angels were not able to bring out the soul of the righteous one by force because the

كلمه من سفر اللاويين فخرج الى البريه (c102r) وصرخ بصوت عال قايلا يا الله انفذ لي موسى يعرفني هذه الكلمه. فهل ذلك صحيح وهل داوود وموسى حضرا¹⁵²⁹ ام ملاك يشبهها.

386 **قال المفسر** ثم من يقول ان الاتبيا والرسل والقديسين الكاملين يرسلون من الفردوس الى (a75v) القديسين في بعض الاوقات لكرامتهم وفرح رجاهم وقت نياحتهم. وهذا كما ان الملايكه يرسلون للمستحقين لوراثه¹⁵³⁰ الحياة¹⁵³¹ كما كتب رسول وكما قال الطوباني بولس المفسر. كما ان القديسين في هذه الحياة¹⁵³² يرسلون بارادة¹⁵³³ مخلص الكل لخلاص الخطاه وكذلك بعد نقلتهم من هنا. وكما ان القديسين دفعات كثيره يخطفون الى الفردوس بعقولهم وهم بعد في الجسد هكذى دفعات كثيره يرسلون من الفردوس بنفوسهم الى القديسين هنا الرىح والكرامه.¹⁵³⁴ فداوود وموسى ارسلا كما كتب في اخبار (b95r) القديسين¹⁵³⁵ من اناس حكما¹⁵³⁶ ابرار. ولو لم يكن موسى هو المرسل بنفسه فلمذا طلب الفاضل القديس انطونيوس حضوره¹⁵³⁷ ولم يطلب حضور ملاك يفهمه. وقد شهد الانجيل ان موسى وايليا ظهرا للرسل ولم يقل ملايكتهما ولا شك ان الروحانيات للروحانيين.¹⁵³⁸ وليس كل احد روحانيا فليس كل احد يقدر على فهم هذه الروحانيات وقبولها. فالنفساني في فكرته ينسب هذه الظهورات الملايكه بشبه¹⁵³⁹ القديسين.

387 **قال الاخوه** فباي¹⁵⁴⁰ ترتيل رتل داوود هو واصحابه المزامير حتى خرجت نفس المتوحد من جسده بنشاط وفرح.

388 **قال المفسر** بزي الروحانيين¹⁵⁴¹ الذي هو اعلا من الحواس الجسديه. كترتيل الملايكه القديسين كما قال انبا اشعيا عن واحد الاثنيعشر¹⁵⁴² الجوالين¹⁵⁴³ (a76r) اي الذين ينتقلون للنفل. انه قال اذا مليت وتكاسلت امضي الى السما¹⁵⁴⁴ وانظر حسن الملايكه العجيب وتسبحتهم لله بغير فتور واتنعم بلحانهم واصواتهم ومن لذتها¹⁵⁴⁵ احسب جميع الارضيات عندها رمادا وزبلا. وبامر الله ما قدر الملاكين يخرجان نفس البار غصبا لان النبي يقول كريم امام

Prophet said: 'Precious before the Lord is the death of his righteous ones'.[407] When it discerned the spiritual chant it came out joyfully and eagerly because of the greatness of the delight."

389 **The Brothers asked:** "A certain holy man asked God to see all the Fathers. He saw them all except Antony and he said to Him: 'The ones I see have a place that would make Antony [with] God there'."[408]

390 **The Exegete replied:** "Either his mind was taken up to Paradise and he saw them, or they came to him spiritually and he saw them mentally, or an angel showed them to him in a vision. He did not see Antony for two reasons: the first is in order for him to be humble so that he does not become proud and is fought with thinking, in the sight of all the Fathers, of comparing himself with God, and in order to attain the sought-after perfection from God. The second is because of the greatness of Antony and the shortcomings of this holy man in discerning him in his glory."

391 **He also said:** "The words of the holy man: 'If there is a persecution go to faithful Fathers or stay in your cell', means: 'If you find Fathers then go to them to strengthen you against persecution, and if you do not find a person that you can rely on then stay in your cell and resign yourself to our Lord and strive in your way of life and the Lord will take care of you and guard you'."[409]

392 **He said:** "If two share an abode and they are both merciful and their wills are in agreement then this is good. But if [only] one of them was merciful then they do not mutually share in what they possess. However, if one [of them] wanted that they share in order for the one to benefit from the other then let each one of them be in possession of what they have, to do with whatever they please."

393 **He also said:** "A group from among the lay brothers who love stillness and solitude and who lacked knowledge, when they had heard that some Fathers had no knowledge of books and by the grace of God they mastered the science of books and knowledge of its commentaries, they began to beseech God that He teach them the knowledge of what they wished without learning, and without having to be humble and to learn from the wise holy men until the time of their old age and perfection. In order to censure their pride

الرب موت ابراره. (c102v) ولما ادركت الترتيل الروحاني فمن عظم اللذه خرجت بفرح ونشاط.

389 **قال الاخوه** بعض الشيوخ طلب من الله ينظر جميع الابا فراهم ماخلا انطونيوس وقال له الذي¹⁵⁴⁶ اراهم له موضع ان (b95v) يكون انطونيوس الله هناك.

390 **قال المفسر** اما يكون اختطف عقله الى الفردوس فراهم او اتوا اليه روحانيا فراهم عقليا او اراهم له ملاك في الرويا. ولسببين ما راى انطونيوس احدهما ليتضع ويقاتل بالفكر ليلا يتكبر فراهم في نظر جميع الابا تشبها¹⁵⁴⁷ بالله وحصول كمال مطلوبه¹⁵⁴⁸ من الله. والثاني لعظمت انطونيوس ونقص هذا الشيخ عن ادراكه في مجده.

391 **وقال ايضا** قول الشيخ واذاكان اضطهاد امض الى ابا مومنين او اجلس في قلايتك. يعني ان وجدت ابا امض اليهم ليقووك على الاضطهاد.¹⁵⁴⁹ وان كنت ما تجد انسانا تتكل عليه امكث في قلايتك واسلم نفسك لربنا واحرص في تدبيرك والرب يهتم بك ويحرسك.

392 **وقال** اذا اشترك اثنان في المسكن فان رحومين (a76v) وارادتها متفقه لجيد وان كان احدهما رحيما فلا يشتركا فيما لها لكن ان اراد ان يشتركا من اجل انتفاع الواحد بالاخر فليكن كلمنها مالكا لما له يصنع فيه ما يشا.

393 **وقال ايضا** ان قوما من الاخوه العلمانيين المحبين الهدو والانفراد غير عارفين لما سمعوا ان بعض الابا لم يكن لهم علم بالكتب وبنعمت الله استطوا في علم الكتب ومعرفت تفاسيرها صاروا يطلبون (b96r) من الله ان يعلمهم معرفة¹⁵⁵⁰ ما يريدونه من غير تعليم ولا يتضعون ويتعلمون من المشايخ الحكما الى زمان شيخوختهم وكهلهم. والله لاجل تبكيت كبرياهم

God did not grant them the understanding of what they wished and when the demons sensed this neglect they gave them understanding according to their wicked will."

394 **He also said:** "He who affects ignorance for the sake of God is the one who is wise and because of his humility is ignorant towards himself and does not cogitate nor display his wisdom."

395 **He also said:** "He who pictures God before his eyes at all times then the recollection of the fear of God does not allow him to sin."

396 **The Brothers asked:** "Abba Theodore said: 'Many in this age have desired rest before God gave it to them'."[410]

397 **The Exegete replied:** "If brothers enter into [the life of] stillness, after just a few years and limited merits they desire spiritual rest which is only barely given to some Fathers in the time of their old age after many toils and great effort accompanied by trials. As for this repose, it comes through meditation, a rightly-guided heart, pure thoughts, spiritual understanding, purity of heart, sacred light of the mind, constant joy in our Lord, constant meditation on future benefits through the way of life of the spirit. Abba Theodore said to a certain brother: 'I did not find rest in seventy years and you wish to find rest in eight years?'"[411]

398 **He also said:** "Sometimes the struggle knocks down the Perfect so that they recollect the weakness of their natures and do not become proud because of their many virtues and gifts."

399 **The Brothers asked:** "A certain holy man when he had spent fifty years not having eaten bread or having drunk any water except for vegetables said: 'I have slain the yearnings', and another said, 'He did not slay the yearnings but rather he fettered them'.[412] Another holy man said, 'I have died to this world'. A holy man who was his friend said to him: 'Except that the devil has not died from the world and for this reason we must be fearful at all times to the final breath'."

400 **The Exegete replied:** "Through many works, constant prayer, the controlling of thoughts and divine aid a person shackles the devil and places him beneath the feet of his mind. If he becomes neglectful or proud then the devil rises up before him and he becomes more brazen towards him. A group of naive fathers

394 **وقال ايضا** المتجاهل من اجل الله هو الذي يكون حكيما وهو لاتضاعه جاهل عند نفسه وغير مفتكر ولا متظاهر 1552 بحكمته. 1553

لم يعطهم فهم ما ارادوا والشياطين اذا حسوا بهذه التخليه يفهمونهم بارادتهم 1551 الشريره.

395 **وقال ايضا** من يصور الله قدام عينيه في كل وقت لا يدعه تذكار مخافة الله ان يخطي.

396 **قال الاخوه** ان انبا ثادرس قال كثير في هذا الزمان اشتهوا الراحه قبل ان يعطيها الله لهم.

397 **قال المفسر** (c103r) ان اخوا اذا دخلوا الهدو في سنين قليله وفضايل يسيره يشتهون الراحة الروحانيه التي هيهات ان تعطي لبعض الابا في زمان شيخوخيتهم الا بعد اتعاب كثيره وجهاد عظيم مع الامتحان. فاما هذا النياح فهو من الفكره. قلب محتد. (a77r) افكار نقيه. فهم روحاني. طهارة القلب. النور المقدس الذي للذهن. الفرح الدايم بربنا. الهذيذ الدايم في الخيرات العتيده مع تدبير الروح وقد قال انبا ثادرس لبعض الاخوه انا في سبعين سنه ما وجدت راحه وانت في ثمان سنين (b96v) تريد تجد راحه.

398 **وقال ايضا** ان الحرب يخلا بعض الاوقات على الكاملين حتى يتذكروا ضعف طباعهم ولا يتكبروا لكثرة فضايلهم ومواهبهم.

399 **قال الاخوه** بعض الشيوخ لما قام خمسين سنه ما اكل خبز ولا شرب ماء 1554 ما خلا خضرا فقط. قال اني قتلت الاوجاع واخر قال لم يقتل الاوجاع وانما ربطها وشيخ اخر قال مت لهذا العالم. فقال له شيخ 1555 صديق 1556 له الا ان الشيطان ما مات 1557 من العالم. ولهذا ينبغي لنا ان نكون خايفين كل حين الى النفس الاخير.

400 **قال المفسر** بالاعمال الكثيره والصلاة الدايمه وحراسة الافكار والمعونة الالهيه يربط الانسان الشيطان ويجعله تحت قدمي ذهنه. وان توانا او تكبر فالشيطان يقوم قبالته ويزداد عليه جراه فقوم من الابا الساذجين

because of old age, long labor and the aid of God considered that they had been relieved of the struggle with yearnings and demons and thought that they had stood in the perfection of the next world, that the yearnings had died in them and that they had defeated the demons. When a group of discerning Fathers heard this concerning them they went to them and rectified their knowledge. Abba Abraham went to the holy man who ate vegetables, did not eat bread for fifty years and said: 'I slew fornication, the love of silver and vainglory'. He said to him: 'If I discovered a woman in your bed would she appear as other than a woman in your thoughts?' He replied: 'No, however I would fight my thoughts'. He said: 'The yearning is alive, since it needs to be fought, however, it is fettered by works, the fear of God and the grace of aid'. He then said to him: 'If you found gold among stones or heard regarding two brothers that one of them praises you and the other curses you would you consider them both in the same manner?' He replied: 'No, however, I would struggle with my thoughts in order not to take the gold and to serve the one who curses me in the same manner as the one who honors me'. He said: 'The yearning is then alive, for what is dead is not fought and so long as the saints are in this world they are unable to slay yearnings and demons. However, they fetter them and so their effects do not appear. The slaying of yearnings and subduing of the demons in this world belong to God alone. In the next world all the natures of the rational of foul intent and the wicked demons are released'."[413]

401 **The Brothers asked:** "The righteous Apostles were granted the authority to crush all the forces of the Enemy and that nothing harm them. Pachomius said: 'You O Theodore, my son, and those who struggle like you, have fettered Satan like a bird and trampled on him like dust, but when you became neglectful he also rose to fight you'. As for Sylvanus, he fought him until he was also no longer able to subdue him."

402 **The Exegete replied:** "Those who struggle with yearnings and battles in humility are the ones who fetter Satan and trample upon him. Those who have acquired the grace of the Holy Spirit and perfect humility are the ones who subjugate Satan. So long as they are in this world whenever they bow or become neglectful in labor or become lacking in humility they fall. The Lord said to his disciples: 'You are the salt of the earth, but if the salt becomes

من اجل الشيخوخه وطول العمل وعون الله راوا انهم قد استراحوا من القتال مع الاوجاع والشياطين وظنوا انهم قد وقفنوا في كمال العالم العتيد وماتت منهم الاوجاع وغلبوا الشياطين. وقوم (a77v) من (b97r) الابا الفهمين 1558 لما 1559 سمعوا عنهم مضوا 1560 اليهم وعدلوا معرفتهم. وانبا ابراهيم مضى 1561 الى الشيخ الذي ياكل الخضر ولم ياكل خبزا خمسين سنه. وقال اني قتلت الزنا ومحبة الفضه والمجد الفارغ. فقال له وجدت امراه في مرقدك هل تكون في افكارك كانها غير امراه. قال لا لكن اجاهد افكاري. قال فالوجع حي. اذ هو يحتاج الى مجاهده ولكنه مربوطا (c103v) بالاعمال والخوف من الله ونعمة المعونه. ثم قال له فاذا وجدت ذهبا مع مجاره او سمعت عن اخوين ان احدهما يمجدك والاخر يسبك هل تنظرهما بالسوا. 1562 قال لا لكني احارب افكاري ان اخذ الذهب وان اخدم الذي يسبني كالذي يكرمني. قال فالوجع حي. فان الميت لا يحارب وما دام القديسون في هذا العالم فلا يقدرون ان يقتلوا الاوجاع والشياطين. لكنهم يربطونهم فلا يظهر اثرهم. وقتل الاوجاع وقهر الشياطين في هذا العالم هو للاله 1563 وحده. وفي العالم العتيد تنعتق جميع طبايع الناطقين في النيه الرديه والشياطين الشريره.

قال الاخوه فالرسل الابرار قد دفع لهم سلطان على ان يدوسوا كل قوات العدو ولا يضرهم شي. ويكوميوس قال انت يا ابني ثادرس 1564 والمجاهدون مثلك ربطتم ابليس مثل العصفور ودستموه مثل (b97v) التراب. ومتى (a78r) توانيتم قام لقتالكم ايضا. واما سلوانا فقتله حتى انه ما بقى يقدر يغلبه ايضا. 401

قال المفسر الذين يجاهدون مع الاوجاع والقتال باتضاع هم يربطون ابليس ويدوسونه. والذين اقتنوا نعمة روح القدس والاتضاع الكامل هم يستعبدون ابليس. وما داموا في هذا العالم متى مالوا او توانوا في العمل او نقصوا في الاتضاع سقطوا. فان الرب قال لتلاميذه انتم ملح الارض فاذا 402

insipid it is thrown out and trampled on'.[414] The angels too if they become proud or their love of God and the fulfillment of His will diminishes then they would fall. A testimony to this is Satan when he became proud, as the Prophet said. Paul the Apostle said: 'If we Apostles or the angels of Heaven should evangelize you outside of that which we have evangelized you, the evangelist would be damned'.[415] As long as we are flesh and blood and our struggle is with those not of flesh and blood: with chiefs, tyrants, the governors of this dark world, and wicked spirits, then we must persist in labor and humility. We must compare those who are in stillness and solitude with those monks who are in a community of communion, and to compare the monks with lay people in the virtuous way of life. Similarly, we must compare the perfect holy men with the solitaries, and to compare the lay people with the monks, and the monks with the solitaries, and the solitaries with the perfect Fathers in the labor of virtue as a far as possible."

403 **The Brothers asked:** "A brother said to Abba Poemen: 'Everywhere I go I find help'. He replied: 'God also helps the bearers of swords in this life, for if we find ourselves in islands of terror there is help, for He would deal with us according to His mercy'."[416]

404 **The Exegete replied:** "If a group of brothers who labor and do not possess knowledge were praised by many people, or they went to places and found people who welcomed them and offered them respite, or they were protected a number of times from trials and injuries, they think that God is protecting them from trials and injuries because He is pleased with their excellent way of life and effort in works of virtue, and He makes them noble in people's eyes so that they honor them and offer them respite. When Abba Poemen wished to rectify this brother's lack of knowledge he said to him: 'In the next world every person is recompensed according to his worthiness and labor. In this world, however, not only are the good honored, given repose, protected and cared for but also the sinful, and not only the weak but also the strong'. As is written: 'The king is not saved by the multitude of his army, neither are great men delivered by their extensive power. The safety of a horse is false, for he does not deliver his rider by the greatness of his strength'.[417] God, therefore, cares for the good and the sinful, and he helps the strong and the weak."

فسد الملح يطرح خارجا ويداس. والملايكة ايضا لو تكبروا او نقصوا من حب الله ومن تكميل ارادته لسقطوا.^1565 ويشهد بهذا ابليس لما تكبر. وكما قال النبي. وقول بولس الرسول ان اثرنا نحن الرسل او ملايكة السما نبشركم بغير ما بشرناكم به. فيكون المبشر محروما. فما دمنا لحما ودما^1566 وجهادنا مع من هم غير لحم ودم مع اراكنة والمسلطين^1567 وضابطي هذا العالم المظلم والارواح^1568 الشريره. فينبغي لنا مداومة العمل والاتضاع ينبغي ان نكون نشبه للذين في الهدو والوحده (c104r) الى الرهبان الذين في مجمع شركه. ونشبه الرهبان الى العلمانيين^1569 في تدبير^1570 الفضيله. وكذلك نشبه الشيوخ الكاملين الى المتوحدين. وان نشبه العلمانيين بالرهبان والرهبان بالمتوحدين والمتوحدين (b98r) بالابا الكاملين في عمل الفضيله حسب الامكان.

403 قال الاخوه قال اخ لانبا بجن في كل موضع امضي اجد معونه. فقال له (a78v) واصحاب السيوف ايضا يعينهم الله في هذه الحياة.^1571 فان وجدونا في الجزاير المخيفه معونه. فهو يصنع معنا برحمته.

404 قال المفسر ان قوم من الاخوه العمالين^1572 وليس لهم علم اذا مدحوا من كثيرين او مضوا^1573 الى مواضع فوجدوا من يقبلهم وينيحهم او حفظوا دفعات من التجارب والمعاطب يظنون ان الله لرضاه بتدبيرهم الجيد ونشاطهم في اعمال الفضيله يحرسهم من التجارب والمعاطب ويجعل لهم في اعين الناس كرامه ليكرموهم وينيحوهم.^1574 ولما اراد انبا بجن ان يعدل قلة معرفة هذا الاخ قال له ان في العالم الاتي يجازى كل انسان بقدر استحقاقه وعمله. واما في هذا العالم فليس الابرار فقط تكرم وتنيح وتحفظ وتعان بل والخطاه وليس الضعفا فقط بل والاقويا. كما كتب ان الملك ما يخلص بكثرة قوته ولا الجبابره ينجوا^1575 بكثرة قوتهم. وباطل خلاص الفرس وليس بكثرة قوته ينجي راكبه. فالله يهتم بالبار والخاطي ويساعد القوي والضعيف.

405 **The Brothers asked:** "Abba Macarius said: 'If you do not have the virtue of the soul then strive after the virtue of the body, then the virtue of the soul will be added to you'.⁴¹⁸ He also commanded the same regarding prayer and humility."

406 **The Exegete replied:** "If you have not reached the point of concerning yourself with God and His benefits in your mind then strive at first to physically distance yourself from people and do not converse with the wicked thoughts that stir within you. This resembles the words of Abba Isaiah that stillness gives birth to stillness, meaning that through the stillness of the body a stillness of the mind is born. If you are unable to pray the spiritual prayer, then strive to acquire a pure prayer from a pure heart. If you have not reached this point then strive in your stillness to say the Psalms and to complete the seven prayers with many prostrations. If you have not reached the humility of mind which the Perfect possess, concerning which the Lord said: 'Learn from me for I am meek and humble of heart',⁴¹⁹ meaning, 'In my inner mind', then strive to acquire the physical humility which the novices possess."

407 **The Brothers asked:** "What is the [meaning of the] statement of that holy man to that brother: 'Reveal to me and show me your shot'?"⁴²⁰

408 **The Exegete replied:** "What is written in the old copies is, 'Your spear', not, 'Your shot'. That is, reveal the blow which the devil wounded you with so that you do not hide the wound causing it to penetrate and putrefy. The brother said: 'My thoughts do not allow me to reveal them'. Abba Poemen said something similar: 'The devil delights in nothing more than if brothers hide their thoughts from their Fathers and do not reveal them to them'.⁴²¹ After this statement he said to the brother: 'If your thoughts do not allow you to reveal your weakness and shortcomings to the Fathers then beseech God that He grant you humility so that you reveal your secrets to your Fathers without difficulty or timidity and that you receive healing through them from the Lord'."

409 **The Brothers asked:** "The holy man said: 'He who teaches but does not labor is like a rough granite basin filled with water from which many drink and much of their filth is cleansed while it becomes more and more fetid'."⁴²²

405 **قال الاخوه** انبا مقار (b98v) قال ان كان ليس لك فضيلة الروح فاحرص من اجل فضيلة الجسد. وحينيذ يزداد لك فضيلة^{1576} الروح. وكذلك امر في الصلاه والاتضاع.

406 **قال المفسر** ان كنت ما وصلت ان تهتم بالله وبخيراته بعقلك فاحرص في الاول ان تبعد من الناس بجسدك ولا تتكلم مع الافكار الشريره (a79r) التي تتحرك فيك. وهذا كقول انبا اشعيا ان الهدو (c104v) يلد الهدو. يعني بهدو^{1577} الجسد يلد هدو الذهن. وان كنت ما تقدر تصلي صلاه الروحانيه فاجتهد ان تقتني صلاه نقيه من قلب نقي. وان كنت ما وصلت الى هذا فاحرص في هدوك^{1578} في خدمة المزامير. وتكميل الصلوات السبع بالمطانيات^{1579} الكثيره. فان كنت ما وصلت الى اتضاع الذهن الذي للكاملين الذي عنه قال الرب تعلموا مني فاني وديع ومتضع بقلبي اي بذهني في الباطن.^{1580} فاحرص على ان تقتني اتضاعا^{1581} جسدانيا الذي للمبتديين.^{1582}

407 **قال الاخوه** ما قول ذلك الشيخ لذلك الاخ اكشف لي وارني رمياتك.

408 **قال المفسر** المكتوب في النسخ القديمه رمحك لا رمياتك. اي اظهر^{1583} الضربة التي جرحك بها^{1584} الشيطان ليلا تخفي الجرح فيغل وينتن. والاخ قال ما تتركي افكاري اكشفها. ولمثل هذا قال انبا (b99r) بجمن ان الشيطان ما يفرح بشي مثل ما^{1585} يفرح اذا^{1586} تخفي الاخوه افكارهم عن ابايهم ولا يظهروها لهم. وبعد هذا القول قال للاخ ان كانت افكارك ما تتركك ان تكشف ضعفك ونقصك للابا فاطلب من الله ان يمنحك اتضاعا لكي بغير صعوبه ولا حشمه تكشف خفاياك لاباىك^{1587} وتقبل على ايديهم الشفا من الرب.

409 **قال الاخوه** قال الشيخ من يعلم وما يعمل يشبه الحوض الصوان الخشن الملو ماء^{1588} الذي منه يشرب كثيرين وتتنقا كثير من اوساخهم وهو لاهرا ولاهرا.

410 **The Exegete replied:** "This means that he who preaches to and teaches many and does not act according to God's commandments resembles the garden basin which contains water and from which many drink, and inside which others wash their filth and with which things are watered, while it does not 'drink', nor is it cleansed from its filth nor watered. Similarly, he who preaches to others and does not counsel himself does not benefit from the knowledge that he has while others do."

411 **He also said:** "Some Fathers fear death when it comes such as the one who at the time of his death kept saying many times: 'Do not fear going down to Egypt, O Jacob',[423] in order to be strengthened by this statement.[424] Arsenius was afraid and cried, while Agathon said: 'I am standing before the throne of Christ and I am very scared and I consider myself to have kept the commandments of our Lord as far as I was able'. Yet the Judgment of God is one thing and the judgment of people another and there is no one who is free of fear and quaking on the day of the Trial and the Judgment."[425]

412 **The Brothers asked:** "Why was it written that a brother went to Abba Poemen and conversed with him about spiritual and heavenly matters but he turned his face away from him and did not reply. And when he spoke to him about the yearnings of the soul he answered him joyfully saying: 'Now you have spoken well! Open your mouth and I will fill it with good things'."[426]

413 **The Exegete replied:** "This was said and written in order to instruct the solitaries not to leave off from speaking about the knowledge of yearnings and virtues and to search instead, like the educated, for the knowledge of the meaning of books, and to converse like the Perfect holy men regarding its teaching and education. For this reason Abba Evagrius said: 'Examine as though sick those who desire good health, and talk about the law of the fear of God and the virtuous way of life not about knowledge of God, except if you find one who leads such a way of life and is able to understand it, in which case speak to him'. The Prophet John said: 'There is nothing in the knowledge of wisdom that equals the knowledge of liberation from yearnings, and he who is able to drive out from himself one yearning then this is better for him than being able to drive out an army of demons from the insane'.[427] This

410 **قال المفسر** يعني الذي يعظ ويعلم كثيرين (a79v) وما يعمل وصايا الله يشبه الحوض[1589] الذي في البستان الذي فيه الما ومنه يشرب كثيرين. واخرون يغسلون فيه اوساخهم وبه تلين اشيا. وهو فما يشرب ولا ينقى من اوساخه ولا يلين. وكذالك الذي يعظ غيره ولا يعظ نفسه لا ينتفع بما فيه من العلم وغيره ينتفع به.

411 **وقال ايضا** ان بعض الابا يخافون الموت وقت[1590] حضوره مثل الذي كان يقول عند وفاته دفعات كثيره لا تخف يا يعقوب ان تنزل الى مصر ليتعزا بهذا القول. وارسانيوس خاف وبكا. واجاثن قال انا واقف قدام منبر المسيح وانا خايف كثيرا واحسب انا حفظت وصايا ربنا كما (c105r) قدرت. الا ان حكم الله شي وحكم الناس شي (b99v) اخر وليس من يفلت من الخوف والرعده في يوم الامتحان والحكم.

412 **قال الاخوه** لماذا كتب ان اخا مضا الى انبا بجمن وتحدث معه في الروحانيات والسماويات[1591] فحول وجهه عنه وما جاوبه. ولما كلمه عن الاوجاع النفس جاوبه بفرح[1592] قايلا الان قلت جيدا افتح فاك واملاه[1593] خيرات.

413 **قال المفسر** هذا قيل وكتب من اجل تعليم المتوحدين لكيلا يتركوا الكلام في معرفة الاوجاع والفضايل ويفتشوا مثل المتعلمين[1594] عن معرفة[1595] معاني الكتب او يتكلمون مثل الشيوخ الكاملين في تعليمها وتفهيها ولهذا قال انبا وغريس الخصوا كالمرضى[1596] الذين يشتهون الصحه. وتكلموا على ناموس مخافة الله وعلى تدبير الفضيله (a80r) لا على معرفة الله الا ان وجدت من يدبر هذه ويقدر يفهمها فقل له. وقال يوحنا النبي ليس في معارف الحكمه شي يوازن معرفة الخلاص من الاوجاع. ومن يقدر يطرد من نفسه وجعا واحدا[1597] خير له من ان يقدر على اخراج عسكر شياطين[1598] من المجانين. فهذه هي

is true wisdom which the Creator formed in the nature of human beings in this life, and we do not find written about our Lord nor about His Apostles 'Blessed are the wise in disputations', however, we find in the Psalm which is spoken through the Holy Spirit: 'Blessed are those who are without blemish in the way and they walk in the law of God. Blessed are those who seek His testimony and follow Him with all their heart'.[428] After a person is cleansed from impurities, he then becomes suitable for every divine wisdom to be ingrained in him. For this reason the Fathers did not allow for novices and the young to leave off from meditating on the salvation of their souls and [instead] to occupy themselves with reading philosophical books or to become knowledgeable in disputations and commentaries. This is so that their minds do not become filled with thoughts and imaginations resulting in them ceasing from the remembrance of God, meditating on the Last Judgment, concerning themselves with the uprightness of the soul, striving to do the work of the Lord, and pursuing the love of the Sweet Beloved who is Christ, to Him be glory."

414 **The Brothers asked:** "Why did Abba Ammon the Virgin say to Antony: 'I see that I have more works than you, why then did your name spread more than mine among the people?' Antony replied to him: 'This is because I love God more than you'."[429]

415 **The Exegete replied:** "They did not intend [to proffer] thoughts but rather [to give] instruction because they had both been forerunners in the solitary way of life and in desert dwelling, therefore, they wished to reveal to those who would become solitaries after them that the spiritual way of life is higher than the bodily way of life because physical labors liberate the solitary from the yearnings of the body and its virtue becomes his own. Mental striving grants him purity of heart and pureness of mind and strengthens the mind in the expelling of wicked thoughts, both satanic and human, and brings him to constant prayer without distraction which raises him to divine light. The memory does not spread of everyone who is virtuous since no one knew Abba Paul during his lifetime, the first of the solitaries, who, because of his virtue, Antony once called the Prophet Elijah, at another time John the Baptist, and at another Paul the Apostle."

الحكمة الحقيقيه التي صنعها الخالق في طبع البشر في هذه الحياة.1599 ولم نجد مكتوبا عن ربنا ولا عن رسله. طوبى للحكما1600 في المجادلات. لكنا وجدنا في المزمور1601 المقول بروح القدس طوبى للذين بلا عيب في (b100r) السبيل السالكين في سنة1602 الله. طوبى للذين يفحصون عن شهادته ويتبعونه بكل قلوبهم. ومن بعد ان ينقى الانسان من الادناس حينيذ يصلح لان ينقش فيه كل حكمة الاهيه. ولهذا ما فسحت الابا للمبتديين1603 والشبان ان يتركوا1604 الهذيذ في خلاص نفوسهم ويشتغلوا بقراة الكتب الحكميه ولا بمعرفة المجادلات والتفاسير ليلا تمتلى عقولهم1605 من الافكار والخيالات فيبطلوا من تذكار الله. والتفكر في الدينونه والاهتمام باستقامة النفس (c105v) والاجتهاد في عمل الرب. والجرى خلف الحب الحلوا والمحبوب الذي هو المسيح له المجد.

414 **قال الاخوه** لماذا قال انبا امون البتول لانطونيوس ارى ان لي اعمال اكثر منك فكيف شاع اسمك عند الناس اكثر (a80v) مني. فقال له انطونيوس لاني احب الله اكثر منك.

415 **قال المفسر** ما قصدا الافكار لكن التعليم لانها سبقا في تدبير الوحده وفي سكنى البريه. فارادا ان يكشفا لمن يتوحد بعدهم.1606 ان التدبير1607 النفساني اعلا من التدبير الجسداني لان الاعمال الجسمانيه تعتق المتوحد من اوجاع الجسد. وتصير الفضيله له ملكه. والجهاد الذهني يمنحه طهارة القلب ونقا الذهن ويقوي العقل1608 على طرد الافكار الشريره الشيطانيه والبشريه. ويوصله الى صلاة الدايمه (b100v) بغير طياشه فيرتفع الى نور1609 الالهي وليس كل فاضل يشيع ذكره. لان انبا بولا بكر المتوحدين الذي لفضله سماه انطونيوس دفعه ايليا النبي. ودفعه يوحنا المعمداني.1610 ودفعه بولس الرسول. في حياته ماكان احد من الناس يعرفه.

416 **The Brothers asked:** "How did the heathen priest know of the mental way of life such that he said to that solitary: 'You do not see visions nor does your Lord reveal His secrets to you even if you had labored in stillness with fasting and vigils, [for] so long as your thoughts are not pure this would be in vain'."[430]

417 **The Exegete replied:** "When the Fathers heard this they said that God had permitted him to say this in accordance with the Fathers' teaching of the brothers, and that only a lack in purity of thoughts creates a distance from God. The youth and the simple might make statements above their knowledge for the instruction of the Perfect. For example, that child who said to his mother when Abba Macarius passed by with some brothers: 'One who is wealthy loves me and I hate him, and one who is poor hates me and I love him'.[431] Abba Macarius was amazed and he knew that God had spoken through the tongue of the child in order to educate the brothers. He explained to them that God is the wealthy one through His gifts and authority, and the devil is the poor one and because of his weakness requires artifice and deception against people. Also, as that maiden who said to Arsenius: 'If you are a solitary then go to the mountain'. He began to reproach himself saying: 'O Arseni', and, 'Arseni, if you are a monk then go to the mountain'."[432]

418 **The Brothers asked:** "Once every year Arsenius would eat fruit and thank God,[433] while Abba Evagrius would not eat any."

419 **The Exegete replied:** "The difference in the actions of the Fathers is for two reasons: for their own gain and to benefit others. Abba Evagrius did not eat fruit in order to adhere to asceticism and to teach the brothers. Given that Arsenius was a laborer he wished to inform them that fruit is not unclean as the heretics say, and not forbidden from monks as those who do not know think. God created it in order [for us] to benefit from it and be grateful for it as Paul the Apostle said."[434]

420 **He also said:** "The sin that stirs in the heart of the monk, if he does not whisper with it in his mind, lose it in his heart, and bring it forth to existence through his action, then after a given duration of his heart's struggle with it, his mind becomes illuminated, he is liberated from the yearnings and he rejoices in God."

416 **قال الاخوه** من اين علم كاهن الحنفا تدبير الذهن حتى قال لذلك المتوحد ما تنظرون مناظر ولا يكشف لكم ربكم اسراره ولو كان لكم اعمال في الهدو من صوم وسهر ما لم تكن لكم افكار نقيه كان ذلك باطلا.

417 **قال المفسر** ان الابا لما سمعوا هذا قالوا ان الله جعله يقول هذا موافقة للابا في تعليم الاخوه. وانه[1611] لا يبعد من الله الا عدم نقا الافكار. وقد تقول الصبيان والسذاج اقوالا اعلا من معرفتهم لتعلم الكاملين. كما قال ذالك الصغير لامه عندما جاز انبا (a81r) مقاره ومعه اخوه. ان غنيا واحدا[1612] يحبني وانا ابغضه. ومسكينا واحدا[1613] يبغضني وانا احبه. فتعجب انبا مقاره وعرف ان الله تكلم على لسان الصغير من اجل تادب الاخوه. وفسر (c106r) لهم ان الله هو الغني في مواهبه وسلطانه والشيطان هو المسكين ولضعفه يحتاج الى الحيله والى المخادعه للناس. وكما قالت تلك الصبيه لارسانيوس ان كنت متوحدا امض الى الجبل. فجعل يبكت نفسه قايلا يا ارساني. وارساني ان كنت راهبا امض الى الجبل.

418 **قال الاخوه** ان ارسانيوس كان في كل (b101r) سنه ياكل من الثمرات دفعه وشكر الله. وانبا وغريس ما كان ياكل منها شي.

419 **قال المفسر** اختلاف افعال الابا يكون لسببين. لربحهم ولنفع غيرهم. فانبا وغريس لم ياكل الفاكهة ليثبت في النسك ويعلم الاخوه. وارسانيوس مع كونه عمالا[1614] اراد ان يعرفهم ان الفاكهة غير نجسه. كما تقول الهراطقه وغير محرمة[1615] على الرهبان كما يظن من لا معرفه له. وان الله خلقها للانتفاع بها والشكر عليها كما يقول بولس[1616] الرسول.

420 **وقال ايضا** ان الخطيه التي تتحرك في قلب الراهب اذا[1617] لم يتوسوس معها في ذهنه ويضيعها في قلبه ويخرجها للوجود بفعله. فبعد زمان معروف لجهاده منها قلبه[1618] ويستنير[1619] ذهنه وينعتق من الاوجاع ويفرح بالله.

421 **The Brothers asked:** "Abba Poemen said: 'It is written: For two or three transgressions of Tyre, the fourth I will not desist from them.'[435] The first is to think of evil, the second is to submit to the thought, the third is to fulfill it, and the fourth is for the thought to materialize through action'."[436]

422 **The Exegete replied:** "He understood the written words spiritually, related to yearnings, as is the custom of the Fathers, and he presented them to demonstrate that committing sin necessitates the anger of God. Every sin begins with the stirring of a wicked thought in the heart, either a bodily stirring or the recollection of an action in the past or through the provocation of the devil. This first stirring which is present is neither considered to be a sin nor innocent. If the solitary does not drive it away from his heart with natural indignation, prayer, and beseeching God's aid but rather leaves it to linger in his heart for a period of time, then this is the first cause of sin. His loving acceptance of this thought and whispering with it in delight is the second cause. If he brings it out as speech such as abusing a brother with his tongue after hating him in his heart, or talking with a woman lustfully after having desired to sin with her, then this is the second cause [sic]. If he strikes with his hand or physically fornicates then this is the fourth cause. Concerning this he said: 'God does not withdraw from him in His anger', that is, he who does not fear God and refrains from the thought of sin then it sticks in his heart, and if he does not expel it or drive it away then he welcomes it in his thought with delight and love, then brings it forth in speech, then acts upon it with his limbs and insolently risks God's patience towards him, and loses His grant of respite for him in order to repent from the first and second and third [causes]. Then the wrath of God will come upon him according to the magnitude of the sin and its consummation."

423 **The Brothers asked:** "A brother said to a holy man: 'I wonder does the devil fight us now as he did the forefathers?' He replied: 'He now fights more because his time is near and he is agitated'.[437] Antony said: 'God does not allow the devil to bring a hard war upon this generation because it is weak'.[438] A certain Father said: 'The last generation will not labor at all and many trials will come upon them and those who are tested among them will be greater than us and our Fathers'."[439]

421 **قال الاخوه** (a81v) قال انبا بيمن مكتوب على ذنوب صور اثنان او ثلثه.[1620] والرابع لا ارجع عنهم. فالاول ان يفتكر الشر. والثاني ان يطاوعه فكره. والثالث ان تكميله. والرابع ان يخرج الفكر الى الفعل.

422 **قال المفسر** انه اخذ قول المكتوب[1621] روحانيا على الاوجاع كعادة الابا وغرضه ان يبين ان فعل الخطيه يوجب سخط الله. وابتدي كل خطيه تحرك الفكره الشريره في القلب (b101v) اما من حركة الجسد او من تذكار ما تقدم فعله او من تحريك الشيطان. وهذه الحركه الاوله الحاضره لا تعد خطيه ولا برا. واذا (c106v) لم يطردها المتوحد من قلبه بالغضب الطبيعي والصلاه وطلب عون الله ويتركها تبطى في قلبه زمانا. فهذه اول اسباب الخطيه. وقبوله لهذه الفكره بمحبه والتوسوس معها بالتذاذ هو السبب الثاني. واذا اخرجها الى الكلام بها مثل ان يشتم الاخ بلسانه بعد ان ابغضه بقلبه.[1622] او يتكلم مع امراه في الشهوه بعد اشتهى الخطيه معها. فهذا هو السبب الثاني.[1623] واذا ضرب بيده او زنا بجسده فهذا هو السبب الرابع. وعن هذا قال ان الله ما يرجع عنه بغضبه اي الذي ما يخاف الله فيترك فكر الخطيه يثبت في قلبه ولا يطرده ويبعده. ثم يقبله في فكره بلذه ومحبه. ثم يخرجه الى الكلام به. ثم يكمل (a82r) فعله بجوارحه ويجسر على طول روح الله عليه بجساره. ويخسر امهاله له ليتوب في الاول والثاني والثالث. فان غضب الله ياتي عليه[1624] على قدر كبر الخطيه وتكميلها.[1625]

423 **قال الاخوه** ان اخا قال لشيخ ترى الشيطان يحاربنا الان مثل الاولين فاجابه انه يقاتل الان ازيد لانه قد دنا زمانه فهو قلق. وانطونيوس قال ان الله ما يدع الشيطان ياتي بالحرب (b102r) الصعب على هذا الجيل لانه ضعيف. وبعض الابا قال ان الجيل الاخر ما يعمل شيا[1626] وستاتي[1627] عليهم تجارب كثيره ويكون الممتحنون منهم اعظم منا ومن ابائنا.

424 **The Exegete replied:** "Abba Sisoes said: 'The devil now fights more than [against] the forefathers', and he meant by 'forefathers' the prophets and the righteous who were in the Old Testament as was written in the Gospel: 'Or one of the forefathers'.[440] He meant by 'now' the time of the Apostles and the Fathers who came after them, because in the New Testament the perfect way of life appeared and the demons' way of life was disclosed as a result of which they became bitter and agitated and they battled harder. Antony prophesied about us because we are less than the Fathers in our enthusiasm for labor and the love of God. Because of our weakness the demons do not cease to fight us as with the Fathers. As for the others, they are the ones about whom the Lord said: 'Because of the chosen ones, those days will be cut short'."[441]

425 **The Brothers asked:** "Abba Poemen said: 'This is the work of the monastic life: discernment, toil, and poverty. For it is written: If these three men were there, Noah, Job, and Daniel, as I live says the Lord.[442] Noah resembles poverty, Job resembles the toil of labor, and Daniel resembles discernment. If the solitary acquires these three then God lives in him'."[443]

426 **The Exegete replied:** "This means that these three more than the remaining virtues free the solitary from all his yearnings, purify his heart, illuminate his mind, make of him an abode for God, and Christ will be alive in him at all times. As Paul the Apostle said: 'It is not I who am alive but Christ who is alive in me',[444] meaning, there is no remembrance of love other than the remembrance of Christ's love. He means that, 'He who is poor, toils in virtue, and acquires discernment then I, the Christ, dwell in him', meaning, 'I will be his life and he will be worthy of seeing me'."

427 **He also said:** "The Lord said: 'He who does not leave everything and follow me is not worthy of me'.[445] The Apostles said: 'We have left everything and followed you'.[446] Leaving everything in order to follow the Lord and to fulfill obedience to Him and love for Him [is divided] into three levels, some more elevated than others. The first is for a person to leave his home, country, ancestors, family, and race and to come to the monastery of the brothers. The second, is for him to enter a cell, to live in solitude away from the brothers for stillness of thought, and to move away from sight, sound, and conversation. The third, is for him to enter the spiritual

424 **قال المفسر** ان انبا شيشاي قال ان الشيطان يقاتل الان اكثر من الاولين وعنى بالاولين[1628] الانبيا والصديقين الذين كانوا في العتيقة كما كتب في الانجيل او واحد من الاولين. وعنى بالان زمان الرسل والابا بعدهم. لان في الحديثه ظهر التدبير (c107r) الكامل وانكشف تدبير الشياطين. فتمرروا وقلقوا وصعبوا القتال. وانطونيوس تنبى[1629] علينا نحن لانا[1630] ناقصون عن الابا في حرارة الاعمال والمحبة لله. ومن اجل ضعفنا لم تخلا الشياطين على قتالنا كالابا. واما الاخرون فهم الذين قال الرب عنهم. ومن اجل المختارين قصرت تلك الايام.

425 **قال الاخوه** قال انبا بجن ما هذا هو فعل الحيات الذي للرهبنه.[1631] لافراز[1632] والتعب والمسكنه. (a82v) فقد كتب ان يكن هناك هولاى الرجال الثلثه.[1633] نوح وايوب ودنيال. انا حي قال الرب. فنوح هو شبه المسكنه. وايوب[1634] شبه تعب الاعمال. ودانيايل[1635] شبه[1636] الافراز. فان اقتنى المتوحد هذه الثلثه[1637] فالله[1638] ساكن فيه.

426 **قال المفسر** يعني ان هذه الثلثه[1639] اكثر من باقي الفضايل تعتق[1640] المتوحد من كل اوجاعه وتنقي قلبه وتنير ذهنه وتجعله مسكنا لله. ويكون المسيح حيا فيه في كل حين. كما (b102v) قال الرسول بولس لست انا الحي بل المسيح هو الحي في. اي ليس في تذكار اخر حبا غير تذكار حب المسيح. فهو يعني ان من كان فقيرا ويعمل في الفضيله ويقتني الافراز فانا المسيح اسكن فيه. اي اكون حياته ويستحق ان يراني.

427 **قال ايضا** ان الرب قال من لا يترك كل شي ويتبعني فما يستحقني. والرسل قالو قد تركنا كل شي[1641] وتبعناك. فترك الاشيا كلها من اجل اتباع الرب وتكميل طاعته ومحبته في ثلث مراتب. بعضها ارفع من بعض. الاولى ان يبعد الانسان من مسكنه ووطنه وابايه واهله وجنسه وياتي الى دير الاخوه. والثانيه ان يدخل الى القلايه ويتوحد من الاخوه لهدو الفكره ويبعد عن النظر والسماع والحديث. والثلثه ان (c107v) يدخل الى

way of life, to eliminate foul thoughts from his mind, not to converse with any of them in his mind, and not allow them to linger in him but to expel them when they first become present. He who leaves these matters shares in the words of the Apostles to the Lord: 'We have left everything and followed you'."

428 **The Brothers asked:** "Abba Alonis said: 'Had I not demolished my self I would not have been able to build my soul'."[447]

429 **The Exegete replied:** "Meaning, he demolished it when it was an abode for yearnings then built it into a palace of virtue. This is the one who attains the love of God from above. He also said: 'No one can know which yearning his soul is sick with and how many satanic thoughts his mind is tied to until he lives in the stillness of solitude. Because of his release when in stillness from the confusion which comes upon him from outside, he perceives the thoughts which stir inside of him. Then, if he wills, he is able to control them and keep them from lingering inside him, rather, he expels them through prayer and the aid of the Lord'."

430 **The Brothers asked:** "The holy man said: 'Do not think about the person whom your heart is pleased with'."[448]

431 **The Exegete replied:** "That is, if you are the disciple or servant of a holy man or if you repeatedly enter and leave [the cell of] one of the Fathers for your profit and the salvation of your soul, and you see a certain shortcoming in him like a person who is bent over, dying and being attacked by the devil, then do not place that shortcoming before your mind's eyes. For the devil is eager for this in order to make you fall into haughtiness towards him, and stop you from benefiting from him. Just as you must not despise your eyes if you see uncleanliness in them, or your head if residue issues from it through the nose, similarly, it is not appropriate for you to despise the possessor of many virtues for the sake of a small shortcoming which you see in them either through human weakness or from combat with the demons. It is possible that God's dispensation was withdrawn from him so that he would not become proud because of his many works and divine gifts and in order to be humble and benefit. Just as it is inevitable that a little smoke appears in the glow of the fire because of the substance which attaches to it and appears in it, even if the oil and the wick were unadulterated yet they do not reach the degree of purity of

التدبير الروحاني فيبعد من عقله الافكار الرديه ولا يتحدث مع شي منها في ذهنه. ولا يتركها تبطي معه بل يطردها (a83r) في ابتدا حضورها. فالذي يترك هذه الامور يكون مشاركا للرسل في قولهم [1643] للرب قد تركنا كل شي [1644] وتبعناك.

428 **قال الاخوه** قال انبا الونيس [1645] لولا هدمت [1646] ذاتي ما قدرتُ ابني نفسي.

429 **قال المفسر** اي هدمها لما كانت مسكنا لاوجاع ثم بناها جوسقا للفضيله. هذا الذي يصل من اعلاه (b103r) الى حب الله. وقال ما يقدر احد يعرف باي وجع [1647] نفسه مريضه وبكم فكر شيطاني عقله مرتبط حتى يسكن في هدو الوحده. فلفرجته في الهدو امن التشوش الوارد عليه من خارج يدرك ما يتحرك فيه [1648] من الافكار وحينيذ ان شا قدر ان يحرسها ولا يدعها تبطي معه. بل يطردها بالصلاة ومعونة الرب.

430 **قال الاخوه** قال الشيخ ان الانسان الذي قد رضي قلبك به لا تكفر فيه.

431 **قال المفسر** اي ان كنت تلميذا او خديما لشيخ او كنت تدخل وتخرج عند احد الابا لربحك وخلاص نفسك فاذا رايت فيه بعض نقص مثل انسان ومايل [1649] ومايت ومقاتل من الشيطان فلا تجعل ذلك النقص قدام عيني ذهنك. فان الشيطان حريص على هذا ليسقطك في الكبريا عليه. ويعدمك الربح منه. فكما انه ما ينبغي ان تحتقر بعينيك اذا ما ظهر لك فيها القذا. او براسك اذا ما صدر عنه الفضلات من الانف. وهكذى ما ينبغي لك ان تحقر صاحب الفضايل الكثيره من اجل نقص يسير تراه فيه اما من ضعف البشريه (a83v) او من حرب الشياطين. وعساه تدبير الله تخلا عليه لكيلا يتكبر باعماله الكثيره او مواهبه الالهيه. وليتضع ويرح. [1650] وكما ان النار من اجل الماده التي تتعلق بها وتظهر فيها لا بد ان يظهر في نورها دخان يسير (b103v) ولو كان الدهن (c108r) والفتيله صافيتين الا انهما لا يبلغان مقدار صفا

the fire's glow, [thus] blackening it a little. The same is the case with the saints so long as they are in this physical world and in this dense and weak body, then it is inevitable that a few shortcomings mingle with what they have and in their minds [a little] wicked thinking. Even if their bodies were tempered with all that can be tempered in this life and even if their minds were purified to the limit that they are able to attain in terms of yoking the body and battling pernicious yearnings, as Abba Macarius said: 'The perfect solitary should not become proud because of his perfection but should know that so long as he is currently in the body then his smoke remains with him', meaning, his inclinations will remain with him and sins will stir in him. As Abba Evagrius said: 'Many solitaries have perished because they did not understand or believe that just as grace is with them so too is the smoke of sin'."

432 **The Brothers asked:** "Antony said: 'If the hire did not put a covering over the eyes of the animal it would draw back and eat its own feces. Similarly, a covering was made for us through the dispensation of God so that if we do good we do not view it as good lest we delight in it, causing it to perish. For this reason we sometimes fall into unclean thoughts in order to see them and accuse ourselves such that they become like a covering for the few good things that we perform which would not then perish'."[449]

433 **The Exegete replied:** "For this reason not all the saints were granted spiritual visions even though they had many virtues not because God is not pleased with their virtues, rather, in order for them not to become proud resulting in their virtues perishing and being deprived of the good things prepared for them. For this reason too the demons are let loose on them and they fight them with impure thoughts and through intimidation and blows in order to train them to recognize their weakness and to be fearful so long as they remain in this life, to think at all times about their shortcomings and to be distracted from thinking about their virtues or the shortcomings of others and to be humble, to beseech God for His forgiveness and aid thus preserving their virtues until they are glorified through them in the eternal world where no thief traverses and no worm corrupts and they exist in eternal bliss."

نور النار ان يكدرها^{1651} قليلا. هكذى القديسون ما داموا في هذا العالم الحسي في هذا الجسد الكثيف الضعيف. فلا بد من ان يخالط^{1652} بما لها نقصا يسيرا وذهنهم فكرا شريرا. ولو تلطفت اجسادهم بكل ما يمكن من تلطيفها في هذه الحياة^{1653} ولو^{1654} تنقت عقولهم غاية ما يقدرون على^{1655} الوصول اليه (a84r) من مقارنة الجسد ومقاتلة^{1656} الاوجاع الخبيثه كما قال انبا مقار ينبغي للمتوحد الكامل ان لا يتكبر من اجل كماله بل يعرف انه ما دام حالا في الجسد فدخانه معه اي ميلانه معه والخطايا تتحرك فيه. وكما قال مار وغريس ان كثير من المتوحدين هلكوا لكونهم ما فهموا ولا صدقوا انهم كما النعمه معهم وكذالك^{1657} دخان الخطيه ايضا.

432 **قال الاخوه** قال انطونيوس لولا ان الاجير وجعل الغطا على عيني البهيمه كانت ترجع وتاكل خراها. وهكذى نحن جعل لنا الغطا بتدبير الله. فاذا عملنا خيرا ما ننظره خيرا ليلا نغتبط به فيبيد. ولهذا نقع^{1658} اوقاتا في افكار دنسه لنراها ونلوم انفسنا. فتكون كالغطا لما نصنعه من الخير اليسير فما يبيد.

433 **قال المفسر** ومن اجل هذا لم يمنح جميع القديسين المناظر الروحانيه. (b104r) وان كانت لهم فضايل كثيره ليس لان الله ما يسر بفضايلهم لكن لكيلا^{1659} يتكبروا^{1660} فتهلك فضايلهم ويعدموا الخيرات المعده لهم. ولهذا ايضا تخلا الشياطين عليهم فيقاتلوهم^{1661} بالافكار^{1662} الدنسه والتخويف والضرب ليتادبوا ويعرفوا ضعفهم ويخافوا ما داموا في هذه الحياة.^{1663} ويفتكروا كل حين مناقصهم ويشتغلوا عن التفكر في فضايلهم او مناقص غيرهم ويتضعوا. ويطلبوا من الله غفرانه وعونه فتنحفظ لهم فضايلهم الى حين تمجيدهم بها في العالم الدايم (a84v/c108v) حيث لا ينقب سارق ولا يفسد سوس ويكونوا في النعيم الدايم.

434   **The Brothers asked:** "Why did God not allow Abba Theodore to serve according to the rank of his ministry but rather said to him: 'If you are able to be like a pillar of light then go and minister'."450

435   **The Exegete replied:** "If he wished to minister according to his rank as all people [do] He would not have forbidden him for two reasons: the first is lest he become proud having received the ministry from God, and the second is for God to reveal the scope of the priesthood so that the proud, insolent, disdainful and impure keep away from it."

436   **The Brothers asked:** "What is the meaning of the statement by Abba Benjamin: 'Had Moses not gathered the sheep into the fold he would not have been able to see Him that is in the bush'."451

437   **The Exegete replied:** "This is because Moses gathered together the sheep in one fold so as not to have fearful thoughts concerning their scattering when he went to see that amazing sight. Similarly, if one of the solitaries wishes to acquire the purity of heart with which he is able to see God and view the amazing light then he must not leave anything his thought can attach to and his memory can be preoccupied with. He must distance himself from the world, from its senses and from its yearnings and persevere in stillness. [He must] gather his thoughts from all distraction and loss, and focus the vision of his mind to a single view of God. Such a one is worthy of purity of heart and clarity of mind and enjoys seeing visions of our Lord, glory be to Him."

438   **He also said:** "Just as the force and development of the body into the shape of its form is not from foodstuff but from a hidden force in it, so too the force and perfection of the soul in the fear and love of our Lord is not a coincidental physical action and a mere habit that lacks discernment but rather derives from the way of knowledge, that is, from good exposition and the mental way of life which is the guarding of thoughts, prayer, humility, and meditating on God."

439   **He also said:** "If you are in a state of stillness and persevere in spiritual labor and the devil becomes envious of you and wishes to expel you from your cell and impede your virtues then he stirs in you either the thought of food or sleep ahead of time or of visiting someone or seeing a holy man, and you see that it is not necessary,

434	**قال الاخوه** لماذا ما فسح الله لانبا تادري ان يخدم درجة خدمته بل قال له ان كنت تقدر تكون كمثل عامود نور امض اخدم.
435	**قال المفسر** لو اراد يخدم درجته مثل كل الناس ما منعه لامرين. الواحد لكيلا يتكبر بكونه قبل الخدمه من الله. والاخر ليظهر الله مقدار الكهنوت وتكف عنه المتكبرين والمتجاسرين والمتهاونين والدنسين.
436	**قال الاخوه** ما معنى قول انبا بنيامين[1664] لولا ضم موسى الغنم الى الحظير ماكان يقدر يبصر الذي في العوسج.
437	**قال المفسر** لان موسى ضم الغنم في حظير واحد لكيلا يبقى له فكر في الخوف من تبددها عند (b104v) مضيه لروية ذلك[1665] المنظر العجيب[1666]. اي وكذلك المتوحدون اذا يريد احدهم ان يقتني نقاوة القلب التي[1667] بها يعاين الله ونظر النور العجيب فينبغي له ان لا يدع له[1668] شيا يتعلق به فكره ويشغله تذكره فيبعد من العالم ومن حواسه ومن اوجاعه ويداوم الهدو. ويضم فكرته من كل الطياشه والتبدد ويجمع نظر ذهنه الى نظر واحد عند الله. فهذا يستحق طهارة القلب[1669] ونقا الذهن ويتنعم في رويا مناظر ربنا له المجد.
438	**وقال ايضا** كما ان قوة الجسد ونموه على شكل تصويره ليس من جسم الغذا بل من قوة الخفيه فيه كذلك[1670] (a85r) قوة النفس وكمالها في مخافة ربنا ومحبته ليس من الاعمال الجسمانيه كيف ما اتفق وكالعاده فقط بلا افراز بل من تدبير المعرفه اي من (c109r) العرض الجيد والتدبير الذهني الذي هو حراسة الافكار والصلاه والاتضاع والهذيذ في الله.
439	**قال ايضا** اذا كنت في الهدو ومداوما لعمل الروحاني ويحسدك[1671] الشيطان ويريد يخرجك من قلايتك ويعيقك من فضايلك فيحرك فيك فكرا اما اكلا او نوما قبل الوقت او افتقاد انسان او نظر شيخ ورايت انه ما ينبغي ولكن[1672]

that it is not the time for it and you reject that thought, then he waits a little and stirs it in you a second time. When you reject it a second time, he then waits a little and stirs it for a third time. At this point know that it is from the devil and that he wishes to impede you from your work, therefore, quickly stop, act courageously, and prostrate before our Lord, pray, and ask for His help and mercy."

440 **He also said:** "Constantine the King said: 'I thank Christ because He granted me in my days three divine lights: Mar Antony, Mar Alonis, and Mar Eugenius'. When Alonis came from Syria to Antony he said to him: 'Good is your coming O morning star that rises early',[452] meaning, just as the morning star is more radiant than the other stars so too is Alonis more perfect in the light of grace than the solitaries. He, therefore, wished to make known to him the glory of his way of life and his light and said to him: 'Peace be to you O pillar of light which supports the inhabited world'. This is not Hilarion who was sent by his parents at the age of fifteen years to Alexandria in order to learn literature and philosophy. When he heard about Antony's courage he went to him and stayed with him for two months, changed his attire and became a monk. After two months he went to his country. In his biography it is written that there was in Egypt a disciple of our Lord Jesus called Antony who was great in his days, and in Palestine Hilarion was young in years. If they went to Antony from Syria because of an illness or other matter he would say to them: 'Why did you weary yourselves and come to me when my son Hilarion is with you?'"

441 **The Brothers asked:** "A brother asked a holy man: 'How is it that some people labor, yet do not receive grace as did the forefathers?' He replied: 'Because the love of the one would lift the other to the heavens but now love has become corrupt and the one drags the other down to the lowest pit'."[453]

442 **The Exegete replied:** "He means by grace the gift of healing and exorcism which used to be granted to the solitaries in order to strengthen them and benefit others. Now, when the good have passed away and faith no longer exists on the earth and love has diminished among the majority, as is written, then these gifts [also] diminished and the saints who were worthy of this grace began to

ما هو وقته وتلقي عنك ١٦٧٣ ذلك الفكر. فيصبر قليلا ثم يحركه فيك ثانيا. ١٦٧٤ (b105r) وتلقيه ثانية. فيصبر قليل ثم يحركه ثالثا. فاعلم حينيذ انه من الشيطان وانه يريد تعويقك من عملك فقف عاجلا وتحرك بشجاعه واسجد قدام ربنا وصلي واطلب عونه ورحمته.

٤٤٠ **وقال ايضا** ان قسطنطين الملك قال ١٦٧٥ اشكر المسيح لان في ايامي وهب لي الله ثلثة ١٦٧٦ انوار الهيه. ١٦٧٧ مار انطونيوس ومار الونيس ١٦٧٨ ومار اوجين. ١٦٧٩ ولما اتاى ١٦٨٠ الونيوس من الشام الى انطونيوس قال له حسنا جيت يا كوكب الصبح الذي يشرق باكرا. اي كما ان كوكب الصبح اكثر نورا من باقي النجوم كذلك الونيوس اتم في نور النعمه من المتوحدين فاراد (d136r) ان ١٦٨١ يعرفه مجد تدبيره ونوره. فقال له السلام لك يا عمود ١٦٨٢ النور الذي حمل المسكونه وليس هذا هو اللاريون (a85v) الذي ارسل من ابايه وهو ابن خمسة عشر سنه الى الاسكندريه ١٦٨٣ ليتعلم الادب والحكمه. ولما سمع بشجاعة انطونيوس مضى اليه واقام عنده شهرين وغير زينه وصار راهبا. ١٦٨٤ وبعد الشهرين مضى ١٦٨٥ الى بلده. وفي سيرته مكتوب كان لربنا يسوع تلميذ بمصر (c109v) اسمه انطونيوس كبير في ايامه. وبفلسطين اللاريون (b105v) حدنا في سنه. وكانوا اذا مضوا الى انطونيوس من الشام من اجل مرض او شي ١٦٨٦ يقول لهم لماذا تعبتم وجيتم الى ولادي اللاريون عندكم.

٤٤١ **قال الاخوه** ان اخا سال شيخا كيف اناسا يعملون وما ياخذون النعمه مثل الاولين. فاجابه لان حب الواحد كان يجذب الاخر الى العلو. والان الحب فسد والى اسفل يجذب الواحد الاخر.

٤٤٢ (e138v) **قال المفسر** يعني بالنعمه موهبة الشفا واخراج الشياطين. وكانت تعطى للمتوحدين ولتعزيتهم ولنفع اخرين والان لما فنى الايمان على الارض وقلت المحبه من الاكثرين كما هو مكتوب قلت هذه المواهب وصار القديسون (d136v) الذين يستحقون ١٦٨٧ هذه النعمه

receive them in their souls in a spiritual and hidden manner, and its effects do not appear in action because this wicked generation is not worthy."

443   **Marginal note:** "It is possible that it disappeared the result of the later generation being divested of it because of their being convinced of its permanence in the first generation who resembled them, as took place with the miracles of faith or the cautioning of the later generation from being damaged by it through pride, intellect, and because of the many vocations which are inferior to the first generation. It is possible that they, I mean the later generation, do not need miracles because of their intelligence and firmness of faith as the Apostle said: that signs were for those who did not believe in order for them to believe.[454] In this manner they receive the Beatitude from the Lord who says: 'Blessed are those who have not seen and have believed'."[455]

444   **The Brothers asked:** "Abba Jacob said: 'He who teaches his neighbor before asking him is the same as the one who rebukes him'."[456]

445   **The Exegete replied:** "He who does not become a head and is not made a teacher and in general has not acquired the rank of learning, neither in terms of his position nor his knowledge nor from his actions nor from experience in his old age, and dares to teach then his teaching is not accompanied by the action of grace and the student does not profit from him. He who teaches without being asked to do so and for no reason, insisting on benefiting the listeners, is ignorant."

446   **The Brothers asked:** "Sylvanus said: 'Do not wish to be a believer'."[457]

447   **The Exegete replied:** "If he wished to be castrated, meaning: 'If the devil presses you in the struggle with fornication do not cut off your sexual organ and do not wish that you had been castrated from the womb of your mother, rather, remain fixed in the struggle, expect victory, and hope for reward'."

448   **He also said:** "If the brothers sat with the Fathers in order to learn the way of life of thoughts and the struggle with yearnings and the Fathers saw that they were illuminated with knowledge, despised yearnings, and were exalted in the Spirit, then they do not

يقبلونها في نفوسهم قبولا خفيا روحانيا. ولا تظهر اثارها بالفعل لعدم استحقاق هذا الجيل الشرير.[1688]

443 **حاشيه** ويجوز ان يكون قد اختفى في تعريه المتاخرين[1689] بتيقنهم ثبوتها الاولين امثالهم[1690] كما جرى في ايات الايمان[1691] او الحذر[1692] (a86r) على المتاخرين[1693] من الضرر بها بالكبريا والفكر وبكثره القاصدين لكونهم دون الاولين. ويجوز ان يكونوا اعني المتاخرين[1694] لذكايهم وثبوت ايمانهم لا يحتاجون للايات[1695] كما قال الرسول ان الايات كانت لغير المومنين حتى امنوا. وبهذا ينالون الطوبا من الرب القايل طوبا للذين لم يروا وامنوا.

444 **قال الاخوه** (b106r) قال انبا يعقوب ان الذي يعلم صاحبه قبل ان يساله هو مساو[1696] مع الذي يبكته.

445 **قال المفسر** (c110r) الذي لم يصير راسا ولا جعل معلما وبالجمله ما اقتنى رتبت التعليم لا من درجته ولا من معرفته ولا من اعماله ولا من تجربته في كبر سنه. (e139r) ويتجاسر على التعليم ما يصحب تعليمه فعل النعمه ولا يربح المتعلم منه. ومن يعلم من غير ان[1697] يطلب منه ومن غير سبب موجب لنفع السامعين فهو جاهل.

446 **قال الاخوه** قال سلوانوس لا ترد[1698] ان تكون مومنا.

447 **قال المفسر** ان[1699] اراد مخصيا (d137r) اي اذا ضغطك[1700] الشيطان في قتال الزنا لا تقطع منك عضو التناسل ولا ترد ان تكون مخصيا من بطن امك بل اثبت في الجهاد وانتظر الغلبه وترجا الجزا.

448 **وقال ايضا** ان الاخوه كانوا اذا جلسوا عند الابا ليتعلموا تدبير الافكار وقتال الاوجاع فاذا راوهم الابا نيرين في المعرفه وهم مبغضين للاوجاع[1701] ويجلون[1702] بالروح ما

allow them to be [present] at all times and with all the thoughts. When thoughts of human and satanic yearnings stir in them they cast them away, rather, they command them to leave them to linger in them a little in order to discern their stirring and recall the knowledge of how to combat them so that they and many [others] might profit, as Abba Joseph said to Abba Poemen: 'If thoughts and yearnings stir in you then give and take with them and discern their deception and train to combat them. The weak and foolish, however, do not benefit from having the thoughts of yearnings linger in them, on the contrary, it is better for them to expel them as soon as they begin to stir in them with indignation, prayer and wakefulness'."[458]

449 **The Brothers asked:** "A holy man said: 'He who does not have the instrument of the craft of labor, whether the instrument of spiritual labor through which he finds strength from God in his soul or the instrument of bodily labor, then he cannot persevere very long in his cell'."[459]

450 **The Exegete replied:** "The bodily refers to fasting, vigils, prostrations, suffering, tears, the prayers of the hours, and reading the sacred books concerning the teachings of the holy men. From these and their like the solitary acquires [the ability] to stay in the cell. As for the spiritual, this refers to perseverance, delight, love, faith, and humility. From these and their like he acquires strength in his solitude."

451 **The Brothers asked:** "A holy man said that he labored in [spiritual] struggle for twenty years until he saw all people as equal. How can a person attain this?"[460]

452 **The Exegete replied:** "The Perfect attain this through prayer, struggle, and humility and just as biological fathers consider their children equally in their sympathy and love towards them, and desire the good for all of them, delight in their joy and are sad with them, both the young with the old among them, and the strong with the weak, the handsome with the ugly, the good with the sinful, so too is this the case of God with people. He loves them and desires the good for all of them equally. Even though He remains with the good more than with the sinners He, nevertheless, also tends to the affairs of the sinners because He said that He appeared in order to call sinners not the righteous.[461] Because the

يفسحون لهم ان¹⁷⁰³ يكونوا في كل (a86v) الاوقات. ومع كل الافكار. عندما تتحرك فيهم افكار الاوجاع البشريه والشيطانيه يلقونها عنهم بل يامرونهم ان يتركونها تبطي معهم قليلا. وييزوا حركتها ويتذكروا بمعرفة جهادها لكي ينتفعوا وينتفعوا¹⁷⁰⁴ كثيرين كما قال انبا يوسف لانبا بمين اذا تحرك¹⁷⁰⁵ (b106v)فيك¹⁷⁰⁶ الافكار والاوجاع خذ واعط معهم وميز مكرهم وتدرب في جهادهم. واما الضعفا والبله فلا خيره لهم من ان تبطي معهم افكار (e139v) الاوجاع. بل الاصلح ان يطردوها عنهم من مبدا تحريكها فيهم (c110v) بالحرد والصلاه واليقظه.

449 **قال الاخوه** قال شيخ ان الذي ما له الة الفلاحه العمل لا الة الفلاحه¹⁷⁰⁷ الروحانيه التي بها يجد عزاء¹⁷⁰⁸ من الله في روحه ولا الة (d137v) الاعمال الجسدانيه. فما يصبر كثيرا في قلايته.

450 **قال المفسر** اما الجسدانيه فالصوم والسهر والمطانيات والتالم والدموع وصلوات¹⁷⁰⁹ الساعات والقراة في الكتب المقدسه في تعليم الشيوخ. فمن هذه وامثالها¹⁷¹⁰ يقتني المتوحد المكث في القلايه. واما الروحانيه بالصبر والفرح والحب والايمان والاتضاع. فهذه وامثالها يقتني العزا في الوحده.

451 **قال الاخوه** ان شيخا قال انه عمل في الجهاد عشرين سنه حتى ينظر جميع الناس¹⁷¹¹ بالسوا. فكيف يصل الانسان الى هذا.

452 **قال المفسر**(a87r) انما يصل الى هذا الكاملون بالصلاه والجهاد والاتضاع وكما ان الابا الجسدانيين ينظرون اولادهم بالسوا في الشفقه عليهم والمحبه لهم وايثار الخير لجميعهم والفرح لفرحهم والحزن معهم الكبار منهم والصغار والاقويا والضعفا¹⁷¹² والحسان¹⁷¹³ والقباح¹⁷¹⁴ والابرار (e140r) والخطاه. وهذه ايضا حال الله مع الناس يحبهم ويريد الخير (b107r) لجميعهم بالسوا. وان كان يلزم الابرار اكثر من الخطاه الا انه يعتني بمصالح الخطاه ايضا لانه قال انه ظهر لكي يدعو الخطاه لا الصديقين. ولان

heavenly Father bestows graces on the good and the evil, so too the perfect Fathers, who seek to resemble God in love according to their capacity, love in equal measure the creatures that resemble their Creator."

453 **He also said:** "The knowledge of books is divided into two parts: the inner which is called spiritual and the outer which is called human. The human is acquired from the teacher through an eagerness to teach [sic]. The spiritual is gained from the Spirit by the good through an eagerness to perform pious deeds and [attain] purification from yearnings, such as with Saint Basilius and his brother Gregorius, the Miracle Worker, the Theologos, Cyril, and Severus, for they all performed pious deeds in solitude along with their book learning. They, therefore, acquired learning in its two parts and they took care not to fall into pride such as those who toiled until they became rich in human knowledge but neglected the performance of pious deeds such as Arius and Nestorius."

454 **The Brothers asked:** "Why do those Fathers who toil become in their old age like children in their state of purity, simplicity, and meekness?"[462]

455 **The Exegete replied:** "This is because the virtue which is placed in the nature of the soul appears in children because of their being devoid of wicked thoughts, love of yearnings and combat with the demons. If the Fathers become purified from this in the period of their old age through the effort of physical and mental labor and the aid of divine grace then their virtue is also revealed and they became worthy of the Kingdom of Heaven as in the words of our Lord: 'If you do not convert and become like these children you will not enter the Kingdom of Heaven'."[463]

456 **The Brothers asked:** "How should lay people think so that they do not complain about the solitaries if they see or hear about their lapses."[464]

457 **The Exegete replied:** "By thinking that fire, which is radiant in its nature, will inevitably have smoke mixed into its glow if it attaches itself to dense or fine matter, and that when wheat is planted in the earth with it sprouts darnel and thorns. The solitaries likewise wish to resemble the spiritual angels yet they have bodies. But because bodies are dense, weak, with inclinations, accompanied by

الاب السمائي¹⁷¹⁵ ينعم على الاخيار والاشرار (d138r) وهكذى¹⁷¹⁶ الابا الكاملون (c111r) المتشبهون بالاله في الحب حسب امكانهم يحبون بالسواء¹⁷¹⁷ المخلوقين¹⁷¹⁸ على شبه خالقهم.

453 **وقال**¹⁷¹⁹ **ايضا** معرفة الكتب على قسمين الجوانيه تدعى الروحانيه والبرانيه تدعى الانسانيه. والانسانيه تقتني من المعلم بالحرص في التعلم.¹⁷²⁰ والروحانيه انما يستفيدها الابرار من الروح بالحرص في عمل البر والنقا من الاوجاع كالقديس باسليوس¹⁷²¹ وغريغوريوس اخيه والعجايبي والثاولوغوس وكيرلس¹⁷²² وسويرس فانهم عملوا البر في الوحده مع تعلمهم الكتب. فاقتنوا المعرفه بقسميها واحتفظوا من سقطة الكبريا التي سقط الذين تعبوا حتى صاروا اغنيا في المعرفه الانسانيه (a87v) وتوانوا في عمل البر مثل اريوس ونسطوريوس.

454 **قال الاخوه** لماذا تصير الابا العمالين¹⁷²³ في (e140v) شيخوخيتهم مثل الاطفال في النقا والبساطه والوداعه.

455 **قال المفسر** لان الفضيلة الموضوعه في طبع النفس تظهر في الاطفال لخلوهم من الافكار الرديه ومحبة الاوجاع وقتال الشياطين. (b107v) والابا اذا تنقوا من ذلك في زمان شيخوخيتهم بجهاد (d138v) الاعمال الجسمانيه والذهنيه ومعونة النعمة الالهيه ظهرت ايضا فضيلتهم واستحقوا ملكوت السما. كقول ربنا اذ¹⁷²⁴ لم ترجعوا وتكونوا مثل هولاي¹⁷²⁵ الصبيان ما تدخلون ملكوت السموات.¹⁷²⁶

456 **قال الاخوه** كيف تفكر العلمانيون حتى لا يشكوا في المتوحدين اذا نظروا او سمعوا زلاتهم.

457 (c111v) **قال المفسر** بان يفكروا ان النار التي هي بطبعها منيره لا بد ان يخالط نورها دخان اذا تعلقت بمادة كثيفه او لطيفه وان الارض يزرع فيها القمح فينبت معه الزوان والشوك. وان المتوحدين كذلك يريدون يكونون مثل الملايكه الروحانيين وهم جسمانيون.¹⁷²⁷ فمن اجل ما في الجسم من الكثافه¹⁷²⁸ والضعف والميلان وما يصحبهم من

necessary needs and are fought by the demons, they firstly withdraw unwillingly and secondly, remorsefully. They should consider that the sin might be through God's dispensation, that they are deprived of aid in order for them to recognize their weakness so as not to fall into pride and haughtiness. They should consider that the virtuous ones in the Old and New Testaments who had the aid of grace established for them, such as Aaron and Peter, also experienced this [lapses/slips] in order for them to recognize their weakness and for people to know that they are human like them in order to forgive the afflicted one but not that which has developed in them. Christ is distinguished from people since no human being can say as he did: 'Who among you convicts me of sin?'[465] and: 'The devil comes to me and has nothing in me'."[466]

458 **The Brothers asked:** "How did the Fathers used to chant the Psalms of the Holy Spirit spiritually without distractions?"[467]

459 **The Exegete replied:** "By training their souls during their prayers in their cells to guard their minds, to gather their thoughts from distraction, and to discern the Psalms with understanding such that they do not leave a word without having looked into its meaning as was written: 'Blessed are the people who know how to praise you',[468] and they chanted for Him and praised Him with understanding. [This is] not a lay person's view like that of the commentators Basilius, Chrysostom, Gregorius and their like, but a spiritual one like the vision of the solitary Fathers who take all the Psalms with them for their way of life that concern yearnings, virtues, and combat with the demons."

460 **The Brothers asked:** "A brother said to a holy man: 'If I were in pure lands and the time of prayer came should I return?' He replied to him: 'What rich person will return to poverty?'"[469]

461 **The Exegete replied:** "The pure country is that which [blessed] Mark calls 'the free atmosphere'. There are brothers who purify their hearts with acts of struggle receiving as a result pure prayer and their minds are illuminated by the light of grace thereby increasing the remembrance of God and spiritual understanding more than usual. He who is standing in this atmosphere when the time of communal prayer comes, the Fathers do not allow him to leave this sweet remembrance in order to chant the Psalms with the

الحوايج الضروريه وقتال الشياطين معهم يزولون كارهين اولا ونادمين ثانيا. وبان يفكروا ان الاتهم قد تكون بتدبير من الله بان تتخلا (e141r) المعونه عنهم ليعرفوا ضعفهم لكيلا يسقطوا في الكبريا والفخر. وبان يفكروا (a88r) بان افاضل[1729] العتيقه والحديثه الذين قد ثبتت معاضدة[1730] النعمه لهم كهارون وبطرس.[1731] قد عرض لهم ذلك لكي يعرفوا هم ضعفهم وتعرف الناس انهم بشر مثلهم (d139r) ويعذروا المتعب دون[1732] بالناشيه بهم ويتميز للناس المسيح عنهم اذ لا يقدر احد من ابنا البشر يقول كما قال هو من منكم يوبخني على خطيه والشيطان ياتي وليس له في[1733] شي.[1734]

458 قال الاخوه وكيف كانوا الابا يرتلون بمزامير الروح[1735] القدس روحانيا بلا طياشه.

459 قال المفسر بان يعودوا نفوسهم في صلواتهم[1736] في قلاليهم بحراسة اذهانهم وجمع عقولهم من الطياشه وتميز المزامير بفهم حتى لا يتجاوزوا الكلمه من دون النظر الى معناها كما كتب طوبا للشعب الذي يعرف تسبيحك[1737] ورتلوا له ومجدوه بفهم. وليس نظرا علنانيا كنظر المفسرين باسليوس فم الذهب (c112r) وغريغوريوس وامثالهم لكن روحانيا كنظر الابا[1738] المتوحدين الذين ياخذون جميع المزامير على تدبيرهم[1739] في الاوجاع والفضايل وقتال الشياطين (e141v) معهم.

460 قال الاخوه ان اخا قال لشيخ ان كنت في بلاد صافيه ووصول وقت الصلاه ها[1740] ارجع فاجابه من هو في الغنى يرجع الى المسكنه.

461 قال المفسر البلد الصافي هو الذي يدعوه مرقس الجو الحر. (a88v) فمن الاخوه من ينقي قلبه باعمال الجهاد (d139v) فينال الصلاة النقيه ويستنير ذهنه بنور النعمه ويزيد بتذكار الله والفهم الروحاني اكثر من العاده. فمن كان واقفا في هذا الجو (b108v) وبلغ وقت الصلاة الجامعه لم تفسح له الابا ان يترك هذا الذكر الحلو ويرتل المزامير مع

brothers. On the contrary, they command him to persevere in that station until the remembrance passes since the service of the Psalms is possible at all times, however, clarity of the mind and purity of the heart in prayer does not occur at all times and not whenever a person wishes it is he able to achieve it because it is a gift from God. If a person was praying and this profit occurs to him then he should not reject the gift of God and fulfill his own volition. As for the novices who have not reached this degree then if they were praying... that remembrance, they leave the profit of their prayers and it is possible that that remembrance was proposed to them through the enticement of the devil. For this reason the novices should reveal their way of life to the Fathers who are knowledgeable in discernment, mentioning to them the cause of the remembrance and how it occurred to them, at what time, and how many times a night they are seized by the demons. He said: 'Remembrance is the attaching of thought to God'."

462 **The Brothers asked:** "Why do the solitaries need to beg from the lay people[470] given that our Lord made a covenant with them when He said: 'Seek first the Kingdom of God, and His righteousness; and all this will be provided to you'."[471]

463 **The Exegete replied:** "This is for the benefit of the lay people and the solitaries because for the lay faithful giving alms is their greatest act of goodness and their almsgiving consists of that which is external to themselves, I mean their possessions, whereas the solitaries give themselves as alms, I mean the labor of their minds and limbs, for the purpose of fulfilling love between them and for each to benefit from the other concerning what each is in need of from the other. The lay help the solitaries with their almsgiving and possessions, and the solitaries assist the lay through their prayers and supplications for them. Through material things they share with the solitaries in what is earthly, while through spiritual matters [the latter] share with the lay in what is heavenly. For this reason our Lord said: 'Make for yourselves friends of the money of unrighteousness, so that when it has been spent, they may receive you into their eternal dwellings'.[472] And the Apostle said: 'Let your abundance be a supply for their want, and their abundance be a supply for your want'.[473] In this manner our Lord acted with his disciples, and He commanded us to imitate them because it is written that the wealthy women, 'Were ministering to Him with

الاخوه. بل يامرونه ان يصبر على المقام حتى يعبر التذكار لان خدمة المزامير¹⁷⁴² ممكنه كل وقت. واما صفا الذهن ونقا القلب في الصلاه فما يكون في كل وقت. ولاكلما اراده الانسان قدر عليه لانه موهبه من الله. واذاكان انسان في الصلاه ويحصل له هذا الربح فلا ينبغي له ان يطرد موهبة الله ويكمل ارادته هو. واما المبتدين الذين لم يصلوا الى هذا الحد فاذاكانوا في صلواتهم...¹⁷⁴³ ذالك¹⁷⁴⁴ التذكار. يتركون ربح صلوتهم¹⁷⁴⁵ وقد يكون ذلك التذكار عرض لهم بغواية الشيطان فلهذا ينبغي للمبتدين ان يكشفوا تدبيرهم للابا العارفين بالافراز. فيذكروا لهم سبب (e142r) التذكار وكيف صار لهم واي وقت وكم مره ليلا يطغوهم الشياطين. وقال التذكار هو ارتباط الفكر بالله.

462 **قال الاخوه** لماذا تحتاج المتوحدون¹⁷⁴⁶ الى الشحاده من العلمانيين وقد عاهدهم ربنا بقوله¹⁷⁴⁷ اطلبوا اولا ملكوت الله وبره وهذا كله تزادونه.

463 **قال المفسر** لربح العلمانيين (d140r) والمتوحدين (a89r) لان المومنين العلمانيين الصدقه هي اكبر برهم وصدقتهم هي بما هو خارج عن ذواتهم اعني بمالهم. والمتوحدون يصدقون بذواتهم اعني بعمل (b109r) عقولهم واعضايهم (c112v) فلتام المحبه بينهم وانتفاع كل فريق من الاخر بما يقدر عليه احوج بعضهم لبعض. والعلمانيون يتمتون بالمتوحدين بصدقاتهم وباموالهم.¹⁷⁴⁸ والمتوحدون يتمتون بالعلمانيين¹⁷⁴⁹ بصلواتهم عنهم وطلباتهم لهم بالجسدانيات يشاركون المتوحدين في الارضيات وبالروحانيات يشاركون العلمانيين في السمايات. ولهذا قال ربنا اتخذوا لكم اصدقا من مال الظلم حتى اذا فنى يقبلونكم في مظالهم الابديه. وقال الرسول ليكون عنكم ما فضل سداد لنقصهم وما يفضل عنهم سداد لنقصكم. وهكذى فعل ربنا وتلاميذه. وقد امرنا بالتشبيه بهم لانه قد كتب ان النسا الاغنيا كان (e142v) يخدمنه

their possessions',⁴⁷⁴ and it is mentioned that they had a coffer which contained the alms of the faithful. For this reason the solitary should not be blamed for taking alms in order to fulfill his necessary need if he is unable to fulfill it through the work of his hands along with the labor of his way of life in his solitary life."

464 **He also said:** "The Fathers said: 'If because of the weakness of your body the result of accidental illness during your youth or natural illnesses during your adulthood you are not able to carry out physical work in the same way that you labor in the work of the soul which is the way of life of the mind, then, if you are unable to fast from food, fast from foul thoughts, and if you are unable to stand and pray with many Psalms then position your mind in front of God in hidden and pure prayer and be meek and humble in your heart, sweet, forgiving, merciful, patient, devoted and thankful. Do not judge anyone in your thought or distress anyone with your tongue. These and their like are not impeded by physical weakness'."

465 **The Brothers asked:** "The holy man said: 'If you see a youth desiring in his fancy to ascend to Heaven then hold on to his leg and cast him down to the earth from there for this is better for him'."⁴⁷⁵

466 **The Exegete replied:** "This resembles the words of Abba Isaiah: 'If the mind wishes to ascend to the cross before the senses are guided away from weakness then God's wrath will come upon him because he began an action that is above his level'.⁴⁷⁶ Certain novice brothers infringe on actions which are above their power and degree, and they do not wish to learn and obey the instruction of the Fathers. Before they fulfill the period in the coenobium as they should, they dare to enter the cell as is written in the book of *The Paradise* regarding a brother who immediately upon wearing the monastic garb secluded himself, and the Fathers then went and brought him out without any trouble. Then there are others who seek seclusion in hermitages without it being of any benefit. Others at the outset of their stillness copy the Fathers in the elevated spiritual way of life before they complete the bodily way of life. If all these do not reveal their thoughts to the Fathers and receive the necessary correction from them but on the contrary they follow a

باموالهن¹⁷⁵⁰ وذكر ان كان معهم صندوق. والذي فيه كان من صدقات المومنين فلهذا ليس يخذه المتوحد ان ياخذ الصدقه ليكمل بها ضرورة حاجته اذا لم يقدر يكملها من عمل يديه مع عمل تدبيره في هذه¹⁷⁵¹ وحدته.

464 **وقال ايضا** قالت الابا ان كنت لضعف جسدك اما بالامراض العرضيه في صباك او بالامراض الطبيعيه في كبرك لا تقدر تعمل اعمال¹⁷⁵² الجسد كما كنت فاعل في اعمال (d140v) النفس الذي (a89v) هو تدبير الذهن. فان كنت ما تقدر تصوم من الاطعمه فصوم من الافكار الرديه. وان (b109v) كنت ما تقدر تقف وتصلي بمزامير¹⁷⁵³ كثيره فاوقف¹⁷⁵⁴ عقلك قدام الله في الصلاة الخفيه النقيه وكن وديعا¹⁷⁵⁵ ومتضعا¹⁷⁵⁶ في قلبك حلوا غفورا رحيما صبورا ودودا شكورا. لا تدن بفكرك ولا تحزن بلسانك احدا.¹⁷⁵⁷ فهذه وامثالها لا يمنعها ضعف الجسد.

465 **قال الاخوه** قال شيخ اذا رايت صبيا يشتهي بهواه ان يصعد الى السما فامسك برجله واطرحه الى الارض من هناك فهو خير له.

466 **قال المفسر** هذا يشبه قول انبا اشعيا من قبل ان تهدي الحواس من الضعف اذا اراد العقل يصعد الى الصليب فغضب الله ياتي عليه لانه ابتدا في فعل اعلا من درجته. (c113r) فقوم من الاخوه المبتدين يتعدون على فعل اعلا من قوتهم (e143r) ودرجتهم وما يريدون ان يتعلموا ويطيعوا وصية الابا. فقبل ان يكملوا الزمان كما ينبغي في الشركه يجسرون يدخلون القلايه كما كتب في كتاب الفردوس من اجل اخ¹⁷⁵⁸ انه لما لبس الاسكيم حبس نفسه. وان الابا مضوا اخرجوه بالهوان. وثم اخر يطلبون الحبوس¹⁷⁵⁹ في الصوامع وليس فيها رج. واخرون في بداية¹⁷⁶⁰ هدوهم يتشبهون بالابا¹⁷⁶¹ في التدبير العالي الروحاني من (d141r) قبل يكملوا التدبير الجسداني وهولاي¹⁷⁶² كلهم اذا لم يكشفوا افكارهم (a90r) للابا ويقبلون التعديل الواجب منهم بل

way of life according to their whim then the demons will possess them and mock them."[477]

467 **He also said:** "Do not be influenced by reputation relayed by people and as consequence reside in an recognized monastery, or as a result become the disciple of a renowned father. However, it is good if you intend to reside in the mentioned monastery because of the great benefit involved and the ease with which virtuous work is undertaken in it, or to become the disciple of a famous father in order to learn from his wisdom, profit from his virtue, lead a way of life according to his prescription, and to take good strength through his prayer and blessing."

468 **He also said:** "Being dead to the world as the Apostle said[478] is to abolish all preoccupations with all worldly concerns and that a person should not concern himself with anything else nor request or covet or desire anything other than to reach perfect love in God our Lord Jesus Christ. Then he would be able to fulfill the prescription of the Apostle who said: 'Love your Lord',[479] 'Be joyful in your hope, patient in affliction',[480] 'Do not be worried about or bent on anything, but direct your full attention to the Lord in every prayer and supplication before Him',[481] glory be to Him forever."

469 **The Brothers asked:** "The Fathers of the Scete desert were summoned by Theophilos the Patriarch of Alexandria in order to pray and purify a temple of idols. While they were eating he placed before them the meat of a calf which they ate in simplicity. The Patriarch then took a piece and presented it to the holy man who was close to him saying: 'This is a nice piece', [to which they all responded]: 'Up to this point we have been eating it not because it is meat', and none of them tasted it any longer.[482] Why did the Patriarch give the meat to the Father to eat? And why did they obey him and eat? And why when he said: 'This is a nice piece', did they not eat any more?"

470 **The Exegete replied:** "There were many heretics in Egypt and Alexandria of various opinions all of whom used to accuse the solitaries thinking that they followed the wicked view of the Manicheans because they prohibit marriage and the eating of meat. In addition a group of children… the Church not knowing that they were making complaints against them and accusing them in

467 **وقال ايضا** لا توثر السمعه^{1764} من الناس فتسكن لاجلها في^{1765} دير مشكور او تتلمذ بسببها لاب مذكور. واما ان قصدت السكن في الدير المذكور لكثرة^{1766} الربح وتيسر عمل الفضيله فيه والتلمذه للاب المشهور لتتعلم من حكمته وتربح من فضيلته وتتدبر بوصيته وتعتضر^{1767} بصلاته وبركته تجيدا.

يتدبروا^{1763} بهواهم. فان (b110r) الشياطين يتسلمونهم ويضحكون بهم.

468 **قال ايضا** الموت العالم كما قال الرسول هو ابطال جميع الهموم بجميع الاهتمامات العالميه وان لا يهتم الانسان بشي^{1768} اخر ولا يطلب ولا يشتاق ولا يشتهي غير الوصول الى الحب (e143v) الكامل في الله بربنا يسوع المسيح. وحينيذ يقدر يكمل وصية الرسول بقوله كونوا محبين لربكم فرحين برجايكم صابرين في الشدايد لا تهتموا بشي وتحرصوا على شي بل جميع همكم القوه الى الرب بكل صلاه وكل طلبه قدامه له المجد الى الابد.

469 **قال الاخوه** لان الابا بريه الاسقيطي استدعوا من ثاوفيلوس بطريرك الاسكندريه ليصلوا ويطهروا (c113v) بربا^{1769} الاصنام. وفيها هم ياكلون احضر (d141v) قدامهم لحم عجل فاكلوا بسذاجه فاخذ البطرك قطعه^{1770} ودفعها للشيخ القريب منه وقال له هذه قطعه مليحه^{1771} نحن الى الان ناكله لا لانه (a90v) لحم. (b110v) وما رجع احد يذوقه منهم. فلماذا اطعم البطرك الاب اللحم^{1772} ولماذا اطاعوه واكلوا ولماذا لما قال هذه قطعة مليحه ما رجعوا ياكلوا.

470 **قال المفسر** في مصر والاسكندريه^{1773} كان هراطقه كثيرون مختلفوا الاراء^{1774} كانوا كلهم يلومون المتوحدين ويظنون انهم على راي المنانيه^{1775} المرذول لانهم يحرمون للزيجه واكل اللحم. وايضا قوما^{1776} من الاولاد ...^{1777} الكنيسة غير عارفين كانوا يشكوا فيهم ويلومهم^{1778}

the words of Paul in his first letter to Timothy. This husband states that in the final age one by one they will become distant from the good faith and will follow after the spirit of prayer and the teaching of the demons.[483] These, who [take on] the form of lies, oppress, and lie while they are perverted in their minds and abstain from marriage and keep away from the food which God created for use and in gratitude by those who believe and know the Truth, since everything which God created is good and nothing is vile if it is gratefully [received] because it is purified through the words of God and prayer. Many who used to hear these words became suspicious of the monks as a result of which all the monasteries in the land of Egypt were ordered to eat meat one day each year which is on the Feast of the Fifty. This was advised by Abba Evagrius in the verse homilies which begin: 'O inheritors of God, listen to the words of God according to what He says. Do not say today is a feast therefore drink wine or tomorrow is the Feast of the Fifty therefore eat meat for this the Fathers used to do in order to remove from themselves the accusation of those people'. When the Fathers visited the Patriarch in Alexandria he ordered that meat be placed before them so that if the philosophers, all the heretics, and the ignorant who are suspicious from among the children of the Church hear that the monks are eating meat with the Patriarch, then the accusation of the heretics and the suspicion of the children of the Church would disappear in the words of Paul the Apostle: 'And that I be without the error of the Jews and the Gentiles and belong to the Church of God'.[484] For this reason the Patriarch commanded them to eat it and they also obeyed him and ate it in simplicity, thankfulness, and prayer. However, when he said to one of them 'This is a nice piece', meaning a succulent piece, they stopped eating and said: 'We were eating in order to remove the accusation of those who are not with us and the suspicion of those who are with us, and not because we had an appetite for succulent meat. On no single day did we ever satiate ourselves with dried and soft bread. We therefore ate what was presented to us in simplicity and now that another assumption has arisen which is that we ate it because it was nice and succulent, we have stopped tasting it because the Apostle said: "Eat everything set before you without inquiry for the sake of conscience."'[485] Therefore, if anyone says to you: 'This is an offering', then do not eat it for the sake of the one who told you and for the sake of the

بقول بولس في رسالته الى طيماثاوس الاولى. هذا الزوج يقول (e144r) ان في الزمان الاخير يبعد واحد واحد من الامانه ويمضون خلف روح الصلاه وخلف تعليم الشياطين. هولاى الذين في شكل الكذب ويطغون ويقولون كذبا وهم محروفون1779 في سريرتهم ويمتنعون من الزيجه ويبتعدون من الاطعمة التي خلقها الله للاستعمال والشكر للذين يامنون ويعرفون الحق لان كلما خلق الله هو حسن وليس شي1780 مرذول اذا كان بالشكر لانه يظهر بكلام الله وبالصلاه. وكثير ممن كان يسمع هذه الاقوال يتشككون في الرهبان. فامرت1781 جميع الاديره بارض مصر ان يكونوا ياكلون اللحم في كل سنه يوما1782 واحدا وهو عيد الخمسين.1783 والى هذا اشار انبا وغريس (b111r) في الميمار1784 الذي اوله يا وارثي الله اسمعوا قول الله بقوله لا تقولوا ان اليوم عيد (a91r) فاشرب خمرا. او غدا عيد الخمسين فاكل لحما. فهذا انما كان الابا يصنعوه ليبطلوا عنهم لوم اولايك1785 فلما دخل1786 الابا الى البطرك بالاسكندريه1787 امر بان يوضع قدامهم لحم حتى اذا سمعوا الفلاسفه وكل (c114r) الهراطقه وغير العارفين المتشككين من اولاد البيعه ان الرهبان ياكلون اللحم مع البطرك فيزول لوم الهراطقه وشك اولاد البيعه بقول بولس1788 (e144v) الرسول واكون بلا عثره اليهود والشعوب ولبيعة الله. فلهذا امرهم البطرك باكله.1789 واطاعوه هم ايضا واكلوه بسذاجه وشكر وصلاه. ولما قال لاحدهم هذه قطعة مليحه اي سمينه امتنعوا من الاكل وقالوا نحن انما اكلنا لنقطع لوم الخارجين عنا وشك الداخلين معنا وليس لانا اشتهينا لحما سمينا. نحن ولا يوما واحد شبع: خبزا1790 يابسا وسليحا فنحن اكلنا بسذاجه ما قدم لنا والان فاذ قد حصل ظن اخر وهو انا اكلناه من اجل انه مليح وسمين. فما بقينا نذوقه لان الرسول1791 قال1792 كلما يوضع قدامكم كلوه بلا فحص من اجل النيه. فان قال لكم (b111v) احد هذه ذبيحه فلا تاكلوه من اجل الذي قال لكم ومن اجل

intention. I am not referring to your intention but rather the intention of the person speaking to you, and why should my freedom be judged based on the intention of another?"

471 **The Brothers asked:** "Why did Paul the Apostle praise faith, hope and love more than the other remaining virtues and said that love is the greatest?"[486]

472 **The Exegete replied:** "All the virtues function within three steps: the way of life of the body, the way of life of the soul, and the spiritual way of life. These three [steps] are [however] restricted to faithfulness, hope and love. Faithfulness is true belief in God and belief in His words. Hope is the mind's constant contemplation of the Lord and on the benefits of His promises. Love is the uniting of the mind with God and preferring Him over everything else. In the beginning, if a person listened to the teachers, read books, and was aided by grace in a concealed manner then he would become righteous through the benefits prepared for the good and the punishments prepared for the wicked, at which time he would reject the world, come to the monastery, and act in accordance with the Lord's commands among the brothers with upright intent. This is the way of life of faith, which is of the body, and is the first way of life. Then, if he succeeded in bodily labor he would gain the hope of the benefits of the Kingdom of Heaven, enter into the stillness of solitude in his cell, combat the yearnings and demons in his thoughts, and pray without abating. His mind would become fixed in meditation on the Lord and contemplating Him. This is the way of life of hope, which is of the soul, and the second way of life. Then, if his heart became purified from foul thoughts, his mind was illuminated through effort, his prayer was freed from distraction, the divine light radiated for him during his prayer, his thinking was protected by the love of Christ, and he attained spiritual prayer, then this is the spiritual way of life, which is the final way of life, and is greater than the former two."

473 **He also said:** "I have answered your question with unembellished discourse and with a method that is not opaque for three reasons. The first is because ornamented speech does not befit the solitaries as Abba Evagrius said: 'Logical discourse is not suitable for our way of life'. The second is because explaining the sayings to certain solitaries is appropriate [by means of] the *Commentary* lest another

النيه وليس اقول عن نيتكم بل عن نية القايل لكم ولماذا حريقي تدان من نية اخر.

471 **قال الاخوه** لماذا مدح الرسول بولص الايمان والرجا والمحبه اكثر من باقي الفضايل (a91v) وقال ان المحبه اعظم.

472 **قال المفسر** ان جميع الفضايل تعمل في ثلثة[1793] درجات. في التدبير الجسداني والتدبير النفساني والتدبير الروحاني. وهذه الثلثة[1794] محصوره في الامانه والرجا والمحبه. والامانه هي الاعتقاد[1795] الحق في الله والتصديق لاقواله. والرجا هو نظر العقل دايما (e145r) الى الرب والى خيرات مواعيده. والمحبه هي اتحاد العقل بالله وايثاره على كل ما سواه. ففي البدايه اذا سمع الانسان من المعلمين وقرا في الكتب ووازرته[1796] النعمه خفيا فصدق بالخيرات المعده للابرار والعقوبات المعده للاشرار. حينيذ يرفض العالم (c114v) وياتي الى دير ويعمل وصايا الرب بين الاخوه بنية مستقيمه. فهذا هو تدبير الايمان وهو التدبير الجسداني وهو التدبير الاول. ثم ان انجح في العمل الجسداني صار له رجا خيرات ملكوت السموات[1797] (b112r) ودخل الى هدو الوحده في قلايته وجاهد الاوجاع والشياطين في[1798] (d142r) افكاره[1799] وصلا بلا فتور. وثبت عقله في الهذيذ في الرب والنظر اليه. فهذا هو تدبير الرجا وهو التدبير النفساني وهو التدبير الثاني. ثم اذا تنقى قلبه من الافكار الرديه واستنار[1800] ذهنه في الجهاد وخلصت صلاته من الطياشه واضا له النور الالهي في صلاته وحميت[1801] فكرته في حب المسيح ونال الصلاة الروحانيه. وهذا هو (a92r) التدبير الروحاني وهو التدبير الاخير وهو اعظم من التدبيرين المتقدمين.

473 **قال ايضا** اني قد كملت ارادة مسالتكم[1802] بكلام غير منمق ونظام غير متعمق (e145v)[1803] الثلثة[1804] اسباب. احدها لان المتوحدين لا يليق بهم لفظ مزوق كقول انبا وغريس ان كلام المنطق لا يصلح لتدبيرنا. وثانيها لان افهام بعض المتوحدين للاقوال انما يلايمها التفسير لكيلا تحتاج الى

commentary be required such as for those who are affected in their speech and composition. Thirdly, because the sayings of the Fathers, which is the subject of the *Commentary*, were not made by them through the external wisdom of speech, and its author Palladius did not write it [*The Paradise*] according to the method of logical composition. It is, therefore, necessary that I imitate them in speech and writing because the purpose is to benefit the reader and the listener and not [gain] the praise of the commentators because I am not imitating the superficial philosophers in terms of envy and self-aggrandizement when they use figurative language but rather the Fathers in terms of love and humility."

I ask you, therefore, for the sake of the love of our Lord Jesus Christ to pray for me, weak sinner that I am, that I may obtain success and assistance from the Lord for obeying him, that I may gain the Lord's satisfaction before death and His mercy on the dreaded Day of Judgment that is filled with glory, Amen. Glory be to the Father, and to the Son, and to the Holy Spirit, the One God for ever and ever, Amen.

474   The *Compendium* of the *Commentary on the Book of Paradise* is complete. What is explained at the end of the book is that it was summarized from a very damaged copy written by one who did not have continuous practice in the Arabic language from Syriac into Arabic.

تفسيرا اخر كالذين يتصنعون في كلامهم وتصنيفهم. [1805] وثالثها [1806] لان كلام الابا الموضوع التفسير لم يصنعوه بحكمة الكلام البرانيه. وبلاديوس [1807] كاتبه لم يكتبه على طريقة التصانيف المنطقيه. فوجب ان اتبعهم في الكلام والنظام لانه بقصد منفعة القاري والسامع لا مدح المفسرون لاني لا اتشبه (b112v) بالفلاسفه البرانيين في الحسد والتعظم اذ [1808] يرمزوا (d142v) بل بالابا في المحبة والاتضاع.

وانا اسالكم من اجل محبة ربنا يسوع المسيح ان تصلوا علي انا العاجز الخاطي لكي اجد من الرب توفيقا ومعاضده على طاعته لاجد رضى (c115r) الرب قبل الموت واجد رحمه في يوم الحكم المخوف المملوا مجدا امين. والمجد للاب والابن والروح [1809] القدس الاله الواحد الى ابد الابدين ودهر الداهرين امين.

474 كمل ما اختصر من كتاب تفسير الفردوس. ما شرح في اخر الكتاب انه اختصر (a92v) من نسخة سقيمه جدا اخراج من لا [1810] عادة له مستمره (e146r) باللغة العربيه من اللسان السرياني الى العربي. [1811]

INDEX OF BIBLICAL REFERENCES

Note numbers refer to the endnotes found in the Notes to the English Translation.

Genesis
 1:1 n44
 1:6–8 n45
 5:1 n95
 19:22–26 n35
 46:3 n423
Exodus
 17:11 n86
 31:15 n148
Numbers
 12:1–16 n205
Deuteronomy
 21:18–21 n217
 29:29 n372
1 Samuel
 17 n227
2 Samuel
 21:15–17 n228
 22:17–20 n60
 23:15 n313
1 Kings
 13:20–25 n120
 19:19–20 n36
Job
 2:1–10 n255
Psalms
 13:1 n363
 18:29 n393
 25:1–2 n361
 27:1 n360
 33:16–17 n417
 36:6 n371
 38:1 n365
 42:2 n57
 42:7 n59
 49:20 n97
 62:10 n213
 65:4 n26
 66:12 n60
 68:1 n364
 70:1 n362
 89:2 n56
 89:15 n468
 101:2 n58
 104:15 n214
 116:12 n342
 116:15 n407
 119:1–2 n428
 119:47 n152
 119:64 n152
 128:5 n25
 140:5 n324
 141:2 n82
 141:8 n83
 143:6 n81
Proverbs
 23:29–30 n215
Ecclesiastes
 2:15 n252

Sirach		11:29	n114, n129, n249, n419
19:20–24	n224		
Isaiah		12:42–44	n140
6:6–7	n72	13:4	n28
45:18	n380	13:7	n21
Jeremiah		15:14	n335
1:6–10	n251	16:24	n18
7:22	n251	18:3	n463
12:5	n402	19:21	n4, n13, n131
Ezekiel		19:27	n446
14:14	n442	20:11–13	n172
18:24	n368	22:37	n479
Daniel		23:12	n259
3:19–30	n232	23:13	n338
6:16–24	n232	24:22	n441
Amos		24:28	n272
1:9	n435	24:45–47	n5
Matthew		25:29	n99
3:16	n189	25:31–34	n47
5	n165	25:34–36	n33
5:3	n347, n348	26:14–15	n121
5:4	n216	26:28	n345
5:5	n348	Mark	
5:7	n157	1:10	n189
5:8	n159, 384	4:4	n28
5:9	n158	9:23	n260
5:13	n414	10:31	n306
5:21–22	n165	10:47	n325
5:22	n164	10:49	n326
5:24	n377	11:25–26	n310
5:27–28	n165	12:41–43	n168
5:39	n243	Luke	
5:44	n202, 397	2:36–38	n167
5:48	n96	3:22	n189
6:10	n383	5:32	n254, n369, 461
6:14	n309		
6:33	n471	6:28	n202
7:1	n339	6:37	n309, n376
9:9	n37	7:37–50	n170
10:30	n379	7:39	n115
10:37–38	n445	7:47	n116
10:37	n16, n399	8:3	n474
10:38	n130	9:19	n440
		10:19	n106

10:26–28	n144
10:27	n15
11:23–25	n140
11:27–28	n250
12:7	n379
14:11	n259
14:26	n16, n17
14:26–27	n400
14:27	n248
15:31–32	n20
16:8	n11
16:9	n19, n472
17:37	n272
18:9–13	n117
18:9–14	n169
18:13	n318
18:14	n259
21:1–4	n168
22:48	n118
23:40–43	n119, n171
23:43	n46
24:50	n84

John
1:29	n343
1:32	n189
3:16	n113
5:44	n182
8:34	n282
8:46	n465
9:2	n403
9:3	n404
11:41	n84
12:26	n14
13:12	n287
13:25	n138
14:21	n387
14:23	n146, n320
14:30	n466
15:5	n78
17:1	n84
20:29	n455

Acts
2:3	n190
2:38	n375
7:60	n203

Romans
12:1	n12
12:12	n480
13:8	n307
13:10	n144

1 Corinthians
2:4	n222
3:18	n223
7:1	n134
7:7	n133
7:32–33	n135
10:27	n485
11:1	n132
11:24	n344
13:4–8	n305
13:8	n111
13:13	n486
14:22	n454

2 Corinthians
1:3–11	n253
6:8	n183
8:14	n473
12:2	n43, n87
12:9	n210
12:10	n209

Galatians
1:8	n415
2:15–16	n484
2:20	n444
6:14	n184

Philippians
2:8	n112
4:6	n481
4:17	n434

Colossians
2:20	n478
3:1	n85

1 Thessalonians
4:17	n273

2 Thessalonians
1:4–6	n201

1 Timothy
2:8	n80

3:1	n61	James	
4:1	n483	1:15	n281
6:16	n388	2:8	n144
2 Timothy		2:17	n98
2:24	n246	2:26	n98
Titus		1 John	
1:15	n321, n330	2:15	n145
Hebrews			
6:18–19	n303		

INDEX OF NAMES, TERMS AND SUBJECTS

Note numbers refer to the endnotes found in the Notes to the English Translation.

Abba Ammon 38, 72, 86, 140, 156, 168, 184, 242
Abba Apellen 56
Abba Apollo 70, 72
Abba Hilarion 256
Abba Isidore 52, 54, 72, 126, 164, 178, 188
Abba John the Less 104, 120, 148, 184
Abba Muthues 184
Abba Nastir 18
Abba Pachomius 32, 64, 72, 114, 126, 152, 184, 234
Abba Pambo 16, 18, 20, 22, 158
Abba Paphnutius 28, 42, 74, 110, 142
Abba Poemen 122, 134, 136, 138, 140, 152, 154, 156, 166, 170, 174, 176, 190, 194, 200, 202, 204, 222, 224, 236, 238, 240, 246, 248, 260
Abba Sarmata 88, 92
Abba Sisoes 56, 68, 86, 88, 98, 118, 120, 122, 136, 154, 162, 198, 200, 206, 214, 248
Abba Theodore 64, 96, 100, 184, 214, 232, 234, 254
Abba Timath 184

Accusation/to accuse 82, 154, 156, 170, 216, 252, 270, 272
Ammonius 38
Anoint oneself with oil 156
Apparitions 228
Arcadius (emperor) n143
Assembly 98, 112
Babai the Great n147
Basil of Caesarea n277, n278
Become righteous/good 90, 160, 274
Blessed Eustathius 48
Canon, rule (monastic) 182
Celestial sphere 40
Community 78, 80, 82, 98, 106, 112, 164, 170, 186, 216, 218, 226, 236
Consolation 92, 152, 154, 182, 188
Contemplation 30, 32, 46, 78, 134, 150, 202, 274
Dissolute 102, 136, 142, 170, 194, 216, 218, 226
Desert (wilderness) 34, 40, 42, 44, 50, 56, 62, 72, 82, 86, 88, 92, 102, 122, 152, 154, 168, 170, 208, 218, 220, 228, 242
Diocles 42, 44

Discernment 48, 158, 174, 248, 254, 266
Divinity 42, 44
Durable 40
Effort 32, 46, 50, 52, 56, 70, 72, 84, 138, 144, 166, 172, 176, 232, 236, 262, 274
Enanisho n1, n64
Evagrius 38, 42, 60, 62, 64, 66, 74, 76, 80, 94, 102, 130, 132, 134, 138, 140, 142, 156, 176, 180, 184, 186, 192, 194, 198, 210, 216, 240, 244, 252, 272, 274
Expectation 44
Fathers 16, 18, 22, 24, 28, 30, 36, 40, 42, 44, 46, 52, 54, 56, 62, 70, 72, 74, 76, 78, 84, 86, 90, 92, 98, 100, 102, 106, 112, 114, 116, 118, 124, 132, 136, 140, 142, 148, 150, 152, 156, 158, 162, 164, 166, 168, 174, 176, 178, 184, 186, 188, 190, 192, 196, 202, 206, 212, 214, 218, 220, 230, 232, 234, 236, 238, 240, 242, 244, 246, 248, 250, 258, 262, 264, 266, 268, 270, 272, 276
Favor 66, 90, 126, 132, 148, 160, 188
Fervent 40, 78, 124, 172, 206, 228
Fervor 74, 84, 92, 118, 134, 210
Firmament 40
Fornication 34, 38, 40, 42, 56, 62, 72, 74, 82, 108, 112, 114, 134, 136, 152, 154, 172, 180, 184, 186, 188, 190, 192, 194, 196, 202, 234, 246, 258

Grace 30, 32, 34, 36, 38, 44, 52, 54, 58, 66, 70, 74, 78, 80, 82, 84, 90, 98, 100, 102, 108, 110, 116, 118, 122, 124, 130, 132, 148, 168, 182, 194, 196, 198, 200, 202, 210, 212, 214, 224, 230, 234, 252, 256, 258, 262, 264, 274
Holy man 34, 62, 72, 78, 82, 84, 86, 96, 98, 110, 114, 116, 120, 122, 124, 128, 134, 138, 144, 148, 150, 152, 156, 158, 160, 162, 164, 166, 180, 182, 186, 188, 192, 202, 204, 210, 212, 214, 216, 222, 230, 232, 234, 238, 246, 250, 254, 256, 260, 264, 268, 270
Humility 38, 44, 46, 48, 50, 54, 58, 60, 62, 68, 70, 74, 79, 88, 90, 106, 122, 126, 128, 132, 150, 160, 164, 166, 168, 170, 172, 174, 178, 182, 184, 186, 200, 218, 232, 234, 236, 238, 254, 260, 276
Indignation (positive)/anger (negative) 36, 54, 60, 90, 104, 108, 134, 136, 154, 174, 176, 192, 196, 216, 218, 246, 260
Intention 18, 20, 22, 32, 44, 88, 90, 92, 114, 124, 136, 138, 202, 204, 222, 224, 234, 259, 274
John of Lycus 38
John of Thebaïs 156
John, the seer of Thebaïs 94
Kalmiran 184
Lazy 98, 114, 140, 228

INDEX

Leader, head, director/Lead, guide, direct 24, 174, 180, 204
Look after (take care of/care for, please, concern oneself with) 40, 42, 74, 94, 126, 186, 230, 238, 266, 270
Macarius n52
Make the sign of the cross on 56, 64, 208
Mar Eugenius 208, 256
Martyrdom n233
Master 16, 18, 68, 202, 204
Meditation 32, 82, 86, 116, 118, 120, 126, 134, 146, 154, 180, 186, 232, 242, 254, 274
Nitria, Monastery of n70
Palladius 42, 48, 50, 76, 152, 208, 276, n54
Paulinus 46, 48, n63
Phantasms, visions 104, 118, 130, 152, 244, 252, 254
Phantom, phantasm 48, 64, 66, 100, 188
Phantoms 150
Prayer 74, 196, 216, 266, 270
Prayer times 44, 274
Prostration 62, 110, 146, 184, 204, 208, 222, 224, 238, 260
Purified 44, 86, 110, 116, 118, 138, 144, 146, 164, 170, 174, 194, 212, 214, 248, 252, 272, 274
Recollection 86, 108, 120, 122, 134, 152, 154, 170, 174, 182, 198, 232, 246
Remorse 34, 124, 158, 160, 170, 196, 204, 206, 216, 218

Repose 20, 60, 100, 104, 110, 130, 132, 206, 214, 228, 232, 236
Resolution 44
Righteous, good 38, 40, 46, 60, 74, 118, 120, 122, 128, 160, 168, 200, 212, 230, 234, 236, 260, 274
Righteousness, goodness 16, 74, 200, 266
Sacrament(s) 34, 40, 50, 150, 204
Scetis Valley, Scete 42, (52), 56, 92, 100, 114, 140, 142, 164, 214, 226, 270
Silvanus 32
Sisoes of the Rock 184
Sky/heaven 26, 28, 30, 34, 36, 38, 40, 54, 56, 58, 62, 116, 118, 144, 146, 150, 162, 164, 168, 184, 190, 210, 212, 214, 228, 236, 240, 262, 266, 268, 274, n42
Solitary 26, 28, 30, 32, 34, 36, 38, 46, 48, 50, 54, 56, 58, 60, 62, 64, 68, 70, 72, 74, 76, 78, 84, 92, 98, 100, 104, 108, 112, 116, 118, 124, 130, 134, 136, 138, 140, 144, 146, 150, 152, 154, 156, 158, 162, 166, 168, 172, 174, 176, 178, 180, 184, 186, 190, 194, 198, 200, 202, 204, 208, 210, 216, 220, 224, 226, 228, 236, 240, 242, 244, 246, 248, 252, 254, 256, 260, 262, 264, 266, 268, 270, 274
Solitude (seclusion/isolation) 20, 22, 28, 32, 40, 56, 58, 76, 78, 80, 92, 94, 102, 104, 112, 122, 150, 156, 158, 164, 166, 168, 178,

184, 198, 204, 218, 220, 230, 236, 242, 248, 250, 260, 262, 274
Spiritual states   42, 54, 58, 90, 112, 118, 144, 150, 178, 210, 220, 222, 228, 232, 240, 250, 262, 266, 268, 274
Steadfast   114, 130, n56
Stillness   16, 18, 20, 22, 26, 30, 40, 46, 48, 54, 62, 78, 80, 82, 84, 86, 92, 94, 96, 98, 100, 102, 106, 122, 138, 146, 152, 156, 158, 172, 174, 220, 222, 224, 230, 232, 236, 238, 244, 248, 250, 254, 268, 274
Suffering (pain)   62, 154, 166, 170, 182, 196, 198, 204, 206, 260
Sylvanus   36, 52, 118, 126, 234, 258
Talents (gifts)   46, 50, 58, 156, 162, 178, 210, 212, 232, 244, 250, 256
Tebansis   184
Theodore of Mopsuestia   n62, n67, n382
Theodosius the Great   n142
Verse homilies   272
Way of life, direction, economy, dispensation   16, 18, 20, 22, 24, 26, 28, 30, 32, 34, 48, 50, 56, 58, 62, 68, 72, 78, 82, 84, 90, 94, 102, 106, 112, 114, 124, 126,

128, 132, 144, 150, 154, 156, 162, 166, 168, 174, 182, 188, 190, 192, 198, 206, 208, 212, 220, 222, 224, 230, 232, 236, 240, 242, 244, 248, 250, 252, 254, 256, 258, 264, 266, 268, 270, 274
Weariness, laziness   30, 78, 84, 92, 104, 108, 168
Wisdom   28, 30, 32, 44, 96, 116, 126, 128, 224, 232, 240, 242, 270, 276
Withdraw (leave, depart, bring out)   28, 34, 36, 38, 42, 44, 68, 70, 74, 76, 82, 84, 86, 100, 102, 106, 112, 118, 132, 138, 146, 152, 156, 168, 198, 226, 228, 230, 246, 250, 264
Worthiness   40, 176, 216, 236
Yearnings, pain   38, 40, 42, 52, 54, 56, 58, 60, 62, 72, 78, 80, 86, 94, 96, 100, 104, 108, 112, 114, 116, 118, 124, 134, 136, 142, 144, 146, 152, 166, 170, 172, 174, 178, 180, 182, 186, 188, 190, 192, 194, 196, 204, 206, 214, 226, 232, 234, 240, 242, 244, 246, 248, 250, 252, 254, 258, 260, 262, 264, 274
Zacchaeus   18, 22, 26, 34

GLOSSARY OF PROPER NAMES AND KEY CONCEPTS

Abba Ammon	انبا امون
Abba Apellen	انبا ابلوان
Abba Apollo	انبا بلوان
Abba Hilarion	الونيوس
Abba Isidore	انبا ايسيدرس
Abba John the Less	انبا يوحنا القصير
Abba Muthues	انبا ماطيس
Abba Nastir	انبا نستير
Abba Pachomius	ابا باكوم
Abba Pambo	ابا بموي
Abba Paphnutius	القديس ببنوده
Abba Poemen	انبا بيمن
Abba Sarmata	انبا سرمطا
Abba Sisoes	انبا شيشاي
Abba Theodore	انبا ثادري
Abba Timath	انبا تمايوا
Accusation / to accuse	لوم / لام
Ammonius	امونيس
Anoint oneself with oil	تمرّغ

Apparitions	ظهورات
Assembly	الجماعة
Become righteous or good	تبرر
Blessed Eustathius	الطوباني اسطاتيس
Canon, rule (monastic)	قانون
Celestial sphere	فلك
Community	مجمع
Consolation	عزا
Contemplation	نظر
Dissolute	منحل
Desert	بريّة
Diocles	دموقلاس
Discernment	افراز
Divinity	لاهوت
Durable	دايمة
Effort	جهاد / اجتهاد
Evagrius	وغريس
Exegete	مفسر
Expectation	قنية
Fathers	الابا
Favor	دالة
Fervent	بغير فتور
Fervor	حرارة
Firmament	جَلَد
Fornication	زنا

GLOSSARY

Grace	نعمة
Holy man	شيخ ، الشيخ
Humility	اتضاع
Indignation (positive) / anger (negative)	غضب
Intention	نيّة
John of Lycus	يوحنا الاسيوطي
John of Thebaïs	حنا التبايسي
John, the seer of Thebaïs	يوحنا النبي
Kalmiran	قلزمي
Lazy	محلول
Leader, head, director / Lead, guide, direct	مدبّر / دبّر
Look after	يهتمّ
Make the sign of the cross on	رسم على
Mar Eugenius	مار اوجين
Master	اسطى (استاذ)
Meditation	هذيذ
Palladius	بلاديس / فلاديس
Passionate	حارّة
Paulinus	بولا
Phantasms, visions	مناظر
Phantom, phantasm	خيال ج. خيالات
Phantoms	فناطس
Prayer	طلبة
Prayer times	مواعيد
Prostration	مطانية ج. مطانيات

Purified	تتنقّى
Recollection	افتكار
Remorse	ندم
Repose	نياح
Resolution	عزيمه
Righteous, good	أبرار
Righteousness, goodness	بر
Sacraments	سراير
Scetis Valley, Scete	اسقيطي
Silvanus	سلوانوس
Sisoes of the Rock	صاحب الصخرة
Sky/heaven	سماء
Solitary	متوحد
Solitude	وحدة
Spiritual states	روحانيات
Steadfastness	برهم
Stillness	الهدوا
Suffering	وجع
Sylvanus	سلوانا
Talents	مواهب
Tebansis	تبايس
Verse homilies	ميمر / ميامر
Way of life; direction; economy; dispensation.	تدبير
Weariness, laziness	ملل
Wisdom	حكمة

GLOSSARY

Withdraw	خرج
Worthiness	حري / حريته
Yearnings, pains	اوجاع
Zacchaeus	زكى

BIBLIOGRAPHY

J.S. Assemanus, *Bibliotheca Orientalis Clementino-Vaticana*, III/1. Rome, 1725.

A. Baumstark, *Geschichte der syrischen Literatur mit Ausschluß der christlich-palästinensischen Texte*. Bonn, 1922.

E.A.W. Budge, *The Paradise or Garden of the Holy Fathers [...]*, 2 vols. London, 1907.

R. Draguet, *Commentaire du Livre d'abba Isaïe (logoi I–XV) par Dadišo Qaṭraya*, in *CSCO*, 326–327, Scr. Syr. 144–5. Louvain, 1972.

———, *Commentaire anonyme du Livre d'abba Isaïe (fragments)*, in *CSCO*, 336–337, Scr. Syr. 150–151. Louvain, 1973.

F. Graffin, "Une page retrouvée de Théodore de Mopsueste," pp. 29–34 in *A Tribute to Arthur Vööbus: Studies in Early Christian Literature and Its Environment, Primarily in the Syrian East*. Edited by Fischer, Robert H.. Chicago, Illinois: The Lutheran School of Theology at Chicago, 1977.

A. Guillaumont and M. Albert, "Lettre de Dadisho' Qaṭraya à Abkosh sur L'Hesychia," in E. Lucchesi and H.D. Saffrey, *Mémorial A-J. Festugière*. Geneva, 1984, pp. 235–245.

R. Kitchen, "Dadisho Qatraya's *Commentary on 'Abba Isaiah'*. The *Apophthegmata Patrum* Connection," in *StPatr* 41, 2006, pp. 35–50.

A. Mingana, *Woodbrooke Studies*, vol. 7, 1934.

D. Phillips, "The Syriac Commentary of Dadisho' Qatraya on the *Paradise of the Fathers*. Towards a Critical Edition," in *BABELAO* 1, 2012, pp. 1–23.

I.E. Rahmani, *Studia Syriaca*, I. Charfet, 1904.

V. Rosen, *Notices sommaires des manuscrits arabes du Musée Asiatique*, I. St. Petersburg, 1881, pp. 6–12.

E. Sachau, *Verzeichniss der syrischen Handschriften der Königlichen Bibliothek zu Berlin*, vol. II. Berlin, 1899.

A. Scher, "Notice sur la vie et les oeuvres de Dadisho' Qaṭraya," *Journal Asiatique*, 10:7, 1906, pp. 103–111.

N. Sims-Williams, "Dādišo' Qaṭrāyā's Commentary on the *Paradise of the Fathers*," in *Analecta Bollandiana*, 112, 1994, pp. 33–64.

E. Tisserant, "Philoxène de Mabboug," in *DThC* 12, 1935, pp. 1521–1522.

W. Witakowski, "Filekseyus, the Ethiopic version of the Syriac Dadisho Qatraya's Commentary on the Paradise of the Fathers," in *Rocznik Orientalistyczny*, 59, 2006, pp. 281–296.

Notes to the Garshuni Text

Mario Kozah

---

¹ والروح : a, f / وروح : b, c.

² الاه : a / الا: b, c.

³ الاه واحد. ابتدي باختصار كتاب اخبار الرهبان المصريين وشرحه لفيلكسينوس السرياني اسقف منبج بمعونة صلاواتهم المقدسه الاول خمس عشر ورده: ساقطة f.

⁴ ولما : a, c / ولماً: b, f.

⁵ رجَل : a, f / رجلاً b : / رجلا: c.

⁶ تنيّح : a, c / تنيّح b: /تنيح: f.

⁷ الف : f.

⁸ قلبها : a, c /قلوبهمَا : b /قلبيها: f.

⁹ يرضيا: f.

¹⁰ جميعه: زائدة f.

¹¹ وتعلَم : a, c /وتعلمُّ : b /وتعْلِم: f.

¹² الهدوا : a, b /الهدو: c /الهدووا: f.

¹³ الغربا : a, b, f /الغرباء: c.

¹⁴ المرضَى : a /المرضي: b /المرضا: c /المرضي: f.

¹⁵ ويتيّحهم : a, c /ويئيّحهم : b /وكل من يتفق ويتيّحهم: ساقطة f.

¹⁶ وهكنا: a, b, f / وهكنى: c.

¹⁷ هو: f.

¹⁸ لها: f.

¹⁹ ايليا: f.

²⁰ عمل : ساقطة b.

²¹ كتدبير : a, b, f / بتدبير : b.

²² ابرهيم : a, c /اباهيم : b, f.

²³ الوصيه التي لربنا القايل: f.

DADISHOʿ QAṬRAYA'S COMPENDIOUS COMMENTARY

24 كاملاً: a, c, f/ كاملٌ: b.
25 طعامهم: f.
26 لذلك: a, c, f/ لذالك: b.
27 هكذا: f.
28 عليَّ: c/ علتي: a/ علي: b, f.
29 قليل: f.
30 اليه: ساقطة b.
31 لها: f.
32 النعيم: ساقطة f.
33 الشيخ: f.
34 واحدا: f.
35 يكملت: f.
36 فتتساوَيا: a, c, f/ فتساويّه: b.
37 النيةِ: a/ النية: c/ النيه: b, f.
38 استطاعته: f.
39 كلشي: a/ كل شي: b, f/ كلشي: c.
40 من: f.
41 بشيّ: a, c/ بشياً: b/ بشي: f.
42 من: زائدة f.
43 زكا: f.
44 ايليا: f.
45 مريم: f.
46 ايليا: a, c/ اليا: b.
47 تدبير: ساقطة a.
48 ابراهيم: f.
49 زكا: f.
50 حنه: ساقطة a.
51 تدبير ابرهيم وزكي وعمل حنه ومريم افضل من: ساقطة b.
52 ابرهيم: a/ ابراهيم: b, c, f.
53 كان كاملاً في: a, f/ كان كاملا في: c/ كامٌل كان: b.
54 تقبله: f.
55 ان يكون: زائدة a, b, c.
56 مزمع ان يكون: ساقطة b.
57 داود: a, c/ داوود: b, f.
58 ايليا: f.

NOTES TO THE GARSHUNI TEXT

⁵⁹ نستير: a, c/ استير: b/ يستير: f.
⁶⁰ به: f.
⁶¹ له: ساقطة f.
⁶² ابرهيم: a, c/ ابراهيم: b, f.
⁶³ داوود: a, b/ داود: c.
⁶⁴ وداوود كان متضعا: ساقطة f/ وايليا كان يوتر الهدو: زائدة f.
⁶⁵ ابرهيم: a, c/ ابراهيم: b, f.
⁶⁶ يدوس: f.
⁶⁷ داواود: a/ داود: b/ داوود: c, f.
⁶⁸ الهدو: f.
⁶⁹ بفرح: f.
⁷⁰ الهدو: f.
⁷¹ يصبر: f.
⁷² الشيطان: b/ الشياطين: a, c, f.
⁷³ بصبر: b, f/ بصابر: a, c.
⁷⁴ ويشكر: f.
⁷⁵ من: f.
⁷⁶ اخ: زائدة f.
⁷⁷ يقدر: ساقطة f.
⁷⁸ الهدو: f.
⁷⁹ او: ساقطة f.
⁸⁰ الهدو: f.
⁸¹ الذي: a, c, f/ التي: b.
⁸² خدمته: f.
⁸³ من: b, c, f/ ومن: a.
⁸⁴ لا: f.
⁸⁵ هولاً: f.
⁸⁶ الثلثه: a, c/ الثلاثه: b/ التلته: f.
⁸⁷ هكذا: f.
⁸⁸ في: f.
⁸⁹ حال: زائدة b.
⁹⁰ الواحده: f.
⁹¹ الهدو: f.
⁹² هو: f.
⁹³ الهدو: f.

94 قد: ساقطة f.
95 ثم: a, c/تم: b, f.
96 الهدو: f.
97 واحدًا: a, c/واحدٌ b/واحد: f.
98 ويرذل: زائدة f.
99 فاما: a, c, f/وامَا: b.
100 الهدو: f.
101 هدو: f.
102 فمضى: a, c, f/فضا: b.
103 واحد: a, c, f/واحدٌ: b.
104 القديسين: f.
105 عسلاً: f.
106 الهوا: f.
107 الافاضل: a, c, f/الافصال: b.
108 الثاني: ساقطة f.
109 قال: f.
110 فلما: f.
111 هو: f.
112 لما ساووا: f.
113 الشيخ: f.
114 تدبيره: a, c, f/تدبيرهما: b.
115 كل من: f.
116 يبيع جميع ما له: f.
117 يضم: a, c, f/يصوم: b.
118 دايمًا: a, f/دايمٌ: b/دايما: c.
119 العنيه: f.
120 مصليًا: a, c, f/مصلّي: b.
121 من يقدر: زائدة b.
122 وله زوجه واولاد ان يصنع: زائدة f.
123 تساويه: f.
124 هو: زائدة f.
125 هدو: f.
126 يساوو: f.
127 تدبير: a, c, f/تدابير: b.
128 زكا: f.

129 كلاهما: f.

130 قصدان: f.

131 الرب: f.

132 ويقدر: f.

133 تفاوت: f.

134 تفاوت: f.

135 يتصرى: f.

136 يهدوا: f.

137 بنيه: f.

138 غير: زائدة f.

139 ناقصاً: f.

140 لا: f.

141 كذلك: a, c, f /كذالك: b.

142 الواحده: f.

143 وتنيح: f.

144 تمجيد: f.

145 كمال: f.

146 يغصب: a, c /يغضب: b, f.

147 الثالث: ساقطة f.

148 قال: f.

149 وتدبير: f.

150 يتصدق: f.

151 بين: ساقطة b.

152 الاقويا: a, c, f /الاقويّه: b.

153 القرضه: a, c, f /القرضا: b.

154 ربا: a, c, f /ربه: b.

155 ايضا: زائدة f.

156 على: ساقطة f.

157 قوته: f.

158 الشيخ: f.

159 دعى: f.

160 العلمانيين: a, c, f /العلمانيّن: b.

161 النور: a, c, f /الور: b.

162 جيلهم هذا: f.

163 سهلة: a, c, f /سهلت: b.

164 فضيلة: a, c, f /فضيلت: b.
165 لله ووانهم ضعايه: f.
166 كوصية: f.
167 بولص: ساقطة f.
168 ان: ساقطة f.
169 اتريد: a, c /ان تريد: b /تريد: f.
170 بع: a, c, f /بيع: b.
171 هو: ساقطة f.
172 والقديسين طلبوا: f.
173 يكون: f.
174 واتركوا: f.
175 ابأ: a, c, f /ابٌ: b.
176 امراةٌ: a, c, f / امرةٌ: b.
177 بنين: f.
178 اخاه: زائدة f.
179 كل يوم: f.
180 للضايق: f.
181 العلمانيين: f.
182 مظالهم: a, c, f /مظالكم: b.
183 السماء: a /السما: b, f /السماء: c.
184 كل حين: f.
185 الى: ساقطة b.
186 مع: f.
187 العلمانيين: a, c, f /العلمانيّين: b.
188 بين: f.
189 والعباد: f.
190 زكا: f.
191 غصبته: f.
192 شيّ: a, c /شيأً: b, f.
193 اضعاف: زائدة f.
194 لانه: ساقطة f.
195 كلشيّ: a, c /كل شي: b, f.
196 طاعتهُ: a, c, f /طاعتك: b.
197 مريم: f.

NOTES TO THE GARSHUNI TEXT

198 مريم: b, c /مريام: a.
199 وتلاميذه. ومزيم جالسه تسمع كلام الرب: ساقطة f.
200 نسيبا: f.
201 هكذا: f.
202 يحسون: a, c, f /يحسبون: b.
203 للمتوحدين: f.
204 في: a, c /افي: b.
205 هكذى: a, c /هكذا: b, f.
206 الجسماني: a, c, f /الجساماني: b.
207 عمل: ساقطة f.
208 ولمحبت الملايكه الروحانيين اعلا من عمل البشريين: ساقطة a, c, f.
209 لمحبة: a, c /لمحبّت: b.
210 والمحبه لله: f.
211 للمخلوقين: f.
212 هكذا: f.
213 وافضل: ساقطة f.
214 العلمانيين: a, c, f /العلمانيّن: b.
215 ايضا: ساقطةً f.
216 قناياهم: f.
217 صناعاتهم: a, c, f /صناعتهم: b.
218 بشبوك: f.
219 محبة: a, c, f /محبت: b.
220 وحده: f.
221 الخلق: f.
222 اشيًا: b, f /اشياء: c /a, c.
223 كثيره: ساقطة f.
224 باشيا: f.
225 ولا يتعزى: f.
226 الاهيا: f.
227 امض: a, c, f /امضي: b.
228 الضيعة: a, c /الضيعه: b, f.
229 تلتين: f.
230 عن: f.
231 وتلاتت: f.

301

232 ثلثة :a, c/ ثلاثه :b/ ثلاثة: f.
233 يخدمونني: f.
234 الغربا: ساقطة f.
235 يسبقوني: f.
236 الغربا: f.
237 بوجه :a, c, f/ في وجه: b.
238 انسان: f.
239 بنوده: f.
240 اوريشليم :a/ اورشلم :b/ اورشليم :c/ ايروشليم: f.
241 جيدا: f.
242 يقتدر :a, c, f/ يقدر: b.
243 في: ساقطة b.
244 بنوده: f.
245 نفسه: زائدة f.
246 طوبى :a, c/ طوبا :b, f.
247 ارسانيوس :a, b, f/ ارسانيس: c.
248 ارساني :a, c, f/ ارسانيوس: b.
249 يمكنه: f.
250 بما: f.
251 صوت: f.
252 عن: f.
253 قال الاخوه: f.
254 العابد :a, c, f/ العباد: b.
255 قال الشيخ: f.
256 الا ان: f.
257 ثلثة :a, c/ ثلاثة: b.
258 على ثلثة اقسام: ساقطة f.
259 ثلثة :a, c/ ثلاثة: b.
260 على ثلثة اقسام: ساقطة f.
261 وجعل العلمانيين على ثلاثة اقسام: زائدة f.
262 فهولا :b, c/ فهولا~: a/ فهولاً: f.
263 فيبرد: f.
264 هولاي :b, f/ هولا~: a/ هولاء: c.
265 معلمين: f.

NOTES TO THE GARSHUNI TEXT

266 السموات: f.
267 فيوثر: a, c/ فيورث: b/ فيور: f.
268 بالعمل: f.
269 فصعد الشوك: ساقطة f.
270 فهولاي: b/ فهولاي: c/ فهولاـﻪ: a/ فهولاً: f.
271 العلمانيين: a, c, f/ العلمانين: b.
272 واهتمامه: f.
273 كالصلاة: a, c, d, e/ كالصلاه: b/ كالصلا: f.
274 ان: ساقطة b, d, e.
275 مخادعات: a, b, d, e, f/ مخادعاة: c.
276 وايضا: زائدة f.
277 قال: f.
278 يكون: f.
279 صلاه: a, c, d, f/ صلاة: e/ صلاتهُ: b.
280 يقتني: f.
281 فهذه: f.
282 الثلثه: a, c, d, e/ الثلاثه: b/ التلته: f.
283 ثلثة: a, c, d, e/ ثلاثة: b/ تلاتة: f.
284 ثلثين: a, c, d, e/ ثلاثين: b/ تلتين: f.
285 الى: f.
286 يتبت: f.
287 فيها: ساقطة f.
288 ثلثون: a, c, d, e/ ثلاثون: b/ تلتين: f.
289 واخر: f.
290 على: f.
291 جزٍ: a/ جزءا: b/ جز: c/ جزٌ: d/ جزّ: e/ خبزا: f.
292 واحدا: f.
293 فيصير: a, c, f/ ويصير: b, d, e.
294 هكذا: f.
295 وايضا: f.
296 تدبيرهم: b, c, e/ تدبيراتهم: a, c, f.
297 يتساووا: a, c, d, e, f/ يتساوًا: b.
298 شبابه: f.
299 استقامة: a, c, d, e, f/ استقامت: b.

300 النية: a, c, d, e / النيه: b, f.
301 لله: ساقطة a, c, f.
302 يرجع: f.
303 بداياته: a, d, e / بدايته: b, c, f.
304 هموم: ساقطة f.
305 لست: a, b, d, e / ليست: c, f.
306 قد: زائدة f.
307 في المحبه: f.
308 والمحبه الى ربنا: b, d, e / ولمحبه لربنا: a / والمحبة لربنا: c / في المحبه لربنا: f.
309 والتذكر: a, b, c, d, f / التذرع: e.
310 وعيده: a, c / وعيَّده: b, d, e / ولوعيده: f.
311 توانى: f.
312 وسقط: f.
313 في: f.
314 بالمعاضدة: a, b, c, f / بالمعارضة: d, e.
315 الالهيه: ساقطة f.
316 نشيط في الفضيله ثم توانا في خلاصه: ساقطة f.
317 بخوموس: f.
318 سلوانس: f / نشيط في الفضيله ثم توانا في خلاصه: زائدة f.
319 بخوموس: f.
320 سلوانس: a, c, f / سلوانوس: b, d, e.
321 يحيى: a, b, d, e, f / يحيا: c.
322 حياة: a, c, d, e / حيات: b / حياه: f.
323 مستقيمه: f.
324 سلوانس: a, c, f / سلوانوس: b, d, e.
325 وشهد: f.
326 بخوميوس: f.
327 واخ: f.
328 توانى: f.
329 انه: زائدة f.
330 فوقه: f.
331 يده: f.
332 ويقبلها: f.
333 ويضعها: f.

NOTES TO THE GARSHUNI TEXT

334 اليدين: f.
335 الى: ساقطة f.
336 الغاب: a, b, c, f/ الجيب: d, e.
337 فشاوروا: f.
338 الهه: a, c, d, e/ الاهه b/ الاله: f.
339 فاجاب: f.
340 كان: ساقطة b.
341 هذا: زائدة f.
342 من شدة: f.
343 كفر: a, c, d, e, f/ وكفر: b.
344 لذلك: a, c, d, e/ لذالك b/ ساقطة f.
345 الهه: a, c, d, e/ الاهه: b, f.
346 تلات: f.
347 فلا: f.
348 من القتال: زائدة f.
349 هكنا: f.
350 البر: f.
351 قال الاخون: f.
352 المتوانون: f.
353 المتوحدين: a, c, d, e, f/ المتوحدون: b.
354 يكون: f.
355 الشيخ: f.
356 كفضل: f.
357 زك: f.
358 الاسخريوطي: f.
359 يستحس: f.
360 ايضا: ساقطة f.
361 صالح: ساقطة b.
362 كثيرا: a, c/ كثير: b, d, e/ كثيرا: f.
363 بثلثة: a, c, d, e/ بثلاثة: b/ بتلعه: f.
364 رووس: f.
365 صوت: b, d, e/ صوتا: a, c, f.
366 تبتخي: f.
367 ساعة: a, c, d, e/ ساعتا: b/ ساعه: f.
368 واحده: a, c, d, e, f/ واحداً: b.

DADISHO' QAṬRAYA'S COMPENDIOUS COMMENTARY

369 وممّا يدل على: f.
370 السماْ b, d, e, f: a/ السمإ / السماء: c.
371 الذي b, d, e: a, c, f/ الذين: a.
372 فكسيتموني: f.
373 تغربت d, b, a, e/ تجربت: c/ وغريب: f.
374 ومرضت وحبست فزرتموني: ساقطة b.
375 هولاي b, d, e: a/ هولا/ هولاء: c/ هولاً: f.
376 في: ساقطة f.
377 ذلك b, c, d, e, f/ ذالك: a.
378 ذكرا: f.
379 يخدمونه a, c, d, e, f/ يخدموه: b.
380 المعد: f.
381 كنالك a, b, d/ كذلك: c, e, f.
382 ذوي: f.
383 اصطادهم: f.
384 متلها: f.
385 اومر: f.
386 متلها: f.
387 ايليا: f.
388 هولاي b, d, e/ هولا: a/ هولاء: c/ هولاً: f.
389 يطلبون: f.
390 تجذبهم: f.
391 ضيق يأتي عليهم في العالم ومن اجل: f.
392 اللالهيه: f.
393 وتتوانى b, d, e/ تتوانى: a, c/ يتوانا: f.
394 عليهم: f.
395 فنسال d, e, f/ فنسل: a, c/ فسال: b.
396 امين: ساقطة f.
397 قال: f.
398 جيد: f.
399 تبتت: f.
400 الكتب a, c, f/ الكتاب: d, e.
401 من الكتب الالهيه ومن: ساقطة b.
402 المبتدين a, c, d, e, f/ المتديّن: b.

NOTES TO THE GARSHUNI TEXT

403 عن: f.
404 السما: b, d, e /السموات: a, c, f.
405 نسال: b, d, e, f /نسـل: a, c.
406 عن ما: f.
407 يعسر: f.
408 المسايل: a, b, c, d, f /المسال: e.
409 الشيخ: f.
410 بمعونة: a, c, d, e /بمعونت: b /بمعونه: f.
411 جميعها: f.
412 الرب: f.
413 قال: f.
414 امونيوس: f.
415 الزني: f.
416 اعضايه: f.
417 الشيخ: f.
418 محاربة: a, c, d, e, f /محاربه: b.
419 تبطل: f.
420 يعتصبوه: f.
421 الاسقنه: b, d, e /الاسقافه: a, c /الاسقيه: f.
422 لينقص: a, b, d, e /لينقض: c, f.
423 شخصه: a, c, d, e, f /شخص: b.
424 وهكذى: a, c, d, e /هكنا: b, f.
425 الصلاوات: a, c, d, e /الصلوات: b, f.
426 احد: f.
427 عبر: a, b, c /عبَّر: d, e, f.
428 انبا: f.
429 له: ساقطة f.
430 الذهن: a, c, e, f /للذهن: b, d.
431 يرى: زائدة f.
432 شي: b, d, e /شيأ: a, c, f.
433 قال: f.
434 الشيخ: f.
435 كيف قال: f.
436 انطونيوس: b, c, d, e, f /انطولنطيوس: a.

437 انه راى: f.
438 بولس: f.
439 صاعدين: f.
440 من اجل: a, c, d, e, f/ مناجل: b.
441 السما: f.
442 دعى: f.
443 فالاولى: f.
444 التوره: b, d, e /التوراه: a, f/ التوراة: c.
445 البد: f.
446 التي: f.
447 الله به: ساقطة f.
448 المياه: f.
449 الثالثه: a, c, d, e /الثالث: b /التالته: f.
450 بولس: f.
451 نفوس: a, c, b, f /نفس: d, e.
452 تكون: ساقطة f.
453 للمجازاه: f.
454 وحنينا: f.
455 يكون: f.
456 للص: b, c, d, e, f /الص: a.
457 انه: زائدة f.
458 قال: f.
459 تعلم: f.
460 الشياطين: a, c, f /الشيطان: b, d, e.
461 قال المفسر لان حرب الشياطين: ساقطة f.
462 تكون: f.
463 وانما: f.
464 يقتني: f.
465 والخلاوه: f.
466 وفيها: f.
467 قال: f.
468 لما: f.
469 ان: ساقطة f.
470 الشيخ: f.
471 الماي: b /الماء: e /الماْ: d /الماء: c /الملا: a /الما: f.

NOTES TO THE GARSHUNI TEXT

472 او يوكل: f.
473 بعد التناول: f.
474 كانت: f.
475 يقولون: a, c /يقولوا: b, d, e /تقول: f.
476 قال: f.
477 بنى: a, c, f /بنا: b, d, e.
478 اليا: a, c, d, e /الى: b /ايليا: f.
479 لهم مدبر: f.
480 فارسل اليه من الله: f.
481 ثلثة: a, c, d, e /ثلاثة: b /تلاتة: f.
482 وحلفوه ان: f.
483 بهن: a, d, e, f /بهم: b, c.
484 قال المفسر: ساقطة f.
485 لثلاثه: f.
486 كترهن: f.
487 يوثرن: ساقطة b /يوترن: e, f.
488 يعيشوا: f.
489 عليهم: f.
490 بهم: f.
491 جلى: e.
492 ما فى: f.
493 بنى: a, c, f /بنا: b, d, e.
494 لهم: f.
495 دير: f.
496 بهم: f.
497 ديرهم: f.
498 حركة: a, c, e /حرك: b, d /حركات: f.
499 القتلات: a, c, d /القتالات: b, e, f.
500 للناس: f.
501 الناس والملايكه والشياطين: a, c, e, f /للناس وللملايكه وللشياطين: b, d.
502 بغضته: f.
503 الشيطان: a, c /للشيطان: b, d, e, f.
504 وينسبون خيرهم: ساقطة f.
505 للشرير: c, f.
506 الى: زائدة f.

507 هذه: a, b, c, d/ هدم: e, f.
508 الامر: f.
509 قومٌ: b.
510 عن قوم: ساقطة f.
511 لنا: زائدة f.
512 ومجده: زائدة f.
513 الالهيته التي لا تعد ولا تحصى من المبتدا الى المنتهى: زائدة f.
514 قال: f.
515 ذلك: ساقطة f.
516 الشيخ: f.
517 مناجل: b.
518 ماري: f.
519 الذي: f.
520 الاسقيط: f.
521 هو: ساقطة b, f.
522 وقع: f.
523 التي: f.
524 ايدي: f.
525 قال: f.
526 او شيطان: f.
527 فلاديس: a, c/ فلاديوس: b, d, e/ بلاديوس: f.
528 العقل البشري: f.
529 قال ديوقلاس: f.
530 قال: زائدة f.
531 والفعل: f.
532 المفسر: ساقطة f.
533 تذكّر: f.
534 وجوده ورحمته: f.
535 وحكمته وجودة رحمته: ساقطة b.
536 القواطع: c, f.
537 ضعف: f.
538 وقتاً وقتاً: a, c, e/ وقتٌ وقتًا: d/ وقتٌ وقتٌ: b/ وقتا ووقتا: f.
539 من: f.
540 بالقراة: a, c/ في القراة: b, d, e/ بالقوه: f.
541 ويكمل: f.

NOTES TO THE GARSHUNI TEXT

542 قال: f.
543 العباد: ساقطة f.
544 نورا: f.
545 الاهي: f.
546 تنتقي: f.
547 اضي: f.
548 ابراهم: a /ابراهام: f.
549 وحنينا: f.
550 العرس: f.
551 الشيخ: f.
552 وعزمه: f.
553 وان: f.
554 الى هنا: f.
555 قلبه: f.
556 الشيطان: f.
557 ومن: ساقطة f.
558 تتقدم: f.
559 هكذا: f, c/ c.
560 للقايه: f.
561 ثبت: f.
562 يثبت: f.
563 يا رب يا الله: f.
564 حق: زائدة f.
565 في نسخة السريانيه متى اتي وانظر وجهك: حاشية a, c.
566 ابني: a, b, c, d, e / انني: f.
567 بلا: f.
568 الي: a, f /ايّ: c /اليّ: b, d, e.
569 الان: b, d, e /لا: a, c, f.
570 هولاي: b, d, e /هولا: c /هولا: a /هولاً: f.
571 بطيا: زائدة: c.
572 طرق: a, c /طريق: b, d, e, f.
573 بعضهم: a, c, f /بعض عنهم: b, d, e.
574 معرفه: f.
575 واخرتني: f.
576 هذه: f.

577 وبالا: f.
578 قال: f.
579 بولس: f.
580 فقد اشتهى: f.
581 صلى: f.
582 الشيخ: f.
583 الله ربنا: f.
584 اعطى: f.
585 تمنع: f.
586 فاضلا: b.
587 صالح: ساقطة e, d.
588 الرياسه: f.
589 واخاف: f.
590 تضرد: f.
591 لتلمذة: f.
592 يخبر: f.
593 احدا: a, c, e, f/ احد: b, d.
594 قدر: f.
595 وينبغي: f.
596 اسقفية: a, c, f/ الاسقفيه: b, d, e.
597 مجدها: f.
598 وينبغي: a, c, f/ فينبغي: b, d, e.
599 دراية الكتب: f.
600 خمسة: f.
601 منجل: f.
602 علمه: f.
603 متضعا: a, c, f/ متضع: b, d, e.
604 موثرا للهدوا: f.
605 سال: a, c, f/ فسال: b, d, e.
606 لكيف: f.
607 اذ: c, f/ اذى: a/ اذا: b, d, e.
608 كاتب: a, c, f/ كتاب: b, d, e.
609 اسطائيوس: c/ اسطانيوس: f.
610 الصلاه: f.
611 تبين: a, c, f/ تبان: b, d, e.

NOTES TO THE GARSHUNI TEXT

612 الشيخ: f.
613 مقاريوس: a, b, c, f/ مقاريس: d, e.
614 الشمس: f.
615 رطوبة: a, c, f/ رطوبت: b, d, e.
616 هكذى: a, c/ هكذا: b, d, e, f.
617 كمالهم: a, c/ كمالها: b, f/ كمالما: d/ كمالها: e.
618 قال انها: f.
619 يظن: f.
620 خيالا: a, c, f/ خيالٌ: b, d, e.
621 بشرًا: f.
622 حقيقيًا: f.
623 يروشليم: f.
624 يرى: a, c, f/ يرا: b, d, e.
625 من: f.
626 زماننا: b, d, e/ زمانانا: a, c.
627 تم: a, c/ كل: b, d, e.
628 نسخة: a, c, e/ نسخت: b, d.
629 الام: a, c/ الوله: b, d/ الاولى: e.
630 اربعون: a, c/ اربعين: b, d, e.
631 قالوا: b, d, e/ قالت: a, c.
632 بلاديس: a, b, c/ بلاديوس: d, e.
633 قسيس: b, c, d, e/ قسيسا: a.
634 شماس: b, c, d, e/ شماسا: a.
635 السارفيم: a, c/ الساروفيم: b, d, e.
636 للملايكة: b, c/ الملايكة: a, d, e.
637 ملكيزادق: d, e/ ملكيزدق: b/ مليزادق: a, c.
638 سلوا: b.
639 كتاب: b, d, e/ كاتب: a, c.
640 الاسكندر: b.
641 المجدم: b, d, e/ المجرم: a, c.
642 قال: a, c/ قالوا: b, d, e.
643 موسا: b.
644 قدرة: b.

645 كان: ساقطة b.

646 شيا: a, c/شي: b, d, e.

647 نضرة: d, e/نظرة: b/نصرة: a, c.

648 من: ساقطة b.

649 بثلاثة: b.

650 كفر: a, c/فكر: b, d, e.

651 كذلك: a, c/كذالك: b, d, e.

652 الشيطان: b.

653 الروح: a, c/روح: b, d, e.

654 الحركة: a, c/الحركت: b, d, e.

655 كذالك: a, c/كذلك: b, d, e.

656 يشفى: a, c/يشفا: b, d, e.

657 بمجدر: b.

658 امور: b.

659 امور: b.

660 اشإ: a.

661 ايديهم: b.

662 داوود: b, d, e/داود: a, c.

663 بسطة: b.

664 قرابانا: b.

665 للمساء: a, c/المسا: b, e/للمسا: d.

666 السماء: a/السما: b, c, d, e.

667 وقتا طويلا: a, c/وقت طويل: b, d, e.

668 هذه: a, c/هنا: b, d, e.

669 ابكي: b.

670 حركة: a, c/حركت: b, d, e.

671 فاتاه: a, c/فاتوه: b, d, e.

672 اعطيوا: a, c/عطيوا: b, d, e.

673 الاقويا: a, c/الاقويه: b, d, e.

674 ذلك: e.

675 قالوا: b.

676 عليّ: c.

677 وافتقرة: b.

678 من: ساقطة b.

314

NOTES TO THE GARSHUNI TEXT

679 والروح: a, c /وروح: b, d, e.
680 التوراة: a, c /التوره: b, d, e.
681 ابوكَ: b.
682 السماوي: b, d, e /السماي: a, c.
683 اختارة: b.
684 ميتا: b.
685 انه: ساقطة b.
686 منتفعا: b.
687 بمن : b, e.
688 السماي: a.
689 تغرقها: a, c /تغرقةَ: b, d, e.
690 القنايا: a, c /القنايه: b, d, e.
691 من: ساقطة a, c.
692 التسع فضايل: b, d, e /الفضايل التسع: a, c.
693 لذلك: a, c, d /لذالك: b, e.
694 ان: b.
695 صلوات: a, d, e /صلاوات: b, c.
696 بتعبا: b.
697 بالصلوات: b, d /بالصلاوات: a, c, e.
698 الدهن: e.
699 داوم: b, d, e /دوام: a, c.
700 اكِل: a, c /افضل: b, d, e.
701 غلبت: b, d /غلبة: a, c, e.
702 الدهن: e.
703 للمتوحد: a.
704 شرورًا: a, c /شرور: b, d, e.
705 ترد: a, c /تزداد: d, e /تزاد: b.
706 ذلك: b, d, e /ذالك: a, c.
707 ذالك: a, b /ذلك: c, d, e.
708 الثلثه: a, c /الثلاثه: b, d, e.
709 هكذا ليس: c.
710 حركاتهم: e.
711 لمحبيه: c /للمحبيه: a, b, d, e.
712 شيا: b.

315

713 تاراه: a.
714 يخيفون: a, c /يخافون: b, d /يكفون: e.
715 فنلك: b, e /فذالك: a, c, d.
716 تادرس: c.
717 خيالا: b.
718 بطالا: b /بطال: d, e /باطلا: a, c.
719 سلطانا: a, c /سلطان: b, d, e.
720 تراات: a, b, d, e /ترات: c.
721 ثلثة: a, c /ثلاثة: b, d, e.
722 الصليب: a.
723 كانوا: b.
724 للشياطين: d, e /الشياطين: a, b, c.
725 نعمه: زائدة a, c.
726 ثم: c.
727 تم اختصر عليه من الجز الثاني ولله المنة علي: ساقطة e.
728 قالوا: b.
729 بولص: b.
730 باشياء: a, c /باشياء: b, d, e.
731 للصليب: b.
732 انه: زائدة b.
733 كنلك: a, d /كذالك: b, c, e.
734 علم: b.
735 الامره: b, d, e /المراه: a, c.
736 الاشيا: b, d, e /الاشياء: a, c.
737 فاري: a, c.
738 له: b.
739 كنلك: a, c, d /كذالك: b, e.
740 لمصلي: b.
741 يهودى: b.
742 هكنا: b, c /هكنى: a, d, e.
743 ذالك: a, c.
744 ذلك: a, b, d /ذالك: c, e.
745 ذلك: a, c, d /ذالك: b, e.
746 لصا: b.

NOTES TO THE GARSHUNI TEXT

747 ذالك: a, c, d / ذلك: b, e.
748 ذالك: a, c, d / ذلك: b, e.
749 ذالك: b, c, d / ذلك: a, e.
750 اولا: a, c, e / اول: b, d.
751 موسا: b.
752 مبتدايه: b.
753 مايتا: a, c / ميت: b, d, e.
754 قالوا: b.
755 ذالك: a, b, c, d / ذلك: e.
756 ذالك: a, b, c / ذلك: d, e.
757 صلاوتهم: a.
758 قالوا: b.
759 عند: b.
760 العضو: a, b, c, d / العضوا: e.
761 نظروا شيطان الزنا: ساقطة b.
762 يتدمر: e.
763 يجلس: ساقطة b.
764 بهذا: a, c / في هذا: b, d, e.
765 مبتدى: b.
766 ذالك: a, b, d / ذلك: c, e.
767 باسرها: b, d, e / باسره: a, c.
768 للذين: b, d, e / الذين: a, c.
769 الوفا: a, c / الوف: b, d, e.
770 كل: a, c.
771 ابا هور راس: a, b, c / ابا هو راس: d, e.
772 كنا: d / كنا: b, e / كد: a, c.
773 ثلاثة: b.
774 ثلاثة: b.
775 ثلاثة يدبر الف: b.
776 البهنساء: c / البهنساءِ: a / البهنساءَ: d / البهنساءُ: b / البهنساء: e.
777 كل ما: e.
778 الطاهره: b.
779 عالمين: b.
780 للمراتين: a, c / المراتين: b, d, e.

DADISHOʿ QAṬRAYA'S COMPENDIOUS COMMENTARY

781 للنص a, b, d, e/ الص: c.
782 زيدا: b.
783 لمن: b.
784 العالمين: b.
785 فليثبتهم: b, d, e/ فليثبهم: a, c.
786 العالمين: b.
787 الما: b/ الماء: e/ الماءَ: d/ المابي: c/ الماءِ: a.
788 مواضعا: b.
789 ماء: e/ اماءَ/ اماءِ: d/ اماءِ: a, c/ اما: b.
790 فليرجع: b.
791 ذلك: e.
792 الماء: e.
793 ينّشف: ساقطة b.
794 الاعضا: b, d, e/ الاعضاء: c/ الاعضاءِ: a.
795 الماء: c, e/ الماءَ: d/ الماء: b/ الماءِ: a.
796 لان كثرة شرب الما: زائدة b.
797 الماء: c, e/ الماءَ: d/ الما: b/ الماءِ: a.
798 الاعضا: b, c, d, e/ الاعضاءِ: a.
799 كوكبا: b.
800 الذين: b.
801 بلاديوس: a, c/ بلاديس: b, d, e.
802 قال الاخوه: ساقطة e.
803 قالوا الاخوه: ساقطة b.
804 والانفراد: زائدة b.
805 "قصر" في الفارسية.
806 للبر: b, d, e/ البر: a, c.
807 كامل: b.
808 عادته: b.
809 المرضى: a, c/ المرضا: b, d, e.
810 الروسا: b, d, e/ الروساء: c/ الروساءِ: a.
811 العمل: e/ المللل: a, c, d/ الملل: b.
812 الجدوي ؟
813 التدبر: d/ التدبير: d, e/ التدرب: a, c.
814 ذلك: b, c, e/ ذالك: a, d.

NOTES TO THE GARSHUNI TEXT

815 الجمع: b.

816 الواحده: b.

817 سلطنت: b.

818 قامة: a, c /قامت: b, d, e.

819 مرتيبين: a, c, d /مرتيبن: b, e.

820 ثلث: b.

821 التدرب: a, b, d, e /لتدرب: c.

822 الهدو: a, c, d /الهدوا: b, e.

823 به: d, e.

824 يكمل: ساقطة b.

825 في: ساقطة b.

826 الدرب: e.

827 السابعه: b.

828 موسا: b.

829 خرجا: a, c /خرجوا: b, d, e.

830 بتعاليم: b.

831 كثيرين: b.

832 الى القلايه: a, c /للقلايه: b, d /القلايه: e.

833 عليها: a, c /عليه: b, d, e.

834 من حواسه وطياشة: زائدة b.

835 اولّ: b.

836 ما: ساقطة b.

837 الدعو: b, d, e /الذي: c /الدعوة: a.

838 معناه: b.

839 تجرب: c.

840 فاحيني: a, c, d /فاحييني: b, e.

841 اي: ساقطة b, d, e.

842 اللسان: b.

843 المبتدي: b, d, e /للمبتدي: a, c.

844 ثلاثة: b.

845 سلطانا: a, c /سلطان: e /سلطانٍ: b, d.

846 ذاك: a, c /ذالك: b, d, e.

847 يعملون: b.

848 في: زائدة a.

849 الثلاثه: b.

850 ليعدوهم: b.

851 المرضى: a, c /المرضا: b, d, e.

852 بعد: b, d, e /بعدم: a, c.

853 فلعدموا: b.

854 الثلاثه: b.

855 ذالك: d.

856 بالملل: a, c /بالعمل: b, d, e.

857 الملل: a, c /العمل: b, d, e.

858 خدمة المرضى: a, c, e /خدمة المرضا: d /خدمت المرضا: b.

859 بالاوفق: a, b, c /فالاوفق: d, e.

860 لهولاني: a.

861 داوم: a, c /دام: b, d, e.

862 للنقية: a.

863 بريه: a, c /البريه: b, d, e.

864 بابتدا: b.

865 هيني: b.

866 الهديد: b, e.

867 الخلطت: d, e.

868 ذلك: b, c, e /ذالك: a, d.

869 شهرا: b.

870 تراا: a, c /ترايه: b, d, e.

871 انسانان: b.

872 مضا: b.

873 افكاري: b.

874 متوا: b.

875 بالوصايا: c.

876 تزني: e.

877 زني: a, c /زنا: b, d, e.

878 فقد زنا في قلبه بها: b.

879 فلا: ساقطة b.

880 فذلك: b, e /فنالك: a, c, d.

881 بتقدم؟

882 كثرت: b.

NOTES TO THE GARSHUNI TEXT

883 اظهرت: a, b, c / اظهرة: d, e.
884 كثرة: a, c / كثرت: b, d, e.
885 فهولا: b, c, e / فهولاتَ: d / فهولاتِ: a.
886 الساعة الحادية عشر: a, c / الحادية عشر ساعة: b, d, e.
887 الشيطان: b, d, e / الشياطين: a, c.
888 في: ساقطة b.
889 الملل: a, c / العمل: b, d, e.
890 الذهن: a, c, d / الدهن: b, e.
891 وقاتا: b.
892 حدة: زائدة b.
893 كذلك: e.
894 من: b.
895 جاء: c, e / جاءتَ: d / حاءِ: a / جا: b.
896 رااه: b, d, e / راءه: a, c.
897 فلما: b.
898 مقار: c.
899 اكي: b.
900 اراده: e, d, b / ارادات: a, c.
901 به: b.
902 و: ناقصة b.
903 ذالك: a, b, d / ذلك: c, e.
904 اطيماتوس: b.
905 فرجوا: b.
906 اخره: b, d, e / اخرى: a, c.
907 مضا: b, d, e / مضى: a, c.
908 لهدى: b.
909 لذالك: b.
910 المراة: a, c / الامراة: b, d, e.
911 لثاوفيلوس: b, d, e / لثاوفلس: a, c.
912 يودي: e.
913 ضعيفا: a, c / ضعيف: b, d, e.
914 ولا: b.
915 بالحرا: b, e / بالحراتَ: d / بالحراتِ: a / بالحراء: c.
916 فكيف: b, d, e / كيف: a, c.

917 المراياه a, c, d / المرايه: b, e.
918 الذين: ساقطة b.
919 للعالم: b, d, e/العالم: a, c.
920 تادرى: b.
921 رئس: b.
922 و: ساقطة b, d.
923 مضى a, c/مضا: b, d, e.
924 الريس: b.
925 هكنا: b, d, e/هكذى: a, c.
926 مرضات: b.
927 فلمذا: b.
928 موسا: b.
929 ينيح: b.
930 الاخوه: b, d, e/اخوه: a, c.
931 هولاي: e/هولا~: d/هولاء: c/هولا: b/هولا: a.
932 الجمع: b.
933 كلواحد: b.
934 بعض: a, d, e/بعضا: b, c.
935 يثاره: a, c, d/يتاره: e/يثراه: b.
936 صارة: b.
937 الطوبانيون: b.
938 قلاية: b.
939 فصار: b, d, e/صار: a, c.
940 ذلك: a, c, e/ذالك: b, d.
941 الماء: b.
942 حيات: b.
943 الله دايما. فاذا ابطا فى المدينه انقطع تذكره: ساقطة b.
944 قيامة: a, c, e/قيامت: b, d.
945 الاديرا: b.
946 يدفعان: a, c/يدفعون: b, d, e.
947 افكارها: a, c/افكارهم: b, d, e.
948 هكنا: b, d, e/هكذى: a, c.
949 ربحهم: b.
950 فى افكار: b, d, e/بافكار: a, c.

NOTES TO THE GARSHUNI TEXT

951 كهاتين: e.
952 قلايت: b.
953 كانوا: a, c /كانا: b, d, e.
954 مضى: a, c /مضا: b, d, e.
955 ثلثة: a, c /ثلاثة: b, d, e.
956 كذلك: a, c /كنالك: b, d, e.
957 النسا: e /النساً: d /النساء: c, b /النساِ: a.
958 لصورت: b.
959 للمتوحد: b, d, e /المتوحد: a, c.
960 الثلاثة: b.
961 للفتيه: b, c, d, e /الفتيه: a.
962 هكنا: b.
963 مهتدي: a, c /مهتد: b, d, e.
964 ذلك: b, d, e /ذالك: a, c.
965 المجمع: b.
966 ذلك: b, e /ذالك: a, c, d.
967 يعلمه: b.
968 شيا: b.
969 اغاش: b /اجاثان: e.
970 حجر: b.
971 ثلثة: a, c /ثلاثة: b, d, e.
972 كذلك: a, b, c /كنالك: d, e.
973 حرصة: b.
974 تشبهوا: a, c, e /تشبهو: b, d.
975 فمنعهم: c.
976 مد: b, d, e /ما: a, c.
977 للنصارى: b, d /النصاره: e /النصارى: a, c.
978 الثلاثة: a, d, e /لثلثة: c /الثلاثة: b.
979 مقاتلهم: b.
980 زيادة: a, c, e /زيادية: b, d.
981 ابطات: a, c /ابطت: e, b, d.
982 على على: a.
983 حركت: b.

984 فهو ضيق القتال واذا دامة حركة تذكار الاوجاع بغير انقطاع فهو مداومه القتال واذا حصل في اثنا القتال سقوط: زائدة b.
985 ويغلب: ساقطة b.
986 فانواع: b.
987 القدس: d, e/ روحالقدس: b/ الله: a, c.
988 راى: b.
989 فرا: c/ فراا: b/ فرا: b, d, e.
990 يعني بالفعل: زائدة b.
991 الرجاء: a, c/ رجاا: b, d, e.
992 صلواتهم: b.
993 يوم واثنين وثلاثه: d, e/ اليوم والاثنين والثلثه: a, c/ اليوم واثنين وثلاثه: b.
994 من: b, d, e/ ان: a, c.
995 يتيحون: b.
996 قوتك: b, d, e/ قوتي: a, c.
997 عشبا: a, c/ عشب: b, d, e.
998 الحيات: b.
999 بحياتك: a, c, e/ في حياتك: b, d.
1000 سببا: b.
1001 للغضب: b, d, e/ الغضب: a, c.
1002 فيجب: b, d, e/ يجب: a, c.
1003 الابا: زائدة b.
1004 ثلاثة: b.
1005 ثلاثة: b.
1006 ان: b, d, e/ اذ: a, c.
1007 الشيخ: a, c, e/ للشيخ: b, d.
1008 فرفع: b.
1009 كاس فهرب واحد: ساقطة b.
1010 فانكسف: e.
1011 راس: a, c/ رايس: d/ ريس: b, e.
1012 التجاره: b.
1013 نكسه: b/ نخسه: e.
1014 ارادت: b.
1015 ليحردوا: b.
1016 يتشبهون: b.

NOTES TO THE GARSHUNI TEXT

1017 بالمتسكين: b.
1018 بحرقيه: b.
1019 اللذات: b.
1020 والرسول: a.
1021 حاربونا: b.
1022 شيخوخيتهم: a, c / شيخوختهم: b, d, e.
1023 بمقتضى: a, c / بمقتضا: b, d, e.
1024 هكنا: a, c / هكذى: b, d, e.
1025 الجيشه: b.
1026 الاجسار: a, b, c, d / الاجساد: e.
1027 في هذينه معه الله: d, e / في هديده معه الله: b / في الهذيذ مع الله: a, c.
1028 اخ: ساقطة b / اخا: d, e / اخ: a, c.
1029 في: ساقطة b.
1030 خسرني خسرة: b.
1031 يكونوا: a, c / يكونا: b, d, e.
1032 ثلثة: a, c / ثلاثة: b, d, e.
1033 ذلك: b, c, e / ذالك: a, d.
1034 نحطها: b.
1035 فيحب: c.
1036 المساكين: زائدة b, d, e.
1037 يفارق: b.
1038 الشعوبي: a, c / الموبي: b, d, e.
1039 ثلثة: a, c / ثلاثة: b, d, e.
1040 غرت: a, c / غرتوا: b, d, e.
1041 فماذا: a, c / فاذا: b, d, e.
1042 وقتا: b.
1043 له: b.
1044 اتى: a, c / اتا: b, d, e.
1045 هولاء: b.
1046 الثالثه: b.
1047 كا: b, c, e / كأ: d / كـ: a.
1048 كثير: b, d, e / كثيرا: a, c.
1049 كا: b, d, e / كاء: c / كـ: a.
1050 نوعا: b.

1051 من: زائدة b.
1052 احكامه كالعبيد. والكاملين يحبون الله: ساقطة d, e.
1053 اباهم: a, c /اباييم: b, d, e.
1054 قال فلا: b.
1055 مرضى: a, c /مرضا: b, d, e.
1056 اي: a, b, c /ان: d, e.
1057 مرضى: a.
1058 بالطبخ: b.
1059 سمايون: a, c /سماينون: b, d, e.
1060 وحدهم: b, c, d, e.
1061 سلونا: a, d, e /سلوانا: b, c.
1062 الحيات: b.
1063 الحيات: b.
1064 طوبى: a, c /طوبا: b, d, e.
1065 للبطن: b, d, e /البطن: a, c.
1066 حملك: a, c, d /حملتك: a, e.
1067 احدا: b.
1068 فلمنا: b.
1069 احد: a, c, d /احدا: b, e.
1070 الحكيم: b, d, e /الحكم: a, c.
1071 شيا: b.
1072 اعطى: a, c /اعطا: b, d, e.
1073 هولاي: c /هولاء: b, e /هولا: a /هولاً: d.
1074 انهم: ساقطة b.
1075 هكنى: a, c /هكنا: b, d, e.
1076 تنسقل: b, d, e /تنصقل: a, c.
1077 كثيرا: b.
1078 مضى: a, c /مضا: b, d, e.
1079 يضي: c.
1080 التلميذه: a.
1081 بصلوتهم: a, c /بصلاواتهم: b, d, e.
1082 العشرين: a, d, e /العشرون: b, c.
1083 ينقي: b.
1084 اراد: a, c /ارادوا: b, d, e.

NOTES TO THE GARSHUNI TEXT

1085 كل شي: b.
1086 كل شي: b.
1087 للمومن: b, d, e /المومن: a, c.
1088 مستطاع: a, c, e /مستطاع: b, d.
1089 الشيطان: a, b, c /للشيطان: d, e.
1090 ياتيه: b.
1091 الشياطين: b.
1092 الثالثه: b.
1093 الاولى: a, c /الاوليه: b, d /الاوله: e.
1094 ان: ساقطة b.
1095 كذلك: c, b /كذالك: a, d, e.
1096 معرفة: a, c /معرفت: b, d, e.
1097 وان: b.
1098 العدو: a.
1099 واحده: b, d, e /واحدا: a, c.
1100 للعدو: c, d, e /العدو: a, c.
1101 واحدة: b.
1102 واحده: b, d, e /واحدا: a, c.
1103 فليتذ: b.
1104 في: زائدة b.
1105 واعطي: e.
1106 و: ساقطة b.
1107 قال المفسر: a, c, e /المفسر قال: b, d.
1108 حركت: b.
1109 الخله: a, c /البله: b /ساقطة d, e.
1110 الضعفا: a.
1111 يطردوها: a, c, d /يطردونها: b /يطردها: e.
1112 قليلا: a, c, e /قليل: b, d.
1113 الدوران: a, c /الزوران: b, d, e.
1114 الحرر: a.
1115 قال: a, c /قالوا: b, d, e.
1116 الشعر: a, c /المر: b, d, e.
1117 عند: ساقطة a, c.
1118 ومضا: b, d, e /مضى: a, c.

1119 كذالك: b.
1120 الصلاه: ساقطة a.
1121 يختصمان: a, c, d/ يخاصمان: b/ يتخاصمان: e.
1122 بعد: ساقطة c.
1123 الوقت: a, c/ للوقت: b, d, e.
1124 عادة: a, c/ عادت: b, d, e.
1125 البي: b.
1126 انتقلت: a, c/ انتقلة: b, d, e.
1127 خاسر: b.
1128 من: a, c/ عن: b, d, e.
1129 الروح: ساقطة b, d, e.
1130 القربان: a, c/ القرابين: b, d, e.
1131 الشبه: b.
1132 الحبس: b.
1133 حيث: a, c/ حيث تكون: d, e/ حتى تكون: b.
1134 الصبيان: b, d, e/ الصبي: a, c.
1135 كل: b.
1136 النسا: b, c, e/ النسإ: a/ النساً: e.
1137 للمتحذرين: a, c/ المتحذرين: b, d, e.
1138 ابراهيم: b.
1139 قال: زائدة a.
1140 غريغريوس: c.
1141 كذلك: c.
1142 الى: ساقطة b.
1143 كذلك: a, c/ كذالك: b, d, e.
1144 افكاراً: b.
1145 يقاتلك: a, c/ يقاتل لك: b, d, e.
1146 فلانه: b.
1147 سماها: a, c/ وسماها: b, d, e.
1148 قالوا: a.
1149 طويلا: b.
1150 الاداره: b.
1151 فتلد: b, d, e/ تلد: a, c.
1152 كلت: b.

NOTES TO THE GARSHUNI TEXT

1153 المره: a, c/الامراة: b, d, e.
1154 خرجة: b.
1155 الى: ساقطة b.
1156 كملة: b.
1157 باعضا: b, e/باعضاء: c/باعضاً: d/باعضاٍ: a.
1158 قليلا قليل ازجره: b, d, e/قليلا ازجره قليلا: a, c.
1159 نظر عقلك: a, c/نظرك عقلك: b/عقلك: ساقطة d, e.
1160 دايما: a, c/دايم: b, d, e.
1161 فليحيد؟ / فليحير: a, c, d/فليحرد: b, e.
1162 المطانيات: a, c/الماطونيات: b, e/الماطونات: d.
1163 العبوديه: a, c/العبديه: b, d, e.
1164 النفس: a, c/والنفس: b, d, e.
1165 ذالك: b.
1166 اولا: a, c/اول: b, d, e.
1167 يقاتلونها: b.
1168 المفسر قال: b, d.
1169 فتركه: b.
1170 الله: d, e/الاه: a, c/ساقطة b.
1171 الماي: c/الما: b/الماْ: a/المأ: d/الماء: e.
1172 معا: a, c/معان: b, d, e.
1173 المفسر قال: b, d.
1174 ذلك: a, c/ذالك: b, d, e.
1175 مضى: a, c/مضا: d, e.
1176 قتال فناطس الشياطين مع صديقه. فانه مضى معه الى قلايته ليعينه. فصار عليه: ساقطة b.
1177 الثلاثه: b.
1178 ازيد: ساقطة a, c.
1179 الكل: b.
1180 تحربت: b.
1181 منه: b.
1182 العبيد: a, b, d, e/البعيد: c.
1183 كالبعيد: a, b, c, d/كالعبيد: e.
1184 اثني عشرة: a, c/اتناعشر: d, e/اتنعشر: b.
1185 بلاديوس: b, d, e/بلاديس: a, c.

329

1186 الباء: b, e/ الماء: d/ الملا: a, c.
1187 النسِا: a, c/ النسا: e/ النسأ: d/ النسا: b.
1188 قتلت: b.
1189 الافكار: b.
1190 شيخا: a, c/ شيخ: b, d, e.
1191 اجاتان: e.
1192 اخا: a, c/ اخ: b, d, e.
1193 ان: ساقطة.
1194 ابراهيم: b.
1195 النسا: b.
1196 الصبى: a, c/ الصبا: b, d, e.
1197 بافكار: a, c/ في افكار: b, d, e.
1198 قريبان: b.
1199 معها: ساقطة b.
1200 من: ساقطة b.
1201 في: ساقطة b.
1202 للكاملين: a, c/ الكاملين: b, d, e.
1203 ساعة: a, c/ ساعت: b, d, e.
1204 يخرج: b.
1205 المنظر: b.
1206 ثلث: a, c/ ثلاثة: b, d, e.
1207 شيا: b.
1208 ثلاثة: b.
1209 منه: b.
1210 مما: b.
1211 لا محب: b, d, e/ لمحب: a, c.
1212 يبغضه: b.
1213 قال: زائدة b, d, e.
1214 اجل: ساقطة b.
1215 إنالك: b.
1216 يصنع: b.
1217 بره: a, c/ برره: b, d, e.
1218 الاخرى: a, c/ الاخوه: e/ الاخرا: b, d.
1219 فيصعب: b.

NOTES TO THE GARSHUNI TEXT

1220 الحيات: b.

1221 مضى: a, c/ مضا: b, d, e.

1222 ثلاثة: b.

1223 فما فعل وساله المذموم الفعل ان يعمل لها شبكه: ساقطة b.

1224 فقالا: a, c/ فقالوا: b, d, e.

1225 مننا: b.

1226 المرسه: b.

1227 وقطع الافكار: زائدة b.

1228 لصوم: b.

1229 كما: ساقطة b, d, e.

1230 المبتديون: a, c/ المبتديين: b, d, e.

1231 ذالك: b.

1232 قطع: c.

1233 و: ساقطة b.

1234 من: زائدة b, e.

1235 بوصيتين: a, c/ في وصيتين: b, d, e.

1236 الذي في: ساقطة a, c.

1237 السما: b, d, e/ السماء: c/ السما: a.

1238 لم يغفر لكم: ساقطة a, c.

1239 الاوليين: b.

1240 مثل: b, d, e/ مثال: a, c.

1241 بما: c/ بما: a/ في ما: d, e/ في ماء: b.

1242 عن: a, c/ ان عن: d, e/ ان: b.

1243 فاشتهى: a, c/ فاشتها: b, d, e.

1244 مضى: a, c/ مضا: b, d, e.

1245 ماء: b, c/ ما: e/ ماً: d/ ما: a.

1246 ماء: c/ ما: a/ ما: b, d, e.

1247 ثلاثة: b.

1248 رجال واخذوا معهم ثلاثة: زائدة b.

1249 الماء: b.

1250 لكيلا: a, c/ لكي لا: b, d, e.

1251 لخزن: b.

1252 ذلك: a, c, e/ ذالك: b, d.

1253 ما: b, e/ ماً: d/ ماء: c/ ما: a.

1254 مبلولا: a, c/ مبلول: b, d, e.
1255 بما: b.
1256 مناجل: b.
1257 فتارت: c.
1258 القديس: e.
1259 فيما: a, c/ في ما: b, d, e.
1260 اصايهم: b.
1261 انسان: b, d, e/ الانسان: a, c.
1262 تحسب: a, c, d/ فيحسب: b, e.
1263 بمعنى: a, c/ في معنى: b, d, e.
1264 حرصنا: b.
1265 الى نقص: a, c/ نقص الى: b, d, e.
1266 و: ساقطة b.
1267 اشياء: c/ اشياءً: a/ اشيا: b, d, e.
1268 هنا: a, c/ هرا: b, d, e.
1269 المتوحدين: b.
1270 كذلك: a, c/ كذلك: b, d, e.
1271 الاعمال: a, c/ اعمال: b, d, e.
1272 يابن: a, c/ يا ابن: b, d, e.
1273 داوود: b, d, e/ دوود: a, c.
1274 اتصل: b.
1275 روح: b.
1276 عظيما: a, c/ عظيم: b, d, e.
1277 افتخارا: a, c/ افتخار: b, d, e.
1278 نتضع: a, c/ نتتضع: b, d, e.
1279 ان: ساقطة b.
1280 شر: a, c/ شرا: b, d, e.
1281 اثنيعشرة: a, c/ اثنعشر: b/ الاثناعشر: d, e.
1282 اسال: e, b, d/ اسل: a, c.
1283 ابعاده: b.
1284 من اجل المسيح. فاذا عبرت هذه الحروب: زائدة a, b, c.
1285 كلشيا: b.
1286 ينسى: b.
1287 حرر: b.

1288 الها: a, c / بالله: d, e / الاه: b.
1289 يرى: ساقطة b, d, e.
1290 احتقرهم: b.
1291 ملامتهم: a, b, c / ملامهم: d, e.
1292 تنقص: b.
1293 ببالە: a, c / في بالە: d, e / في باليە: b.
1294 تميز: b.
1295 نشيط: b.
1296 بغض: b.
1297 فما: a, c / فم: b, d, e.
1298 كلحين: b.
1299 ذلك بان: a, c / ذلك ان: d, e / ذالك ان: b.
1300 الحفره: a, c / الحفيره: b, d, e.
1301 لثلثة: a, c / لثلاثة: b, d, e.
1302 حقير من: a, c, e / يحقير من: d / يحقر من: b.
1303 جميع: زائدة a.
1304 بالاحرى: b.
1305 وانما: a, c / انما: b, d, e.
1306 اخا: b.
1307 داخلا: b.
1308 للمتوحد: b, d / المتوحد: a, c, e.
1309 الكمال: a, c, d / الكامل: b, e.
1310 لا: ساقطة b.
1311 سقطت: b.
1312 معرفة: a, c / معرفت: b, d, e.
1313 يوصلوا: a, c / يصلوا: b, d, e.
1314 حدر: a, c / حرد: b, d, e.
1315 والاتضاعه: b.
1316 للشيخ: b, d, e / الشيخ: a, c.
1317 عنده: b.
1318 سببا: a, c / سبب: b, d, e.
1319 العا: b.
1320 المطانيات: a, c / الماطانيات: d, e / الماطونيات: b.
1321 نظرت: a, c / نظرتوا: b, d, e.

1322 باسما: b, e/ باسماء: c/ باسمأَ: d/ باسمِاٍ: a.
1323 فاضله: a, c/ فضاله: b, d, e.
1324 هو: ساقطة b.
1325 القزي: b.
1326 بور: b.
1327 الحيات: b.
1328 شعيا: a, c/ اشعيا: b, d, e.
1329 السماء: a, c/ السما: c, d, e.
1330 شهوت: b.
1331 شهوت: b.
1332 اخا: b.
1333 جمعه: a, c/ جمعهم: b, d/ جميعهم: e.
1334 متكلا: a, c/ متكل: b, d, e.
1335 صلوا: a, c/ صلو: b, d, e.
1336 منه: a, c/ عنه: b, d, e.
1337 ارجع: a, c/ رجع: b, d, e.
1338 مضى: a, c/ مضا: b, d, e.
1339 ظاهرا: a, c/ ظاهر: b, d, e.
1340 الاعضاء: c.
1341 يخذعونه: c.
1342 غصبا: a, b, c/ غصب: d, e.
1343 راى: b.
1344 بالفعل: a, c/ بفعل: b, d, e.
1345 ان: ساقطة b.
1346 نقاوة: b, d, e/ نقاة: a, c.
1347 عقلِه: ساقطة b.
1348 التي: a, c/ الذي: b, d, e.
1349 كل: ساقطة b.
1350 الى السطح: a, c/ للسطح: b, d, e.
1351 اولا: a, c/ اول: b, d, e.
1352 يعطيان: a, c/ يعطون: b, d, e.
1353 كان: زائدة b.
1354 هذا التذكار. لكن ليس لكل احد: ساقطة b.
1355 اتى: a, c/ اتا: b, d, e.

NOTES TO THE GARSHUNI TEXT

1356 a: على.
1357 b: مناجل.
1358 b: بطارة.
1359 a, c, e: بنقاوة/ b, d: بنقاة.
1360 a, c: اولا/ b, d, e: اول.
1361 b: فكرت.
1362 a, c: يضغتك/ b, d, e: يطغك.
1363 ينبغي له ان يصرف الفكرة الدنسه بالصلاه من حركتها. والمبتدي الذي ما وصل بعد الى الصلاة الذهنيه: ساقطة b.
1364 a, c: للعدو/ b, d: للعدوا/ e: العدو.
1365 a, c, d: اعانانا/ b, e: اعداينا.
1366 b: منيتنا.
1367 b: يقدرو.
1368 في المخطوطتين D و E هناك جزء كبير من النص مفقود من هذه النقطة وهو ما يساوي تقريباً من المخطوطة B الصفحات من وجه الورقة 81 الى وجه الورقة 105.
1369 a, c: ذالك/ b: ذلك.
1370 a, c: بالفناطس/ b: بالفناطيس.
1371 a, c: قف/ b: اقف.
1372 كما: ساقطة c.
1373 a, c: الحياة/ b: الحيات.
1374 a, c: اذ/ b: اذا.
1375 b, c: عليي/ a: علي.
1376 a, c: قم/ b: قوم.
1377 a, c: الاولى/ b: الاوله.
1378 a: كذلك/ b, c: كذالك.
1379 a, c: الاستنصار/ b: الاستنطار.
1380 a, c: الهي/ b: لاهي.
1381 a, c: انصرني/ b: انظرني.
1382 b: ذلك/ a, c: ذالك.
1383 a, c: دايما/ b: دايم.
1384 a, c: توبخني/ b: تادبني.
1385 a, c: الشيطان/ b: الشياطين.
1386 a, c: الطهاره/ b: الطاهره.
1387 a, c: الابد/ b: ابد الابدين.

1388 تابا: a, c/ تابوا: b.
1389 الاخرى: a, c/ الاخر: b.
1390 النير: a, c/ نير: b.
1391 كذلك: a, c/ كذالك: b.
1392 الوله: a, c/ الاولى: b.
1393 قم: a, c/ قوم: b.
1394 قمت: a, c/ قمتوا: b.
1395 كذلك: a, c/ كذالك: b.
1396 مضاددة: a, c/ مجاددة: b.
1397 لمغفرة: c/ المغفرة: a, b.
1398 الخطايا: a, c/ للخطايا: b.
1399 قال الاخوه: b, c/ قال المفسر: a.
1400 علماني: a, c/ علمانيا: b.
1401 هكذا في المخطوطات والارجح: لا.
1402 كذلك: a, c/ كذالك: b.
1403 الى ساقطة b.
1404 معلمه: a, c/ معلمهم: b.
1405 لان: a, c/ الان: b.
1406 غلبة: a, c/ غلبت: b.
1407 اجله: ساقطة b.
1408 صلاة: a, c/ صلات: b.
1409 يقبله: a, c/ ويقبله: b.
1410 ليعتمد: a, c/ ليتعمد: b.
1411 لمغفرة: a, c/ لمغفرت: b.
1412 كباير: a, c/ كبار: b.
1413 قوانينه: a, c/ قوانينهم: b.
1414 اولا: a, c/ اول: b.
1415 صالح: a, c/ اصلح: b.
1416 بذلك: a, c/ بذالك: b.
1417 المفلحه: b, c/ الفلحه: a.
1418 جسد: a, c/ الجسد: b.
1419 وما: b/ ما: a, c.

NOTES TO THE GARSHUNI TEXT

1420 هذه الحياة: a, c /هذا الحيات: b.
1421 لا: ساقطة b.
1422 ولا: a, c /لا: b.
1423 الحياة: a, c /الحيات: b.
1424 لنا من عمل: ساقطة b.
1425 الحياة: a, c /الحيات: b.
1426 اقاموهم: a, c /اقامُهم: b.
1427 محصاه: a, c /محصيه: b.
1428 اما: b /واما: a, c.
1429 اللهي: a, c /الله: b.
1430 الماء: c /الملا: b /الملا: a.
1431 ذلك: a, c /ذالك: b.
1432 بارادة: a, c /بادارت: b.
1433 يشكرون: a, c /يشرکون: b.
1434 فقط: ساقطة b.
1435 الحياة: a, c /الحيات: b.
1436 فذلك: a, c /فذالك: b.
1437 لاثبات: a, c /الاثبات: b.
1438 العازار: a, c /العازر: b.
1439 طابيثا: a, c /طبيثا: b.
1440 الفردوس: a, c /الفرديس: b.
1441 ايام: ساقطة b.
1442 الشيطان: a, c /الشياطين: b.
1443 ايمانه: a, c /امانتيهم: b.
1444 نارا: a, c /نار: b.
1445 احد: a, c /واحد: b.
1446 للقديسين: b /القديسين: a, c.
1447 الى: a, c /على: b.
1448 وعنها: b.
1449 لتاتي: b /لتاتٍ: a, c.
1450 كل حين: a, c /كلحين: b.
1451 هكذى: a, c /هكذا: b.
1452 حدود: a, c /نحدود: b.

337

1453 فراى: a, c/ فراا: b.
1454 الذي يشرق في عقول الصديقين فاما الطبع الالهي: زائدة b.
1455 المتحد: a, c/ المتوحد: b.
1456 بولس: a, c/ بولوس: b.
1457 للملايكه: b/ الملايكه: a, c.
1458 استنارت: a, c/ استرة: b.
1459 واوقاتا: b, c/ اوقاتا: a.
1460 يشغلوه: a, c/ يشغلون: b.
1461 فاحس: a, c/ نحس: b.
1462 للذي: a, c/ الذي: b.
1463 الذين: a, c/ اللذين: b.
1464 يلزمون: b/ يلزون: a, c.
1465 هنا: a, c/ هاذا: b.
1466 ثلثه: a, c/ ثلاثه: b.
1467 او: زائدة b.
1468 الحياة: a, c/ الحيات: b.
1469 احدهما: b/ احدهم: a, c.
1470 الذين: b/ للذين: a, c.
1471 حرصه: a, c/ حصره: b.
1472 بلسانه: a, c/ في لسانه: b.
1473 كثيرين: a, c/ كثيره: b.
1474 كذلك: a, c/ كذالك: b.
1475 ثلثه: a, c/ ثلاثه: b.
1476 اخضعهم: a, c/ اخضاعهم: b.
1477 كذلك: a, c/ كذالك: b.
1478 هكذا في المخطوطات والارجح: ولا.
1479 طاعة: a, c/ طاعت: b.
1480 رووسا: a, c/ روسا: b.
1481 مروسا: b, c/ مرووسا: a.
1482 الثلثه: a, c/ الثلاثلاث: b.
1483 الثلثه: a, c/ الثلاثه: b.
1484 ان: a, c/ لان: b.

NOTES TO THE GARSHUNI TEXT

1485 الاضطراب: a, c /اضطراب: b.
1486 الحكم: ساقطة b.
1487 في: ساقطة b.
1488 العلمانيين: a, c /العلمانين: b.
1489 لاقلاهم: a, c /لاقلالكم: b.
1490 جاوا: b, c /جااوا: a.
1491 معهم: a, c /معه: b.
1492 متعنر: a, c /معتنر: b.
1493 التي لي: a, b /لي التي: c.
1494 ثلثة: a, c /ثلاثة: b.
1495 اجزاء: c /اجزا: b /اجزا: a.
1496 في: a, c /فهي: b.
1497 العلو: a, c /العلوا: b.
1498 لذة: a, c /لذت: b.
1499 الطاعه: زائدة a.
1500 المنحة: a, c /المحنة: b.
1501 فلا: ساقطة b.
1502 كبريا: a, c /كبريه: b.
1503 لان: a, c /لا: b.
1504 للنساء: c /للنسا: b /للنسا: a.
1505 مضى: a, c /مضا: b.
1506 بمن: ناقصة a, c.
1507 ثلثة: a, c /ثلاثة: b.
1508 متساويا: a, c /متساويان: b.
1509 معرفة: a, c /معرفت: b.
1510 فسح: a, c /فسك: b.
1511 بمن: c /بمن ايوب: a, b.
1512 الريح: a, c /الحرب: b.
1513 فالتسليم: a, c /فتسليم: b.
1514 امسكوهم: a, c /اسكوهم: b.
1515 اذ اطعمهم: c /اذا طعمهم: b /اذاطعمهم: a.
1516 الى: a, c /الذي: b.
1517 سالمين: a, c /سالمون: b.

1518 فيريحون: a, c / بيريحون: b.
1519 ان: ساقطة b.
1520 التشبه: a, c / المتشبه: b.
1521 ذالك: a, b / ذلك: c.
1522 الضباع: a, c / السباع: b.
1523 للقديس: b / القديس: a, c.
1524 جريتك: a, c / اجريتك: b.
1525 يسالون: b / يسلون: a, c.
1526 اليه: a, c / اليهم: b.
1527 ترضى: a, c / ترضا: b.
1528 الهنا: a, c / لاهنا: b.
1529 حضرا: a, c / حضر: b.
1530 لورائه: a, c / لوراثها: b.
1531 الحياة: a, c / الحيات: b.
1532 الحياة: a, c / الحيات: b.
1533 بارادة: a, c / بارادت: b.
1534 موسى: a, c / موسا: b.
1535 يكن: ساقطة b.
1536 موسى: a, c / موسا: b.
1537 حضوره: a, c / حضرونه: b.
1538 للروحانيين: a, c / للروحانين: b.
1539 بشبه: a, c / كشبه: b.
1540 فباي: a, c / فاي: b.
1541 الروحانيين: a, c / الروحانين: b.
1542 الاثنيعشر: a, c / الاثنعشر: b.
1543 الجوالين: a, c / الجولين: b.
1544 السما: a, c / السما: b.
1545 لذتها: a, c / لذاتها: b.
1546 الذي: ساقطة b.
1547 تشبيها: a, c / تشبه: b.
1548 مطلوبه: a, c / مطلبه: b.
1549 الاضطهاد: a, c / لاطهاد: b.

NOTES TO THE GARSHUNI TEXT

1550 معرفة: a, c /معرفت: b.
1551 بارادتهم: a, c /فارادتهم: b.
1552 متظاهر: a, c /متظاهرا: b.
1553 بحكمته: ساقطة b.
1554 ماء: c /ما: a /ما: b.
1555 اخر قال مت لهنا العالم. فقال له شيخ: ساقطة b.
1556 صديق: a, c /صديقا: b.
1557 مات: a, c /امات: b.
1558 الفهمين: a, c /المفهمين: b.
1559 لما: a, c /لوا: b.
1560 مضوا: a, c /مضو: b.
1561 مضى: a, c /مضا: b.
1562 بالسوا: a, c /في السويه: b.
1563 للاه: a /للالاه: b /لناله: c.
1564 تادرس: c.
1565 لسقطوا: a, c /ليسقطوا: b.
1566 دما: a, c /دم: b.
1567 المسلطين: a, c /المسلطون: b.
1568 الارواح: a, c /الاروح: b.
1569 الى: ساقطة b.
1570 العلمانيين: a, c /العلمانين: b.
1571 الحياة: a, c /الحيات: b.
1572 العمالين: a, c /العاملين: b.
1573 او مضوا: ساقطة b.
1574 ينيحوهم: a, c /ينحوهم: b.
1575 ينجوا: a, c /يزيجوا: b.
1576 فضيلة: a, c /فضيلت: b.
1577 يهدو: a, c /يهداو: b.
1578 في هدوك: ساقطة b.
1579 بالمطانيات: a, c /في الماطونيات: b.
1580 الباطن: a, c /البطن.
1581 ائضاعا: a, c /ائضاع: b.
1582 للمبتدين: a /المبتدين: b, c.

1583 لي: زائدة b.
1584 بها: ساقطة b.
1585 ما: ساقطة b.
1586 يفرح اذا: ساقطة a, c.
1587 لاباياك: a, c /لاباك: b.
1588 ماء: c /ما: b /مإ: a.
1589 الحوض: b, c /للحوض: a.
1590 وقت: a, c /عند: b.
1591 السماييات: a, c /السمايات: b.
1592 بفرح: a, c /في فرح: b.
1593 املاء: a, c /املا: b.
1594 المتعلمين: a, c /متعلمين: b.
1595 معرفة: a, c /معرفت: b.
1596 كالمرضى: a, c /كالمرضا: b.
1597 وجعا واحدا: a, c /وجع واحد: b.
1598 عسكر شياطين: a, c /الشياطين: b.
1599 الحياة: a, c /الحيات: b.
1600 للحكما: a, b /الحكما: c.
1601 المزمور: ساقطة b.
1602 السنة: a, c /سنة: b.
1603 للمبتدين: a /المبتدين: b, c.
1604 يتركوا: a, c /يتركوه: b.
1605 عقولهم: a, c /عقوله: b.
1606 بعدهم: a, c /بعدها: b.
1607 التدبير: a, c /تدبير: b.
1608 العقل: a, c /العقول: b.
1609 الالهي: زائدة b.
1610 المعمداني: b, c /المعمدني: a.
1611 وانه: a, c /عند: b.
1612 واحدا: a, c /واحد: b.
1613 واحدا: a, c /واحد: b.
1614 عالا: a, c /عاملا: b.
1615 محرمة: a, c /محرومة: b.

342

1616 بولس: a, c/ بولوس: b.
1617 اذا: a, c/ اذ: b.
1618 قلبه: ساقطة b.
1619 ويستنير: a, c/ يستنير: b.
1620 ثلثه: a, c/ ثلاثه: b.
1621 المكتوب: a, c/ المكتو: b.
1622 بقلبه: a, c/ في قلبه: b.
1623 هكذا في المخطوطات والأرجح: الثالث.
1624 ياتي: ساقطة b.
1625 عليه: a, c/ اليه: b.
1626 شيا: a, c/ شي: b.
1627 ستاتي: a, c/ سياتي: b.
1628 بالاولين: a, c/ في الاولين: b.
1629 تنبى: a, c/ تنبا: b.
1630 لانا: a, c/ لاننا: b.
1631 للرهبنه: b/ الرهبنه: a, c.
1632 لافراز: a, c/ الافراز: b.
1633 الثلثه: a, c/ الثلاثه: b.
1634 هو: زائدة b.
1635 دانيايل: a/ دنيال: c/ دانيال: b.
1636 شبه: ساقطة b.
1637 الثلثه: a, c/ الثلاثه: b.
1638 فالله: a, c/ الله: b.
1639 الثلثه: a, c/ الثلاثه: b.
1640 تعتق: a, c/ اتعتق: b.
1641 كل شي: a, c/ كلشيا: b.
1642 شي: a, c/ شيا: b.
1643 قوطم: a, c/ قلوبهم: b.
1644 كل شي: a, c/ كلشيا: b.
1645 الونيس: a, c/ الوانيس: b.
1646 هدمتَ: زائدة b.
1647 وجع: a, c/ وجه: b.
1648 فيه: ساقطة b.

1649 ومايل: ساقطة b.
1650 يرج: a, c/ليرج: b.
1651 يكدرها: a, b/يكدراها: c.
1652 يخالط: a, c/يخالج: b.
1653 الحياة: a, c/الحيات: b.
1654 ولو: a, c/وتلو: b.
1655 على: ساقطة b.
1656 مقاتلة: a, c/مقاتلت: b.
1657 كذلك: a, c/كذلك: b.
1658 نقع: a, c/نوع: b.
1659 لكيلا: a, c/ليلا: b.
1660 يتكبروا: a, c/يتكبرو: b.
1661 فيقاتلوهم: a, c/فيقاتلونهم: b.
1662 بالافكار: a, c/فالافكار: b.
1663 الحياة: a, c/الحيات: b.
1664 بنيامين: a, c/بنيامن: b.
1665 ذلك: a, c/ذالك: b.
1666 كذلك: a, c/كذلك: b.
1667 التي: a, c/الذي: b.
1668 له: ساقطة b.
1669 القلب: b, c/للقلب: a.
1670 كذلك: a, c/كذلك: b.
1671 يحسدك: a, c/حدسك: b.
1672 انسان: a, c/انسا: b.
1673 عنك: ساقطة b.
1674 ثانيا: a, c/ثانيه: b.
1675 قال: ساقطة b.
1676 ثلثة: a, c/ثلاثة: b.
1677 الهيه: a, c/الاهيه: b.
1678 الونيس: a, c/الونيس: b.
1679 اتى: a, c/اتا: b.
1680 الونيوس: a, b/الونيس: c.
1681 المخطوطتان D و E اللذان إنقطعتا سابقا تستأنفان من هنا.

NOTES TO THE GARSHUNI TEXT

1682 عمود: a, c /عامود: b, d, e.
1683 الاسكدريه: b.
1684 راهبا: a, c /راهب: b, d, e.
1685 مضى: a, c /مضا: b, d, e.
1686 شيا: b.
1687 القديسين: b.
1688 الرجل: b.
1689 المختارين: b.
1690 امثالها: b.
1691 الايام: b.
1692 الحذر: c /للحذر: a /الحرد: b, d, e.
1693 المختارين: b.
1694 المختارين: b.
1695 الايات: b.
1696 مساو: a, c /مساوا: b, d, e.
1697 ان: ساقطة b.
1698 تريد: b, d, e /ترد: a, c.
1699 ان: ساقطة a, c.
1700 اغضبك: b.
1701 الاوجاع: c.
1702 يجعلون: e.
1703 ان: ساقطة b.
1704 ينتفعوا: a, c /ينتفعون: b, d, e.
1705 تحركت: c /تحركة: a, b, d, e.
1706 فيك: ساقطة b.
1707 الفلاحة: ساقطة b.
1708 عزاء: c /عزا: b, e /عزا: d /عزا: a.
1709 صلوات: c /صلاواة: a, e /صلاوات: d /صلوات: b.
1710 امثالها: ساقطة b.
1711 الناس جميعهم: b, d, e / جميع الناس: a, c.
1712 الضفا: b.
1713 الحسان: c /الاحسان: a, b, d, e.
1714 القباح: a, c /القباح: b, d, e.
1715 السماني: a, c /السماوي: b, d, e.

1716 هكذا: b.
1717 بالسواء: c/ بالسوا: b, d, e/ بالسوا: a.
1718 امكنهم يحبون بالسوا المخلوقين: زائدة b.
1719 قال: b.
1720 هكذا في المخطوطات والأرجح: التعلم.
1721 باسليوس: a, c, d/ باسيليوس: b/ باسيلليوس: e.
1722 كريلس: b.
1723 العمالين: a, c/ العاملين: b, d, e.
1724 هكذا في المخطوطات والأرجح: إذا.
1725 هولاء: b.
1726 السموات: a, c/ السماوات: b, d, e.
1727 جسمانيون: a, c/ جسمانيين: b, d, e.
1728 الكفه: b.
1729 افاضل: a, c/ افضل: e/ افضال: b, d.
1730 تثبت: b.
1731 معاضدت: b.
1732 بطروس: b.
1733 المتعب دون: a, c/ المتعبدون: b, d, e.
1734 في: b.
1735 شي: a, c/ شيا: b, d, e.
1736 الروح: a, c/ روح: b, d, e.
1737 صلواتهم: b.
1738 تسبحك: b.
1739 الابنا: a, c/ الابا: b, d, e.
1740 تدبيره: b.
1741 هكذا في المخطوطات والارجح: هل.
1742 مع الاخوه: زائدة b.
1743 فراغ: هنالك فراغ في المخطوطتين A و C مما يشير الى أن جزءاً من النص مفقود. في المخطوطة E ليس هنالك إنقطاع في النص ولكن هنالك ما يشير الى الإنقطاع في المعنى.
1744 ذلك: e.
1745 صلوتهم: a, c/ صلواتهم: b/ صلاواتهم: d, e.
1746 المتوحدين: b.
1747 بقولهم: b.
1748 وباموالهم: a, c/ باموالهم: b, d, e.

NOTES TO THE GARSHUNI TEXT

1749 بالعلمانيين: a, c/ بالعلمانيون: b, d, e.
1750 باموالهم: b.
1751 هداو: d.
1752 اعمال: a, c/ افعال: b, d, e.
1753 بمضامير: b.
1754 فاوفق: b.
1755 وديعا: a, c/ وديع: b, d, e.
1756 متضع: b.
1757 احد: b.
1758 اخا: b.
1759 الجبوس: a, c/ الحبس: b, d, e.
1760 بدايت: b.
1761 بالاب: b.
1762 هولا: b.
1763 يتذكروا: e.
1764 السمعنه: b.
1765 في: ساقطة b.
1766 لكثرت: b.
1767 هكذا في المخطوطات والأرجح: وتعتضد.
1768 بشيا: b.
1769 أي: برية. معبد مصري قديم.
1770 قطعه: a, c/ قطعت: b, d, e.
1771 مليحله: b.
1772 اللحم: b, c, e/ اللحم: a, d.
1773 و: ساقطة b.
1774 الاراء: b, c/ الارا: a/ الارآ: d/ الارا: e.
1775 المنايه: b.
1776 قوما: a, c/ قوم: b, d, e.
1777 تم الإشارة الى الفراغ في المخطوطة A بإشارة ~.
1778 يلوموهم: b.
1779 محرفون: b.
1780 شي: ساقطة b.
1781 هنالك ثلاث أوراق ناقصة في المخطوطة D.
1782 يوما: a, c/ يوم: b, e.
1783 الخمسين: a, c, e/ الخمسون: b.

1784 المجار: a, c/ المجر: b, e.
1785 اولايك: a, c/ اوليك: b, e.
1786 دخل: a, c/ دخلوا: b, e.
1787 بالاسكدريه: b.
1788 بولس: a, b, c/ بولص: e.
1789 باكله: a, c/ باكلها: b, e.
1790 خبز: b.
1791 الرسل: b.
1792 قال: ساقطة a, c.
1793 ثلاثة: b.
1794 الثلاثه: b.
1795 اعتقاد: b.
1796 وارثه: b.
1797 السموات: a, c/ السماوات: b, e.
1798 يستأنف النص في المخطوطة D من هذه النقطة.
1799 افكاره: ساقطة b.
1800 استانار: b.
1801 حميت: a, c/ حمية: b, d, e.
1802 مسالتكم: b, d, e/ مسلتكم: a, c.
1803 متغمق: c.
1804 الثلاثه: b.
1805 تصانيفهم: b.
1806 ثلاثها: b.
1807 بلاديوس: b, d, e/ بلاديس: a, c.
1808 اذا: b.
1809 الروح: a, c/ لروح: b, d, e.
1810 الا: e.
1811 ونقلت هذه النسخه من نسخه (كان قد نقلت على نسخه: زائدة c) بدير القديس العظيم في القديسين اب جميع الرهبان ابا انطونيوس صلاته تعمنا امين: زائدة a, c.

كل هذا الكتاب على يد الخاطي افريم ابن زكر من بيت قس ابراهيم في شهر تموز ستة ايام سنة 1843 مسيحيه: زائدة e.

كاتبه بالاسم كاهن وبالفعل خاطي مذنب صلو علي وكان بسنه ܡܐ ܐܠܦܐ الف وخمسمايه وخمسه واربعون يونانيه ولله الحمد ابدا لدهور امين: زائدة c.

NOTES ON THE ENGLISH TRANSLATION

MARIO KOZAH AND SULEIMAN MOURAD

1 The author of this work is in fact Enanisho (seventh century), the East Syriac author responsible for the collection of lives of desert Fathers known in English as *The Paradise of the Holy Fathers*, edited and translated by E. A. Wallis Budge, *The Paradise or Garden of the Holy Fathers* […], 2 vols., London, 1907.

2 This commentary is in fact by Dadishoʿ Qaṭraya. See Introduction.

3 E. A. Wallis Budge, *The Paradise or Garden of the Holy Fathers* […], 2 vols., London, 1907. Vol. I, p. 108, "The Histories of the Natural Brethren Paesius and Isaiah."

4 Matthew 19:21.

5 Matthew 24:45–47.

6 E. A. Wallis Budge, *The Paradise*, vol. II, pp. 283–284.

7 E. A. Wallis Budge, *The Paradise*, vol. I, p. 109.

8 E. A. Wallis Budge, *The Paradise*, vol. II, p. 65.

9 E. A. Wallis Budge, *The Paradise*, vol. II, pp. 8–9.

10 E. A. Wallis Budge, *The Paradise*, vol. I, p. 109.

11 Luke 16:8.

12 Romans 12:1.

13 Matthew 19:21.

14 John 12:26.

15 Luke 10:27.

16 Luke 14:26; Matthew 10:37.

17 Luke 14:26.

18 Matthew 16:24.

19 Luke 16:9.

20 Luke 15:31–32.

21 Matthew 13:7.

22 E. A. Wallis Budge, *The Paradise or Garden of the Holy Fathers* […], 2 vols., London, 1907.

²³ The Garshuni has "teach him."
²⁴ E. A. Wallis Budge, *The Paradise*, vol. I, pp. 360–361.
²⁵ Psalms 128:5.
²⁶ Psalms 65:4.
²⁷ E. A. Wallis Budge, *The Paradise*, vol. II, p. 318.
²⁸ Mark 4:4 and Matthew 13:4.
²⁹ E. A. Wallis Budge, *The Paradise*, vol. I, p. 278.
³⁰ E. A. Wallis Budge, *The Paradise*, vol. I, pp. 284–287.
³¹ E. A. Wallis Budge, *The Paradise*, vol. II, p. 258.
³² E. A. Wallis Budge, *The Paradise*, vol. I, pp. 266–267.
³³ Matthew 25:34–36.
³⁴ E. A. Wallis Budge, *The Paradise*, vol. II, p. 187.
³⁵ Genesis 19:22–26.
³⁶ 1 Kings 19:19–20.
³⁷ Matthew 9:9.
³⁸ E. A. Wallis Budge, *The Paradise*, vol. I, p. 105.
³⁹ Ibid.
⁴⁰ E. A. Wallis Budge, *The Paradise*, vol. I, p. 106.
⁴¹ E. A. Wallis Budge, *The Paradise*, vol. I, p. 170.
⁴² The word *heaven* has to be understood in this discussion in its original meaning of sky.
⁴³ See 2 Corinthians 12:2.
⁴⁴ See Genesis 1:1.
⁴⁵ See Genesis 1:6–8.
⁴⁶ See Luke 23:43.
⁴⁷ See Matthew 25:31–34.
⁴⁸ E. A. Wallis Budge, *The Paradise*, vol. II, p. 287.
⁴⁹ E. A. Wallis Budge, *The Paradise*, vol. I, p. 124.
⁵⁰ E. A. Wallis Budge, *The Paradise*, vol. I, pp. 142–144.
⁵¹ E. A. Wallis Budge, *The Paradise*, vol. I, p. 178.
⁵² These are in fact the words of the blessed Macarius: see E. A. Wallis Budge, *The Paradise*, vol. II, p. 287.
⁵³ The Scetis Valley (i.e., valley of the ascetics), also known as Wadi al-Natrun, is located in northwestern Egypt where several monasteries have existed since the third century. The Scetis Desert is the desert around the Scetis Valley, and was a popular retreat for many Christian monks and hermits pursuing solitary life away from their monasteries and Egyptian society.
⁵⁴ Palladius of Galatia (born c. 363) is the author of the *Lausiac History*.

55 This is a possible reference to a similar account concerning blessed Ammon. Cf. E. A. Wallis Budge, *The Paradise*, vol. I, p. 377.

56 See Psalms 89:2: "Forever I will keep my steadfast love for him, and my covenant with him will stand firm."

57 See Psalms 42:2.

58 See Psalms 101:2.

59 See Psalms 42:7.

60 This is a likely reference to 2 Samuel 22:17–20 or Psalms 66:12.

61 See 1 Timothy 3:1.

62 This is a probable reference to Theodore of Mopsuestia (d. 428) known to have written a work on priesthood.

63 This is a probable reference to Paulinus (d. 388) who was a claimant to the See of Antioch from 362–388.

64 This is a reference to Enanisho.

65 E. A. Wallis Budge, *The Paradise*, vol. I, p. 186.

66 E. A. Wallis Budge, *The Paradise*, vol. II, p. 224.

67 *The Book of the Perfection of Disciplines* is a monastic work, extant today in only three other known fragments, written by Theodore of Mopsuestia whose works were translated from Greek into Syriac in Edessa in the first half of the fifth century and who enjoyed a great deal of authority in the Church of the East being quoted extensively by authors such as Dadishoʿ. See F. Graffin, "Une page retrouvée de Théodore de Mopsueste", pp. 29–34 in *A Tribute to Arthur Vööbus: Studies in Early Christian Literature and Its Environment, Primarily in the Syrian East*. Edited by Fischer, Robert H.. Chicago, Illinois: The Lutheran School of Theology at Chicago, 1977.

68 E. A. Wallis Budge, *The Paradise*, vol. I, p. 214.

69 E. A. Wallis Budge, *The Paradise*, vol. I, p. 197.

70 Parnouj Monastery was the Coptic name of the large Monastery of Nitria, north of the Scetis Valley and southeast of Alexandria.

71 E. A. Wallis Budge, *The Paradise*, vol. I, p. 100.

72 See Isaiah 6:6–7.

73 E. A. Wallis Budge, *The Paradise*, vol. I, p. 234.

74 E. A. Wallis Budge, *The Paradise*, vol. I, p. 278.

75 *The Paradise of the Desert Fathers* known in its Arabic version as *Bustān al-Ruhbān* or *The Garden of the Monks*.

76 E. A. Wallis Budge, *The Paradise*, vol. I, p. 196.

77 E. A. Wallis Budge, *The Paradise*, vol. I, p. 216.

78 Meaning, "Without me you can do nothing." See John 15:5.

79 E. A. Wallis Budge, *The Paradise*, vol. I, p. 217.

[80] See 1 Timothy 2:8.
[81] See Psalms 143:6.
[82] See Psalms 141:2.
[83] See Psalms 141:8.
[84] See Luke 24:50, and John 11:41 and 17:1.
[85] See Colossians 3:1.
[86] See Exodus 17:11.
[87] See 2 Corinthians 12:2.
[88] E. A. Wallis Budge, *The Paradise*, vol. II, p. 25.
[89] Cf. E. A. Wallis Budge, *The Paradise*, vol. II, p. 290.
[90] E. A. Wallis Budge, *The Paradise*, vol. I, p. 237.
[91] E. A. Wallis Budge, *The Paradise*, vol. I, p. 143.
[92] E. A. Wallis Budge, *The Paradise*, vol. II, p. 292.
[93] E. A. Wallis Budge, *The Paradise*, vol. II, p. 292.
[94] E. A. Wallis Budge, *The Paradise*, vol. I, p. 243.
[95] See Genesis 5:1.
[96] See Matthew 5:48.
[97] See Psalms 49:20.
[98] See James 2:17 and 26.
[99] See Matthew 25:29.
[100] E. A. Wallis Budge, *The Paradise*, vol. II, p. 305.
[101] E. A. Wallis Budge, *The Paradise*, vol. II, pp. 294–295.
[102] E. A. Wallis Budge, *The Paradise*, vol. II, p. 295.
[103] E. A. Wallis Budge, *The Paradise*, vol. II, p. 296.
[104] E. A. Wallis Budge, *The Paradise*, vol. II, p. 296.
[105] E. A. Wallis Budge, *The Paradise*, vol. II, p. 300.
[106] See Luke 10:19.
[107] E. A. Wallis Budge, *The Paradise*, vol. I, p. 304.
[108] E. A. Wallis Budge, *The Paradise*, vol. I, p. 225.
[109] E. A. Wallis Budge, *The Paradise*, vol. I, p. 251.
[110] A location in the inner Nitrian desert.
[111] See 1 Corinthians 13:8.
[112] See Philippians 2:8.
[113] See John 3:16.
[114] See Matthew 11:29.
[115] See Luke 7:39.
[116] See Luke 7:47.
[117] See Luke 18:9–13.
[118] Meaning his betrayal of Jesus: see for example Luke 22:48.

[119] Meaning the thief who was crucified on the right side of Jesus: see Luke 23:40–43.

[120] See 1 Kings 13:20–25.

[121] Meaning the thirty silver coins that Judas received for betraying Jesus: see Matthew 26:14–15.

[122] E. A. Wallis Budge, *The Paradise*, vol. II, p. 118.

[123] E. A. Wallis Budge, *The Paradise*, vol. I, p. 342.

[124] E. A. Wallis Budge, *The Paradise*, vol. I, p. 348.

[125] E. A. Wallis Budge, *The Paradise*, vol. I, p. 341.

[126] E. A. Wallis Budge, *The Paradise*, vol. I, p. 351.

[127] E. A. Wallis Budge, *The Paradise*, vol. I, p. 334.

[128] Coptic: *Pemdje*.

[129] See Matthew 11:29.

[130] See Matthew 10:38.

[131] See Matthew 19:21.

[132] See 1 Corinthians 11:1.

[133] See 1 Corinthians 7:7.

[134] See 1 Corinthians 7:1.

[135] See 1 Corinthians 7:32–33.

[136] E. A. Wallis Budge, *The Paradise*, vol. II, p. 150.

[137] E. A. Wallis Budge, *The Paradise*, vol. I, p. 358.

[138] John 13:25.

[139] E. A. Wallis Budge, *The Paradise*, vol. II, p. 316.

[140] See Matthew 12:42–44, and Luke 11:23–25.

[141] E. A. Wallis Budge, *The Paradise*, vol. II, p. 317.

[142] Roman Emperor from 379 to 395.

[143] Byzantine Emperor from 395 to 408.

[144] See Romans 13:10. See also Luke 10:26–28 and James 2:8.

[145] See 1 John 2:15.

[146] See John 14:23.

[147] A possible reference to the monastic reforms undertaken by Babai the Great (ca. 551–628) recorded in his monastic Canons.

[148] See Exodus 31:15.

[149] E. A. Wallis Budge, *The Paradise*, vol. II, p. 317.

[150] E. A. Wallis Budge, *The Paradise*, vol. II, p. 318.

[151] E. A. Wallis Budge, *The Paradise*, vol. II, p. 318.

[152] See Psalms 119:47 and 119:64.

[153] E. A. Wallis Budge, *The Paradise*, vol. II, p. 319.

[154] E. A. Wallis Budge, *The Paradise*, vol. II, pp. 4–5.

[155] Cf. E. A. Wallis Budge, *The Paradise*, vol. II, p. 94.

[156] E. A. Wallis Budge, *The Paradise*, vol. II, pp. 93–94.
[157] See Matthew 5:7.
[158] See Matthew 5:9.
[159] See Matthew 5:8.
[160] E. A. Wallis Budge, *The Paradise*, vol. II, p. 320.
[161] E. A. Wallis Budge, *The Paradise*, vol. II, pp. 320–321.
[162] E. A. Wallis Budge, *The Paradise*, vol. II, p. 5.
[163] E. A. Wallis Budge, *The Paradise*, vol. II, p. 5.
[164] See Matthew 5:22.
[165] See Matthew 5, especially 5:21–22 and 5:27–28. These sayings are not placed here in the order they appear in Matthew, and belong to Jesus' Sermon on the Mount.
[166] Elizabeth: wife of Zachariah and mother of John the Baptist.
[167] The Prophetess Anna: Luke 2:36–38.
[168] See Luke 21:1–4, and Mark 12:41–43.
[169] See Luke 18:9–14.
[170] See Luke 7:37–50.
[171] See Luke 23:40–43.
[172] See Matthew 20:11–13.
[173] E. A. Wallis Budge, *The Paradise*, vol. II, p. 6.
[174] *Parasang* was a measure of distance used in the ancient and medieval Near East (one parasang approximately equals four kilometers).
[175] E. A. Wallis Budge, *The Paradise*, vol. II, p. 14.
[176] E. A. Wallis Budge, *The Paradise*, vol. II, p. 57.
[177] E. A. Wallis Budge, *The Paradise*, vol. II, p. 71.
[178] E. A. Wallis Budge, *The Paradise*, vol. II, p. 14.
[179] E. A. Wallis Budge, *The Paradise*, vol. II, pp. 57–58.
[180] A species of wild plant with a prickly head.
[181] E. A. Wallis Budge, *The Paradise*, vol. II, p. 281.
[182] See John 5:44.
[183] See 2 Corinthians 6:8.
[184] See Galatians 6:14.
[185] E. A. Wallis Budge, *The Paradise*, vol. II, pp. 110–111.
[186] E. A. Wallis Budge, *The Paradise*, vol. II, p. 8.
[187] E. A. Wallis Budge, *The Paradise*, vol. II, p. 9.
[188] E. A. Wallis Budge, *The Paradise*, vol. II, p. 146.
[189] See John 1:32. See also Matthew 3:16, Mark 1:10, and Luke 3:22.
[190] See Acts 2:3.
[191] E. A. Wallis Budge, *The Paradise*, vol. II, p. 321.
[192] E. A. Wallis Budge, *The Paradise*, vol. II, p. 321.

193 E. A. Wallis Budge, *The Paradise*, vol. II, p. 6.
194 E. A. Wallis Budge, *The Paradise*, vol. II, p. 25.
195 E. A. Wallis Budge, *The Paradise*, vol. II, p. 249.
196 E. A. Wallis Budge, *The Paradise*, vol. II, p. 323.
197 E. A. Wallis Budge, *The Paradise*, vol. I, p. 234.
198 E. A. Wallis Budge, *The Paradise*, vol. II, p. 324.
199 E. A. Wallis Budge, *The Paradise*, vol. II, p. 14.
200 E. A. Wallis Budge, *The Paradise*, vol. II, p. 324.
201 See 2 Thessalonians 1:4–6.
202 See Matthew 5:44 and Luke 6:28.
203 See Acts 7:60.
204 E. A. Wallis Budge, *The Paradise*, vol. II, p. 325.
205 See Numbers 12:1–16. The punishment was Miriam being struck with leprosy.
206 E. A. Wallis Budge, *The Paradise*, vol. II, p. 326.
207 E. A. Wallis Budge, *The Paradise*, vol. II, pp. 15–16.
208 E. A. Wallis Budge, *The Paradise*, vol. II, p. 16.
209 See 2 Corinthians 12:10.
210 See 2 Corinthians 12:9.
211 E. A. Wallis Budge, *The Paradise*, vol. II, p. 17.
212 E. A. Wallis Budge, *The Paradise*, vol. II, p. 18.
213 See Psalms 62:10.
214 See Psalms 104:15.
215 See Proverbs 23:29–30.
216 See Matthew 5:4.
217 See Deuteronomy 21:18–21.
218 E. A. Wallis Budge, *The Paradise*, vol. II, p. 19.
219 E. A. Wallis Budge, *The Paradise*, vol. I, p. 130.
220 E. A. Wallis Budge, *The Paradise*, vol. II, p. 19.
221 E. A. Wallis Budge, *The Paradise*, vol. II, p. 19.
222 See 1 Corinthians 2:4.
223 See 1 Corinthians 3:18.
224 See Sirach 19:20–24.
225 E. A. Wallis Budge, *The Paradise*, vol. II, p. 24.
226 E. A. Wallis Budge, *The Paradise*, vol. II, p. 26.
227 A reference to Goliath: see 1 Samuel 17.
228 A reference to when Ishbi-Benob threatened to kill David, Abishai went and killed him: see 2 Samuel 21:15–17. Ishbi-Benob was not in fact a Gittite.
229 E. A. Wallis Budge, *The Paradise*, vol. II, p. 24.

[230] E. A. Wallis Budge, *The Paradise*, vol. II, p. 10.
[231] E. A. Wallis Budge, *The Paradise*, vol. II, p. 29.
[232] See Daniel 3, especially 3:19–30 (Daniel's companions—Hananiah (Shadrach), Mishael (Meshach) and Azariah (Abednego)—were thrown by King Nebuchadnezzar into a fiery furnace but were not harmed), and Daniel 6, especially 6:16–24 (Daniel was thrown by King Darius into the Lions' den but was not harmed either).
[233] A probable reference to the Christian martyrs who were killed during the Roman persecution of the third century.
[234] E. A. Wallis Budge, *The Paradise*, vol. II, p. 26.
[235] E. A. Wallis Budge, *The Paradise*, vol. II, p. 201.
[236] E. A. Wallis Budge, *The Paradise*, vol. II, p. 15.
[237] E. A. Wallis Budge, *The Paradise*, vol. II, p. 30.
[238] E. A. Wallis Budge, *The Paradise*, vol. II, p. 311.
[239] E. A. Wallis Budge, *The Paradise*, vol. II, p. 31–32.
[240] E. A. Wallis Budge, *The Paradise*, vol. II, p. 33.
[241] E. A. Wallis Budge, *The Paradise*, vol. II, p. 33.
[242] E. A. Wallis Budge, *The Paradise*, vol. II, p. 41.
[243] See Matthew 5:39.
[244] E. A. Wallis Budge, *The Paradise*, vol. II, p. 45.
[245] E. A. Wallis Budge, *The Paradise*, vol. I, p. 194–195.
[246] See 2 Timothy 2:24.
[247] E. A. Wallis Budge, *The Paradise*, vol. II, p. 49.
[248] See Luke 14:27.
[249] See Matthew 11:29.
[250] See Luke 11:27–28.
[251] See Jeremiah 1, especially 1:6–10. Cf. also Jeremiah 7:22.
[252] See Ecclesiastes 2:15.
[253] See 2 Corinthians 1:3–11.
[254] See Luke 5:32.
[255] Satan asked God to test Job: see Job 2:1–10.
[256] E. A. Wallis Budge, *The Paradise*, vol. II, p. 54.
[257] This commentary by Dadishoʿ on the twenty-six discourses of Abba Isaiah has been edited and translated by René Draguet: R. Draguet, *Commentaire du Livre d'abba Isaïe (logoi I–XV) par Dadišo Qaṭraya*, in *CSCO*, 326–327, Scr. Syr. 144–5. Louvain, 1972. However, all the extant manuscripts of this work only reach the end of the commentary on the fifteenth discourse. Interestingly, a later anonymous commentary in Syriac which is in fragmentary form incorporates sections from the subsequent discourses by Dadishoʿ proving that he did in fact complete this work.

The statement we have here by Dadishoʿ provides further evidence by the author himself that his commentary on the twenty-six discourses of Abba Isaiah consisted of at least twenty-five discourses confirming that he almost certainly completed the work. It also confirms that the commentator or "Exegete" as we have translated the word *mufassir* in this *Compendious Commentary on the Paradise of the Egyptian Fathers* is indeed the voice of Dadishoʿ.

[258] E. A. Wallis Budge, *The Paradise*, vol. II, p. 54.
[259] See Matthew 23:12, and Luke 14:11 and 18:14.
[260] See Mark 9:23.
[261] E. A. Wallis Budge, *The Paradise*, vol. II, p. 56.
[262] E. A. Wallis Budge, *The Paradise*, vol. II, p. 304.
[263] E. A. Wallis Budge, *The Paradise*, vol. II, p. 59.
[264] E. A. Wallis Budge, *The Paradise*, vol. II, p. 60.
[265] E. A. Wallis Budge, *The Paradise*, vol. II, p. 198.
[266] E. A. Wallis Budge, *The Paradise*, vol. II, p. 60.
[267] E. A. Wallis Budge, *The Paradise*, vol. II, p. 67.
[268] E. A. Wallis Budge, *The Paradise*, vol. II, p. 61.
[269] E. A. Wallis Budge, *The Paradise*, vol. II, p. 321.
[270] E. A. Wallis Budge, *The Paradise*, vol. II, p. 63.
[271] E. A. Wallis Budge, *The Paradise*, vol. II, p. 64.
[272] See Luke 17:37; and Matthew 24:28.
[273] See 1 Thessalonians 4:17.
[274] E. A. Wallis Budge, *The Paradise*, vol. II, p. 66.
[275] E. A. Wallis Budge, *The Paradise*, vol. II, p. 128.
[276] E. A. Wallis Budge, *The Paradise*, vol. II, p. 219.
[277] Basil of Caesarea, c. 328–378.
[278] *The Questions of the Brothers* is the late fourth century Syriac translation of Basil of Caesarea's *Asketikon*. See A. M. Silvas, *Basil of Caesarea. Questions of the Brothers*. Brill, 2014.
[279] Only two of Basil's letters in early Syriac translation have thus far been published.
[280] E. A. Wallis Budge, *The Paradise*, vol. II, p. 67.
[281] James 1:15.
[282] John 8:34.
[283] E. A. Wallis Budge, *The Paradise*, vol. II, p. 115.
[284] E. A. Wallis Budge, *The Paradise*, vol. II, p. 250.
[285] E. A. Wallis Budge, *The Paradise*, vol. II, p. 76.
[286] E. A. Wallis Budge, *The Paradise*, vol. I, p. 267.
[287] See John 13:12.

[288] E. A. Wallis Budge, *The Paradise*, vol. I, p. 305.
[289] E. A. Wallis Budge, *The Paradise*, vol. I, p. 130.
[290] E. A. Wallis Budge, *The Paradise*, vol. II, p. 83.
[291] E. A. Wallis Budge, *The Paradise*, vol. II, p. 84.
[292] E. A. Wallis Budge, *The Paradise*, vol. II, p. 80.
[293] E. A. Wallis Budge, *The Paradise*, vol. II, p. 84.
[294] E. A. Wallis Budge, *The Paradise*, vol. II, p. 66.
[295] E. A. Wallis Budge, *The Paradise*, vol. II, p. 324.
[296] E. A. Wallis Budge, *The Paradise*, vol. II, p. 281.
[297] E. A. Wallis Budge, *The Paradise*, vol. II, p. 83.
[298] E. A. Wallis Budge, *The Paradise*, vol. II, p. 52.
[299] E. A. Wallis Budge, *The Paradise*, vol. II, p. 82.
[300] E. A. Wallis Budge, *The Paradise*, vol. II, p. 13.
[301] E. A. Wallis Budge, *The Paradise*, vol. II, p. 94.
[302] E. A. Wallis Budge, *The Paradise*, vol. II, p. 95–96.
[303] Hebrews 6:18–19.
[304] E. A. Wallis Budge, *The Paradise*, vol. II, p. 98.
[305] 1 Corinthians 13:4–8.
[306] Mark 10:31.
[307] Romans 13:8.
[308] E. A. Wallis Budge, *The Paradise*, vol. II, p. 95.
[309] Luke 6:37; Matthew 6:14.
[310] Mark 11:25–26.
[311] E. A. Wallis Budge, *The Paradise*, vol. II, p. 100–101.
[312] E. A. Wallis Budge, *The Paradise*, vol. II, p. 92–93.
[313] 2 Samuel 23:15.
[314] E. A. Wallis Budge, *The Paradise*, vol. II, p. 217.
[315] E. A. Wallis Budge, *The Paradise*, vol. II, p. 93.
[316] E. A. Wallis Budge, *The Paradise*, vol. II, p. 104.
[317] E. A. Wallis Budge, *The Paradise*, vol. II, p. 105.
[318] Luke 18:13.
[319] E. A. Wallis Budge, *The Paradise*, vol. II, p. 106.
[320] John 14: 23.
[321] Titus 1:15.
[322] E. A. Wallis Budge, *The Paradise*, vol. II, p. 107.
[323] E. A. Wallis Budge, *The Paradise*, vol. I, p. 273–275.
[324] Psalms 140:5.
[325] Mark 10:47.
[326] Mark 10:49.
[327] E. A. Wallis Budge, *The Paradise*, vol. II, p. 120.

328 E. A. Wallis Budge, *The Paradise*, vol. II, p. 108.
329 E. A. Wallis Budge, *The Paradise*, vol. II, p. 298.
330 Titus 1:15.
331 E. A. Wallis Budge, *The Paradise*, vol. II, p. 293.
332 E. A. Wallis Budge, *The Paradise*, vol. II, p. 69.
333 E. A. Wallis Budge, *The Paradise*, vol. II, p. 163.
334 E. A. Wallis Budge, *The Paradise*, vol. II, p. 108.
335 Matthew 15:14.
336 E. A. Wallis Budge, *The Paradise*, vol. II, p. 113.
337 E. A. Wallis Budge, *The Paradise*, vol. II, p. 140.
338 Matthew 23:13.
339 Matthew 7:1.
340 E. A. Wallis Budge, *The Paradise*, vol. II, p. 327.
341 E. A. Wallis Budge, *The Paradise*, vol. II, p. 112.
342 Psalms 116:12.
343 John 1:29.
344 1 Corinthians 11:24.
345 Matthew 26:28.
346 E. A. Wallis Budge, *The Paradise*, vol. II, p. 125.
347 Matthew 5:3.
348 Matthew 5:3 and 5:5.
349 E. A. Wallis Budge, *The Paradise*, vol. II, p. 126.
350 E. A. Wallis Budge, *The Paradise*, vol. II, p. 126.
351 E. A. Wallis Budge, *The Paradise*, vol. II, p. 126.
352 E. A. Wallis Budge, *The Paradise*, vol. II, p. 126–127.
353 E. A. Wallis Budge, *The Paradise*, vol. II, p. 127.
354 E. A. Wallis Budge, *The Paradise*, vol. II, p. 61.
355 E. A. Wallis Budge, *The Paradise*, vol. II, p. 85.
356 E. A. Wallis Budge, *The Paradise*, vol. II, p. 131.
357 E. A. Wallis Budge, *The Paradise*, vol. II, p. 133.
358 E. A. Wallis Budge, *The Paradise*, vol. II, p. 134.
359 E. A. Wallis Budge, *The Paradise*, vol. II, p. 206.
360 Psalms 27:1.
361 Psalms 25:1–2.
362 Psalms 70:1.
363 Psalms 13:1.
364 Psalms 68:1.
365 Psalms 38:1.
366 E. A. Wallis Budge, *The Paradise*, vol. II, p. 136–137.
367 E. A. Wallis Budge, *The Paradise*, vol. II, p. 139–140.

[368] See Ezekiel 18:24.
[369] Luke 5:32.
[370] E. A. Wallis Budge, *The Paradise*, vol. II, p. 139.
[371] Psalms 36:6.
[372] Deuteronomy 29:29.
[373] E. A. Wallis Budge, *The Paradise*, vol. II, p. 217.
[374] E. A. Wallis Budge, *The Paradise*, vol. II, p. 206.
[375] Acts 2:38.
[376] Luke 6:37.
[377] Matthew 5:24.
[378] E. A. Wallis Budge, *The Paradise*, vol. II, p. 142.
[379] Luke 12:7; Matthew 10:30.
[380] See Isaiah 45:18.
[381] E. A. Wallis Budge, *The Paradise*, vol. II, p. 146.
[382] This is a probable reference to Theodore of Mopsuestia (d. 428).
[383] Matthew 6:10.
[384] Matthew 5:8.
[385] E. A. Wallis Budge, *The Paradise*, vol. II, p. 145.
[386] E. A. Wallis Budge, *The Paradise*, vol. II, p. 144.
[387] John 14:21.
[388] See 1 Timothy 6:16.
[389] E. A. Wallis Budge, *The Paradise*, vol. II, p. 214–215.
[390] E. A. Wallis Budge, *The Paradise*, vol. II, p. 11.
[391] E. A. Wallis Budge, *The Paradise*, vol. II, p. 10–11.
[392] E. A. Wallis Budge, *The Paradise*, vol. II, p. 199–200.
[393] Psalms 18:29.
[394] E. A. Wallis Budge, *The Paradise*, vol. II, p. 173.
[395] E. A. Wallis Budge, *The Paradise*, vol. II, p. 172–173.
[396] E. A. Wallis Budge, *The Paradise*, vol. II, p. 166.
[397] See Matthew 5:44.
[398] E. A. Wallis Budge, *The Paradise*, vol. II, p. 151.
[399] Matthew 10:37.
[400] Luke 14:26–27.
[401] E. A. Wallis Budge, *The Paradise*, vol. II, p. 153.
[402] Jeremiah 12:5.
[403] John 9:2.
[404] John 9:3.
[405] E. A. Wallis Budge, *The Paradise*, vol. II, p. 154–155.
[406] E. A. Wallis Budge, *The Paradise*, vol. II, p. 164.
[407] Psalms 116:15.

408 E. A. Wallis Budge, *The Paradise*, vol. II, p. 165.
409 E. A. Wallis Budge, *The Paradise*, vol. II, p. 159.
410 E. A. Wallis Budge, *The Paradise*, vol. II, p. 174.
411 E. A. Wallis Budge, *The Paradise*, vol. II, p. 48.
412 E. A. Wallis Budge, *The Paradise*, vol. II, p. 178.
413 E. A. Wallis Budge, *The Paradise*, vol. II, p. 178.
414 See Matthew 5:13.
415 Galatians 1:8.
416 E. A. Wallis Budge, *The Paradise*, vol. II, p. 183.
417 Psalms 33:16–17.
418 E. A. Wallis Budge, *The Paradise*, vol. II, p. 192.
419 Matthew 11:29.
420 E. A. Wallis Budge, *The Paradise*, vol. II, p. 184.
421 E. A. Wallis Budge, *The Paradise*, vol. II, p. 298.
422 E. A. Wallis Budge, *The Paradise*, vol. II, p. 184.
423 Genesis 46:3.
424 E. A. Wallis Budge, *The Paradise*, vol. II, p. 187.
425 E. A. Wallis Budge, *The Paradise*, vol. II, p. 280.
426 E. A. Wallis Budge, *The Paradise*, vol. II, p. 188–189.
427 E. A. Wallis Budge, *The Paradise*, vol. II, p. 280–283.
428 Psalms 119:1–2.
429 E. A. Wallis Budge, *The Paradise*, vol. II, p. 193.
430 E. A. Wallis Budge, *The Paradise*, vol. II, p. 157.
431 E. A. Wallis Budge, *The Paradise*, vol. II, p. 211.
432 E. A. Wallis Budge, *The Paradise*, vol. II, p. 78.
433 E. A. Wallis Budge, *The Paradise*, vol. II, p. 157.
434 Philippians 4:17.
435 Amos 1:9.
436 E. A. Wallis Budge, *The Paradise*, vol. II, p. 194.
437 E. A. Wallis Budge, *The Paradise*, vol. II, p. 172.
438 E. A. Wallis Budge, *The Paradise*, vol. II, p. 205.
439 E. A. Wallis Budge, *The Paradise*, vol. II, p. 195.
440 Luke 9:19.
441 Matthew 24:22.
442 Ezekiel 14:14.
443 E. A. Wallis Budge, *The Paradise*, vol. II, p. 196.
444 Galatians 2:20.
445 See Matthew 10:37–38.
446 Matthew 19:27.
447 E. A. Wallis Budge, *The Paradise*, vol. II, p. 202.

[448] E. A. Wallis Budge, *The Paradise*, vol. II, p. 202.
[449] E. A. Wallis Budge, *The Paradise*, vol. II, p. 203–204.
[450] E. A. Wallis Budge, *The Paradise*, vol. II, p. 204.
[451] E. A. Wallis Budge, *The Paradise*, vol. II, p. 316.
[452] E. A. Wallis Budge, *The Paradise*, vol. II, p. 177.
[453] E. A. Wallis Budge, *The Paradise*, vol. II, p. 210.
[454] 1 Corinthians 14:22.
[455] John 20:29.
[456] E. A. Wallis Budge, *The Paradise*, vol. II, p. 216.
[457] E. A. Wallis Budge, *The Paradise*, vol. II, p. 160.
[458] E. A. Wallis Budge, *The Paradise*, vol. II, p. 198.
[459] E. A. Wallis Budge, *The Paradise*, vol. II, p. 222.
[460] E. A. Wallis Budge, *The Paradise*, vol. II, p. 311.
[461] See Luke 5:32.
[462] E. A. Wallis Budge, *The Paradise*, vol. II, p. 307.
[463] Matthew 18:3.
[464] E. A. Wallis Budge, *The Paradise*, vol. II, p. 307.
[465] John 8:46.
[466] John 14:30.
[467] E. A. Wallis Budge, *The Paradise*, vol. II, p. 312.
[468] Psalms 89:15.
[469] E. A. Wallis Budge, *The Paradise*, vol. II, p. 305–306.
[470] E. A. Wallis Budge, *The Paradise*, vol. II, p. 304.
[471] Matthew 6:33.
[472] Luke 16:9.
[473] 2 Corinthians 8:14.
[474] Luke 8:3.
[475] E. A. Wallis Budge, *The Paradise*, vol. II, p. 302.
[476] E. A. Wallis Budge, *The Paradise*, vol. II, p. 302.
[477] E. A. Wallis Budge, *The Paradise*, vol. II, p. 303.
[478] Colossians 2:20.
[479] Matthew 22:37.
[480] Romans 12:12.
[481] Philippians 4:6.
[482] E. A. Wallis Budge, *The Paradise*, vol. II, p. 257–258.
[483] 1 Timothy 4:1.
[484] See Galatians 2:15–16.
[485] 1 Corinthians 10:27.
[486] 1 Corinthians 13:13.

www.ingramcontent.com/pod-product-compliance
Lightning Source LLC
Chambersburg PA
CBHW052140300426
44115CB00011B/1460